Life after Death
According to the Orthodox Tradition

LIFE AFTER DEATH
According to the Orthodox Tradition

JEAN-CLAUDE LARCHET

TRANSLATED FROM THE FRENCH
BY G. JOHN CHAMPOUX

HOLY TRINITY PUBLICATIONS
The Printshop of St Job of Pochaev
Holy Trinity Monastery
Jordanville, New York

Printed with the blessing of His Eminence,
Metropolitan Hilarion First Hierarch
of the Russian Orthodox Church Outside of Russia

Life after Death According to the Orthodox Tradition,
Second Edition Format © 2021 Holy Trinity Monastery
Text © 2012 Jean-Claude Larchet
Revised Text, 2nd edition © 2021 Jean-Claude Larchet

Originally published as
La vie après la mort selon la Tradition orthodoxe.
Paris: Les Éditions du Cerf, 2001.

The first English language edition
was published by the Orthodox Research Institute.

PRINTSHOP OF
SAINT JOB OF POCHAEV

An imprint of

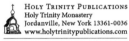

HOLY TRINITY PUBLICATIONS
Holy Trinity Monastery
Jordanville, New York 13361-0036
www.holytrinitypublications.com

ISBN:978-0-88465- 477-3 (paperback)
ISBN: 978-0-88465-483-4 (ePub)

Library of Congress Control Number: 2021918542

Scripture passages taken from the New King James Version.
Copyright © 1982 by Thomas Nelson, Inc. Used by permission.
Psalms taken from *A Psalter for Prayer*, trans. David James (Jordanville, N.Y.:
Holy Trinity Publications, 2011). Apocryphal passages taken from the
Orthodox Study Bible (OSB). Copyright © 2008 by Thomas Nelson, Inc.
Used by permission.

Cover photo: Fresco by Archimandrite Cyprian (Pyzhov)
"The Resurrection of Lazarus,"
Holy Trinity Monastery Cathedral, Jordanville, New York.

CONTENTS

PREFACE

D EATH IS A great mystery. This fact, as so many philosophers have stressed, is our future's only certainty, but also one of the greatest uncertainties as to its nature and after-effects.

Scripture underscores the unforeseeable character of death ("You know neither the day nor the hour" [Matt. 25:13]). It gives indications about its origin (Rom. 5:12). It heralds the future resurrection of the body and the eternal life of the Kingdom to come, but it gives practically no information about the period that separates the death of each person from the last and universal Judgment, and from the resurrection that must occur at the end of time. It is also remarkable that, in the accounts of the resurrections of the widow of Nain's son (Luke 7:11–16) and Lazarus (John 11:1–43), nothing is said about what they experienced between their death and return to life. Finally, it is clear that God does not permit the dead to reveal their condition to the living, even to helpfully warn them. Christ Himself even says this through a parable: for that "they have Moses and the prophets; let them hear them" (Luke 16:29). These last two facts, however, cannot be interpreted as a prohibition in principle made by God to men about speaking of conditions beyond the grave. In the first case the silence of Scripture is explained by the fact that it focuses on what is essential in the two events: the resurrection of two people by Christ, pointing to the resurrection to come and at the same time proving God's ability to do this. In the second case, the impossibility for the dead to speak of their lot has received on behalf of several Fathers[1] this explanation: the devil would have profited from this situation by giving rise to false apparitions and producing false testimony; under his instigation or under the effect of mental illnesses, some of the living would be made to pass for the dead returned to life, and people would have found more turmoil and deception than profit in so confused a situation.[2] The word placed by Christ in Abraham's mouth: "They have Moses and the prophets; let them hear them" is not so much a prohibition against being interested in the after-death condition of human beings as an invitation to carefully examine the Scriptures on this subject,[3] and be attentive to the visions and words of the prophets, and to the testimony and teachings of the saints, which, in their entirety, comprise the necessary indications.

Actually, an in-depth examination and an exegesis adapted from several scriptural passages, the parable of Lazarus, and the rich man in particular (Luke 16:19–31), yield substantial teachings.[4] The *Sayings* and *Lives* of the Fathers (who, in a broad sense, can be likened to the prophets spoken of by Christ) include a certain number of accounts, visions, and revelations concerning the condition and progress of souls after death. In their commentaries many of the Fathers clarify previous data. Lastly, the Church's funerary rituals in their temporal arrangement (especially their celebration on the first, third, ninth, and fortieth days), in their material forms, and prayer texts (all composed by inspired fathers), help us to see how the Church perceives death as it draws near, in the moment of its arrival; and in what follows, how it treats the bodies of the deceased, and how it looks upon the state of their soul.

These items of tradition are certainly scattered about and often elliptical. However, gathered together, compared, and synthesized, they ultimately enable us to define with rather fine precision the manner in which Christianity represents life after death to itself.[5]

Does the disclosure of this representation in all its breadth and detail go against a duty of reserve that Scripture, through its discretion, seems to teach us?

This discretion has a certain pedagogical aim: it teaches us to believe without seeing, it tells us that it is more important to prepare for death and the hereafter than to know its nature, especially since it is hard to imagine, in our present state, a very different condition.[6] However the Fathers, who have thought it good, in being inspired and authorized by the Holy Spirit, to relate or comment on certain revelations about the hereafter, are also responding to a pedagogical aim, but an aim of a different nature, by giving signs to those for whom they are necessary or useful. It is appropriate to discern human times (Luke 12:56) and needs, and adapt the Church's teaching. This does not mean that the latter varies in its basics, but that it makes the expression of an immutable truth correspond to the demands of circumstance, by more or less explaining this truth, by more or less insisting on one or another of its aspects.

People have always wished to know what there is beyond death, and the different philosophies and religions have always more or less responded to this need. Christianity's relative silence is another matter, for this silence too is rich in teachings: it requires of men a deeper and purer faith that knows how to dispense with signs. But, to those who ask for signs (Matt. 12:39, Mark 8:12), Christianity has often given them to rouse and strengthen our faith.

The enormous success enjoyed today by books collecting accounts of post-mortem experiences and claiming to draw teachings from them (like those of Dr. Raymond Moody and Elizabeth Kübler Ross) is not the expression of an unhealthy curiosity, but of a real and legitimate disquiet over the subject of death and the condition that follows it.

Should Christianity leave to secular authors, the sects, or non-Christian religions the monopoly on teaching about death and beyond-death conditions, with, as a consequence, a wide dissemination of fanciful beliefs on this subject? Should it, without good reason,[7] place that rich patrimony accumulated on this subject over the course of time under a bushel?

On this question as on others, there is the embarrassed silence of Christian theologians, insecure and ashamed in the face of modern materialism and scientism. Hoping to make a good impression on agnostics, they advocate 'demythologization' in the name of a faith that wishes to be pure (but most often only succeeds in being abstract and empty). This only contributes to alienating people from church and proves advantageous to those sects and religions unafraid of displaying their beliefs. For, like it or not, responses brought by religions to the question of death have always held an important place in the motivations of religious belief, not only because people seek in religion an assurance and consolation when faced with the prospect of death,[8] but also because death is surely one of the chief problems posed by human life, and precisely because the meaning of existence depends on the solution given to this problem.

The great success enjoyed, in the United States, by Christian authors (like Father Seraphim Rose[9]), who have responded to the spread of false beliefs about death and beyond with the teachings of the Christian tradition, indicates the path to follow for pastoral care and catechesis.

In this work, we will present the teachings from the Orthodox Church tradition. On a few points, these teachings differ significantly from those of the Catholic and Protestant confessions. Some divergences between eastern and western traditions have existed since the fifth century, but were considerably accentuated since the twelfth when the West, to borrow an expression from the historian Jacques Le Goff, 'invented Purgatory'.[10] The Latin tradition is however, in its depths, in perfect agreement with the Eastern tradition. Also, even if in our references we give the greatest space to the Greek Fathers, we will surely cite convergent or complementary teachings and testimonies of the Latin Fathers and hagiographers of antiquity.

We hope in this way to make better known to Orthodox the teachings of their own often scattered about and poorly known tradition,[11] and also to acquaint Catholic or Protestant readers with teachings unknown to them or which long ago ceased being within the compass of their faith, but nevertheless belong to the rich patrimony of an ancient Christian tradition which, in its origins, is or should be common to all.

Before beginning our account, one more detail seems necessary: concerning the hereafter, the Fathers express themselves most often in a symbolic manner. The reason for this is that they are dealing, as we have said, with an existential condition of which we have no experience in our present life, and for that reason is impossible to represent directly. According to the very principles of symbolism invisible and spiritual realities are often represented by visible and material realities. Indications of places and times especially should not be taken literally, this having to do with states or conditions of existence that elude space and time, or more exactly are situated—giving heed to another principle of symbolism: the analogical relationship between the symbol and what it symbolizes—in a spatiality and temporality different than those conditioning our perception in our earthly life. Bear in mind this detail especially when we see Paradise and Hades or the Kingdom of Heaven and Hell designated as places, when their experience will be described in terms of delights or material torments, or again when the different stages of post-mortem life will be evoked in terms of a number of days.

Chapter One

DEATH: ORIGIN AND SPIRITUAL MEANING

1 The First Cause of Death: The Ancestral Sin.

The Fathers are unanimous in considering that God has not created death.[1] Already the author of the Book of Wisdom had taught: "For God did not make death, neither does He have pleasure over the destruction of the living. For He created all things that they might exist, and the generations of the world so they might be preserved" (Wisdom of Solomon 1:13–14, LXX, OSB). Death has no positive reality: it only exists through loss of life; it forms a part of those evils that only exist by the loss and absence of the good. Now God has created the world entirely good and gave mankind life as a benefit.

Was man for all that immortal? Many Fathers reply in the affirmative[2] and consider death totally foreign to the very nature of man, but others hesitate to assert this.[3] Basing themselves on the verse of Genesis (2:7) according to which "God formed man of the dust of the ground," the latter, careful to maintain the distinction between the created and the uncreated, suppose that the human body was in its earliest origins and according to its own nature an unstable, corruptible, and mortal composite. "Man is by nature mortal, inasmuch as he is made out of what is not," writes St Athanasius of Alexandria[4] who asserts that, at origin, men "were of a corruptible nature."[5] Some Fathers prefer to say then, in a nuanced fashion, that man was created "for incorruption,"[6] or "for immortality,"[7] or it was part of his nature to tend to participate in divine immortality;[8] again, they speak of a 'promised'[9] incorruptibility and immortality, indicating that they were not definitively acquired from the outset like they would have been if they were properties attached to man's very nature. The Fathers meant to affirm in fact that the incorruptibility and immortality of the first man were due to divine grace alone. Soon after having created man from the dust of the earth, God, says the Book of Genesis, "breathed into his nostrils the breath of life; and man became a living being" (Gen. 2:7): the Fathers have seen the soul in this breath, but also the divine Spirit.[10] This is because the first man was imbued with divine energies, because his soul and body possessed supernatural qualities. Thus St Gregory Palamas notes that divine grace "made up for what was deficient in our nature with [Its] many bounties."[11] It is also by this grace that the body was made incorruptible and immortal.[12] St Athanasius speaks of man living an "immortal life" insofar as "having the grace of Him that gave it, having also God's own power from the Word of the Father,"[13] and he notes that men were "by nature corruptible, but... by the grace following from partaking of the Word" they "escaped their natural state,"[14] and "because of the Word dwelling with them, even their natural corruption did not come near them."[15]

However, having been created free, man relied on his will to preserve or not this grace, and so either remain in this incorruptibility and immortality conferred on him, or, to the contrary, lose them by rejecting it.[16] So, when the Fathers affirm that man was created incorruptible and immortal, they do not mean that he could not know corruption or death, but that he had by grace and free choice the possibility of not being corrupted and dying. For his incorruptibility and immortality to be maintained and definitively appropriated, man had to preserve the grace given to him by God, remain united with Him while availing himself of the commandment God had given him to this effect (cf. Gen. 2:16–17). [18] Thus, St Gregory Palamas writes: "From the beginning ... if, waiting patiently for it, he kept the commandment, he would be able to share through the [grace given him] in a more perfect union with God, by which he would live for ever with Him and obtain immortality."[19]

We understand then why the Fathers often say that originally and until sin man was truly neither mortal or immortal. St Theophilus of Antioch writes: "But some one will say to us, Was man made by nature mortal? Certainly not. Was he, then, immortal? Neither do we affirm this. But one will say, Was he, then, nothing? Not even this hits the mark. He was by nature neither mortal nor immortal. For if He had made him immortal from the beginning, He would have made him God. Again, if He had made him mortal, God would seem to be the cause of his death. Neither, then, immortal nor yet mortal did He make him, but, as we have said above, capable of both; so that if he should incline to the things of immortality, keeping the commandment of God, he should receive as reward from Him immortality, and should become God; but if, on the other hand, he should turn to the things of death, disobeying God, he should himself be the cause of death to himself. For God made man free, and with power over himself."[20] St Athanasius of Alexandria notes: "Knowing once more how the will of man could sway to either side, in anticipation He secured the grace given them by a law and by the spot where He placed them ... So that, if they kept the grace and remained virtuous, they might still have ... the promise of incorruption ... but that if they transgressed and turned back, and became evil, they might know that they were incurring that corruption in death which was theirs by nature: no longer to live in paradise, but cast out of it from that time forth to die and to abide in death and in corruption."[21] St Gregory Palamas even sees in the divine commandment a means given by God to man for avoiding corruption and death as well as for preserving his freedom,[22] and stresses that immortality and death, incorruptibility and corruption depend in fact on man's choice[23] for God, having created man free, could not hinder what he chose to do or become.[24] According to the Fathers, it is then solely in man's personal will, in the bad use he has made of his free choice, in the sin he has committed in paradise that we must search for death's origin and cause.[25] Their teaching follows that of St Paul: "through one man sin entered the world, and death through sin," (Rom. 5:12, cf. 1 Cor. 15:21). Thus, St Theophilus of Antioch notes: "for the first man, disobedience procured his expulsion from Paradise ... for his disobedience did man ... at last fall a prey to death."[26] St Maximus likewise affirms: "the deviance of free choice introduced ... mortality in Adam's nature."[27] And St Gregory Palamas, to the question: "What is the origin of our infirmities, illnesses, and all our other troubles, including death? Whence does death come?" replies: "From our original disobedience to God, from the transgression of the commandment God gave us, from our Ancestors' sin in God's paradise. Disease, illness, and the whole burden of different kinds of temptations are the result of sin. On account of sin we put on 'tunics of skin' (Gen. 3:21): our infirm mortal bodies were beset with pain. We moved into this temporary, perishing world, and were sentenced to live lives full of suffering and misfortune. Sickness is like a rough, up-hill road on which sin set the human race. Death is the last stopping-place on this way, the final lodging."[28]

By choosing to follow the suggestion of the Evil One to become "like gods" (see Gen. 3:5), that is gods outside of God, Adam and Eve were themselves deprived of grace and have henceforth lost the qualities that they owed to it and that conferred on them in some manner a supernatural condition.[29] "Transgression of the commandment," writes St Athanasius, "turn[ed] them back to their natural state,"[30] that is to the dust of the earth from which they were fashioned (Gen. 2:7),[31] in accordance with what God said to Adam: "Till you return to the ground, for out of it you were taken; for dust you are, and to dust you shall return." (Gen. 3:19).

The evils suffered by Adam and Eve as a result of sin are not then for the Greek Fathers, as they are for a certain number of the Latin Fathers, a divine punishment. They are rather in keeping with the logic of their willed deprivation of communion with God which had made them sharers in His divine characteristics. By separating themselves from the Good they have exposed human nature to all the evils;[32] more precisely, by turning away from Life and depriving themselves of it, they have introduced death into themselves. St Gregory of Nyssa writes: "This abandoning of the good, once accomplished, had for a consequence the advent of all forms of evil: the turning away from life provoked death; privation of light entailed obscurity; for want of virtue, evil appeared. And so all forms of the good were replaced by a series of contrary evils. This departure from the good introduced in its train every form of evil to match the good (as, for instance, on the defection of life there was brought in the antagonism of death; on the deprivation of light darkness supervened); in the absence of virtue vice arose in its place, and against every form of good might be reckoned a like number of opposite evils."[33] The same author notes again: "In the same way the enemy, by craftily mixing up badness in man's will, has produced a kind of extinguishment and dullness in the blessing, on the failure of which that which is opposed necessarily enters. For to life is opposed death."[34] St Basil of Caesarea likewise notes: "Death is a necessary consequence of sin. Death draws nigh to the extent that one distances oneself from life, which is God; death is the privation of life: Adam, in separating himself from God, has exposed himself to death."[35] And St Maximus the Confessor: "The first man, for not having wished to be fed [from the Word of life], was inevitably estranged from divine life, and in return another one, engendering death, befell him."[36]

In the first place death affected the soul of man, who became passible, grew corrupt, and perished from being separated from God and deprived of divine life.[37] Next it is transmitted by the soul to its body. This two-fold death, spiritual and corporeal, is signified, remarks St Athanasius, by the insistent character of the formula that Genesis attributes to God warning Adam and Eve (Gen. 2:17): "in the day that you eat of it [the tree of the knowledge of good and evil] you shall surely die."[38] St Gregory Palamas clarifies this from the same perspective: "The death, however, that befell the soul because of the transgression not only crippled the soul… it also rendered the body itself subject to fatigue, suffering and corruptibility, and finally handed it over to death. For it was after the dying of his inner self brought about by the transgression that the earthly Adam heard the words, 'for you are earth, and to earth you will return' (Gen. 3:17–19)."[39]

According to the Fathers, following in this the teaching of the Holy Scriptures, Adam and Eve have transmitted to all their descendants the evils that affected their nature in the wake of their sin, with mortality in first place.[40] Adam was in fact the archetype, principle, and root of human nature and held it as a whole principally within himself.[41] A certain number of Fathers note that this transmission is made through biological life at the time of conception[42] and is therefore inevitable.[43] Since then all men are born passible, corruptible, and mortal, and no one can escape this destiny that St Maximus the Confessor calls 'the law of sin'[44] for it follows from sin, or again 'law of nature'[45] for it becomes inherent to fallen human nature as a whole. Here St Paul's teaching must be recalled: "through one man sin entered the world, and death through sin, and thus death spread to all men" (Rom. 5:12).

2 The Spiritual Ambivalence of Death.

A) *Death's Positive Aspect.* Although spiritual death has only negative aspects, some advantages relative to the new situation introduced by ancestral sin can be found in physical death. St John Chrysostom notes in this way: "However death was introduced here below by sin, that does not hinder God making it serve to our profit;"[46] he sees in death then "a grace rather than a chastisement."[47]

If man had known spiritual death without knowing the death of his body, numerous disadvantages would have resulted.

First, he would have been able to put up with this situation and live continually in carelessness, whereas the prospect of death and ignorance of its falling due can lead him to gauge the limits of this life and prepare himself for the future life, to develop a feeling of spiritual urgency and penitence.

Second, his immortality would also have aroused in him a feeling of pride and would seem to confirm the tempter's false promise: "ye shall be as gods" (Gen. 3:5, KJV), whereas the fact of having to return to the earth contributes to making him become aware of his limits as a creature, of his intrinsic weakness, of his nothingness when deprived of God's grace, and brings him to humility.[48]

Third, without the prospect of death, remarks St John Chrysostom, their "bodies would have been excessively loved; and most men would have become more carnal and gross."[49]

Fourth, without death man's deteriorating situation following on the ancestral sin would have been eternal. Thus, St Basil writes that God "has not hindered our dissolution so that our infirmity is not lasting by the mere fact of its immortality."[50]

This is so for bodily infirmities. Thus, St John Chrysostom notes: "If the body were to remain always in the sorry state to which it is reduced in this life, we would have to weep."[51] Clearly we must recognize that "it is not only the body, but the corruption of the body that death destroys", and that death, positively, signifies "corruption destroyed for ever."[52] By permitting death, God thus providentially prepares for the future restoration, through Christ, of the paradisal state and even the establishing by Him of a loftier state wherein man will become definitively incorruptible and immortal, [53] knowing that the grain should die to give birth to a new plant (cf. John 12:24, 1 Cor. 15:35–44).

But this is even more valid for spiritual infirmities. Thus several Fathers affirm that death is permitted "to prevent evil from becoming immortal."[54] With death sin also dies. St John Chrysostom stresses this paradox: the child kills its own parent since it is sin that gave birth to death.[55] St Maximus the Confessor stresses that the advent of death, providentially, has constituted for fallen man a certain form of liberation and has, paradoxically, contributed to preserving him, since it has allowed "the power of the soul to be not eternally confined to its movement against nature, which would not only be the utmost degree of evil and the manifest elimination of man's identity, but even the clear negation of divine goodness."[56] The same author says again that God has allowed death to occur because He "judged that it was not right for humanity, having abused free choice, to have an immortal nature."[57]

Summarizing the foregoing considerations, St Maximus writes: "I do not think that the limit of this present life is rightly called death, but rather release from death, separation from corruption, freedom from slavery, cessation of trouble, the taking away of wars, passage beyond confusion, the receding of darkness, rest from labors, silence from confused buzzing, quiet from excitement, a veiling of shame, flight from the passions, the vanishing of sin, and, to speak briefly, the termination of evils."[58]

For the Fathers, although it springs, insofar as a general phenomenon affecting all humanity, from the sin of the first man and, insofar as a particular phenomenon affecting each person in a singular manner, with phenomena tied to evil indirectly (sickness, corruption…) or directly (killings, wars…), and although God does not prevent this insofar as He respects human freedom even in its most unfortunate forms and consequences, death remains, as to the moment of its arrival, under the control of Providence. They are convinced that each person dies at the time which, spiritually, is the most favorable according to the knowledge and foreknowledge of God. St Maximus the Confessor has developed the idea that every individual receives from God a clearly defined time for living, one offering the maximum possibilities for filling in the distance that separates us from Him.[59] In this way can be explained why some die under the effect of a mild cause, while others remain alive after being struck with serious illness or having passed through the worst dangers. From a different point of view, St John Chrysostom considers that one should not be troubled by death, neither someone "bad and subject to the passions," for it is a providential interruption of the course of his vices, nor someone "good and virtuous," for "he was carried off before evil corrupted his heart, and has passed over to a place where his virtue will be henceforth out of harm's way and where one will no longer be afraid of changing."[60]

The Fathers strongly emphasize that for the just "death is something good"[61] since it enables them to gain access to a life better in all respects.[62] But this perspective is valid above all after Christ accomplished His saving work and is explained by the Fathers in taking this work into account.[63] We will come back to it then, as we have mentioned, restricting ourselves here and in the following section to looking at death as it appears before Christ changes its significance, and therefore also for anyone who considers it outside of Christ.

B) *Death's Spiritual Negativity.* Despite the previously cited nuances, the Fathers and the entire Tradition perceive death overall, before its meaning was changed by Christ, as an evil. Thus St Paul characterizes it as 'enemy' (1 Cor. 15:26).

Death is twice evil, since on the one hand as we have seen it springs from ancestral sin, and is on the other a source of sin.[64]

After the sin of the first man, death is in fact, since its advent, in the devil's power (cf. Heb. 2:14). From a physical vantage point, the devil uses it as a means to exercise his hatred against humanity and spread evil over creation.

From a spiritual vantage point, he utilizes it—just like the natural and non-culpable passions, especially pleasure and suffering [65] —to induce man to sin and lead him to develop within himself unnatural and culpable passions. St Paul can thus speak of those "who through fear of death were all their lifetime subject to bondage" (Heb. 2:15), and even to speak of death because of which "all have sinned" (Rom. 5:12).[66] This idea is taken up again by a certain number of eastern Fathers.[67] Thus Theodore of Mopsuestia remarks that "by becoming mortal, we acquired a greater tendency to sin," and explains that the necessity of satisfying the body's needs leads mortals to the passions, for the latter represent an inevitable means for temporary survival.[68] Theodoret of Cyrrhus extends his teacher's thought. Emphasizing that "mortal beings are necessarily subject to passions and dread, pleasures and vexations, anger and hatred,"[69] he explains how, thinking to escape death in this way, fallen man is led to give himself up to numerous evil passions: "All those born [of Adam] receive a mortal nature; but such a nature possesses countless needs: it requires food, drink, clothing, housing, and various trades. These needs often prompt an excess of the passions and excess begets sin. The divine apostle says then that, Adam having sinned and become mortal through sin, death and sin enter into his race: 'Death, because of which all have sinned, has passed to all men' (Rom. 5:12)."[70] For example, thinking to live more securely and to guarantee health, man accumulates money and shows himself eager to acquire always more of it, falling thus into *philarguria* (avarice) and *pleonexia* (greed); he feeds his own body abundantly, gives himself up to the pleasure of the senses, and cherishes his own body in every way, falling into *gastrimargia* (gluttony), *luxuria* (lust) and in a general manner *philautia* (self-love) the mother of all the passions; he secures his power over things and other people, thinking to thus better assert and establish his own existence and, in so doing, develops the passion of aggression; he seeks, through various works, to become famous, thinking to thus live enduringly in human memory, but in this way falls into vainglory and pride.[71]

The same idea is again found with other Fathers like St John Chrysostom, who stresses that the fear of death exercises a tyranny over all men[72] which incites them to do anything to avoid it;[73] like St John of Damascus for whom man is "enslaved by death through sin,"[74] and like St Gregory Palamas.[75] But St Maximus the Confessor has given it special emphasis in close connection with his soteriologcial doctrine. For Maximus "our forefather's sin… caused the fear of death to rule human nature."[76] Fruit of sin, death also incites man to sin. More precisely, the devil and demons besiege man's passible side, it having appeared subsequent to the ancestral sin, and make use of the natural and non-culpable passions contained in it to develop, out of it, the culpable passions.[77] Now, figured among the natural and non-culpable passions is a revulsion towards death.[78] Out of this the devil and the demons arouse an evil apprehension of death that turns man toward sin and the passions with the illusory goal of avoiding death. Thus, not only physically, but spiritually, death (just like pleasure and sorrow[79]) comes to exercise a domination and tyranny over man that steers the disposition of his will and his choices in the direction of evil.[80]

Revulsion towards death becomes apprehension of death and gives rise to fear, anguish, melancholy, disgust, despair, and worst of all, hatred of God and revolt against Him. Revulsion towards death becomes likewise denial and rejection of death, and the rejection of death leads man to become passionally attached to life—not to true life, but to life according to this world. Conversely, this rejection is itself reinforced by the impassioned attachment of man to the false goods of this world, which he dreads being deprived of by death.[81]

Christ, by His saving economy, has delivered man from death and given him eternal life. This was moreover, in the eyes of the Fathers, the chief goal of his Incarnation. St Gregory of Nyssa writes magnificently on this theme: "Perhaps an exact knowledge of the mystery would let it be said with likelihood that the birth [of Christ] is not the cause of His death, but it is, to the contrary, because of death that God has accepted to be born. It is not in fact the need to live that leads the Eternal to subject Himself to birth, but the desire to call us back from death to existence."[82]

By willingly taking death upon Himself (since He was not naturally subject to it, having been conceived virginally and having therefore escaped the biological transmission of the effects of the ancestral sin[83]), by remaining inaccessible to corruption (since His flesh was that of the divine Word,[84] or since in Him mortal human nature was united to immortal divine nature, benefiting from its energies[85]) and by rising from the dead He has made it so men are not utterly given up to death and corruption, but has acquired for them the grace of the ability to be resurrected at the end of time, with their own body reunited to their soul, but renewed, uplifted to a higher mode of existence, having become incorruptible for ever in a condition no longer subject to the vicissitudes or limits of matter and time.[86]

In the eyes of the Fathers, the death of Christ signifies then 'the death of death,'[87] and His resurrection the victory and perpetual reign of Life—eternal and incorruptible life. On Pascha and in the weeks that follow, the Orthodox Church tirelessly sings: "Christ is risen from the dead, trampling down death by death, and upon those in the tombs bestowing life."

Because He has assumed all of human nature within Himself, it is the body of all men that has escaped corruption and is risen in His own body[88] Christ makes His appearance then as a New Adam who reverses the process of the Fall. "For since by man *came* death, by man came also *came* the resurrection of the dead" (1 Cor. 15:21).

It must be stressed that Christ's victory over death is a physical and not just spiritual reality. Quite really and objectively Christ has destroyed death and is risen in his own humanity and for all mankind; this is not just a subjective view of our faith as so-called Christian theologians, claiming to 'demythologize' Christianity, have maintained in recent decades. Here we must remember the word of St Paul: "If Christ is not risen, your faith is futile" (1 Cor. 15:17), and recall that the Orthodox, according to a very ancient tradition, greet each other at the time of the feast of the Resurrection and in the weeks that follow not only with: "Christ is risen!", but answer this proclamation with: "*Truly* He is risen!"

But for all that it must not be forgotten that Christ's victory over death is equally a spiritual victory.

By His death, Christ has put sin to death and at the same time erased the sins of all mankind.

Christ has also vanquished the spiritual power exercised over humanity by the devil[89] and the demons through the subterfuge of death, and that even before dying—at the time of His passion, His agony, and on the Cross, even though the prospect of death was presented to Him directly and even though the devil proposed all kinds of temptations in connection with this.[90] The devil in fact sought to inspire in Him an evil fear of death, provoke despair, make Him reject the will of God and therefore lead Him astray, have Him revolt against God. Christ overcame these temptations by proving himself inaccessible to them, maintaining His human will unfailingly in accord with the divine will,[91] and has in this way obtained for those who would be united with Him and receive His grace an overcoming of such temptations whenever they occur. Christ's agony in Gethsemane is a crucial moment in this saving process. The sentence of Christ: "My Father, if it is possible, let this cup pass from Me;

nevertheless, not as I will, but as You will" (Matt. 26:39), testifies on His behalf, before the prospect of death, to the rejection of this temptation to yield to His apprehension (expressed in the first part of the formula) by maintaining the accord (expressed in the second part of the formula) of His human will with the divine will of His Father.[92] Christ has in this way indicated to us the way to follow when such a temptation presents itself, but He has also obtained for us the power to overcome it to the extent that we are united to Him. Just as Christ's human will actually received assistance and strength from His divine nature with which His human nature was united,[93] we are assisted and strengthened in our human weakness by the energies of the Spirit that Christ communicates to us if we are united to Him.

Christ's victory over death is therefore His victory over death and corruption as physical phenomena, but also a victory over sin and the passions which are apt to appear and develop with the actual prospect of death and the fear it arouses. This is why the victory of Christ over death not only assumes its meaning for mankind at the end of time, when everyone will be resurrected, or, at present, as a source of hope and a firm assurance that our faith is not futile (cf. 1 Cor. 15:17); it also has an impact from that very moment, on the spiritual life of each Christian, that it liberates from the power of death, sin, the passions, and the devil. This is why the death and resurrection of Christ are presented by Tradition as constituting, for anyone who receives their grace by being baptized, a spiritual death and rebirth, namely the death of the old man and rebirth of the new man (cf. 2 Cor. 5:17). The Scriptures present Christ's victory over death as a victory over sin not only because death is the consequence and seal of ancestral sin, but also because it is for fallen humanity a potential source of sin, an instrument in the hands of the devil for inclining man to sin and to the evil passions, a means by which he causes the law of sin to reign in them. Thus, St Paul writes that Christ has shared in the human condition "that through death He might destroy him who had the power of death, that is, the devil, and release those who through fear of death were all their lifetime subject to bondage" (Heb. 2:14–15).[94]

The Scriptures and the Fathers likewise present Christ's victory over death as a victory over the devil, because death was established in human nature by the acquiescing of the first man to temptation and, hence, to the devil's will, but also because the devil makes use of the fear of death as a tool to dominate man and incline him toward sin and the passions.[95]

We have seen that the Fathers say that death was permitted by God so evil and the evil state of man would not be immortal. But they also say that death was abolished by Him so man's mortal condition would not be endless and his death not eternal: that would have utterly contradicted the plan of God who had created man to live and not to die; that would also mean that "the wickedness of the serpent would have prevailed over the will of God."[96]

By the saving work of Christ, death has lost the definitive character it seemed to have previously. "For no longer now," writes St Athanasius of Alexandria, "do we die as subject to condemnation; but as men who rise from the dead we await the general resurrection of all, 'which in its own times He shall show' [1 Tim. 6:15], even God, Who has also wrought it, and bestowed it upon us."[97] Before the end of time and the general resurrection, death continues to exist for all men, but it has lost its power over those who are united to Christ (through the sacraments and the practice of the divine commandments); it still manifests itself physically, but has ceased being an annihilation to become a rest, a sleep.[98] Spiritually, it has lost its power, it no longer prevails, and especially it no longer inspires a fear inclining us to sin. It is in this strong sense that the Christian is liberated here and now from death. St Athanasius of Alexandria notes: "For that death is destroyed, and that the Cross has become the victory over it, and that it has no more power but is verily dead, this is no small proof, or rather an evident warrant, that it is despised by all Christ's disciples, and that they all take the aggressive against it and no longer fear it; but by the sign of the Cross and by faith in Christ tread it down as dead ... Before men believe Christ, they see in death an object of terror, and play the coward before it. But when they are gone over to Christ's faith and teaching, their contempt for death is so great that they even eagerly rush upon it, and become witnesses for the Resurrection the Savior has accomplished against it ... [they] scoff at death, jesting at it, and saying what has been written against it of old: 'O death, where is your victory? O grave, where is your sting?' (1 Cor. 15:55)."[99] St John Chrysostom writes in the same vein: "[Death] is no longer terrible, but has been trodden under foot, has been utterly despised; it is vile and of no account... People of former times were, during their entire life, subject to the fear of death; they were slaves; people today, to the contrary, are delivered from these terrors and laugh at these phantoms that made their ancestors shudder."[100] "You see," he again remarks, "that this death, the sight of which was so dreadful before Jesus Christ, has become contemptible since His resurrection. Through [this resurrection] the stratagems of the devil have lost all their power; through it we are contemptuous of death; through it we put ourselves above this present life; through it, however clothed with a body, we can enjoy the same privileges as the incorporeal powers."[101]

Thanks to Christ, death has radically changed in meaning. St John Chrysostom underscores the paradox: "By death we have become immortal;"[102] "what was the greatest of evils, the chief point of our unhappiness, what the devil had introduced into the world, in a word death, God has turned it to our honor and glory."[103] The same saint again remarks: "Know then how much death inspired fear previously, so that in seeing the scorn in which it is held today you will admire God, the author of this change. Learn of its past might, so that in seeing its present weakness you will give thanks to Jesus Christ who has overthrown it completely. Formerly, nothing was more powerful than it, and nothing more impotent than ourselves, but at present nothing is equal to our power. Do you see what a wondrous change has been accomplished? Do you see how God has rendered weak what was strong and strong what was weak, showing us his power on one side as on the other?"[104]

Besides losing its power to dominate man spiritually, death has ceased being an absolute end to become the beginning of a new life, a life without end. As St Maximus the Confessor says, Christ has made "death into the beginning of our natural transformation into incorruption."[105] In this fallen world, death manifests positively as the moment of passage towards an immortal life [106] and the necessary means to gain access to the better circumstances of the other world where man will know, in body and soul, a superior mode of existence no longer involving the present limitations. [107] Through the saving work of Christ, death is no longer simply a door that closes on earthly life, nor a door that opens into the subterranean abodes of Hades where until that time souls seemed to be confined forever, but a door that opens into the celestial life and enables man to gain access to the Kingdom of Heaven[108] where he will finally be able to receive if worthy, not only with his soul but with his body, the fullness of divine blessings. Death is no longer a fact that reduces human life to nothing, but an event that gives it access to a more real life, to a better,[109] fuller existence,[110] no longer then something that humiliates and annihilates it, but something that uplifts it and endows it with a surplus of being. "The devil had introduced it for our loss, for bringing us back to the earth and so closing off for us any hope of salvation. But, in His turn, Christ has won it back and transformed it," notes St John Chrysostom.[111]

Thanks to Christ, not only is death no longer to be feared, but it becomes paradoxically a desirable reality (certainly not in and for itself, but because it enables the faithful to gain access to a better life closer to God). The Fathers love to cite in this respect the example of the martyrs who anticipate death joyously.[112] Even though it is not sought for (and should not be), at least it is accepted willingly by the Christian who is prepared to welcome it in faith with Christ. One might object and say that such an attitude is not new and is already to be found in such philosophies as Platonism and Stoicism. But there is in fact a great difference. The Christian attitude differs from the Platonic for, as Jean Daniélou so pertinently declares, what it seeks is "not liberation of the soul with respect to the prison of the body, but the liberation of soul and body with respect to bondage to the flesh."[113] It also differs from the Stoic attitude for which the victory over death is a purely intellectual and a psychological victory over those representations that cause us to fear death. On the other hand, what matters to the Christian in his desire, his welcoming of death, is to live with Christ close to the Father. Thus, St Ignatius of Antioch writes: "It is better for me to die in Jesus Christ than to rule the ends of the earth. That is the one I seek; that is the one I desire, who arose for us. But pains of birth have come upon me. Grant this to me, brothers... do not hand over to the world the one who wants to belong to God or deceive him by what is material. Allow me to receive the pure light; when I arrive there, I will be a human... For I write to you while living desiring to die. My passion has been crucified and there is no burning love within me for material things; instead there is living water, which also is speaking in me, saying to me from within: 'Come to the Father.'"[114] Recalling the death of his sister Macrina, St Gregory of Nyssa describes a similar attitude: "As she approached her end, as if she discerned the beauty of the Bridegroom more clearly, she hastened towards the Beloved with the greater eagerness."[115]

In the course of the text, St Gregory relates the dying prayer of St Macrina; her words summarize all the previous considerations: "Thou, O Lord, hast freed us from the fear of death. Thou hast made the end of this life the beginning to us of true life. Thou for a season restest our bodies in sleep and awakest them again at the last trump [1 Cor. 15:52]. Thou givest our earth, which Thou hast fashioned with Thy hands, to the earth to keep in safety. One day Thou wilt take again what Thou hast given, transfiguring with immortality and grace our mortal and unsightly remains. Thou hast saved us from the curse and from sin, having become both for our sakes. Thou hast broken the heads of the dragon [Psalm

73:14] who had seized us with his jaws, in the yawning gulf of disobedience. Thou hast shown us the way of resurrection, having broken the gates of hell, and brought to nought him who had the power of death — the devil."[116]

Chapter Two

The Moment of Death

I. THE TRIAL OF THE COMING DEATH

1 The Nature of the Trial.

We often hear it said that anyone who dies suddenly is very lucky because they did not see death coming and did not see themselves dying. For the Fathers, however, it is grievous to die without being able, even for a few moments, to prepare oneself for death, and it is, to the contrary, a grace of God—which we must ask of Him—to see death coming and have time to put ourselves in an appropriate frame of mind regarding Him. A great Orthodox monk of this century, in a lengthy *Prayer at daybreak* that he had composed, includes this request to Christ: "When Thou shalt be pleased to bring my life to an end, forewarn me that I may prepare my soul to come before Thee."[1]

The desire to die suddenly is spiritually irresponsible, but expresses the fear of having to face death and the presentiment that a difficult trial is involved.

This trial is threefold.

Someone near death feels that he will have to quit this world, be separated from those near and dear, lose everything that he possessed, and be removed from his familiar universe.

He also knows, by the example of those who have died before him, that his body will become inanimate, cold, that it will be buried and decompose. This body will still be his, but he will no longer control it and no longer have any power over it.

He finds himself faced with a condition altogether new with respect to the one he had known up to that time; he has not the least experience of it, and its real nature is totally unknown to him. His future presents itself as a huge dark hole which is about to engulf him. This can only arouse disquiet and even anxiety. The *Canon of Supplication to the Most-Holy Theotokos at the Parting of the Soul from the Body* mentions the fear that seizes the dying at the prospect of this separation: "Great fear now seizes my soul with unspeakable trembling, and it is afflicted as it is about to go forth from the body."[2] Although it might, by faith, be certain that he will continue to live, he cannot know how. He does not know what life without a body is like; he does not know where the soul will find itself and where it will go, in what state it will find itself, whether its condition will be happy or sad. St Macarius of Alexandria relates in this manner some of these anxieties experienced by the dying: "the soul has not as yet experienced a summons as terrifying as that one; it fears the harshness of the path and the change in dwelling-place; likewise it is gripped by sadness for the sight of things and its possessions; it suffers from the separation of the body, its companion; this is something painful for it and it weeps because of the dissolving of its communion with it, seeing itself deprived of its society."[3]

Anyone on the verge of dying is generally in a condition of sickness, infirmity, or debility which makes such questions even more grievous, even more agonizing.

Nietzsche claimed that religion was an invention of feeble man to reassure and console himself in the face of death. Nothing is more false. Surely it is easier for the agnostic and the materialist to face death by telling themselves that it is a mere nothing, an immense sleep from which no one awakens, and after it there is nothing else; while a believer, for whom death opens out upon the prospect of an eternal life, is *a priori* ignorant of its form and content.

Even sanctity does not guarantee anyone serenity before death. The greatest saints are also those who feel themselves the greatest sinners and who most fear what will transpire after death; even though they place their hope in the goodness of God, they also fear that their sins have earned them a place in hell and would have to suffer a wretched condition for eternity. Abba Peter relates these words confided to him by Abba Isaiah as the hour of his death approached: "Fear of this dark hour, when I am thrown before the face of God, oppresses me. No one will hear me. No one will have rest as a prospect."[4] And for his part, Abba Elias acknowledges: "I fear three things: the moment when my soul will leave my body, and when I shall appear before God, and when the sentence will be given against me."[5]

2 The Importance of the Family's
and the Church's Accompaniment of the Dying.

During these moments of disquiet and anxiety, it is especially important for the dying to receive help and support from their circle of family and friends. When, in our day, many people die in solitude, distanced or separated from their family, most often in a hospital's anonymous and cold setting, such an 'accompaniment' is indispensable. Even in the case where the sick person has a diminished awareness or seems to have lost consciousness under the effect of the disease or medication, a simple, even silent presence, if attentive and loving, is an invaluable help. Even more so, the prayer of those closest to him is of great assistance in confronting and overcoming this trial.

The whole ecclesial community is called upon to join together in this prayer and, in these difficult moments, the Church has arranged to be especially present beside the sick, bringing them the support of its prayer and its grace. It has at its disposal two offices: *The Office of Intercession for the Dying* and the *Canon of Supplication to the Most-Holy Theotokos at the Parting of the Soul from the Body.*

The former consists first in the recitation of Psalms 69 and 142, which are read in various offices, but which, in light of these circumstances, show themselves to be profoundly apt: "God, make speed to save me; O Lord, make haste to help me. . . . But I am poor and needy, O God; help me! Thou art my helper and my redeemer, O Lord; make no long tarrying."[6] "Lord, hear my prayer, consider my supplication in Thy truth; hearken unto me in Thy righteousness, And enter not into judgment with Thy servant, for before Thee shall no man living be justified. For the enemy hath persecuted my soul; he hath smitten my life down to the ground; he hath laid me in the darkness, as those that have been long dead, And my spirit is despondent within me, and my heart within me is vexed. I remembered the days of old; I mused upon all Thy works; I exercised myself in the works of Thy hands. I stretched forth my hands unto Thee; my soul gasped unto Thee as a thirsty land. Hear me soon, O Lord, for my spirit faltereth; turn not Thy face from me, ... tell me, O Lord, the way that I should walk in, for I lift up my soul unto Thee. Deliver me from mine enemies, O Lord, for I have fled unto Thee. Teach me to do Thy will, for Thou art my God. Thy good Spirit shall lead me into the land of righteousness. For Thy Name's sake, O Lord, quicken me by Thy truth; Thou shalt bring my soul out of trouble. And of Thy mercy Thou shalt slay mine enemies, and destroy all them that vex my soul, for I am

Thy servant."[7] One Canon (poetic song) in nine odes, composed by St Theodore the Studite, tells of the fear of the dying person at appearing before the dread judgment seat of Christ and asks Him to spare him at the hour of judgment, henceforth pardoning his sins. This prayer has then a strong penitential accent which gives the soul, if alienated from God, a last chance to repent and return to Him: "Turn back, wretched soul, and lament, before the fair-ground of life comes to an end, before the Lord shuts the door of the bridal chamber."[8] In the prayer that follows, the priest asks God that the separation of soul from body which will occur might actually be for the dying "the separation from the fleshly and sinful bonds," and that his soul be welcomed by Him into peace. Another prayer asks God, who is "the repose of our souls and bodies," to "transform into rest the separation of the soul and body" of the dying person, and also to deliver him "from these intolerable sufferings, from his cruel sickness."

The *Canon of Supplication to the Most-Holy Theotokos at the Parting of the Soul from the Body* is "to be recited in the presence of the dying who can no longer speak", and entrusts to the Mother of God all the distress of the dying and asks for her help in very touching accents. "Great fear now seizes my soul with unspeakable trembling, and it is afflicted as it is about to go forth from the body. Comfort it, O Most pure One."[9] "The rending of the bonds, the sundering of the natural law that holds the whole fleshly composition together, causes me anguish and unbearable necessity ... Look down on me from above, O Mother of God, and mercifully attend now unto the visitation that has come upon me, that, gazing on thee, I may depart from the body with rejoicing."[10] "The night of death, dark and moonless, has overtaken me still unready, sending me unprepared on that long and dreadful journey. Let thy mercy accompany me, O Sovereign Lady."[11]

II. PHENOMENA AND EXPERIENCES PRECEDING DEATH

The coming of death is so much more difficult to bear alone since a whole series of phenomena, unknown to a person while living, occur about him and within him.

1 A Review of One's Whole Life.

One of the best known phenomena immediately preceding death is the inner perception, by the dying, of a review of his whole life, every moment of which files past in his consciousness.

Such a phenomenon has been mentioned by secular authors relating the testimonies of people brought back to life after experiencing a near-death state.[12] According to certain testimonies, memories succeed each other at a dizzying rate in their chronological order; according to other testimonies, all the memories present themselves simultaneously and a single glance is enough to take them in. All the testimonies agree in asserting that all the memories present themselves in a quite vivid and realistic, but also precise manner: although the images file past quite rapidly or are presented simultaneously in very large numbers, each of them is precisely perceived and recognized. Some witnesses recall having perceived in this review only the major facts of their existence; others assert that every act of their life was represented, from the most important to the most insignificant.

This phenomenon is equally mentioned by Orthodox authors.[13] Metropolitan Hierotheos Vlachos relates that an important contemporary religious figure has stated that "at the hour of death a person will see even the slightest deed he has done in his life, just as in a fraction of a second one sees a small impurity in a glass of water."[14]

Here a new trial for the dying is encountered: he might on the one hand experience a painful nostalgia upon seeing the happy moments of his past, but above all he is overwhelmed upon seeing all his past sins exhibited to him in an instant. Metropolitan Hierotheos Vlachos notes: "When a person's soul is about to leave the body, the memory of the sins which he has committed in his life comes back to him. It is a truly intolerable state. St John Chrysostom speaks of it. He says that on the last days of a person's biological life 'sins contort his soul', they stir up his soul."[15]

From the spiritual point of view, however, this last trial is also as if a last possibility, a "last chance" given to him to repent, and more generally to define his spiritual attitude with respect to the totality of his life and with respect to God. This review is in fact for the dying like a balance sheet of his life, which presents itself at once as a rapid examination of conscience, and as an overall synthesis of his existence which makes its general meaning apparent, and which for this reason is as if a judgment.[16] The dying person can respond to this by an interior disposition towards repentance (in the face of this balance sheet and the judgment on his failings) and thankfulness (at the sight of everything God has given him during his entire life), expressed by a brief prayer, even if this can no longer be expressed by words, or even an ordinary thought, and amounts to a mere attitude.

2 Supernatural Apparitions, Visions and Auditions.

In certain cases, the moment of death is accompanied by various phenomena of a paranormal and supernatural character perceived only by the dying, the latter gaining access then to modes of extrasensory and supersensible perception and to a form of superterrestrial consciousness, perceptual modes belonging to the other world.[17]

a. One common phenomenon is the perception by the dying of people in his circle of acquaintances and their attitude, even though he no longer has the use of his senses and has lost the ordinary consciousness that connects him to the world by means of the body.[18] St Macarius of Alexandria relates such an experience: "Miserable and weak, the soul sees at that time, while they gather about him from everywhere, brothers, friends, parents helplessly lamenting and weeping; it also perceives the tears, laments, and weeping of those who stand around it."[19] The dying, although they cannot show it, are altogether aware of the reactions and attitudes of the people in their circle, and these people can have a positive or negative impact, a comforting or to the contrary, a shocking and depressing impact. Those who gather about the dying should be aware of this fact and their responsibility.

b. Another phenomenon that might be produced is a vision, by the dying, of other people dying at the same time as themselves in other places, or previously deceased people of their circle. St Gregory the Great remarks: "It frequently happens that a soul on the point of death recognizes those with whom it is to share the same eternal dwelling for equal blame or reward."[20] The same saint cites the case of a monk named John who, just before dying, cried out: "Ursus, come"; his brethren learned later that this was a monk of another monastery who died at the same moment as he himself.[21] Such phenomena of clairvoyance and seeing at a distance presuppose no particular spiritual quality and are experienced as much by sinners as by the just. Thus, St Gregory the Great relates the case of a young man named Eumorphius who, at the moment of dying, commanded his servant: "Go quickly and tell [the adjutant] Stephen to come at once, because our ship is ready to take us to Sicily." Hurrying to the home of this man who lived not far from there, the servant found that he had just died and, returning to his master, likewise found him dead. Sicily as it turns out, in the words of Eumorphius, symbolized hell (by reason of its volcanic activity).[22]

c. A good many patristic writings, especially the *Lives* of the saints, tell of the apparitions of prophets, saints, and even the Mother of God or Christ Himself. These apparitions concern only a minority of the dying. These are, in nearly all cases, people whose holiness of life has made them worthy of being visited by those they have loved and prayed to their entire life, to whom they have devoted their earthly existence, and who come in a visible manner to comfort, console, reassure, and support them[23] in this crucial moment of passage to another world.

The *Life* of St Syncletica relates, in a quite general manner, that a short time before her death she "experienced visions."[24] One *Saying* is seen to be more precise as regards Abba Sisoes who had the privilege of benefiting from a vision of all heaven's inhabitants: "It was said of Abba Sisoes that when he was at the point of death, while the Fathers were sitting beside him, his face shone like the sun. He said to them, 'Look, Abba Anthony is coming.'[25] A little later he said, 'Look, the choir of the prophets is coming.' Again his countenance shone with brightness and he said, 'Look, the choir of apostles is coming.' His countenance increased with brightness and lo, he spoke with someone. Then the old men asked him, 'With whom are you speaking, Father?' He said, 'Look, the angels are coming to fetch me …' [And after a little while] he said to them, 'Look, the Lord is coming and he's saying, "Bring me the vessel [ACTS 9:15] from the desert."' And he soon gave up his spirit."[26] When St Daniel the Stylite was dying, the same phenomenon occurred, but this was from someone possessed who proclaimed in the midst of a crowd: "There is great joy in heaven at this hour, for the holy angels have come to take the holy man with them, besides there are come, too, the honorable and glorious companies of prophets and apostles and martyrs and saints."[27]

St Gregory the Great recounts how his aunt Tarsilla, at the moment of her death, although many people were gathered about her, "suddenly… looked up and saw Jesus coming. She turned to her visitors with a look of great concern. 'Stand back! Stand back!' she exclaimed. 'Jesus is coming.' While she directed her gaze intently on the vision, her holy soul took its leave from the body."[28]

The same saint relates the case of a certain Musa who, before the departure of her soul, saw the Blessed Virgin. "Our Blessed Lady called to her, and little Musa lowered her eyes as she answered with a clear voice, 'I am coming my noble Lady, I am coming to you.' With these words she gave up her soul."[29]

St Gregory the Great, yet again, recounts that Abbot Stephen, just before dying, had a vision of the Apostles: "In an outburst of joy he exclaimed, 'It is good that you come, my lords! It is good! But why do you take the trouble to visit a worthless servant? I come! I come! I am most grateful to you!' Since he kept repeating these words, his friends standing at his side tried to find out to whom he was speaking. Surprised at their question, the sick man answered, 'Do you not see the holy Apostles present here? Do you not see the princes of the Apostles, Peter and Paul?' Then turning again to his vision he said, 'I come, I come.' And with these words he breathed his last. By following the Apostles he bore witness to the fact that he had seen them."[30] The same saint likewise relates the case of a nun named Galla who, a short time before her death, "saw the Apostle Peter standing ... near her bed. Without the least sign of fear, and encouraged by her love, she spoke to him with great joy. 'What is it, my lord?' she said. 'Have my sins been forgiven?' With a most pleasant expression on his face, St Peter nodded in affirmation. 'They are forgiven,' he said. 'Come.'"[31] St Gregory the Great also remarks that "it often happens that the saints of heaven appear to the just at the hour of death in order to reassure them."[32] He cites the case of Bishop Probus who, at the moment of his death, saw the holy martyrs Juvenal and Eleutherius appear to him.[33] Two saints likewise appeared to St Macarius nine days before his death, when weakened from illness he was obliged to take to his bed: "While he was thinking to himself, as was his custom, about his passing away and his meeting God and the judgment that would be passed against him at that time and the place where he would be thrown, two saints suddenly appeared to him, shining brightly with glory and honor, their faces full of joy. When the old man saw them, he kept silent for a while and one of them said to him, 'Don't you know who I am?' Although he studied him, he was unable to clearly make him out on account of the great radiance that shone from him. After a little, he said to the one who had spoken to him, 'I think you're my father, Abba Antony.' Saint Abba Antony said to him, 'Don't you know who this other person is?' Once again he was silent, for he never replied to anything hastily. Abba Antony said to him, 'This is my brother Pachomius, the father of the monks of Tabennesi. We have been sent to summon you. Hereafter take care of your business, for in another nine days you will lay aside the garment of skin [Gen. 3:21] and you will dwell with us. Lift your eyes to heaven and see the place that has been prepared for you to rejoice and enter into rest.' And so the saints withdrew from him."[34] As for St Daniel the Stylite: "Three days before his falling asleep in the middle of the night he was allowed to see at one time all those who had been well pleasing to God."[35]

d. Apparitions of angels and demons are on the other hand not only common, but universal. In fact the soul, when it begins to be detached from the body, "sees the spiritual world that the body had concealed from it. When a person dies, the first thing that presents itself is the world of spiritual beings, of angels and demons, that surround him. There are people who, thanks to a special act of God's goodness, receive this faculty of spiritual vision, —angelophanies[36] for instance—prior to their death. But, at death, everyone gains access to this naturally."[37]

A good many patristic texts affirm that, at the moment when the soul is going to be separated from the body, angels come before the dying to collect his soul and conduct it into the other world,[38] while demons likewise come to try to seize it.[39]

As regards the first, we have previously seen that the dying, St Sisoes said to those about him: "Look, the angels are coming to fetch me."[40] St Gregory Nazianzus notes on the subject of St Basil, in his funeral oration on the latter: "He lay, drawing his last breath, and awaited by the choir on high, towards which he had long directed his gaze."[41] When St Macarius arrived at the moment of his death, an angel "came with large multitudes of incorporeal choirs and said to him, 'Hurry, come, for all those standing around you will testify on your behalf.' And Abba Macarius said in a loud voice, 'Lord Jesus, my soul's beloved, receive my spirit' [Acts 7:59] And so he went to sleep."[42] When Abba Paphnutius was near death, "an angel of the Lord came to him saying; 'Come now, you blessed one, enter yourself into the eternal tabernacles of God. For the prophets have come to welcome you into their choirs.'"[43]

According to patristic testimony, the angels can be more or less numerous, but in general there are at least two. The first is the angel charged with conducting (that is to say accompanying and guiding) the soul into the other world; this is the 'psychopompic' or 'psychagogic' angel.[44] The second is the dying person's guardian angel. "According to the doctrine of the Church, [this latter angel] stands before our death bed and receives our soul ... He becomes visible and accessible to us after [our soul's] separation from the body."[45] These two angels are mentioned in numerous texts. One Russian Orthodox monk, living in the nineteenth century and having had in his youth a 'near-deathexperience'[46] relates: "two Angels appeared at my side; for some reason in one of them I recognized my Guardian Angel, but the other was unknown to me;"[47] a pious pilgrim later informed him that this last angel is the 'meeting angel'. These two angels are also mentioned in the *Life of St Salvius* written by St Gregory of Tours,[48] and in the account of St Theodora found in the *Life of St Basil the Young*: "When I was at the end of my strength I saw two radiant angels of God, who were like youths of inexpressible beauty. They were coming toward me. Their faces were shining, their gaze was full of love; their hair was like snow, white with a golden tinge; their garments glistened like lightning and were girded with gold."[49]

The arrival of demons before the dying and their being perceived are likewise mentioned by certain patristic witnesses. Thus St Gregory the Great tells of the case of a wealthy man who, "a short time before he died ... saw hideous spirits standing before him, threatening fiercely to carry him to the depths of hell."[50] St Theodora relates: "When I drew near the end of my life and the time of my departure had come, I saw a great multitude of demons who had surrounded my couch. Their faces were dark like soot and pitch, their eyes were like glowing coals, their entire appearance was as frightening and evil as fiery hell itself. They began to grow indignant and to make noise like dogs; others howled like wolves. [51] As they looked at me, they were full of anger; they threatened me, kept rushing at me and gnashing their teeth, and appeared ready to devour me. Yet they seemed to wait for a Judge who had not yet come but would do so; they were making ready charts and unrolling scrolls on which were written all my evil deeds. My miserable soul was taken by great fear and trembling. Not only the bitterness of death tormented me but even more the terrible appearance and the cruel demeanor of the frightening demons; these were to me like another death, only a worse one. I kept turning away my eyes in all directions so as not to see their terrible faces, and wished not to hear their voices, but I was unable to be rid of them. They turned everywhere and there was no one to help me."[52]

The *Canon of Supplication to the Most-Holy Theotokos at the Parting of the Soul from the Body* contains an echo of this type of apparition: "Make known thy mercy unto me, O thou pure and renowned Refuge ... and deliver me from the hands of demons, for many dogs have surrounded me:"[53] "noetic roaring lions have surrounded me, seeking to carry me away and bitterly torment me."[54]

These apparitions arouse in the soul, according to its state and spiritual tendencies, more or less fear. They are also then a trial, not only—which is understandable—when an apparition of frightening demons is involved, for these angels too assume for sinners a terrifying aspect; additionally, the dying person is aware at this time that in any case they are about to take the soul away from the body and from this world. Thus, St Macarius of Alexandria affirms: "Just as, when servants are sent by an earthly king to bring a man into his presence, when they come to take him and make known to him the king's command, this man fears the arrival of these servants who are to seize and without pity force him to go along with them, so too, when angels are sent to take a man's soul, whether he is just or a sinner, it is frightened in the presence of those who are to carry it off and hasten to seize it."[55] St John Chrysostom likewise mentions at several points the fear aroused by angels at the moment of death. He states that a person is "completely dazzled" at their arrival.[56] He also remarks that some of the dying seem terrorized, for this apparition is a sign that they soon must appear before the judgment seat of Christ: "Is it not this that fills the spirit of the dying with apparitions and frightful visions, which they themselves relate to us and the sight of which they cannot endure? In their despair they produce such violent efforts that they shake their whole bed and overturn it. They cast wild glances to every side on those who stand around them. One sees without what the soul is suffering within when it struggles against leaving the body, *or when it cannot endure the presence of the angels which have come for it.*"[57] And he adds: "If the glance of certain people often make us tremble with fear, what will we do when the angels come to us with menacing eye, and when the heavenly powers separate us from all present things?"[58]

It is likely, though, that St John Chrysostom is darkening the picture here for a pastoral reason: to incite his listeners to prepare themselves for death by detaching themselves, from now on, from this world and purifying themselves spiritually, so to appear with a pure conscience "before the dread judgment seat of Christ." Other texts present the coming of the angels in a more positive light and stress that their function is, before leading the soul of the deceased away, to help the one dying. Thus, in the *Life* of St Syncletica, it is specified that a little before her death she benefited from the assistance of angels.[59]

Venerable Bede, relating the account of one dying man, mentions the apparition of angels and demons at the same time, and attributes to them the recapitulation of the good and bad actions of a lifetime which, at the approach of death, is experienced by every person in their conscience; involved here is a prefiguration of the examination the soul will undergo later, at the time of its passage through the aerial toll-houses:[60] "A short time ago ... two most handsome youths came into my house and sat down near me, one at my head and one at my feet. One of them drew out a very beautiful but exceedingly small book and gave it to me to read. On looking into it, I found all the good deeds I had ever done written down, but they were very few and trifling. They took the volume back but said nothing to me. Then suddenly there appeared an army of evil spirits with horrible faces; they surrounded the outside of the house, also filling almost the whole of the interior, and they too sat down. Then the one who seemed to be chief among them, judging by his dark and gloomy face and by the fact that he occupied the chief seat, took a volume of enormous size and almost unbearable weight, horrible to behold, and ordered one of his followers to bring it to me to read. On reading it I found all my sins written down very clearly but in hideous hand-writing: not just my sins of word and deed but even my slightest thoughts. He said to the glorious white-robed men who sat by me, 'Why do you sit here since you know that this man is certainly ours?' They said, 'You speak the truth.'" [61]

e. Other extraordinary phenomena can accompany death.

—The dying person can hear noises of supernatural origin; sometime he alone perceives them, sometimes those about him perceive them at the same time. According to patristic testimony demons, when they manifest themselves, do so with a certain uproar, but the coming of angels or saints makes a noise analogous to the bursting in of a group of people[62] which can frighten the dying by its unexpected character.

—The dying can also hear songs which those who tell of them characterize as 'angelic' or 'heavenly'. Thus St Gregory the Great affirms that "frequently the sound of heavenly singing accompanies the death of the elect."[63] He recounts the case of a certain Servulus who, "realizing that death was near ... asked the strangers and guests to stand and recite with him the psalms for the dying. While he was chanting the psalms with them, awaiting death, he suddenly interrupted their prayer with a frightened cry. 'Listen', he said. 'Do you not hear the beautiful hymns resounding in heaven?' As he turned his mind to follow the melodies resounding within him, his soul was freed from the body."[64] He also recounts the case of the nun Romula who, before dying, heard the voices of two choirs, "the men singing the psalms and the women the responses. While these ceremonies for her departure were celebrated ... the soul of Romula was set free from the body to be conducted directly to heaven. And as the choirs escorted her soul, rising higher and higher, the sound of their singing gradually diminished" for the other people present who had perceived this singing as well.[65] In his *History of the Monks* Theodoret of Cyrrhus states that St Theodosius "migrated to the angelic choir."[66]

—The dying can also have visions of light.[67] The apparitions of Christ, the Mother of God, the Apostles, and saints take place within a sparkling light.[68] The angels that come before the dying are quite luminous to the point of dazzling them, as St John Chrysostom notes.[69] But this can likewise be the case with demons who, as Scripture says and as confirmed by the experience of the saints, can disguise themselves "as angels of light" (cf. 2 Cor. 11:14) for the purpose of deceiving man.

3 The Risks of Illusion.

As regards all these supernatural apparitions and perceptions, there is a significant risk of illusion.

Obviously, on the one hand, there are counterfeits to these in the form of deliriums or hallucinations possibly engendered by the dying person's state of illness, or of imaginative projections corresponding either to one's desires or fears. We will return to this point later.

On the other hand, the dying person who has not previously learned, as Scripture says, how to 'discern spirits' (1 Cor. 12:10), to "not believe every spirit, but test the spirits, whether they are of God" (1 John 4:1), might be unaware of the true nature of the apparitions and take for an apparition of Christ, a saint or an angel, the apparition of a demon who counterfeits one or the other. According to the Fathers, in fact, although angels always appear to men under the same form and such as they are, conversely the demons appear to them under multiple forms and assume numerous disguises.[70] Their goal is then to deceive people, especially at this crucial time of death when the last moment of one's eternal destiny is being played out. In general this involves giving the dying a reassuring vision of their future, dissipating their fear of God's judgment, and doing so in such a way that they do not repent at the very moment when a last possibility of repenting is offered.

From this point of view, the accounts of near-death experiences presented in some recent books should be viewed with much prudence and discernment, as much to their form as to the conclusions drawn from them.

4 Near-Death Experiences and Their Value.

Near-death experiences are undergone by people: 1) who are revived after being considered clinically dead by their doctors; 2) who, following accidents, serious injuries or illness, are found in a state very close to death; and 3) who, on the verge of dying, are able to give to those about them a description of what they are experiencing. Some of the people belonging to the first two categories are able to retain a memory of what they have experienced and provide a more or less detailed account.

Accounts of this kind have been collected in the 1970s in the United States by Dr. Raymond Moody in a book that has caused a considerable stir: *Life after Life*.[71] Other books of the same type[72] have been also very popular to the extent that, in a non-religious setting, they bring to the public at large insights about an unknown and reputed to be unknowable reality, or more precisely the certainty —independent of any belief—of a life after death, with reassuring conclusions on the nature of the latter.

With regard to what extent such accounts can be trusted and the value to be attributed to their interpretation and to the conclusions drawn from them, three remarks of a methodological order are to be made.

First, if people considered clinically dead have been brought back to life, this is because they were not altogether dead. Hence their accounts cannot be considered testimonies of an experience of death in the strict sense. Nevertheless, they retain all their value as testimonies about experiences of being on the verge of death.

Second, these are seldom raw accounts: they have passed through the filter of memory, with all that this includes of unconscious interpretive factors, endowing memory with a structure and a meaning capable of expressing it conceptually in a coherent narrative. Some of them, moreover, are noticeably reinterpreted in the light of esoteric, occult, or spiritist works.

Third, these accounts are themselves selected and put in perspective by the authors of the works in which they are collected, and are often subjected by these authors to a 'theoretically ideal' interpretive 'model' well-suited for endowing them with unity and coherence,[73] a model that surely reflects the personal opinions of these authors.[74]

Several remarks are necessary regarding the accounts themselves.

In his summary,[75] Dr. Moody includes two chief stages:

1) The dying person begins to perceive a disagreeable noise and at once feels himself conveyed with great rapidity through a kind of dark space. After that he finds himself outside his physical body, but without leaving his immediate physical surroundings; he perceives his own body, as well as the people about him, at a distance, like a spectator.

2) Other beings come to meet him, apparently wanting to come to help him. First he senses the presence of spirits whose role seems to him to consist in facilitating his passage into the other world (some perceive them as parents and friends deceased before them, others as 'guardian angels' or 'spirit guides'). Next "a loving, warm spirit of a kind he has never encountered before—a being of light—appears before him. This being asks him a question, nonverbally, to make him evaluate his life and helps him along by showing him a panoramic, instantaneous playback of the major events of his life."[76]

Dr. Moody is careful to point out however that: 1) despite striking similarities between the different testimonies upon which this summary is based, he finds no two are completely identical; 2) he finds no testimony that includes at once all the details that he presents in his 'composite experience' (for example, sometimes the being of light does not appear and the panoramic vision of one's life takes place independently); 3) none of the elements recorded in the individual testimonies that he has received is to be found again on a regular basis in every account; 4) the order in which a dying person passes through the different states described can differ from the one shown in his 'theoretical model' (for example, several people have declared that they perceived the 'being of light' a little before or at the very moment of leaving their physical body and not, as in his 'theoretical model', some moments later).[77]

The first stage, from the viewpoint of what Orthodox tradition teaches, is not at all surprising[78] and does not call for any particular caution:[79] this is the stage of the separation of the soul from the body (or more exactly its first phase, for this stage, as we will see in the next chapter, lasts a certain time). Man becomes capable of seeing his body from the outside still considering it all the while as his own. Such an experience of disincorporation can also occur on occasions other than death, in various forms of mystical ecstasy for example. This stage is abundantly described in Dr. Moody's book and in the other books of the same kind, which above all are concerned with out-of-body experiences and the immediate *post-mortem* state;[80] on the other hand it is seldom mentioned in

Christian literature because this literature chiefly focuses on the later stages of *post-mortem* life and the soul's final destiny.

The second stage includes elements we have previously indicated on the basis of Orthodox testimony: the dying person's panoramic vision of the events of his life and his perception of those near and dear to him who have died at the same time as himself or before.[81] The mention of a 'being of light' may correspond to one of those apparitions we have mentioned, which all take place in light. But the term 'being of light' and even more so the term 'entity', utilized by Dr. Moody, are generic expressions aimed at collecting under a single label realities variously identified by witnesses and often not identified at all; it gives a false impression that this is a single reality, identical in every case, while different beings are obviously involved. Here is to be found precisely the previously mentioned risk of illusion and confusion.

The experiences described by Dr. Moody have without any doubt a basis in reality and should not be contested in principle,[82] but viewed with discernment as to the interpretations applied. The majority of witnesses do not seem to possess the means for this discernment enabling them to recognize the nature of what has appeared to them. The fact that the 'being of light' may have shown in every instance positive feelings of tenderness and love is not enough to positively identify it (as an angel, a saint, or even Christ): patristic testimony shows that the devil does not always present himself under the form of a hate-filled being, but sometime feigns solicitude and goodness to seduce man and turn him away from God. This is seen for example in the *Life* of holy martyrs Timothy and Maura where the devil appeared to them during the most severe of their tortures, when they were very nearly dead, with the pretended goal of easing their sufferings, but with the actual intent of depriving them of the fruit of their martyrdom.[83] Neither is the appeasing character of the 'being of light' enough to assure us of his positive identity: demons can also, as we have said, present to the dying a serene vision of the beyond in order to divert them from the fear of God and from the repentance necessary for their salvation. The fact that the person appearing to the one who is dying prepares him to appear before God and arouses in him a feeling of repentance is, to the contrary, one factor in support of identifying him as being 'of God'. Notice however that, in the patristic testimonies cited, the saints give to those who do not recognize them the means to identify them.[84]

In general, though, the Fathers possess an aptitude for discernment acquired through the grace of God in the course of long years of ascesis during which they have become enlightened by the lessons of Scripture, the Fathers who have preceded them, and by the counsels of an experienced spiritual father. Besides, the traditional practice of sobriety in eastern spirituality hardly leaves any room for imaginative digressions; many patristic texts show us moreover that the Fathers to whom apparitions occurred at the moment of death not only do not look for them, but prove to be hesitant to accept them and recognize their reality. Patristic testimonies can be considered reliable for these reasons, but also for two other reasons: 1) saints belonging to different eras, and societies have had convergent experiences on this subject; 2) a certain number of the facts described—especially visions and supernatural auditions—have had witnesses among the people gathered about the saints at the moment of their death.[85] To this must be added a certain number of revelations concerning death and the hereafter granted to certain Fathers at various times in their life when the possibility of delirium, in connection with an illness for example, is clearly excluded.

Chapter Three

FROM THE FIRST TO THE THIRD DAY AFTER DEATH: THE SEPARATION OF THE SOUL FROM THE BODY

1 The Nature of Death: The Separation of the Soul from the Body.

Like many other religions or philosophies, Christianity considers death, insofar as an event, to be a separation of the soul from the body by the soul passing outside of the body. This definition of death is constant in patristic writings of every nature[1] and is reflected in the services of the Orthodox Church that precede, accompany, or follow one's demise.

The soul, being for the body the principle of its life (what animates it), its organization, its movement, and its preservation;[2] a body from which the soul is separated becomes inert; it ceases to be an organism: its components lose their unity and their relationships, and dissolve.[3] It is in this sense that man, taken from the earth, returns to it (cf. Gen. 3:19).

As for the soul separated from the body, it continues to exist and to live:[4] it is immortal.[5] Death understood in the sense of a full-fledged reality is then solely the death of the body.[6] The soul, deprived of the body, is also found to be deprived of its faculties connected to the body and to its relationships with it;[7] to be more precise, it is deprived of their activity, these faculties returning so to speak to the state of potentialities, as was the case after conception and before the complete formation of the body, when an individual existed in the embryonic and fetal state, since the soul was wholly present with all its powers, but the body was not sufficiently developed to enable it to exercise them.[8]

2 The Separation of Soul from Body Occurs More or Less Easily.

Separation is a natural process (within the framework of fallen nature), but different supernatural and spiritual factors can interfere in this process to speed and facilitate it or, to the contrary, to slow it, and make it more difficult and painful.

On the one hand, the Fathers deem that the passions weigh down the soul, making its taking flight difficult (which should be understood in a symbolic sense), and fixing it to the body, making it hard for the soul to separate from it.[9] Virtues to the contrary, which bear witness to the absence of the corresponding passions, but also to a positive attachment of the soul to the heavenly world, and to its movement of constant rising towards God, facilitate by contrast the loosing of the soul and its flight.

On the other hand, the angels and demons present to people at the moment of their death (and who often, as we have seen, appear to them) contend for the soul of the deceased when it has not clearly belonged to the one or the other through its spiritual dispositions. While the angels seek to raise up the soul with them, the demons seek on the contrary to keep it in the body and within the bounds of this world, which is so much easier for them when the soul is more attached to the latter things.[10]

3 The Presence of the Soul on Earth during the Three Days Following Death.

A certain number of Fathers or authoritative texts of the Orthodox Church hold that, during the three days that follow 'clinical' death (that is the moment of death insofar as observed and determined from the outside), the soul, in nearly all cases, "remains on earth."[11] Thus this prescription can be read in the *Nomocanon* of Manuel Malaxos: "Let the deceased be commemorated and provisions be distributed to the poor on the third, ninth and fortieth days after death; on the third day, because the souls of the deceased remain on earth until the third day that follows their separation from the body, and can, in the company of their guardian angels, visit any place they wish."[12] This text expresses a very old teaching. St Macarius of Alexandria affirms that the soul, remaining on earth after death, "consoles the people of his household and the body which it has left."[13] He specifies further: "The soul is left for two days with the angels, the ones who have taken it away, in order for it travel with them and go wherever it wishes. If it craves its body, it goes near it for a time in the tomb; [it sometimes also goes] for a time close to its near and dear ones, wherever it was accustomed, and these two days pass in this way while it flies about, circulates and seeks out those who love it, just like a bird seeking its nest. In the same way a virtuous soul likewise goes into those places where it customarily practiced its good actions."[14] St Theognostus restates and develops this teaching of St Macarius.[15] We also find it again with an Orthodox religious figure, St John Maximovich: "For the course of [the first] two days the soul enjoys relative freedom and can visit places on earth which were dear to it."[16] St Theophan the Recluse shares the same concept; he writes to one of his spiritual sons whose sister is dying: "In the first hours and days she will be around you. Only she will not say anything, and you will not be able to see her; but she will be right there."[17]

This last case, however, is not the rule: a certain number of accounts tell of the appearance—either in a state of waking or a dream—of the dead to members of their circle during the first days following their decease.

The third day which, along with the ninth and fortieth days, is strongly valorized within the liturgical setting and in prayers for the dead,[18] and which in ancient Christian texts is accorded more space than the very day of burial,[19] marks the end of this process of separation and access to another stage of *post-mortem* life. In symbolic relation with Christ's resurrection (it too was accomplished on the third day),[20] this is when the raising of the soul to heaven occurs.[21] During the three-day period following death the body has not lost its recognizable form.[22] The ancients thought that during these three days the soul that had been separated from the body was capable of returning, and that the dead person was therefore capable of returning to life.[23] Thus, those accounts that mention a miraculous resurrection almost always situate it in this three-day period.[24] From this also follows the belief and practice according to which a dead person should not be buried before these three days have elapsed.[25] These beliefs should be put in symbolic relation with the fact that Christ's soul was separated from His body for the three days that followed His death in order to descend into hell, before resuming this body on the third day for its resurrection.

This experiences of disincorporation and reincorporation described by the Orthodox faithful[26] or by authors having collected the accounts of near-death experiences[27] can find a justification within the framework of this conception. Thus St Athanasius writes: "How is it that certain people ... die, have visions, and come back to life after two or three days to relate them? This is because their soul has not altogether left the body."[28] This calls for one note of caution however: modern medicine, with its technical apparatus, perceives the moment of death with greater precision than ancient medicine, even though its definition of death remains relative and subject to change[29] and with it too there is a possibility of error.[30] Still, return to a normal life after being clinically dead cannot, in the present state of medical knowledge, be situated beyond a few hours, and even a few minutes in cases where there is no artificial respiration preventing serious and permanent lesions to the brain. This does not, however, contradict the accounts of a miraculous resurrection beyond this period, since in a miracle the laws of nature are surpassed in a transcendent and incomprehensible manner.

4 Death as Process.

The previous remarks show us that death is not considered to be a precise, instantaneous, and irreversible event, as modern medicine tends to do. There is certainly a moment of death that corresponds to what medical science calls 'clinical death', a moment that corresponds for the body to the disappearance of every observable sign of life, and for the soul to its leaving the body. But, as we have just seen, this leaving is not considered to be final before three days, or even complete, as the previously cited declaration of St Athanasius attests: "The soul has not altogether left the body."[31] Orthodox tradition therefore considers death—the separation of soul from body—to be a process[32] unfolding over a period of three days.

5 Ethical Implications.

For friends and relations of the dying person, this conception implies a certain number of duties. The first one, already mentioned, is not to proceed with the burial of the deceased before this three-day period has elapsed. The second is to respect his or her body. For one thing, this explains the importance of the care lavished on the mortal remains within the framework of the funeral rites preceding burial.[33]

Probing, from an Orthodox point of view, into the ethical position regarding organ removal (which our society would like to practice according to its needs), Dr Marc Andronikof is seen to be especially circumspect: this removal, necessarily carried out when the deceased has just been declared clinically dead so that the organs are usable, risks affecting, shocking, and upsetting the dying person when he has not completed the dying-process,[34] and when he is already in a state of suffering over the fact of the separation of his soul from his body.

6 The Ordeal of the Separation of the Soul from the Body.

For the saints, the separation of the soul from the body is not only a easy thing but a source of joy. Thus, St Theognostos writes: "Inexpressible is the soul's delight when in full assurance [*plerophoria*] of salvation it leaves the body, stripping it off as though it were a garment. Because it is now attaining what it hopes for, it puts off the body painlessly."[35]

However, for the ordinary person who would fear it with the approach of death,[36] this separation is now undergone with a certain suffering and is therefore a new ordeal. The liturgical services for funerals refer to the "groaning and agony at the parting of the soul"[37] and lament in this way: "Woe is me! What manner of struggle has the soul when it is parted from the body?"[38] St Macarius of Alexandria refers to this ordeal in these terms: "The soul suffers from its separation from the body, its companion; this is something painful, and it weeps because of the dissolving of its communion with it, since it is deprived of its society."[39] And St John Chrysostom, commenting on St Paul's words: "We who are in this tent groan," not wishing to be set free from the body (2 Cor. 5:4), notes: "Putting off the body appeared to many a grievous thing ... the soul in being separated from it so suffers and laments."[40] The difficulty with being separated from the body and the pain experienced while undergoing this separation are not necessarily the sign of a pathological attachment to the body, of that passion of 'philautia' (impassioned self-love) which St Maximus the Confessor defines as "tenderness for the body" in a negative sense and in which he sees the source for a majority of the other passions. This is above all a natural suffering provoked by the disjunction of the two elements constituting, together and indivisibly, our human nature and which the person bears within himself in a unified manner. This separation is therefore a process against nature;[41] it is in some manner a violence done to the nature and harmony of the human composite, as St John Damascene indicates in the *Canon* he has written for the funeral service of a layperson: "Truly dreadful is the mystery of death, how the soul is forcibly parted from the body, from their harmony, and how their most natural bond of kinship is sundered by the will of God."[42] As also indicated by St John Damascene, this separation process is accomplished by the divine will, the activity of God being providential here since this in fact involves the dissolving of the human composite in its fallen state (that is, a state subject to corruption) to reconstitute it later in a better, incorruptible state. It is in this sense that Father Sergius Bulgakov sees in the "separation of soul and body ...

a sacrament where at the same time the judgment of God is delivered upon the fallen Adam," and the soul is enabled to be "born anew, in the spiritual world."[43] It is this perspective that gladdens the saints or all the faithful who are assured of the renewal promised by Christ, and in whom the anticipated joy of the hoped for new birth makes them forget the pains of this birth.

7 Spiritual Aid from Those about the Deceased and from the Church.

To the extent that the process of the separation of the soul from the body is a painful ordeal, the prayers of those close to the deceased and of the Church are fundamental for helping and consoling anyone undergoing this ordeal. This is why, according to the tradition of the Orthodox Church, these prayers are continuous during the three days following death: members of the deceased's family and friends take turns around him reading and rereading the Psalter in its entirety, and pray that he find rest.

At the time of the funeral services, the Church asks on many occasions for the repose of the deceased person's soul: at this moment, in the moments that follow, and in all his ulterior life where, as we will see, other ordeals and other sources of disturbance and suffering—and these of a spiritual order—await. But he can however be spared this, not only by reason of spiritual qualities acquired during his earthly life, but also by the very fact of the prayers of the ecclesial community on his behalf.

The prayers of the Church and those close to the deceased also have as a goal the making the soul's flight towards heaven easier and helping it gain access to a blessed condition by asking God to pardon the deceased's voluntary and involuntary sins and purify him of his passions.

8 The Spiritual State of the Soul after Death.

After death, the soul remains, in fact, marked by the passions affecting it while alive. St Macarius of Alexandria indicates this symbolically in this way: "The stench of its evil deeds clings to the sinful soul when it has a body; but after its death, these deeds affect it even more, above all assuming the form of darkness and gloom."[44] Through some of these passions the soul remains attached to this world. Certain Fathers symbolically say that it is weighed down with them[45] and so has difficulty taking its flight. St Gregory of Nyssa invites the faithful to do whatever necessary to avoid being affected by such a handicap: "We who are living in the flesh ought as much as possible to separate ourselves and release ourselves from its hold by the life of virtue, so that after death we may not need another death to cleanse us from the remains of the fleshly glue. Then, as if chains have been broken away from the soul, its course may become light and easy towards the good, when no bodily weight drags the soul to itself. So if one should become completely carnal in his mind, devoting all the activity and energy of his soul to the will of the flesh, such a man even when he gets out of the flesh is not separated from its experiences. Those who have spent their time in evil-smelling places do not part with the unpleasantness contracted by that lengthened stay, even if they go out into the fresh air, are not cleansed from the unpleasantness which has adhered to them from prolonged contact. In the same way, even when the transition has been made to the invisible and rarified life, the lovers of the flesh would doubtless be unable to avoid bringing with them some of the fleshly odor. This makes their pangs more grievous, as their soul has become partly materialized from such an environment."[46] And note how in this passage St Gregory of Nyssa explains the existence of ghosts: "There seems to be some support for this opinion in what certain people say, that often around the bodies' graves there appear some kind of shadowy shapes of the departed. If this really happens, it proves that the soul has become more attached than it should be to the present fleshly life, so that even when it is driven out of the flesh it is not willing to fly clean away. It does not even allow its form to be completely changed into invisibility, but stays with its shape even after its shape has been dissolved. Although it has already gone outside of its shape, it wanders longingly in the material places and spends its time in them."[47]

Conversely, the soul purified of its passions is found to be relieved of fleshly encumbrances, freed of its attachments to this world, and meets with no obstacle to being raised on high to the heavenly places after being separated from the body.[48]

In a general manner, one might say that souls, in quitting the body retain the spiritual good or evil acquired in the course of their earthly life, in their relationship with the body, and remain in the spiritual state in which they are found at death. "The souls of the departed," writes Archimandrite Justin Popovich, "enter into the life beyond with the entirety of their contents. 'Their works follow them' (Apoc. 14:13). They enter there with all their thoughts and perceptions, with all their virtues and passions, with all their good qualities and vices, with the whole of their moral universe. Just as they have left this body and earthly life, so they are."[49] Father Justin Popovich sees in this one of the conditions for the preservation of a person's identity: "If death were to change this state of the soul, the person would lose all continuity, and in the life beyond Peter would no longer be recognized as Peter, or Paul as Paul."[50]

It is important to point out that, even though after its death the soul retains the spiritual state that was its own at the moment of death, it is henceforth impossible for it to change this state in any way. There are several justifications for this fact. For Father Justin Popovich, the reason for this is that the soul is separated from its body and deprived of the other conditions of its earthly life which would enable it to lead another manner of life or modify its behavior: "Even if the soul living in the hereafter would want this with its whole being, and whatever its desire might be to change itself so to begin again another life, completely different than the one led on earth, it no longer has the possibility to do so. It can no longer do so because in such a case that body, which is an indispensable component of the human person in exercising its full self-determination and its activity, is lacking, and also because it is now devoid of any earthly environment where it might find the means for salvation. In other words, repenting in the hereafter has become impossible, for what bears its fruits yonder is what has begun here below ... This is indeed what the holy apostle teaches us when he calls this life on earth 'sowing' and life in the hereafter 'reaping' (Gal. 6:7–8)."[51]

9 The Subsistence of the Link between Soul and Body in the Permanence of the Hypostasis.

After the soul has been separated from it, the body does not return purely and simply to nothingness, and its elements, scattered, dissolved and mixed with other material elements, does not become so much 'refuse' for all that. Dionysius the Areopagite emphasizes this,[52] as well as St Gregory of Nyssa who writes: with death, "the sensible part is dissolved but not destroyed, for destruction is a passing into nothingness, whereas dissolution is the return of this part to the elements of the world, out of which it was formed, and its dispersal. That which is found in this state has not perished, even though evading our sensible perception."[53] For St John Chrysostom, this means that death "when it arrives destroys and uses up the corruption; the corruption, I say, not [properly speaking] the body."[54]

It would likewise be a mistake to "think that the link of body and soul is broken forever."[55]

If death puts an end to the natural bond between soul and body as a composite, in return, it allows their natural bond to subsist under a certain form, and their hypostatic bond to subsist in a complete manner. The deceased should not be seen as reduced henceforth to his soul, while his body, consigned to dissolution, would lose any relationship to it and would be no longer anything. Just as the soul is the soul of a deceased person, his body, even in the state of a corpse or skeleton, remains his body. Beyond death, soul and body retain, in their relationship to the person (or hypostasis) whose soul and body they are, a never to be lost and inalienable bond between themselves and with this person (or hypostasis).

St Maximus the Confessor in particular has developed these anthropological considerations. Even after death, he writes, the soul is not completely dissociated from the body, for "the soul, after the death of the body, is not simply called soul, but the soul of a human being, indeed the soul of a certain human being. Even after it has departed the body, the whole human is predicated of it as a part of its form [εἶδος] according to its condition. In the same way, although the body is by nature mortal, because of how it came to be, it is not an independent entity. For the body, after the separation from the soul, is not simply called body, but the body of a man, indeed the body of a certain man, even though it will decompose and be broken down into the elements of which it is composed. For like the soul it has the whole human being predicated of it as part of its form [εἶδος] according to its condition. Therefore the human being is composed of soul and body, for soul and body are indissolubly understood to be parts of the whole human form [εἶδος]. Soul and body came into being at the same moment and their essential difference from each other in no way whatsoever impairs the *logoi* that inhere naturally and essentially in them. For that reason it is inconceivable to speak of the soul and body except in relation to each other. It is only as they come together to form a particular person that they exist ... The relation between them is immutable."[56]

St Gregory of Nyssa broaches this question from another angle. He explains that the soul never forgets the elements of the body when dispersed following death, just as the painter, in mixing colors to produce a new color, does not forget the hue of the colors used to make the mixture,[57] or just as a cattle farmer does not forget the animals that belong to him and knows how to find them when dispersed among the animals of other breeders within the same herd,[58] or again just as the owners of different earthen vessels which have been gathered together and smashed should recognize among the mingled fragments those that were their own property.[59] In death too the soul retains a memory, not only of the body as a whole, but of its different components and remains in a certain fashion present to each of them, however altered from its original state: "The soul knows the individual nature of the elements which joined together in the formation of the body to which is was attached. Even if their nature drives them far away from one another because of their inherent oppositions, repelling each of them from combination with its opposite, none the less the soul will be present with each, holding on to its own by its cognitive power and remaining with it until the separated elements are combined again into the same body to reconstitute what was dissolved. This in a true sense both is and may properly be called 'resurrection.'"[60] Conversely, after the separation of soul and body, the body remains in some manner present to the soul, as St Gregory of Nyssa remarks elsewhere: "For that some signs of our compound nature remain in the soul even after dissolution is shown by the dialogue in Hades [Luke 16:19 ff], where the bodies had been conveyed to the tomb, but some bodily token still remained in the souls by which both Lazarus was recognized and the rich man was not unknown."[61] Despite the various alterations that it may undergo in the course of its earthly existence (through the aging process, for example) and through death (which provokes the dispersal and dissolution of its components), the body possesses a form [εἶδος][62] that remains unchanged and the imprint of which the body preserves continually within itself, including beyond death. And it is thanks to this that, at the time of the resurrection, the different elements will be able to be reassembled and reconstituted to form the risen body. "Differences in the combinations [of matter] produce varying aspects to the form [εἶδος]; this combining is, moreover, no different than the mixture of primary elements (we so name the elements that are the formative principles of everything and by which the human body is also composed). Consequently, since the form [εἶδος] of the body remains in the soul which is as if the imprint with respect to the seal, the materials used to form the shape on the stamp do not remain unknown to the soul, but, in the instant of the resurrection, it receives anew within itself everything in accord with the imprint left in it by the form [εἶδος] of the body. Those elements which, since the beginning, have made up the form will then be entirely in accord with it."[63] The resurrected body will surely be renewed and different from its present condition, but will nevertheless preserve its personal identity and, from this point of view, will be in continuity with the present body, the resurrected person indeed recovering his own body (and not someone else's or another body entirely), but in a different mode of existence. This preservation of personal identity and this continuity should equally subsist, then, between the moment of death and the moment of resurrection, whereas the body's elements are dispersed and profoundly altered, even dissolved. It is not impossible, Gregory of Nyssa writes, "for the elements to come together again with one another and to reproduce the same man ... For if it should not recover its own exactly, it will become a different one in place of the one it was before. Such an event would no longer be a resurrection but the fashioning of a new man. But if the same man must return into himself again, he ought to be altogether the same as himself, taking up again his original nature in all the parts of the elements."[64] This is why St Gregory of Nyssa comes back to his "conception concerning the soul, that whatever elements were joined to the soul at the beginning, it remains with them even after their dissolution, stationed like a guard over its own. When the elements mix with their own kind, the soul does not let go of its own in the subtlety and mobility of its intellectual power. It is not deceived by the small particles of the elements, but it slips away together with its own when they are mixed with their kind. It does not become weak as it passes through small spaces with them, when they are poured out into the universe, but it always remains in them, wherever and however their nature arranges them."[65]

10 The Body's Spiritual Status after Death.

After death the body continues to be in relationship with the soul of the deceased and, whatever its state, continues to belong to that person. Thus it deserves the respect due to the person. In this regard, it is significant that Jesus Christ himself, in the episode where Mary Magdalene poured fragrant ointment on his head, speaks of *His* burial, and not the burial of His body: "For in pouring this fragrant oil on My body, she did it for My burial" (cf. Matt. 26:12). This explains the care lavished on the body after death, in funeral rites especially, when the body is bathed, perfumed, clothed in its own garments, correctly positioned,[66] crowned,[67] blessed, incensed, kissed on the forehead, and honored in various ways.[68] In the Old Testament, burial rites assume a special importance and last up to forty days (see Gen. 50:3). Their value is confirmed in the New Testament by the intervention, after the death of Christ, of the 'myrrhbearing women' and, in an anticipated manner, by the episode where Mary Magdalene pours a very costly fragrant oil on the head of Christ, who replies to the disciples indignant over this waste: "In pouring this fragrant oil on My body, she did it for My burial" (Matt. 26:6–13, Mark 14:3–9).

The close connection of the dead body with the person of the departed also explains why people gather before the grave of the departed, seeing that it contains not only his body, but, in a certain manner, his soul is also present. One prays before the 'remains' as before the whole person.

The close connection that the body of the deceased preserves with its person is also revealed in the fact that the wish for the dying person to abide 'in Abraham's bosom' in the presence of his ancestors or those near and dear who have died before him is accompanied by the wish to be buried beside them or to have their bones placed with theirs. Scripture gives many examples of this. Thus Jacob tells those close to him: "I am to be gathered to my people; bury me with my fathers" (Gen. 49:29).[69] Joseph asks his brothers that, when they go into the promised land, they carry his bones away with them (Gen. 50:24–25). We likewise find many examples in the *Lives* of the saints from antiquity to our own day.[70]

The care lavished on the mortal remains of the departed continue well beyond the time of decease. It is the custom in Greece and other Orthodox countries to exhume with respect the bones of the deceased about five years after his death, wash them with wine and place them in a small chest devised for this purpose; they are next brought to church for a memorial service, then placed in an ossuary in expectation of the resurrection (see Ezek. 37:1–14).

The care lavished on the bodily 'remains' of the deceased, the concern for their preservation, is accompanied by veneration in the case of the relics of saints. The previous considerations enable us to understand this veneration which, in the Orthodox Church, is equivalent to that of the veneration of icons.[71] According to St Gregory of Nyssa's conception presented above, the souls of saints remain to a certain extent present with their relics, as does everyone's soul with their bodily remains. Even more: the relics of a saint are attached to his person, continue to be a part of him; they share, then, in the sanctification and deification of his entire person, soul and body; they are bearers of the divine energies which have sanctified and deified the saint. This is why relics have the power to work miracles, as numerous *Lives* of the saints attest. But obviously relics should not be adored (adoration is due to God alone) or venerated in themselves: they should always be related to the entire person of the saint, and it is the saint who should be venerated through them. Besides, the faithful who venerate relics do so by addressing the person of the saint.

The foregoing arguments explain the Orthodox Church's rejection of the cremation of bodies.[72] This rejection is not new or tied to the development of cremation experienced in modern societies: this has been a usual practice in non-Christian societies for millennia, and was quite widespread in the ancient world at the time of the birth and development of Christianity. From the outset Christians have opted for burial and rejected cremation, and the latter, which was quite widespread in the Roman world, ended up being totally abandoned in the fifth century under pressure from the prevailing Christianity.

In the Old Testament, cremation was considered to be a condemnable act (cf. Amos 2:1) and was practiced as a worsening of the death penalty (cf. Lev. 20:14, 21:9). The patristic tradition, along the same line, generally condemns cremation as an insult to the dead.[73] Respect for the divine word: "For dust you are, and to dust you shall return" (Gen. 3:19) has, to the contrary, contributed in its eyes to the value of burial. Cremation is perceived as an annihilation (that is as a reducing to nothing) of one's mortal remains, which contradicts the concern for preserving the remains of the deceased (especially the bones) in expectation of the resurrection. In this respect, Christian tradition retains as a model the manner in which the body of Christ was, after His death, carefully laid in a new tomb (cf. Matt. 27:57–61, Luke 23:50–56, Mark 15:42–47, John 19:38–42) in expectation of His resurrection. As Father Sergius Bulgakov writes: "The dead body is interred with veneration as the seed of the coming resurrection, and the very ritual of inhumation is held by certain ancient writers to be a sacrament."[74]

The importance of relics and their veneration in the Orthodox Church surely explains in part as well the reserve felt regarding cremation: if the latter had been or were to be practiced systematically, no longer would there be any relics. This would affect not only the relics of the saints, but likewise those of the simple faithful. In fact, according to the liturgical language of the *Ritual*, the word 'relic' is not reserved for the remains of saints, but also for those of all the faithful,[75] whose souls are to a certain extent present with their bodily remains, whose remains stay connected with and always belong to their person, and share in the degree of sanctification obtained by each, the body having been the companion of the soul in the practice of the virtues and the reception of divine grace.

To this one can add that "every dead body ... is capable of being glorified"[76] in the future life after the resurrection in a body which, although new (being a spiritual and heavenly body instead of a psychic and earthly body, (cf. 1 Cor. 15:35–53)), will nevertheless be in continuity with the previous one.

Chapter Four

From the Third to the Ninth Day:
The Passage through the Aerial Toll-Houses

1 The Raising of the Soul to Heaven.

The third day after death is a transition and inaugurates a new, especially important stage. This is why the Church celebrates an office for the deceased on this third day.[1]

We have seen that during the three days following death, according to ancient tradition, the soul remains on earth in a majority of cases. According to this same tradition, it quits the earth on the third day and is raised into the sky by angels. The fact that the soul is led away by angels is mentioned in Scripture: Christ Himself says in the parable of the evil rich man and poor Lazarus: "The beggar died, and was carried by the angels into Abraham's bosom" (Luke 16:22). This ascent into heaven is affirmed by numerous patristic texts (see *infra*).

The teaching that this phenomenon occurs on the third day is encountered less frequently but is sufficiently attested.[2] It is found, for example, in this already cited text by an anonymous eleventh–twelfth century author: "The soul after death remains on earth until the third day. On the third day the angels carry it on high."[3] It is also found in a much older text, attributed to St Macarius of Alexandria, who places this third day, when the soul is raised into heaven, in a symbolic relationship with the third day when Christ was raised, the day of His resurrection, the three days the soul has passed on earth being implicitly placed in symbolic relationship with the three passed by Christ in Hades and the tomb: "On the third day Christ—the One who has been raised from the tomb and resurrected on the third day, Himself, the God of all—ordains that every Christian soul ascend to heaven. Consequently the holy Church observes in a fine manner this tradition of offering prayer and sacrifice for the soul in every place to the God of all."[4]

The angels that accompany and support the soul in its ascent to heaven are the very ones who came to the dying person to gather up his soul and accompanied it during the three days it has remained on earth.

We have seen that these angels are more or less numerous. This is because the Fathers often speak of them in the plural and without specifying their number. Thus, St Gregory of Nyssa notes: "The angels awaited the departure of their souls [from the bodies to which they were attached] for the purpose of conducting them to their destiny."[5] And St John Chrysostom: "At its departure [from the body] the soul, invisible to eyes of flesh, is gathered up by the angels."[6] The guardian angel is present alongside the soul (who is now aware of it) and accompanies it.[7] But the primary role falls to an angel that is more especially charged with the mission of conducting the soul and is called the 'psychopomp' or 'psychogogic angel'.[8] It is to him that St Macrina alludes in the prayer that she addresses to God a little before her death: "Do Thou give me an angel of light to conduct me to the place of refreshment, where is the water of rest, in the bosom of the holy Fathers."[9]

The raising of the soul to heaven by an angel of light is mentioned in numerous texts.[10] In some of them it is specified that these angels are two in number:[11] here we have then the guardian angel and the psychogogic angel.

As seen in the *Lives* of the saints, this phenomenon of the raising of the soul to heaven by angels is frequently perceived by the close disciples of these saints or by holy people some distance away. In many cases, however, this ascent to heaven follows immediately after death: we have noted that the stage when the soul passes three days on earth involves a majority of people, but the saints are often exempted from this by grace, in response to their perfect detachment as to this world and their eagerness to meet with Christ, the object of all their desire.

We can cite the example of St Paphnuntius who "saw [a] man's soul borne up by angels singing."[12] And when St Paphnuntius himself gave up his spirit, "the priests saw him plainly as he was taken up to heaven with the choirs of the just and the angels singing hymns to God."[13] Theodoret of Cyrrhus notes that St Theodosius, "after living a short time, migrated to the angelic choir."[14] The most famous example, because the one most cited, of vision at a distance is St Antony the Great seeing the soul of St Amoun of Nitria "being taken up and conducted to heaven by angels."[15] We can also cite the case of St Cuthbert who saw "a long stream of light break through the darkness of the night, and in the midst of it a company of the heavenly host descended to the earth, and having received among them a spirit of surpassing brightness, returned without delay to their heavenly home:" this concerned angels come to seek the soul of St Aidan to lead him into heaven.[16] And we might even cite the example of St Benedict who "saw the soul of Germanus, Bishop of Capua, in a fiery globe to be carried up by Angels into heaven."[17]

2 The Efforts of the Demons to Seize the Soul.

As numerous patristic texts attest, at the time of the soul's ascent into heaven, the demons seek to steal it away from the angels who have taken charge of it and drag it below to hell.

Certain Fathers show a multitude of angels face to face and on an equal footing with a multitude of demons ready to seize the soul from the time of its departure from the body. Thus we read in a homily of St Cyril of Alexandria: "At the time of the separation of the soul from the body, behold standing before us the army of the heavenly Powers on one side, and the Powers of darkness on the other."[18] When his mother died, St Symeon the Fool addressed this prayer to God: "Grant her angels who will keep her soul safe from the spirits and beasts of the air, evil and unmerciful beings who endeavor to swallow up everything which comes into their midst. Lord, Lord, send out to her mighty guards to rebuke every impure power molesting her."[19]

This concept has been transmitted down to our day in the Orthodox Church.[20]

Certain Fathers affirm that the soul can then be taken in charge and carried away by either angels or demons, according to its spiritual state: the good powers (the angels) have power over it in proportion to its virtues, the evil powers (the demons) have power over it in proportion to its passions, the soul having engendered in the course of its life, by its dealings with one or the other of these powers, a kind of state in common with them which therefore sets its future course.

St Maximus the Confessor only refers to the first of these two aspects: "Remember death and the soul's terror upon its leaving the body, and how the powers of the air and the dark forces come to meet it, all dissociated and cut to pieces in proportion to its disastrous familiarity with them through the play of the passions."[21] St Hesychios of Batos writes in the same vein: "One who fails to pursue watchfulness ... cannot free himself from evil thoughts, words and actions, and because of these thoughts and actions he will not be able to freely pass the lords of hell when he dies."²² Or again St Dorotheos of Gaza, who advises the insensible soul to "retain the thought of the dread judgments of God, to recall that the soul will leave the body and meet the terrifying Powers with which it had committed evil in this short and miserable life."²³ This passage can be related to the one in which Dorotheos notes, in a manner recalling St Maximus's previously cited remark and in a context where the passions are readily identified with the demons that arouse them, that "when at last it goes out of the body [the soul], is alone with its own passions and, in short, it is tormented by them, forever nattering to them and being incensed by the disturbance they cause and being torn to pieces by them."²⁴

St Theognostos only mentions the second aspect:

> Inexpressible is the soul's delight when in full assurance of salvation it leaves the body, stripping it off as though it were a garment. Because it is now attaining what it hopes for, it puts off the body painlessly, going in peace to meet the radiant and joyful angel that comes down for it, and traveling with him unimpeded through the air, totally unharmed by the evil spirits. Rising with joy, courage and thanksgiving."²⁵

As for St Macarius of Egypt, he mentions both aspects:

> If the dark power of the passions and the malice of evil spirits cleaves to a soul, if the invisible spirits of error accompany it and haunt the highways and byways of its thoughts in order to act through the passions, and if this soul becomes their accomplice, when it comes to leave the body, the spirits of error and the Prince who delights in evil, the Ruler of the world of darkness, receives it, takes charge of it and detains it among themselves; it entirely belongs to them, this soul that did their will and accompanied them to the end when in the flesh. And conversely, the soul that accompanies the essence of the desirable and inexpressible beauty of the divine Spirit's light, the soul that accompanies and dwells with the grace of Christ's truth, the soul that has been from its time here below favored with holiness of heart and the indwelling of Christ in the highways and byways of its thoughts, when this soul comes to leave the body, the spirits of the saints in light (receive it) and the King of peace, Christ, who Himself finds His joy in excellent souls, receives this soul and welcomes it into His presence as His very own bride and intimate associate, this soul that has never acted on earth outside of His will.²⁶

The same saint writes elsewhere in the same vein:

> When the soul of man departs from the body, a certain great mystery is there enacted. If a person is under the guilt of sin, bands of demons and fallen angels

approach along with the powers of darkness which capture that soul and drag it as a captive to their place. No one should be surprised by this fact. For if, while a man lived in this life, he was subject to them and was their obedient slave, how much more, when he leaves this world, is he captured and controlled by them? You can understand this, however, from what happens to those on the better side. Indeed, angels even now stand alongside God's holy servants and holy spirits surround and protect them. And when they leave their bodies, the bands of angels receive their souls and carry them to their side into the pure eternity. And so they lead them to the Lord.[27]

The same conception is again found in St Nicetas Stethatos, the disciple of St Symeon the New Theologian:

Envy, bitterness, passionate cowardice and fear are completely foreign to the soul, in no way proper to its nature; these are passions of the soul, not its properties. If the soul goes away in their company when it quits the body for life hereafter, the father of envy and bitterness recognizes it for his own servant thanks to cowardice and fear, and he drags it away alongside himself to the depths of hell. Could anything more unfortunate happen to a soul fallen far from God? But if it has completed the present life in piety and purity, in the exercise of every good and the practice of the commandments of God ... it pitches its tent in the places of the glory of God. Now the divine places of the glory of God are nothing but the Powers from on high and the legions of angels ... By virtue of the charisms [given it by the Holy Spirit], the soul discovers its own dwelling-place and abode among these various dwelling-places of God, which is ascribed to it according to its merit. The reasonable nature of man, perfected by every virtue, enhanced by every knowledge and wisdom of the Spirit, participates in fact with the angelic powers on high through the divine charisms. It is proportionately united with each of them for having communed through reason with them and having drawn into itself what is proper to all ... This is then how the soul is equipped to dwell, after death, at rest in the divine places of the glory of God, as we have stated, in the shadow of the wings of angels.[28]

The same saint writes further in the same vein:

Among the souls that emigrate, some are pure and perfumed [by their virtues], alike to God, filled with divine glory and absolutely immaculate light: these are those of the saints; upon leaving their bodies they shine like the sun because of works of justice, wisdom and purity. These, through the intermediary of angel-friends who lead them away toward the primordial, superessential and immaterial light, a light incomprehensible even to angels, toward God Himself glorified and adored in Father, Son and Holy Spirit by the infinite powers, these ascend, like lights of the third order thanks to lights of the second order ... But other souls, obscured and frightfully plunged in darkness because of the malice of their acts, words and thoughts, their habits, occupations and dispositions, these are the souls of sinners; when they are violently torn from the body, they give off such stench as they have imparted to it in leaving, along with all manner of unpleasantness. These souls, filled with obscurity, stench and rottenness, are dragged away against their will by dark and avenging angels, in the midst of a terrible fear, shaking with fright, to the depths of hell as into a dark prison devoid of consolation. They are handed over to the impure and evil spirits that guard this prison, there where the prince of darkness is held fast by eternal bonds so to be consumed by fire along with his kind, the angels of darkness. They are handed over to them to remain with them eternally in the future; they have, in fact, accepted them as friends during their life in their acts and their words. They have preferred their suggestions, they have implemented them to their own and others' loss.[29]

This conception has been likewise incorporated by the Orthodox Church. We find a significant echo of it in the *Canon of Supplication to the Most-Holy Theotokos at the Parting of the Soul from the Body* celebrated prior to death, but which is intended to prepare the person dying for the trials to be encountered after his decease, and convey to him the Church's intercession to obtain from the Mother of God the help needed to face these trials and come away from them victorious. One series of prayers asks for the assistance of the Mother of God in hindering the demons, who show themselves at that time, from carrying off the soul: "They that shall lead me hence have come, holding me on every side. But my soul shrinks back and is afraid, full of great rebelliousness, which do thou comfort, O pure One, by thy appearance;"[30] "make known thy mercy unto me, O thou pure and renowned Refuge for sinners and them that are contrite, and deliver me from the hands of demons, for many dogs have surrounded me;"[31] "noetic roaring lions have surrounded me, seeking to carry me away and bitterly torment me. Do thou crush their teeth and jaws, O pure One, and save me;"[32] "no one delivers me now, and, in truth, no one helps me. But, do thou help me, O Sovereign Lady, that as one helpless, I not become a captive in the hands of my enemies;"[33] "do thou translate me, O Sovereign Lady, in the sacred and precious arms of the holy Angels, that sheltered by their wings, I do not see the impious, foul and dark form of the demons."[34] One might also cite this prayer that the Church sings on the feast of St John Chrysostom (January 27) which is also addressed to the Mother of God: "Grant me to pass untroubled through the host of noetic satraps and the tyrannic battalion of the lower air in the hour of my departure, that joyously I may cry Rejoice to thee, O Lady: Rejoice thou unshamed hope of all."[35]

3 The Passage through the Aerial Toll-houses or 'Telonies'.

Previously cited patristic texts give us a simplified view of the soul's destiny, carried away by angels or demons according to whether it is closer, by its spiritual state, to the ones or to the others. Other patristic sources show us a detailed and more complex process, utilizing argument and struggle between angels and demons disputing over the soul of the deceased. This is understandable to the extent that, aside from those on the whole rather rare cases of saints who have achieved a perfect purity or those people who have lived continually and deliberately in evil, people for the most part are situated in an intermediate state and produce a balance sheet of their life in which good and evil are intermingled in varying proportions. Angels and demons are each in dispute then to claim for themselves their due portion, the demons seeking to seize the soul and prevent the angels from raising it up to heaven.

One saying of the desert Fathers relates:

> Abba Theophilus said, "What fear, what trembling, what uneasiness will there be for us when our soul is separated from the body. Then indeed the force and strength of the adverse powers come against us, the rulers of darkness, those who command the world of evil, the principalities, the powers, the spirits of evil. They accuse our souls as in a lawsuit, bringing before it all the sins it has committed, whether deliberately or through ignorance, from its youth until the time when it has been taken away. So they stand accusing it of all it has done. Furthermore, what anxiety do you suppose the soul will have at that hour, until sentence is pronounced and it gains its liberty. That is its hour of affliction, until it sees what will happen to it. On the other hand, the divine powers stand on the opposite side, and they present the good deeds of the soul. Consider the fear and trembling of the soul standing between them until in judgment it receives the sentence of the righteous judge."[36]

An experience, anticipating this *post-mortem* experience, was undergone by St Antony the Great while still alive during an ecstasy and is related in this way by his biographer, St Athanasius of Alexandria:

Once when he was about to eat, rising to pray around the ninth hour, he felt himself being carried off in thought, and the wonder was that while standing there he saw himself, as it were outside himself, and as if he were being led through the air by certain beings.[37] Next he saw some foul and terrible figures[38] standing in the air, intent on holding him back so he could not pass by. When his guides combated them, they demanded to know the reason, if he was not answerable to them. And when they sought an accounting of his life from the time of his birth, Antony's guides prevented it, saying to them, 'The Lord has wiped clean the items dating from his birth, but from the time he became a monk, and devoted himself to God, you can take an account.' Then as they leveled accusations and failed to prove them, the passage opened before him free and unobstructed. And just then he [returned to] himself ... Forgetting to eat, he spent the remainder of the day and the entire night groaning and praying. For he was amazed to see how many foes our wrestling involves, and how many labors someone has in passing through the air, and he recalled this is what the Apostle said, *following the prince of the power of the air* [Eph. 2:2]. For in this sphere the enemy holds sway by doing battle and by attempting to stop those who are passing through.[39]

Numerous other texts mention the soul being met by demons in the course of its ascent. Thus, Abba Isaiah writes: "Keep death before your eyes daily, and be concerned about how you will leave this body, pass the powers of darkness that will meet you in the air."[40] In the *Ladder* of St John Climacus, one dying man asks himself: "Will our soul pass through the irresistible water of the spirits of the air?"[41] The more precise idea of a ferreting out and a placing in evidence by demons of a person's evil acts and passions is frequently mentioned as well. St Macarius of Egypt writes in the form of a warning: "When you hear that there are ... dark forces under heaven ... you will remain ignorant of such things unless you receive the pledge of the Holy Spirit. These forces will hold your soul and when you depart from this life will not allow you to rise to heaven."[42] For his part, St Hesychios of Batos notes: "The hour of death will come upon us, it will come, and we shall not escape it. May the prince of this world and of the air find our misdeeds few and petty when he comes, so that he will not have good grounds for convicting us."[43] St Gregory the Great writes: "One must reflect deeply on how frightful the hour of death will be for us, what terror the soul will then experience, what remembrance of all the evils, what forgetfulness of past happiness, what fear, and what apprehension of the Judge. Then the evil spirits will seek out in the departing soul its deeds; then they will present before its view the sins towards which they had disposed it, so as to draw their accomplice to torment. But why do we speak only of the sinful soul, when they come even to the chosen among the dying and seek out their own in them, if they have succeeded with them?"[44]

The beginning of the account of Blessed Theodora, all while presenting the accusations pronounced by the demons against the soul at the departure from its body, strongly insists on the defense employed by the angels, who carefully gather up all the good works of the deceased to counter these accusations:

> [My soul] shuddered and went out of my body. The light-bearing angels immediately took it in their arms. When I looked back I saw my body lying breathless and immovable. I looked at my body like someone who has taken off his clothes and thrown them down; this was a strange feeling. Meanwhile, although the holy angels were holding me, the demons surrounded us and cried: 'This soul has a multitude of sins—let her answer for them!' They kept pointing to my sins, but the holy angels sought out my good deeds; and indeed, with God's help they found all that, by God's grace, I ever did of good. The angels gathered together everything that was good: all those instances when I gave alms to the needy, or fed the hungry, or gave drink to the thirsty, or clothed the naked, or brought into my house and rested there the homeless, or served the servants of God, or brought comfort to the sick or those who were imprisoned; or when I went with diligence to God's house and prayed with all my heart and shed tears, or when I attentively listened to what was read and sung in church, or brought to church incense and candles, or filled with oil the church lamps before the icons, or kissed the icons with awe and reverence; or when I fasted and abstained on Wednesdays, Fridays, or during other fasts, or when I prostrated myself before God and spent nights awake in prayer, or when I sighed to God and wept for my sins, or confessed my sins before my spiritual father with great regret for what I had done, and then tried with all my strength to balance my sins with good deeds; or when I did anything good to my neighbors, when I bore no anger to my enemies, bore no grudges and meekly endured hurts and reproaches, did good in return for evil, humbled myself, felt sorry for those who suffered and commiserated with those to whom anything bad happened, comforted those who were weeping and rendered them assistance, supported any good beginning and tried to turn people away from what was bad; or for myself turned my eyes away from vanity and kept my tongue from oaths, lies, or bearing false witness, or speaking without need—and all my other good deeds, even the least important ones, did the holy angels gather and make ready to put on the scale in order to balance my evil deeds.[45]

Some patristic texts do not mention the defense of the deceased by angels, but present him as summoned to answer his evil judges himself and obliged to secure his own defense before the accusers of bad faith, who may go so far as to accuse him of faults not committed. St John Climacus thus tells of a vision of a certain Stephen, presenting to him beforehand what he would endure after his death:

> On the day before his death, he went into ecstasy of mind, and with open eyes he looked to the right and left of his bed and, as if he were being called to account by someone, in the hearing of all the bystanders, he said: "Yes indeed, that is true; but that is why I fasted for so many years." And then again: "Yes, it is quite true; but I wept and served the brethren." And again: "No, you are slandering me." And sometimes he would say: "Yes, it is true. Yes, I do not know what to say to this. But in God there is mercy." And it was truly an awful and horrible sight—this invisible and merciless inquisition. And what was most terrible, he was accused of what he had not done. How amazing! Of several of his sins, the hesychast and hermit said: "I do not know what to say to this." [46]

This confrontation with crafty slanderers obviously increases the difficulties and risks of the trial endured and makes an angelic and divine assistance so much the more indispensable. St John of Karpathos recalls a context similar to the previous one, but remarks however that the soul of the just, supported by its faith in God and encouraged by the angels that accompany it, is ultimately stronger than its accusers:

> When the soul leaves the body, the enemy advances to attack it, fiercely reviling it and accusing it of its sins in a harsh and terrifying manner. But if a soul enjoys the love of God and has faith in Him, even though in the past it has often been wounded by sin, it is not frightened by the enemy's attacks and threats. Strengthened by the Lord, winged by joy, filled with courage by the holy angels that guide it, encircled and protected by the light of faith, it answers the malicious devil with great boldness: "Enemy of God, fugitive from heaven, wicked slave, what have I to do with you? You have no authority over me; Christ the Son of God has authority over me and over all things. Against Him have I sinned, before Him shall I stand on trial, having His Precious Cross as a sure pledge of His saving love towards me. Flee far from me, destroyer! You have nothing to do with the servants of Christ." When the soul says all this fearlessly, the devil turns his back, howling aloud and unable to withstand the name of Christ. Then the soul swoops down on the devil from above, attacking him like a hawk attacking a crow. After this it is brought rejoicing by the holy angels to the place appointed for it in accordance with its inward state.[47]

One Orthodox tradition going back at least to the fourth century[48] and maintained down to our own day, speaks of the 'telonies,'[49] that is, the 'heavenly custom-houses' or 'aerial toll-booths', and refers to the stages that the soul successively passes through in its ascent. This path of the soul is situated by certain texts between the third and ninth days following death.[50] Each duty station corresponds to a particular passion, a type of misdeed or a kind of sin of which a certain type of demon is the inspirer and which it represents. This conception is connected with an identification, very marked in the work of Evagrius of Ponticus and subsequently reiterated by the whole ascetic tradition of the Orthodox Church, between hierarchically arranged passions and the corresponding demons.[51] As for the 'custom offices' or 'tollbooths', they are sometimes represented in iconography under the form of a ladder with its rungs crossed successively by individuals surrounded by angels and demons, the former drawing them above, the latter drawing them below.[52]

The demons appointed to the different 'custom stations' stop the soul and examine it (certain texts call them 'judges' or 'inquisitors' because of this), going through in some manner its spiritual baggage, demanding that it account for what they find of the misdeeds or passions corresponding to them. Like some corrupt tax-collectors who, in antiquity, dishonestly fleeced the taxpayer by demanding they pay more than they owed,[53] the demons sometimes demand a reckoning from the soul for misdeeds it did not commit. The nature of payment is open to several explanations. According to certain authors, the soul should in some manner pay with itself; in other words, the demons/aerial taxcollectors demand that it give them that portion of itself by which it is comparable to them. Thus we have seen St Maximus the Confessor assert that the soul is "all dissociated and cut to pieces in proportion to its disastrous familiarity with them through the play of the passions,"[54] and that certain Fathers show us the evil soul ultimately carried off by the demons. According to other texts (the majority), the soul must pay the toll-collectors with the good deeds accomplished and the virtues acquired during its life on earth, the former only allowing it to pass when it has presented them with a quantity of good actions superior to the bad deeds of which it stands accused,[55] or a degree of virtue greater than the degree of passion they have found within it. The soul is then assisted and defended by the angels that accompany it; also by the prayers made for it by the living, hence the role of liturgical commemorations for the sake the deceased during this period of its voyage in the afterlife. The already cited anonymous eleventh-to-twelfth century text simply refers to "the inspectors of the air" in whose presence the soul finds itself until the ninth day with its rising up to heaven.[56] Origen proves to be more precise:

> When we depart from the world and this life of ours has been transformed, some beings will be seated at the boundary of the world, as if they were exercising the office of tax collectors,[57] very carefully searching to find something in us that is theirs ... [W]e read in the Apostle, namely, "Repay to all what is owed: tribute to whom tribute is due, taxes to whom taxes are due, honor to whom honor is due" (Rom. 13:7), these words are also to be understood in a spiritual sense ... For this reason we should ponder to what great dangers we are exposed. Otherwise, when we do not have the means to pay the tax, we ourselves might be dragged off on account of the debt. This is what normally happens to those subject to worldly taxes, when someone is imprisoned for his debt and made a slave of the state. How many more of us are destined to be held by tax collectors of that sort![58]

Other texts mention the spiritual obstacles to passing through the toll-houses, the passions or evil deeds that connect the dying person to the demons, and show how, to the contrary, certain virtues and certain good deeds constitute a pass or safe-conduct that enables the soul to leave nothing of itself, or to give the demons who want to seize it no place to lay hold. St Basil of Caesarea, commenting on this verse from Psalm 7: "Lord my God, in Thee have I put my trust; save me from all them that persecute me, and deliver me; lest they seize my soul like a lion, ..." writes:

> The dying person, knowing only that there is only one savior and liberator, cries out: "In Thee have I put my hope, save me" from my weakness "and rescue me" from captivity. For I think that the valiant athletes of God, after having kept up the good fight the whole course of their existence against the invisible enemies and escaping every trap, when they arrive at life's end, are examined by the Prince of this world. If they are found, following the battle, to still have some wounds, stains or remnants of sin, they are detained by him. However, if they are to the contrary whole and untainted, these invincible heroes remain free and are admitted by Christ to the place of rest. The Psalmist is praying therefore for the present life and for the future life. Save me, he says, from those who persecute me here and deliver me there, at the moment of examination, from the fear that [the ruler of this world] might seize my soul like a lion. This is what we can learn from the Lord Himself, who said on the eve of His passion: "The ruler of this world is coming, and he has nothing in Me." He who had not committed any sin said that He had nothing. As for man, it is enough for him to be able to say: "The ruler of this world comes and he will having nothing in me but a small number of little things." [59]

St Diadochos of Photiki affirms that "if we are afraid [at the time of our death], we will not be able to freely bypass the rulers of the nether world. They will have as their advocate to plead against us the fear which our soul experiences because of its own wickedness. But the soul which rejoices in the love of God, at the hour of its departure, is lifted with the angels of peace above all the hosts of darkness."[60] Abba Isaiah notes on the one hand: "Woe to me, woe to me, for in no way have I been freed from Gehenna, those who drag me toward it still bear fruit within me, and all its acts are alive within my heart. Those who overwhelm me in its fire are still active in my flesh, wanting to succeed. I have not yet learned from here my place of destination. The straight way is not yet prepared for me; I have not yet been liberated from the evil spirits in the air who will hinder me on account of their evil deeds that are within me."[61] But on the other hand he writes: "[Love] is precisely the seal of the soul upon death, as [Christ] said to his disciples, 'By this everyone will know that you are my disciples, if you have love for one another' (John 13:35). About what else, then, does he mean that they will know you, other than about the powers of the right[62] and of the left ?[63] If the enemy sees the sign of love accompanying the soul, it keeps a distance from it on account of fear, and then all the holy powers rejoice with the soul."[64] Later he declares that "those who dwell in heaven testify that he has escaped from the princes of the Left, he will be remembered by those heavenly inhabitants."[65] He also teaches that the faithful person "needs to examine himself at all times. Has he escaped to be with those who have withdrawn into the air? Is he free from those in order that he may live again?"[66]

The heavenly 'tax booths' and 'tax collectors' are likewise mentioned by St Macarius of Egypt: "Like the tax collectors who sit along the narrow streets and snatch at the passers-by and extort from them, so also the demons watch carefully and grab hold of souls. And when they pass out of the body, if they are not completely purified, they are not permitted to go up into the mansions of Heaven there to meet their Master. For they are driven down by the demons of the air."[67]

But other Fathers are more precise than the preceding ones. Here is Ephrem the Syrian:

> While the dying person addresses his last words to us, suddenly his tongue is at a loss, his eyes dim, his mouth falls silent, his voice paralyzed when the Lord's troops have arrived, when his frightening armies overwhelm him, when the divine bailiffs invite the soul to be gone from the body, when the inexorable lays

hold of us to drag us to the tribunal … Then the angels take the soul and go off through the air. There stand principalities, powers and leaders of the adverse troops who govern the world, merciless accusers, strict agents of an implacable tax bureau, like so many examiners that await the soul in the air, ready to demand a reckoning, to examine everything, brandishing their claims, that is to say our sins: those of youth and of old age, those intentional and those not so, those committed by actions and those by words or thoughts. Great then is the fear of the poor soul, inexpressible its anguish when it sees itself at grips with these myriads of enemies, who stop it, push and shove it, accuse it, hinder it from dwelling in the light, from entering into the land of the living. But the holy angels, taking the soul, lead it away.[68]

Still more precise is St Cyril of Alexandria, in a homily which will be repeated in summary by St Anastasius of Sinai[69] and quoted by St John Damascene:[70]

What fear, what terror, what strife and what anguish the soul is called to suffer once separated from the body. For we encounter then, on the one hand, the heavenly armies and powers; on the other, the adverse powers, the lords of darkness, the impious masters of the world, the tax collectors, the inspectors and auditors of our deeds that inhabit the air, and with them the murderous devil, overseer of the realm of evil. He lays traps for us like a lion in his den. It is the great dragon, the apostate, hell itself that opens its maw. Because he presides over the empire of darkness, he retains power and, in a certain manner, the judging of the dead: he stops the soul to oppose it, to reproach it for all its faults and failings, in acts and words, conscious or unconscious; he scrutinizes our entire conduct from youth until our last day. How great the soul's fear and terror when it sees itself in the presence of these dreadful and ferocious beings, these pitiless and cruel demons that assail it … just the sight of which is more terrifying than all the other torments! Seeing them, it becomes agitated and distressed, overwhelmed with pain and draws back, flees to the angels of God. The latter take the soul then and carry it away into the air. But it finds there a cordon of duty collectors that bar the route, that seize and stop souls from passing. Now to each station is assigned a particular kind of sin. Here the sins of the tongue and mouth: lies, swearing and perjury, useless words and vain pleasantries, immoderate libations of wine, excessive and misplaced laughter, immodest kisses and lewd songs. But the holy angels that are leading the soul extol in their turn all the good speech that our mouth and tongue have pronounced: prayers, thanksgiving, psalms, hymns and spiritual canticles, lessons in Scripture, in short anything we have offered to God by mouth and tongue. A second station deals with sight, with everything having to do with indecent spectacles, needless and dissolute gazing, misleading glances. The third is that of hearing and everything sullied minds receive through this sense. The fourth is that of smell, in charge of all sensations obtained through those perfumed odors or essences fit only for actresses or prostitutes. The fifth watches for all sins and unruliness owing to a touch of the hands. Other stations lastly inquire into envy and jealousy, vanity and pride, ill-will and anger, fits of ill temper and rage, fornications, adultery, masturbation, homicide and sorcery, in summary into all the other evil actions, the details of which would be out of place here and will be set aside for another time. In short, each disease of the soul, each kind of sin has its inspectors and special accountants. When the soul sees all this then and still more, what fear, terror and affliction it must be in until the sentence is pronounced that assures it of acquittal! This is a painful hour, an hour of groaning and danger that leaves it anxious until the outcome of events. But in fact, the divine powers are there and also confront the impure spirits. The former bring to the fore its good deeds by words and actions, thoughts and intentions. Trembling and fearful, the soul stands in the middle until, according to its acts and words, it is condemned and imprisoned or else justified and set at large. For everyone's sins are chains that bind them. If it is judged worthy, because of its pious life and its conduct in conformity with the will of God, the angels take it and henceforth it proceeds in complete security, having the celestial powers for companions.[71]

The heavenly 'toll-houses' are described in an equally precise manner in this text of Abba Isaiah of Scetis, where the demons of the different tollbooths, who demand a reckoning for the passion they inspire, are identified successively:

How much joy do you suppose fills the soul when a person begins to serve God, and when that person completes the task? Upon his death, he will present his ascetic discipline, and the angels will rejoice with him when they see him rid of the powers of darkness. When the soul leaves the body, the angels journey with it. At that moment, all the forces of darkness come out to meet the soul, wanting to possess it and examining whether it has anything that belongs to them. Then it is not the angels who war against these forces, but the good works that have been achieved which fortify and protect the soul from them, so that it may not be touched by them. If the good works are victorious, then the angels lead the soul, chanting in procession, until it meets God in gladness, and at that time it forgets every worldly labor and ascetic toil. Let us, therefore, do our utmost to work well during this brief lifetime, preserving our ascetic labor from every evil, in order that we may be saved from the hands of the evil spirits of this world, for they are wicked and lack compassion. Blessed is the person in whom nothing is found that belongs to them. His joy, gladness, rest, and crown will be exceedingly great … Dear brothers, let us do our utmost in tears before God, so that his goodness may be merciful to us and grant us strength that we may, in turn, wrestle against the evil spirits that come to meet us in regard to the deeds we have performed. Let us take care, therefore, with all sincerity of heart, and acquire within ourselves a desire for God that will save us from the hands of the evil ones when they come to meet us there. Let us learn to love the poor, because this may save us from avarice when it approaches us. Let us strive to make peace with all people, because this will save us from hate when it approaches us. Let us acquire long-suffering in all things, for this will protect us against negligence when it approaches us. Let us love all people as our brothers, neither allowing any hatred against anyone to enter our heart, nor returning evil for evil (cf. Rom. 12:17), for this will protect us from envy when it approaches. Let us strive for humility in everything, enduring the words of our neighbor when he either hurts or rebukes us, and this will protect us from pride when it approaches us. Let us seek to honor our neighbor, never causing any harm by blaming, and this will protect us from slander when it approaches us. Let us overlook the needs and honors of this world, that we may be saved from jealousy when it approaches us. Let us train our mind in godly study, righteousness, and prayer, that these may protect us from falsehood when it approaches us. Let us purify our heart and body from sinful desire, that we may be saved from impurity when it approaches us. All these [passions] occupy the soul when it leaves the body, and the virtues assist the soul, if the latter has acquired them.[72]

The 'tollbooths' and 'tax inspectors' posted there, which correspond to different passions, are likewise referred to in detail in the *Life* of St John of Cyprus (also called St John the Almsgiver), Patriarch of Alexandria:

[John] always used to talk much about the thought of death and the departure of the soul so that on several occasions those who went in to him with a haughty bearing and laughing face and bold eyes came out from his presence with humble demeanor and a contrite face and eyes filled with tears. He used to say: 'My humble opinion is that it suffices for our salvation to meditate continually and seriously about death and to think earnestly upon the fact that nobody will pity us in that hour nor will anyone travel with us out of this life except our good deeds. And when the angels come hastening down, in what a tumult will a soul then be if it is found unready! How it will beg that it may be allowed a further short span of life, only to hear the words: "What about the time you have lived, have you spent it well?" And again he used to say as though speaking of himself, "Humble John, how will you have the strength to 'pass the wild beasts of the reeds', [Psalm 67:31 LXX], when they meet you like tax collectors? Woe is me, what fears and tremors will encompass the soul when it is called to account by so many keen and pitiless accountants?" And indeed the saintly man had especially noted that which was made known through revelation by St Simeon, the stylite; the words were: "When the soul goes forth from the body, as it rises from the earth to heaven there meet it troops of demons, each in his own regiment. A band of demons of arrogance meet it, they feel it all over to see whether the soul possesses their works. A band of the spirits of slander meets it; they inspect it to see whether it has ever uttered slanders and not repented. Again higher up the demons of harlotry meet it; they investigate whether they can recognize their pursuits in it. And while the wretched soul is being brought to account on its way from earth to heaven the holy angels stand on one side and do not help it, only its own virtues can do that.' [73]

We also find the tax stations mentioned in the account of an out-of-body experience undergone by a mace bearer (*taxiotes*), which is found in the *Lives of the Saints* upon the date of March 28. But we cite here the long version by an anonymous author:

At the time of the patrician Nicetas, this is what happened at Carthage in Africa. There was in the *praetorium* a mace bearer who spent his life in numerous sins. When the plague invaded Carthage, he was moved to compunction and proceeded to move away to a small suburb of the city, with his wife accompanying him as well. Now then the devil, perpetually jealous of man's salvation and repentance, there too drove the mace bearer into adultery with a wife of a farmer who lived in that district. But a few days after his lapse he was stricken with buboes and died. There was a monastery a mile from the suburb. The wife of the mace bearer went there and begged the monks to come. They came and, having taken the body, they buried it in their church. This was around the third hour. Then, while they were chanting at the ninth hour, they heard a voice as if from the depths saying: "Have mercy on me!" Obeying the voice they returned to the tomb. And, having opened it, they found the mace bearer weeping. Soon they lifted him out, freed him from his waxcoated bandages, and questioned him, wanting to know what he had seen and what had happened. Unable to tell them because of profuse moaning, he asked them to bring him to the servant of God Thalassios, who was then the ornament of all Africa. At the time, then, that they had brought him to Thalassios and related the extraordinary event that befell this man, venerable Thalassios, full of divine wisdom, stayed to catechize and console the young man, and for three days he urged him to relate what he had seen. Finally on the fourth day, with difficulty, he was able to loosen his tongue from its moanings and speak distinctly, and he told him with a flood of tears: "I the miserable one, when I was dying, I saw demons[74] who appeared before me. Their appearance was very frightful; my soul beholding them was disturbed. Then I saw two splendid youths, and my soul leaped out into their arms. We began slowly to ascend in the air to the heights, as if flying, and we reached the toll-houses that guard the ascent and detain the soul of each man. Each toll-house tested a special form of sin: one lying, another envy, another pride; each sin has its own testers in the air. And I saw that the angels held all my good deeds in a little chest; taking them out, they would compare them with my evil deeds. Thus we passed by all the toll-houses. And when, nearing the gates of heaven, we came to the toll-house of fornication, those who guard the way there detained me and presented to me all my fleshly deeds of fornication, committed from my childhood up to now. The angels who were leading me said: 'All the bodily sins which you committed in the city, God has forgiven because you repented of them.' To this my adversaries said to me: 'But when you left the city, in the village you committed adultery with a farmer's wife.' The angels, hearing this and finding no good deed which could be measured out for my sin, left me and went away. Then the evil spirits seized me and, overwhelming me with blows, led me down to earth. The earth opened, and I was let down by narrow and foul-smelling descents into the underground prison of hell. Imprisoned there are the souls of sinners, dead for all eternity, as Job said … I was confined in those dark regions, full of terrible sorrows, and wept and bitterly sobbed from the third to the ninth hour. About the ninth hour I saw these two angels who arrived there, and I set about calling them and begging them to take me out of this prison that I might repent to God. They answered me: 'You call in vain. None of those who come here leave or are delivered until the day of the resurrection.' Now then, as I persisted in begging them, in repeating my prayer, and as I promised a sincere repentance, one of them said to the other: 'Do you guarantee that he will sincerely repent to God?' And I saw so to say the other one guarantee and authorize it. Then they took me, brought me back to earth and placed me in my tomb near my corpse. And they told me: 'Enter there where you came out.' Now I saw my soul as if a pearl that shone like a crystal, but the sight of my corpse as if a mire and dark, stinking slime, and I turned away from it in horror. It was hard to enter back into it. The angels said to me: 'You can only do penance by means of the body by which you have sinned.' Once again I begged not to reenter it. At that point they told me: 'Believe us, either enter into your body, or else we will bring to back to the place from which we have led you. Enter now, that you might tell others for their edification what you have seen and suffered.' I then saw myself entering the corpse by the mouth, and soon I began to cry out … This is what fathers worthy of faith have related to us for our edification.[75]

The most precise description we have of the stations of the aerial toll-houses is found in the account of Blessed Theodora, who appears in the *Life* of her spiritual father, St Basil the Young (tenth century), written by another of his disciples, Gregory of Thrace. This passage deserves to be quoted despite its length for, on this question, it is still considered a text of reference:

The holy angels took me up, and we went eastward through the air.

THE FIRST TORMENT "As we were rising from the earth to the heights of heaven, we were first met by the spirits of the first torment. Here the souls are tormented for the sins of idle speech; that is, for speaking without thinking, or speaking what is vile and shameless, or speaking without need or order. We stopped, and many scrolls were brought out on which there were recorded all the words that I had uttered from my youth on, either needlessly or unreasonably, and especially when such words expressed anything unclean or blasphemous, as young people frequently bear on their tongue."

"There I saw recorded all my angry words, foul words, worldly shameless songs, wild cries and laughter. The evil spirits accused me of all this and indicated the time and place, when and where and in whose company I spoke these vain words or evoked the wrath of God by my unseemly words, even though at the time I did not consider such things sinful; and paying no great attention to them did not confess them to my spiritual father, and never repented. Now I kept silent, as if I had lost my voice. I was unable to reply because the evil spirits accused me rightly. But while I was silent in my shame and trembled with fear, the holy angels offered some of my good deeds and, since these were not enough, they added something from the treasure given me by the holy man Basil[76]; and thus they paid my debts at this station."

SECOND TORMENT "Thence we ascended and drew near the torment of lying. Here is tested every lying word: failure to keep oaths, vain use of God's name, failure to keep vows given to God, insincere or false confession of sins, and the like. The spirits of this station are evil and ruthless. They stopped us and began to question us closely. However, I was accused of two things only: first, that I occasionally lied in matters of small importance—something that I did not even consider sinful; second, that, because of a false sense of shame, I sometimes insincerely confessed my sins to my spiritual father. As for false oaths or false witness, none of these, through Christ's grace, was found in me. Here the holy angels put down for my sins some of my good deeds, but the prayers of my spiritual father did even more to save me. We went on."

THIRD TORMENT "We reached the station where souls answer for speaking evil of others and spreading rumors about them. When we were stopped here, I understood how heavy is the sin of speaking evil about one's neighbor, and how great an evil it is to spread bad rumors, judge the deeds of others, damage someone's reputation, slander, give bad words to people, or laugh at other's deficiencies. Such sinners are regarded as antichrists, since even before Christ has judged their neighbors they already allow themselves this right of judgment. In me, however, through the grace of Christ, they did not find many of these sins, for all the days of my life I always diligently strove not to condemn anyone, never to spread falsehoods about people, never to laugh at anyone, and never to give anyone bad words. Only occasionally, when I heard how other people condemn, malign, or laugh, did I too happen to agree with them to some extent in thought, or even, in my carelessness, add my word to what they were saying; but even then I instantly caught myself and stopped. But here I was held responsible even for the inclination. Here also the angels freed me by means of the prayers of the holy man Basil, and we continued to ascend."

FOURTH TORMENT "We reached the station where gluttony is punished, and evil spirits immediately rushed out to meet us, for they hoped to find a victim. Their faces resembled those of sensuous gluttons and despicable drunkards. They walked around us like dogs and immediately showed their count of all the instances when I ate secretly from others, or without need, or when I ate in the morning before I had even prayed and signed myself with the mark of the cross; or when, during the holy fasts, I ate before the church service was over. They also revealed all the instances when I was drunk and even showed us those very cups, goblets, and others vessels from which I became intoxicated at such and such a time, during such and such a feast, with such and such companions. And every other instance of my gluttony was pointed out to me, and the demons already rejoiced, as if they had put their hands on me. I was trembling at the sight of such accusations and did not know how to object. But the holy angels took out enough from what was given to us by the holy man Basil, balanced my sins with this and set me free. When the spirits saw the ransom, they cried out, 'Woe! our labors and hopes have perished!' and threw their records of my gluttony into the air. I, however, rejoiced, and we went on."

"As we were ascending, the holy angels talked among themselves and said words to this effect: 'Truly does this soul have great help from Basil, a man who has pleased God. If it had not been for his prayers, she would have suffered a great deal in those stations of the air.' I took courage and said to them: 'It seems, holy angels, that none of the earth dwellers knows what happens here and what the soul can expect after death.' But the angels replied: 'Does not the divine Scripture testify concerning all of this? It is read in churches and preached by priests. Only those people who are passionately devoted to the vanities of earth take no heed of what they are told, and since they consider daily gluttony and drunkenness to be the greatest pleasure, they eat beyond measure and drink without thinking of the fear of God. Their belly is their God. They have no thought of future life and do not remember what is said in Scripture: "Woe to you who are full, for you shall hunger" (Luke 6:25). "'Still, even the gluttonous can be saved. Those who are merciful and kindhearted to the needy and beggars and help those who ask for help—such men can easily obtain from God forgiveness of their sins, and because of their kindheartedness toward their neighbors, pass the stations of torment without stopping. It is said in Scripture that alms save us from death and cleanse every kind of sin; those who give alms and do justice will be filled with life (Tob 12:9). But he who does not strive to cleanse his sins by good deeds cannot escape the dark tormentors who lead the sinners down to hell and hold them bound until the terrible judgment at Christ's second coming. You, too, would not have escaped here your evil lot, were it not that you have received the treasure of holy Basil's prayers.'"

FIFTH TORMENT "During this conversation we reached the station of sloth, where sinners are accused of all those days and hours which they spent in idleness. Here, too, are detained those who did not work themselves but lived by the labor of others; and those who were hired to work, took their wages, but did not fulfill the duties which they had taken upon themselves. And also are stopped here those who do not care to praise God and are too lazy to go to church on holidays and Sundays, either in the morning or to the Divine Liturgy, or to other church services. And here too people are accused of despondency and general carelessness about things that have to do with the salvation of their souls; this happens to both laymen and those who are ordained. Many are thence led into the abyss. I, too, was accused there of much and could not have freed myself if the holy angels had not balanced my deficiencies by the gifts of the holy man Basil."

SIXTH TORMENT "Thence we came to the torment of stealing, and although we were briefly stopped there, we went on after we had given a small ransom only: for no stealing was found on my record, except some very unimportant occurrences in my childhood, and those stemmed from lack of reason."

SEVENTH TORMENT "We passed without stopping through the station of avarice and love of money. By God's grace I never loved riches. I was content with what God gave me and never was avaricious; on the contrary, I diligently gave to the needy that which I had."

EIGHTH TORMENT "When we rose still higher, we came to the station of usury, where those are accused who lend money for illegal interest. Here, too, are stopped those who gain riches by exploiting their neighbors, those who take bribes, or who by some other way steal indirectly, acquiring what really belongs to others. The tormentors, when they did not find me guilty of such sins, gnashed their teeth with annoyance, but we went on, praising God in the meanwhile."

NINTH TORMENT "Now there lay before us the torment of injustice. Here are punished the unjust judges who acquit the guilty and condemn the innocent, all for the sake of gain; and also those who do not give the appointed wages to those whom they have hired, and the merchants who use false weights and measures, and all the others who are in some way unjust. We, however, by God's grace, passed this station without incurring any grief after we had given only a little bit for my sins in this regard."

TENTH TORMENT "As for the torment of envy, we passed it without giving anything at all in payment, for I never had been envious. Here also people have to face the accusations of lack of love, hatred toward their brethren, unfriendliness, and other manifestations of hatred. Through the mercy of Christ our God, I was found innocent of all these sins; and although I saw the savagery of the demons, I was no longer afraid of them. Joyfully we went on."

ELEVENTH TORMENT "Then we passed the station of pride, where arrogant spirits make accusations of vanity, absolute reliance on oneself rather than on God, disdain of others, and bragging; and here too the souls are tormented for their failure to give proper honor to their parents, their government, or their other superiors appointed by God, and for failure to obey them. Here we put down very little for my sins, and I was free."

TWELFTH TORMENT "As we continued rising toward heaven, we encountered the torment of anger and ruthlessness. Happy is the man who never in his life felt anger. The eldest of the evil spirits was sitting here on a throne, and he was full of anger, ruthlessness, and pride. Ruthlessly and angrily he ordered his servants to torment and accuse me. They licked their chops like dogs and began to point out not only all those occasions when I actually said something angry or unfeeling to anyone, or harmed anyone by my words, but even those instances when I merely looked angrily at my children or punished them severely. All these cases they represented vividly and even indicated the time when everything happened, the persons on whom I poured out my anger, the very words which I then used, and in whose presence I used them. The angels replied to all this by offering part of the treasure, and we went on."

THIRTEENTH TORMENT "After this, the torment of bearing grudges lay before us. Here merciless accusations await those who nurture in their hearts evil thoughts against their neighbors and return evil for evil. God's mercy saved me here too, for I did not tend to have such wicked designs and did not keep in mind offenses of others toward me; on the contrary, whenever I could, I displayed love and meekness toward those who offended me, and thus overcame their evil by my goodness. Here we paid nothing. Joyful in the Lord, we went on."

"Here I dared to ask my angel leaders: 'Tell me how can these terrible rulers of the air know in such detail all the evil deeds of men, and not only the open ones but even those that are secret?' The angels replied: 'Every Christian, as soon as he is baptized, receives from God an appointed guardian angel who guards him invisibly and inspires him night and day to every kind of good deed; he also records all his good deeds, for which that man later can hope to receive from the Lord grace and eternal recompense in the heavenly kingdom. The prince of darkness, who desires to draw into his own destruction the whole race of men as well, also appoints one of his evil spirits to walk in the man's steps and record all his evil deeds. It is his duty to inspire man to such deeds by any vile trickery in his power; and when he succeeds in his designs, he records all the wickedness of which the man has made himself guilty. Such an evil spirit spreads the report of every man's sins to all the stations of torment, and this is how the sins become known to the princes of the air. When the soul parts from its body and desires to go to its Creator in heaven, the evil spirits prevent the soul and show to it its sins. If the soul has done more good deeds than evil, they cannot keep it; but if the sins outweigh the good deeds, they keep the soul for some time, shut it up in the prison where it cannot know God, and torment it as much as God's power allows them, until that soul, by means of prayers of the Church and good deeds done for its sake by those who are still on earth, should be granted forgiveness.'"

"'Those who believe in the Holy Trinity and take as frequently as possible the holy communion of the Holy Mysteries of Christ our Savior's Body and Blood—such people can rise to heaven directly, with no hindrances, and the holy angels defend them, and the holy saints of God pray for their salvation, since they have lived righteously. No one, however, takes care of the wicked and depraved heretics, who do nothing useful during their lives, and live in disbelief and heresy. The angels can say nothing in their defense.'"

"'When a soul proves to be so sinful and impure before God that it has no hope of salvation, the evil spirits immediately bring it down into the abyss, where their own place of eternal torment is also. There the lost souls are kept until the time of the Lord's second coming. Then they will unite with their bodies and will incur torment in fiery hell together with the devils. Note also,' said the angels, 'that this is the way by which only those who are enlightened by faith and holy baptism can rise and be tested in the stations of torment. The unbelievers do not come here. Their souls belong to hell even before they part from their bodies. When they die the devils take their souls with no need to test them. Such souls are their proper prey, and they take them down to the abyss.'"

FOURTEENTH TORMENT "During our conversation we reached the torment of murder, where are accused not only men such as robbers, but even those who have in some way wounded another man, or given him a blow, or pushed him angrily, or shoved him. We gave a little and went on."

FIFTEENTH TORMENT "We passed the torment of magic, sorcery, poisoning, and incantations. The spirits of this station resemble serpents, snakes, and toads. They are frightening and repulsive. By the grace of God, they found nothing of the kind in me, and we went on, accompanied by the shouts of the demons: 'Soon you will come to the torment of fornication; let us see how you will free yourself from it!'"

"As we were rising, I dared to question the holy angels once more: 'Do all Christians pass these torments? Is there no possibility to pass by the torments and not be tested in any of the stations?' The angels replied, 'There is no other way for the souls that rise toward heaven. Every one goes this way, but not everyone is tormented like you; only sinners like you incur the torments, for they have not confessed their sins fully, and moved by a false sense of shame, have kept their really shameful deeds secret from their spiritual fathers. When a man wholeheartedly confesses his evil deeds and repents and regrets them, his sins are invisibly wiped out by God's mercy. When a repentant soul comes here, the tormentors of the air open their books but find nothing written there; the soul, then, joyfully ascends to the throne of God.'"

"'The evil spirits open their records but find nothing written there, for the Holy Spirit has made invisible all the writing. The spirits see this and know that what they have recorded has all been obliterated because of the soul's confession, and they are very much saddened by this. If the man is still alive when his confession has wiped out his sins, the spirits once again try to have an occasion to record some new sins of his.'"

"'Indeed, there is a great source of salvation for man in his confession! Confession saves him from many misfortunes and much unhappiness and gives him the opportunity to pass all the torments with no hindrance and to approach God. Some people do not confess their sins because they hope to have time for salvation and for a remittance of their sins; others are simply ashamed of telling their spiritual father about their sins. They will, however, be severely tested when they pass the stations of torment. There are still other people, who are ashamed of telling everything to one spiritual father. Therefore they choose several and reveal some of their sins to one and others to another, and so on; they will be punished for this kind of confession and will suffer a great deal as they pass from one torment into another.'"

"'If you, too, had made a complete confession of your sins and had been granted remission of them, and had then done all you could to make up for them by good deeds—if you had done all this, you would not have been subjected to such terrible torments in the stations. You were, however, greatly helped by the fact that you have long ago ceased to commit deadly sins and have spent the rest of your life in virtue. You have been helped especially by the prayers of God's holy man Basil, whom you have served greatly and diligently.'"

SIXTEENTH TORMENT "During our conversation, we approached the torment of fornication, where souls are accused not only of actual fornication but also of amorous daydreaming, of finding such thoughts sweet, of impure glances, lustful touches, and passionate strokings. The prince of this torment was clothed in a dirty and stenchful garment befouled by a bloody foam, and there was a multitude of demons standing around him. When they saw me, they marveled that I had already passed so many torments. They brought out the records of all my deeds of fornication and accused me by pointing out the persons, the places, and the times: with whom, when, and where I sinned in my youth. I kept silent and was trembling with shame and fear. The holy angels, however, said to the devils, 'Long ago has she left her deeds of fornication and has spent the remainder of her life in purity, abstinence, and fasting.' But the demons replied, 'We, too, know that she has long ago ceased sinning, but she has not sincerely confessed to her spiritual father and has not received from him proper directions for the penance she should make for her sins. Therefore she is ours! Either leave her to us or ransom her with good deeds.' The angels put down many of my good deeds but even more did they take from the gift given us by the holy man Basil; barely did I save myself from great grief."

SEVENTEENTH TORMENT "We reached the torment of adultery, where are accused of their sins those who are married but do not observe marital fidelity toward each other and do not keep their marriage bed undefiled; here, too, rapes are punished. Besides, here are strictly punished those who have devoted themselves to God and promised to live for Christ alone, but have fallen and failed to keep their purity. I, too, had a great debt here; the evil spirits already had accused me and were about to tear me from the arms of the angels, but the angels began to argue with them and show them all my later labors and good deeds. After some time they rescued me, but with difficulty, and not so much by my good deeds—all of which, down to the last, they deposited here—but rather by the treasure of my father Basil, from which they also took very much to put on the scale to balance my iniquities. Then they took me and we went on."

EIGHTEENTH TORMENT "We approached the station of the Sodomic sins; here souls are accused of all unnatural sins, incest, and other revolting deeds performed in secret—shameful and frightening even to think about. The prince of this torment was more disgusting than any other devil; he was befouled by pus and full of stench. His servants were just like him. The stench that came from them was not to be endured, their ugliness was unimaginable, their cruelty and ruthlessness not to be expressed. They surrounded us but by the grace of God found nothing in me and ran away from us in their shame. We went on."

"The holy angels said to me: 'You have seen, Theodora, the frightening and disgusting torments of fornication! Know then that few are the souls that pass them without stopping and paying their ransom, for the whole world lies immersed in the evils of seductive foulness, and all mankind is sensuous. Few guard against the impurities of fornication and deaden the desire of their own flesh. And this is the reason why few pass here freely; many come as far as this place but perish here. The rulers of the torments of fornication boast that they, more than any of the others, fill the fiery abyss of hell with the souls of men. But you, Theodora, must thank God that you have already passed the torments of fornication by the prayers of the holy man Basil, your father. Now you will no longer fear.'"

NINETEENTH TORMENT "Thereafter we came to the torment of heresies, where are punished those whose reasonings about faith are not right, and also those who turn away from the Orthodox confession of faith, who lack faith, have doubts about it, deny holy things or show a negative attitude toward them, and other sins of this kind. I passed this torment without being tested; we were no longer far from the gates of heaven."

TWENTIETH TORMENT "But here we were met by the evil spirits of the last torment, the station that tests lack of compassion and cruelty of heart. Cruel are the tormentors of this place, and their prince is terrible; dried-up and depressed is his appearance. Here the souls of the unmerciful are tormented without mercy. Even if a man performs the most outstanding deeds, mortifies himself by fasting, prays ceaselessly, and guards and keeps the purity of his body, but is merciless—from this station he is cast down into the abyss of hell and will receive no mercy in all eternity. We, however, by the grace of Christ, passed this place without trouble, for we were helped by the prayers of the holy man Basil."

[new para]"Now we approached the gates of heaven. We entered joyfully, for we had passed unharmed through the bitter tests of the torments. The gates resembled crystal, and the buildings that stood there glistened like stars. The youths who stood there were wearing golden garments. They joyfully received us, for they saw that a soul had escaped from the bitter tests of the torments of the air."[77]

This teaching on the 'telonies' is not the monopoly of the east, but is also found, although in a more discrete manner, among the ancient Fathers of the west.[78] We have seen St Gregory the Great refer to evil spirits examining the soul departed from its body. St Boniface, the Anglo-Saxon apostle to the Germans (eighth century) in one of his letters relates this account of an out-of-body experience undergone by a monk of the monastery of Wenlock:

> Angels of such pure splendor bore him up as he came forth from the body that he could not bear to gaze on them … "They carried me up," he said, "high into the air …" He reported further that in the space of time while he was out of the body a greater multitude of souls left their bodies and gathered in the place where he was than he had thought to form the whole race of mankind on earth. He said also that there was a crowd of evil spirits and a glorious choir of higher angels. And he said that the wretched spirits and the holy angels had a violent dispute concerning the souls that had come forth from their bodies, the demons bringing charges against them and aggravating the burden of their sins, the angels lightening the burden and making excuses for them.
>
> He heard all his own sins, which he had committed from his youth on and had failed to confess or had forgotten or had not recognized as sins, crying out against him, each in its own voice,[79] and accusing him grievously … Everything he had done in all the days of his life and had neglected to confess and many which he had not known to be sinful, all these were now shouted at him in terrifying words. In the same way the evil spirits, chiming in with the vices, accusing and bearing witness, naming the very times and places, brought proofs of his evil deeds … And so, with his sins all piled up and reckoned out, those ancient enemies declared him guilty and unquestionably subject to their jurisdiction.
>
> "On the other hand," he said, "the poor little virtues which I had displayed unworthily and imperfectly spoke out in my defense … And those angelic spirits in their boundless love defended and supported me, while the virtues, greatly magnified as they were, seemed to me far greater and more excellent than could have been practiced by my own strength."[80]

Although the west seems to have forgotten this teaching on the heavenly customs houses, it is still found, on the other hand, in a certain number of by no means minor Orthodox authors, and bears witness to the preservation, in the bosom of the Orthodox Church, of a tradition dating back to the early centuries. It was strongly upheld at the end of the nineteenth century by St Ignatius Brianchaninov, who summarizes it in these simple terms:

> For the testing of souls as they pass through the spaces of the air there have been established by the dark powers separate judgment places and guards in a remarkable order. In the layers of the under-heaven, from earth to heaven itself, stand guarding legions of fallen spirits. Each division is in charge of a special form of sin and tests the soul in it when the soul reaches this division. The aerial demonic guards and judgment places are called in the patristic writing the toll-houses, and the spirits who serve in them are called tax-collectors (Brianchaninov, vol. III, p. 136).[81]

In his *Discourse on Death*, St Ignatius has collected a great number of scriptural, patristic, hagiographic, and liturgical testimonies on this subject. This teaching was also defended in the same period by St Theophan the Recluse.[82] Commenting on verse 80 of Psalm 118: "O let my heart be blameless in Thy statutes, that I be not ashamed," the latter observes:

> The prophet does not mention how and where one 'may not be put to shame.' The nearest 'not being put to shame' occurs during the arising of inner battles. The second moment of not being put to shame is the time of death and the passage through the toll-houses. No matter how absurd the idea of toll-houses may seem to our 'wise men' according to this age, they will not escape passing through them. What do these 'toll-gatherers' seek in those who pass through? They seek whether people might have some of their goods. What kind of goods? Passions. Therefore, in the person whose heart is pure and a stranger to passions, they cannot find anything to wrangle over; on the contrary, the opposing quality will strike them like arrows of lightning … Therefore, it is very doubtful that a soul, as long as there remain in it sympathies for the objects of any passion, will not be put to shame in the toll-houses. Being put to shame here means that the soul itself is thrown into hell. But the final being put to shame is at the Last Judgment, before the Face of the All-seeing Judge.[83]

During this same period, the archimandrite Antony also mentions the examining of souls in the aerial toll-houses that they have to pass through when, accompanied by angels, souls are raised from the earth to heaven. He points out that the evil spirits stop them there to demand a reckoning of their sins, but specifies that, according to the Fathers, all souls are not stopped by the evil spirits: those who are holy and pure freely fly away to the bosom of Abraham.[84]

St Macarius of Moscow concludes, after having presented this topic in his renowned *Dogmatic Orthodox Theology*: "Such an uninterrupted, constant, and universal usage in the Church of the teaching of the toll-houses, especially among the teachers of the fourth century, indisputably testifies that it was handed down to them from the teachers of the preceding centuries and is founded on apostolic tradition."[85] It is also accepted by Father Sergius Bulgakov, who mentions it in his well-known presentation on Orthodoxy,[86] and the famous contemporary Serbian religious figure, Archimandrite Justin Popovich, takes it up again and expounds it in turn in his *Dogmatics of the Orthodox Church*[87] by observing that "numerous testimonies can be found in holy tradition on this topic."[88] Recent Orthodox authors from various backgrounds who have written works on death according to the Orthodox tradition likewise treat it at some length.[89]

The Orthodox Church also refers to this teaching on the 'telonies' in its liturgical services. These prayers are found in the *Octoechos*:

— "O Virgin, at the hour of my death, snatch me from the hands of demons, judgment, accusation, dread testing, the cruel toll-stations, the ferocious prince and eternal condemnation, O Mother of God."[90]

— "When the hour of death will have come for me, be present at my side, protect me, and save me from the terrible demons who seek to instigate my perdition."[91]

—"At the terrifying hour of my death, Holy Virgin, snatch me from accusing demons and from every punishment."[92]

— "Do not hand me over, pure Virgin, to the enemies who vie for my perdition on account of my faults, but, in Thy compassion, from their harmful actions preserve me."[93]

— "At the dread hour of death, snatch me from the midst of accusing demons and from all punishment."[94]

The prayer of St Eustratius, in the Saturday midnight Office, can also be cited:

Now, O Master, let Thy hand shelter me and let Thy mercy come upon me, for my soul is troubled and in sore distress at its departure from this, my wretched and defiled body, lest the counsel of the adversary come upon it and hinder it because of the sins I have committed in this life, whether in ignorance or in knowledge. Be gracious unto me, O Master, and let not my soul behold the gloomy and darksome countenance of the wicked demons, but let thy radiant and luminous angels receive it. Give glory unto Thy holy Name, and by Thy might lead me unto Thy divine tribunal. When I am to be judged, let not the hand of the prince of this world seize me, that he might drag me, the sinner, down unto the deep of Hades; but stand Thou by me and be Thou unto me a Savior and Helper. Have mercy, O Lord, on my soul which hath been defiled by the passions of this life, and receive it cleansed by means of repentance and confession; for Thou art blessed unto ages of ages.[95]

An allusion to the aerial toll-house is likewise found in the *Canon to the Guardian Angel*: "At the dread hour of my death, forsake me not, O my good guardian, but drive away the dark demons who will seek to terrify my trembling soul; defend me from their pursuit when I must perforce pass through the aerial toll-houses, that, preserved unharmed by thee, I may attain unto the paradise I desire."[96]

Various other liturgical texts also contain such an allusion, like this excerpt from the canon of the Mother of God sung during the feast of St John Chrysostom: "Grant me to pass untroubled through the host of noetic satraps and the tyrannic battalion of the lower air in the hour of my departure."[97]

We can likewise cite these prayers from the *Canon of Supplication to the Most-Holy Theotokos at the Parting of the Soul from the Body*, which is meant to prepare the dying person for the trials he will encounter after his death. "Count me worthy to pass, unhindered, by the persecutor, the prince of the air, the tyrant, him that stands guard in the dread pathways, and the false accusation of these, as I depart from earth;"[98] "do thou count me worthy to escape the hordes of bodiless barbarians, and rise through the aerial depths and enter into Heaven, that I may glorify thee unto the ages, O holy Theotokos."[99]

The teaching on the heavenly custom houses or aerial toll-houses has recently occasioned certain criticisms.[100] The latter remain, however, limited and ill-founded.[101] As we have seen, this teaching is widely attested from Christianity's origins down to our own time by a great variety of patristic, hagiographic, and liturgical texts. These criticisms are, however, a warning against possible shifts in its understanding and use, and invites us to give the following clarifications.

1) This teaching is not an article of faith, having been the object on the Church's part of no dogmatic definition.[102] It is rather a *theolegoumenon*, a personal belief. On this point the faithful might very well adopt a certain hesitancy, seeing that life beyond the grave remains a mystery here-below. They can also adhere to an 'abridged' conception that renounces seeing intermediate stages between the moment of death, when the soul is separated from the body, and the latter's appearing before Christ at the Last Judgment. There is in the Church, concerning the soul's destiny after death, not one Tradition, but traditions which, although diverse, are not necessarily irreconcilable and can be equally admissible from the moment that they are not in contradiction

with points upon which the Church has given a dogmatic definition (which is the case, as we will see in the following chapters, for certain later stages of *post-mortem* destiny).

2) This teaching on the aerial toll-houses should not be taken literally and in its materiality, as those who accept it have stressed moreover. St Theophan the Recluse notes that this teaching expresses the reality, but this does not mean that the reality is exactly as described in the texts that mention it[103] We have here a symbolic expression, under a sensible and material form accessible to all, of a spiritual reality which, in our present condition, eludes our experience and, therefore, our full comprehension.[104] As can be observed, the different accounts do not agree on the number and nature of toll-house stations, and the sins and passions cited vary from one account to another: this is because they reflect the inner state, the frame of reference and the experience proper to each author. Therefore we should consider the details of the accounts at a certain remove, not reading and understanding them literally, but always taking their symbolic nature into account and above all seeking out their spiritual significance. St Macarius of Moscow clarifies this: "One must picture the toll-houses not in a sense that is crude and sensuous, but—as far as possible for us—in a spiritual sense, and not be tied down to details which, in the various writers and various accounts of the Church herself, are presented in various ways, even though the basic idea of the toll-houses is one and the same."[105]

Overall, the teaching on the toll-houses and tax-collectors expresses the fact that each person, after his death, will have to render a very precise account of all the sins he has committed in his life and all the passions that reside in him, and of which he has not repented. This will have to be done not only in Christ's presence, but also, beforehand, in the presence of the angels and demons, the latter accusing him and the former coming to his defense.

In this respect the teaching on the aerial toll-houses has a dual pedagogical function: a) to make a person attentive to the importance of each action, not only for his present life but for his future one; and b) to incite a person to repentance. It should be observed that certain confessors in the Orthodox Church have a custom of offering to the faithful the account of St Theodora to help them make their examination of conscience, for the chief sins and passions affecting man are mentioned there.

3) This teaching should not be confused, as some have done, with the Latin conception of Purgatory: nowhere does this involve a gradual purification

in passing through the different toll-houses. In the account of the Blessed Theodora found in the *Life of St Basil the Young*, the toll-houses are often called 'torments', but this is because of the harassment of the demons and the torments their interrogations provoke in the soul.

4) Nor should this be confused with the western conception of the merits through which a person might gain (or pay for) paradise. Good works and the virtues surely assume, in all the accounts we have presented, an important place. It is not however only thanks to one's own virtues that a person can escape the powers of the air which, at the various stages of his ascension, attempt to stop him: it is absolutely indispensable to have at the same time help, aid and assistance from Christ. St Symeon the New Theologian, who addresses this prayer to God, is well aware of this: "You fill me with all blessings, O my God; but all of these will not help me if You will not give me the grace to overcome without confusion the gates of death. If the prince of darkness, when he should come, should not see Your glory surrounding me and be not completely rendered powerless, he with his darkness be not dissipated by Your inaccessible light and if all the opposing powers with him be not put to flight, seeing the sign of Your stamp on me … of what use to me are all these [experiences] which are now taking place in me?"[106] A similar teaching is found in St Hesychios: "If the soul has Christ with it, it will not be disgraced by its enemies even at death, when it rises to heaven's entrance; but then, as now, it will boldly confront them."[107] This is why the Church, in the services preceding death, as a preparation, but also in the services following death, especially the one on the third day, asks for Christ's help in supporting the soul of the deceased in its voyage in the hereafter through the heavenly toll-houses, until it has attained 'a place of rest'.

5) This teaching should not as a result let anyone suppose that, after death, demons would have total power over them. Many of the accounts cited make it quite clear in any case that the demons have no power over the just, and only have power over sinners to the extent that the latter have freely abandoned themselves to their works (acquiring in this way a certain intimacy with them) and have remained unrepentant.

6) The accounts presented here have without any doubt an edifying function: they wish to make the faithful more sensitive to the fact that a reckoning will be demanded of them for each action, whether good or bad, and therefore stress the spiritual importance, for their eternal future, of each act committed here-below. They elicit from the faithful a sense of their own responsibility by stressing the

fact that every person suffers the consequences of one's own faults, one's soul tending toward the condition for which it has shown the greatest affinity during its life. This is a way to say that man has to assume the logical consequences of his own acts not only here-below but even hereafter.

7) These accounts often insist, moreover, on the role played by repentance in breaking a person's ties with the evil actions committed and the passions able to affect him in this world. But they clearly leave another truth in the background: the fact that Christ can forgive the dying person for the evil done in his life if he shows repentance. We should recall here the episode of the repentant thief who asks Christ: "Lord, remember me when You come into Your kingdom," to which Christ replies: "Assuredly, I say to you, today you will be with Me in Paradise" (Luke 23:40–43).

This does not authorize a person to behave however he chooses, thinking he can, at the very moment of his death, count on Christ's forgiveness. The teaching on the 'heavenly custom-houses' is an additional invitation to man to be prepared beforehand for the judgment to come and *post-mortem* life, to purify himself through asceticism, to struggle against his passions by striving, with the aid of grace, to eliminate them completely, to do penance for all past faults so to be found just, without anything in him the Enemy can claim for his own, and so that he can say with Christ to whom he will be united and likened: "The ruler of this world is coming, and he has nothing in Me" (John 14:30).

We can see in this passage of the letter of St Paul to the Ephesians (without it being excluded that this counsel is applied also and first of all to the spiritual life here-below) an invitation to prepare oneself for the encounter, after death, with demons who will demand a settling of accounts with the soul: "Put on the whole armor of God, that you may be able to stand against the wiles of the devil. For we do not wrestle with flesh and blood, but against principalities, against powers, against the rulers of the darkness of this age, against spiritual hosts of wickedness in the heavenly places. Therefore take up the whole armor of God, that you may be able to withstand in the evil day, and having done all, to stand" (Eph. 6:11–13).[108] St Paul refers elsewhere to "the prince of the power of the air, the spirit who now works in the sons of disobedience" (Eph. 2:2).

St John Chrysostom reminds us: "Then we will need many prayers, many helpers, many good deeds, a great intercession from angels on the journey through the spaces of the air. If when traveling in a foreign land or a strange city we are in need of a guide, how much more necessary for us are guides and helpers to guide us past the invisible dignities and powers and world-rulers of this air, who are called persecutors and publicans and tax-collectors."[109]

In the account of Blessed Theodora found in the *Life of St Basil the Young*, the role of the latter's intercession and prayers is strongly emphasized (through the symbol of the pouch of gold containing his prayers) and presented as decisive in securing for the saint a passage without obstacle through the different aerial toll-houses.

But it is first Christ Himself that the faithful should implore as guide, not only in the present life, but also in the future one, by praying to Him without cease as recommended by Hesychios: "Let [the soul] not tire in calling upon the Lord Jesus Christ, the Son of God, day and night until the time of its departure from this mortal life, and He will speedily avenge it in accordance with the promise which He Himself made when speaking of the unjust judge (cf. Luke 18:1-8). Indeed, He will avenge it both in this present life and after its departure from its body."[110]

Chapter Five

FROM THE NINTH TO THE FORTIETH DAY: THE INTRODUCTION INTO THE OTHER WORLD

A T THE END of its voyage through the 'telonies', the soul is introduced into the other world and at that time visits at once, whatever its spiritual state and whatever the result of the examination undergone during its passage through the aerial toll-houses, the heavenly mansions and the abysses of hell.[1]

St Andrew of Crete teaches that even the souls of saints pass through "the dark place [of hell]," so that they might be initiated into the incredible mystery of the divine Economy, that is, the descent of Christ into hell, and might also better understand the extent of Christ's victory over death and hell.[2]

There are few texts on this subject and they sometimes diverge as to the timing of this stage. Some situate it between the third day (when the soul leaves the earth) and the fortieth (when it undergoes the particular judgment);[3] they think then that the crossing of the 'telonies' is complete by the end of the third day. Others situate it between the ninth and the fortieth day, placing the crossing of the 'telonies' between the third and ninth day. This second teaching takes into account the dates assigned since the earliest times by the Church for commemorating the deceased in the period following death: the third, ninth and fortieth (or thirtieth) day,[4] while the first teaching is deficient, losing sight of the ninth day and its significance with regard to the destiny of the deceased.

Among those texts in which we find the second teaching, the already mentioned anonymous text (eleventh–twelfth century) should be cited, a text closely tied to a passage from the *De mensibus* of John the Lydian: "On the third day the angels carry the soul on high. On the ninth day the separation of the soul away from the tax gatherers of the air and the angels occurs. On the fortieth day the soul is led before the divine throne."[5]

The *Revelation* of St Macarius of Alexandria presents the voyage of the soul into the heavenly places and the depths of hell in a detailed manner, but adopts a timeline differing from the previous one: a visit to the heavenly dwellings is situated between the third and ninth day, while the visit to hell between the ninth and fortieth day. St Macarius does not mention, however, any passage through the heavenly toll-houses, but in his text for the identical period extending from the third to the ninth day we see again a common element: the deceased person accused for faults committed during his earthly life, although here these accusations are the work of his own conscience. Here is the text:

> On the third day Christ—the very one raised from the tomb and resurrected on the third day, He himself, the God of the universe—decrees that every Christian soul ascend to heaven. Hence the holy Church beautifully observes this tradition of offering prayer and sacrifice to the God of the universe, on the third day, for the soul in every place. After this soul has adored God, then a command goes out from Him on its account: "Let it be shown all the varied dwellings of the saints, as well as the splendor and delights of paradise!" And when the soul has seen these things and been instructed about them for six days, it admires, is astonished at, and glorifies God, He, the arranger and finisher of these things, and, in seeing them, it is transformed and forgets the distress affecting it in connection with its separation from the body. But another distress and anguish seizes it if it is guilty of sin. The soul in fact sees the praises and delights of these servants of God and begins to be sad, to be distressed as well, and it accuses itself, saying: why have I lived vainly in the perverse world, been trapped by its futile passions, passed the greater part of my life in error producing nothing useful, and why have I not honored and served God as is fitting so to be worthy myself of this joy and glory? Woe is me, the wretched one! Of what use now the houses, goods and possessions I have amassed for myself and own there below? Of what use the vines and olive trees I have planted there? What advantage have I from gold and silver? Woe is me who has served vanity. Woe is me who, for the trifling love of vainglory that I fancied, have inherited eternal poverty. Woe is me, woe is me! How darkened I have become! Woe is me who has no one to help me, no one "who can intercede for me so that I might be worthy of the mercies of God." Then, after it has seen the joy of the righteous as well as the beauty and splendor of paradise during these six days, it is next once more raised up to adore God. The Church thus well and truly observes this law of offering the ninth day prayer and synaxis in memory of the deceased. And, after this second adoration, again a command goes out from the Lord of the universe on its account: "Let it descend to Sheol and be shown the judgments and tortures down there, as well as those infamous and dark places prepared for the wicked and the sinners, weeping and grinding their teeth!" And when the

soul has gone about and spent thirty days in these places, it is afraid, it weeps, and is greatly terrified that, in one of those places, it will be tormented and kept until the coming of the day of judgment. Next, on the fortieth day, the soul again ascends to adore God.[6]

This visit to the heavenly places and to hell is described at greater length in the account of Theodora and Gregory of Thrace found in the life of St Basil the Young. But no precise dating is offered. After visiting hell, Blessed Theodora specifies that it was forty days since she left her body,[7] but nothing is said about the duration of the passage through the aerial toll-houses, about the moment when she fell prostrate before God, or about the time when her visit began.

The relative scarcity of texts in which we see this stage mentioned, the variations in its dating, and the variations we encounter in its presentation remind us: 1) that we are in the realm of a symbolic chronology here, time in *post-mortem* life being different from that here below, if only because the first is tied to the laws of matter and its inertia, while the second, which is spiritual, is not; 2) that we are not in a realm of a dogma precisely defined by the Church in an unequivocal and universal manner, but of *theologoumena*, which can be diverse (without being for all that necessarily contradictory); also there has existed in the Church since its beginnings not a Tradition but traditions on this subject.

The descriptions of hell or heaven found in the texts that mention this stage often seem quite naïve. But they too have a symbolic significance and must not be taken at face value. They aim above all at making the reader understand:

a) that the world hereafter is a world in which the conditions of existence differ radically from ours; the naïve descriptions in the accounts play the same role as naïve architecture in icons, where the buildings depicted have incoherent forms and are uninhabitable: the iconographer is perfectly aware of this but wishes to give the impression of different mode;

b) that the just person finds rest, joy and happiness in heaven, while the sinner finds torment and suffering. What is described materially as experienced by the body, symbolizes what is spiritually experienced by the soul. What is essential here is not the materiality of described facts, this having to do with a realm where the conditions of existence differ from our present conditions of existence and are, approached from the latter, inaccessible to us, but the spiritual teachings that we can draw from the symbols presented prepare our soul for its voyage and then for its life hereafter.

Chapter Six
THE FORTIETH DAY:
THE PARTICULAR JUDGMENT

1 The Particular Judgment.

According to an ancient tradition, on the fortieth day after death the soul undergoes what is called 'the particular judgment'. This judgment is the one for each person after his death; it must be distinguished from the Last or universal Judgment to take place at the end of time, at the time of the second coming of Christ when He will resurrect the bodies and when all people will be summoned to appear before Him.

The teaching on the particular judgment is not a dogma, but rather a *theologoumenon*. This is why not all the Fathers mention it. It has been asserted that we have here "an hypothesis borrowed from Roman Catholic theology by the theologians of Kiev in the sixteenth century,"[1] but all the Catholic theologians do not lay claim to this teaching[2] which has never been the object of an explicit definition of faith in their Church.[3] The belief in Purgatory, which the Orthodox Church does not share, seems to imply such a judgment,[4] but it is equally implied by the belief, admitted by a majority of the eastern Fathers, that the soul is rewarded or chastised, in a non-definitive manner however, soon after its death;[5] it is in fact hard to imagine reward or punishment being ascribed without a judgment taking place. The debate over Purgatory, at the Council of Florence, has led western and eastern theologians to clarify their positions according to their respective points of view. It can be stated then that "nearly all the Greco-Russian theologians assert that the Orthodox Church teaches that there is no particular judgment."[6] But this conception has "remained quite popular in the Greco-Russian Church,"[7] it being based in fact on a certain number of very ancient testimonies.

Among the witnesses to the tradition on this subject, one can cite the already presented anonymous eleventh/twelfth century text: "On the fortieth day after death the soul is led before the throne of God where it receives its sentence, which is to dwell in a place apart until the resurrection of the dead."[8] The same indication is found in the Nomocanon of Manuel Malaxos:[9] "On the fortieth day the soul goes away to adore [God] and it receives its place in conformity with the life it has led on this earth, until the second Parousia of our Lord Jesus Christ."[10] But older texts also attest to this, like the *Revelation* of St Macarius of Alexandria: "On the fortieth day, the soul is again raised up to adore God. Then, in conformity with its works, the Judge of all things commands: 'Let it go into the guard-house!'[11] and there, on this fortieth day, the soul receives the place appropriate to its lot."[12]

As for the dating mentioned by the foregoing texts, we must recall here the importance, besides the third and ninth days, that the fortieth day assumes in the commemoration of the deceased by the Church according to an early tradition[13] attested to, for example, by the *Canons* of Clement[14] or the *Revelation* of St Macarius of Alexandria: "The Church thus beautifully preserves this custom of celebrating on the fortieth day the memory of those who have passed away."[15] This tradition has been preserved down to our own day, and the fortieth day is even, today as formerly, considered to be more important than the preceding ones, and is the occasion for a highly esteemed liturgical service.[16]

A belief in the particular judgment is found again among a certain number of modern Orthodox authors enjoying great authority in the Church.[17] One can cite St Ignatius Brianchaninov, who mentions it in his *Discourse on Death*, but also in *The Arena, Guidelines for Spiritual and Monastic Life*:[18] "The judgment is private for every Christian immediately after his death, and it will be general for all men at our Lord Jesus Christ's second coming to earth."

One might likewise cite Archimandrite Justin Popovich, who has devoted a lengthy explanation to it in his *Orthodox Church Dogmatics*:

> According to the teaching of holy tradition, the last judgment upon the world belongs to Christ the Lord, since He Himself is the Savior of the world: it is said in Holy Scripture that God the Father has committed all judgment to the Son (John 5:22). Christ the Lord will proceed with this judgment upon the world at His second coming, for that is when He will come to judge the living and the dead. This will be the 'last judgment'. But, beforehand, the Lord pronounces a preliminary judgment on each person when he dies and his soul quits this world for the other. This judgment is called the 'particular judgment'. At the time of this particular judgment the Lord assigns to each soul its share in the life beyond the grave, until the universal resurrection of all flesh which will take

place at the second coming of Christ the Lord. At the particular judgment the Lord confers on the souls of the just a temporary and incomplete beatitude, and on the souls of sinners a temporary and incomplete torment. For this judgment the Lord takes into consideration the entirety of soul's moral state at the time of its death: everything the soul bears within itself and with which it has made its entry into the world beyond the grave. What assumes a decisive importance then is the relationship that people maintain with the triune God during their life on earth, with the work of salvation accomplished by Christ the Lord, and with His divine-human body that is the Church. The parable of Lazarus and the evil rich man, presented to us by the Lord, clearly shows that right after death a judgment is pronounced on each person's soul at the conclusion of which it must depart, either to a place of happiness and joy or torment and misery (Luke 16:23–25). One or the other place is assigned as a function of the life this person has led on earth. In his immense longing for Christ, the apostle Paul, the one who had seen heaven, the one who already during his lifetime on earth was raised up to the third heaven, to paradise itself, to contemplate the secrets of the life beyond the grave, resolutely and clearly teaches this on the subject of the particular judgment: it is appointed for men to die only once, and after this the judgment (Heb. 9:27). He again refers to this when he speaks of the reward obtained immediately after death for evangelic work accomplished on earth (Phil. 1:21–24, 2 Cor. 5:1–2, 6, 8).

As for the exact manner in which the particular judgment unfolds, this by its mystery plunges us into the shoreless and bottomless ocean of the divine heavenly mysteries. The mystery of the particular judgment has been only partially revealed to us by God, and so too through the intermediary of the holy Apostles and holy Fathers, for by their God-pleasing lives they have themselves become close to God, members of the household of God (Eph. 2:19). By their christified spirits ('we have the mind of Christ' [1 Cor. 2:16]), they have been able to delve into this heavenly mystery, insofar as it can be revealed to human nature and insofar as it does no harm to the overall mandate of the divine-human economy of salvation.[19]

2 The Author of the Particular Judgment.

Patristic teaching on the particular judgment is not completely uniform. According to the previously cited texts, each soul presents itself before Christ to receive the sentence of His judgment and to have its destiny determined.

However, for the majority of Christian authors who uphold the teaching on the aerial toll-houses, the judging of the soul happens at the very moment of its passage through these way-stations: the soul undergoes a trial in which the demons accuse it and the angels defend it. Two possible outcomes are the result, and these are the sentences meted out to souls: the souls of sinners find themselves detained in the course of their ascent and hurled by the demons into the abyss of hell; the souls of the just continue to ascend and arrive in heaven where they are allowed to fall prostrate before the throne of Christ. Christ Himself hands down the sentence only with respect to the just as, for example, this text of St Theognostos indicates: "Inexpressible is the soul's delight when in full assurance of salvation it leaves the body ... going in peace to meet the radiant and joyful angel that comes down for it, and traveling with him unimpeded through the air, totally unharmed by the evil spirits. Rising with joy, courage and thanksgiving, it comes in adoration before the Creator, and is allotted its place among those akin to it and equal to it in virtue, until the universal resurrection."[20] More exactly, Christ only confirms by His sentence the fortunate lot the just have obtained after successfully passing the 'examination' of the aerial toll-houses, while the lot of sinners was determined by their failure during this same 'examination'.

This means that the particular judgment of a person after his death is actually carried out by angels and demons, or even, strictly speaking, by the demons alone, as might be deduced from numerous patristic texts (which are far from being marginal or conveying extra-Christian influences, but express to the contrary an authentically Christian tradition and date back to earliest times[21]) and the writings of more recent theologians.[22]

This idea that not only seems to withdraw from God his prerogatives as Judge, but entrusts the destiny of souls to evil spirits, might seem shocking at first glance. It must be understood, however, in relation to its context.

On the one hand the authors who think that it is indeed the angels (both good and bad) who judge, specify that they do so in some fashion by delegation, that God judges through their mediation,[23] and therefore that God is still the only judge. Thus, St Ignatius Brianchaninov writes: "At both judgments God Himself is present and judges. At the private judgment He judges by means of angels of light and fallen angels; at the general judgment He judges by means of His incarnate Word."[24] Even though all the Fathers do not give this precise detail, it is obvious that none of them think that the judging of a person can be done outside of the permission and, more generally, the authority of God. For them it is self-evident—for this is a recurring teaching of Scripture from which they would not be exempt—that "there is only one judge" (James 4:12), that

God is "the Judge of all" (Heb. 12:23), and that Christ is "ordained by God to be Judge of the living and the dead" (Acts 10:42).

Thus, in his recounting of a vision of Abba Stephen, in which the accusations the demons will bring against him are shown to him immediately before his death, St John Climacus allocates an essential place to these demons in the trial of the soul and concludes indecisively as to the author (or authors) of the judgment and final sentence: "While [Abba Stephen was] being thus called to account, he was parted from his body, leaving us in uncertainty as to his judgment, or end, or sentence, or how the trial ended." [25] However, he does not lose sight of the fact that in the final analysis judgment depends on God, since he cites this verse from Ezekiel a few lines earlier: "As I find you, I will judge you, saith God" (Ezek. 33:13–20).

3 The Particular Judgment as a Consequence of Human Choices.

This quote leads us to emphasize another fact: the Fathers are anxious, through the considerations they have developed on the aerial toll-houses or the particular judgment, to put man in the presence of his responsibilities by pointing out that he ultimately inherits in the hereafter that lot chosen during his earthly life, or at least the lot toward which the kind of life led here below has oriented him. The examination of the soul while passing through the aerial tollhouses only brings out that toward which the soul is most inclined by its spiritual qualities or spiritual defects, and Christ is only respecting each person's choice of life, each person being thus, in a certain manner, his own judge and the free author of his destiny.

This is frequently highlighted by the Fathers. St Ignatius of Antioch writes to the Magnesians: "All things have an end, these two things are simultaneously set before us—death and life; and every one shall go unto his own place. For as there are two kinds of coins, the one of God, the other of the world, and each of these has its special character stamped upon it, [so is it also here.] The unbelieving are of this world; but the believing have, in love, the character of God the Father."[26] St Justin emphasizes quite strenuously that the destiny of man in the hereafter depends in fact on his free will.[27] Some will object that this idea comes from Plato, who writes in the *Republic*: "The blame is his who chooses. God is blameless" (X, 617e); but St Justin retorts that Plato has himself borrowed this idea from the prophets in whose teaching it is rather common.[28] We find it again in St Irenaeus who writes: "All men are of the same nature, able both to hold fast and to do what is good; and, on the other hand, having also the power to cast it from them and not to do it—some do justly receive praise even among men who are under the control of good laws (and much more from God), and obtain deserved testimony of their choice of good in general, and of persevering therein; but the others are blamed, and receive a just condemnation, because of their rejection of what is fair and good."[29] St Cyprian of Carthage, after having noted that the Lord allows everyone the freedom of their own choices, observes that by this very fact, "even here, before the day of judgment, the souls of the righteous and of the unrighteous are already divided, and the chaff is separated from the wheat."[30] St Gregory of Nyssa stresses that anyone who lives in the passions is depriving himself of spiritual good things in the future life: "He who has definitively pursued pleasure for this life and has not cured his misguided choice by repentance makes the land of the good inaccessible to him hereafter. He digs himself this impassable necessity, like an immense pit which cannot be crossed."[31] St John Cassian affirms that "everyone ... knows that he must be committed to that special task or ministry to which he has given himself in this life as a participant," and "in that everlasting age he will also be the partner of him whose servant and companion he now wishes to be ... For just as the kingdom of the devil is gained by conniving at the vices, so the kingdom of God is possessed in purity of heart and spiritual knowledge by practicing the virtues ... [souls] enjoy a state of existence appropriate to their desserts and actions."[32] Referring to the judgment, St Maximus the Confessor notes that "each person finds himself judge of his own failures."[33] And, in connection with the punishment of sinners, he writes: "We harvest the fruits of our own sowing, and we are sated with our insanity;"[34] "we thus gather up what our actions have earned, or rather we receive the price that our own set disposition deserves ... In short, for each of the evils that we have deliberately willed, its opposite effect that we do not will befalls us."[35] We can likewise cite St Theophylact of Ochrid who writes, in connection with the parable of Lazarus and the evil rich man: "The chasm indicates the separation and the difference that exists between the righteous and the sinners. Just as their choices were far different in this life, so too their dwelling places in the next life are separated by a great distance, each one receiving as his due the reward appropriate to his choices in this life."[36]

---

4 The Particular Judgment as a Judgment of Man by His Own Conscience.

The preceding considerations have led some Fathers to hold that the particular judgment is, at once, both a judgment by Christ or by angels that serve Him as intermediaries, and a judgment of man by his own conscience. Thus, St Cyril of Alexandria, even while presenting the teaching on the aerial toll-houses and the judgment of man by the angels in a detailed manner, writes in this same text: "The one who judges us after death has no need of either accusers, witnesses, or proof, but He places before the eyes of sinners everything that they have said, done, or thought."[37] In a similar vein, we have the lengthy considerations of St Dorotheos of Gaza on the torment suffered by the soul in remembering the sins it has committed on earth and enduring the burden of the passions that accompany it.[38]

5 The Particular Judgment and Universal Judgment.

When the Fathers refer to the judgment, sometimes it is hard to say whether they have in mind the universal Last Judgment (obviously the one referred to most often) or the particular judgment. With good reason one might suppose that the particular judgment is involved when the judgment is shown to immediately follow death and without it being related to the Second Coming of Christ. An allusion to the particular judgment can thus be seen in this remark by St Paul: "It is appointed for men to die once, but after this the judgment" (Heb. 9:27). And numerous assertions by the Fathers can equally be understood in this sense. Thus, St Clement of Rome writes: "Fear Him that *after you are dead* has power over soul and body, to cast them into the gehenna of fire."[39] In the same way this affirmation by St John Climacus can be understood as relating to the particular judgment: "The judgment on our labors we shall know at the time of our death."[40] Likewise these remarks of St John Chrysostom: "If indeed not all understand correctly about the resurrection, still all are in accord about the judgment, the retribution and the courts of the next world, that there is some recompense hereafter for what is done here."[41] "For the awareness of our sins always pricks us, especially at the time when we are about to be led away to the examination of accounts in that terrible court."[42] "It is the Lord of the angels Himself who has come to give us a very precise knowledge of the soul's true state *after our death*. Why seek you the testimony of men when the Judge

Himself, who will ask back from you an account of all the actions of your life, every day cries out to you that He is preparing heaven for the good and hell for the wicked?"[43] "Be most assured that you will appear *upon leaving this life* before a dread tribunal, where we will render an account of all our actions. It is there that we will be condemned if we persist in crime and will receive the crown if we keep watch over ourselves during this life which is so short ... and if we walk in the paths of virtue so to be able to appear with confidence before this great Judge and enjoy the good things promised us."[44] These assertions might seem ambiguous, but the same saint notes elsewhere that God "exercises His justice" twice: "both after death and the moment of resurrection,"[45] thus distinguishing quite clearly between the particular judgment and the universal judgment. Abba Isaiah of Scetis just as likely has the particular judgment in mind when he writes in a more precise manner: "Keep death before your eyes daily, and be concerned about how you will leave this body, pass the powers of darkness that will meet you in the air, and encounter God without hindrance, foreseeing the awesome day of his judgment and reward for all our deeds, words, and thoughts. Everything lies naked and exposed to the eyes of the one with whom we have to reckon."[46] This is confirmed by another text from the same saint: "The one who believes that there is judgment *after death* cannot judge his neighbor in anything at all, because he will himself give account before God about all his actions."[47] Moreover, this same author refers to the meeting with God that follows the passage through the aerial toll-houses.[48] As for St John Damascene, he notes that "men illumined by God declare that with the last breath the actions of men are weighed as in a balance."[49]

Belief in a particular judgment soon after death is implied, we have said, by the belief that the soul receives soon after death reward or punishment, or, if one prefers, belief that after their death the just and sinners are not to be found in the same circumstances. To admit only a universal Last Judgment, to transpire at the end of time with the Second Coming of Christ, would be to admit that, until that moment, the soul is in a state of expectation of an undetermined quality, discontinuous with what it was during its earthly life, a state where it experiences nothing. This is rather unthinkable on the one hand, and in disagreement with the Church's teaching on the other, as we will see in the next chapter devoted to the nature of the intermediate state.

Chapter Seven

FROM THE FORTIETH DAY TO THE LAST JUDGMENT: THE INTERMEDIATE STATE

1 The Nature of the Intermediate State.

After having been judged, the soul while awaiting the Resurrection (when it will be reunited with its renewed body) and the universal Last Judgment, is assigned a temporary abiding-place, whether in Paradise[1] (often also called by the Fathers: 'bosom of Abraham'[2] or 'bosom of the patriarchs,'[3] or even 'heaven') where the souls of the just are gathered, or in Hades[4] (sometimes also called 'hell', according to the Latin translation of the Greek word 'Hades', or even 'abyss'[5]) where the souls of sinners are gathered.[6] For the period that precedes Christ's descent to hell, Hades (*Sheol* in Hebrew) designates, for a majority of the Fathers, the abiding-place of all the dead.[7] It is a place of darkness, servitude (cf. 2 Sam. 22:6, Job 7:9, Pss. 18:6, 48:15–16, 88:49, Isa. 38:10, 1 Pet. 3:19) and corruption which is under the control of Satan. Souls are suffering there (cf. Ecclesiasticus 14:16), but in various degrees: the souls of the just (prophets, patriarchs) are suffering there, but are consoled by the hope of the coming of Christ, while the souls of sinners suffer without consolation.[8] By descending after His death into Hades, Christ, because His human soul was hypostatically united to His divinity,[9] was able to accomplish the feat of 'binding the strong man'; in other words, He vanquished the power of Satan, pardoned the sins of those who believed in Him,[10] and freed all the souls who, since the birth of the first man, were held there. After this victory of Christ over it, Hades has subsisted but has changed its nature: it has become a place of suffering reserved for unrepentant sinners, while the gates of Paradise were opened to the just by Christ.[11] Since then Hades has become no longer synonymous with Sheol but Gehenna.[12]

The fact that, after the death of an individual, his soul is set in one of these two places is revealed by Christ Himself, just as the names and nature of these two places are revealed to us by Him. On the cross He only mentions the latter by simply saying to the good thief: "Assuredly, I say to you, today you will be with me in Paradise" (Luke 23:43). But in the parable of Lazarus the beggar and the wicked rich man, he mentions both places: "The beggar died, and was carried by the angels to Abraham's bosom. The rich man also died and was buried. And being in torments in Hades, he lifted up his eyes and saw Abraham afar off, and Lazarus in his bosom. Then he cried and said, 'Father Abraham, have mercy on me, and send Lazarus that he may dip the tip of his finger in water and cool my tongue, for I am tormented in this flame.' But Abraham said, 'Son, remember that in your lifetime you received your good things, and likewise Lazarus evil things, but now he is comforted and you are tormented. And besides all this, between you and us there is a great gulf fixed, so that those who want to pass from here to you cannot, nor can those from there pass to us.' Then he said, 'I beg you therefore, father, that you would send him to my father's house, for I have five brothers, that he may testify to them, lest they also come to this place of torment'" (Luke 16:22–28).

In this parable, Christ informs us that Paradise, designated here by the expression 'Abraham's bosom', is a place of refreshment,[13] rest,[14] and consolation, while Hades is a place of torments, where the soul endures the torture of 'flames', where it is parched and remains disconsolate. St Paul testifies as well to the existence of Paradise: it was given to him to enter into Paradise and experience it during his ecstasy (2 Cor. 12:1–6). The holy apostle John had a revelation of the presence of the just before Christ in this place: not only the twenty-four elders sitting on thrones, clothed in white robes and bearing golden crowns on their heads (Rev. 4:4), but also the martyrs (Rev. 6:9–11) and those forming "a great multitude which no one could number, of all nations, tribes, peoples, and tongues," standing before the throne of Christ and praising Him (Rev. 7:9).

The qualities of Paradise and Hades, expressed in symbols whose meanings we will explain later, are, based on the parable of Lazarus and the wicked rich man, widely referred to by the Orthodox Church in the texts of different liturgical services for the intention of the deceased.[15] Thus, in the burial[16] and *panikhida*[17] services, the priest, in the name of the Church, asks that the deceased be freed "from the tears and sighing which are in Hades," and in return that they "rest in the bosom of Abraham," that they find "repose, consolation, and blessedness," that they might be "granted repose in a habitation ... of refreshment and peace, in a place whence sickness, sorrow and sighing have fled away."

Two other basic characteristics of these two places are also mentioned in these liturgical services: the luminosity of Paradise and the gloom of Hades, this latter place being indicated by Christ when He speaks of 'outer darkness' (Matt. 8:12; cf. 22:13, 25:30), and by St Peter when he speaks of the 'chains of darkness' (2 Pet. 2:4). And so God is asked that the deceased being commemorated "abide in a place illumined by the face of God," that they be granted "rest in a habitation of light," that they be established "in Paradise where the choirs of the saints and the righteous shine like the stars," that they "find in heaven the splendor of [the divine] brightness."

This teaching that the soul, after death and before the Last Judgment, experiences either reward, rest, consolation, light and blessedness, or punishment, torments, darkness and suffering, is of course to be found among the Fathers. St Macarius of Egypt thus refers to the soul that the Lord "receives ... to His bosom and into His light ... snatch[ing it] from the jaws of darkness," which was its other possible destiny.[18] Elsewhere he mentions the sufferings endured by sinners after their death.[19] St Gregory of Nazianzus thinks that the holy soul, "when, set free from the bonds of the body ... departs hence, at once enjoys a sense and perception of the blessings which await it ... and feels a wondrous pleasure and exultation, and goes rejoicing to meet its Lord ... and so enters on the enjoyment of the bliss laid up for it, of which it has even now some conception,"[20] whereas the sinners are punished soon after their death also.[21] St John Cassian notes that the parable of Lazarus and the rich man clearly shows that "one of these is brought to a most blessed place, the repose of Abraham's bosom, while the other is burned up by the unbearable heat of an eternal fire."[22] Abba Isaiah mentions the sinners who, "when they leave their bodies, go away to torment, while the just "go away with joy to the resting-place of the Son of God."[23] St John Chrysostom notes: "Upon its leaving the body the soul, invisible to fleshly eyes, is gathered up by the angels and established either in the bosom of Abraham, if it is faithful, or else in the prison of Hades, if it is sinful."[24] St Cyril of Alexandria holds that the just enter into heaven immediately after their death,[25] while sinners are immediately punished.[26] Likewise, according to St Dorotheos of Gaza, after death—that is after the soul has left the body—, "the saints are received into places full of light, and angelic happiness proportionate to their own good conduct, [while] the sinners are received into dark and gloomy places, full of horror and petrifying dread, as the saints tell us."[27] St Nicetas Stethatos notes that if the soul, in leaving the body, carries the passions

along with it, "the father of spite and envy recognizes it for his own servan…
and drags it away beside him to the depths of Hades," but "if it has completed
the present life in piety and purity, in the exercise of every good and the practice
of the commandments of Go… it pitches its tent in the places of the glory of
Go… It is full of gladness and experiences a perfect joy in the hope of enjoying
the eternal blessings of God, even before the future restoration and ultimate
return of things divine."[28] St Nicetas later expands on this teaching. In a chapter
entitled: "Where does the soul go after death?" He strongly insists on the fact
that the souls of the just share in the condition of the angels, while the souls of
sinners share in the condition of demons:

> Among the souls that emigrate, some are pure and perfumed, alike to God,
> filled with divine glory and absolutely immaculate light: these are the saints;
> upon departing the body they shine like the sun because of the works of
> justice, wisdom, and purity. These, by the intermediacy of the angel-friends
> who lead them away toward the primal, superessential and immaterial light,
> a light incomprehensible even to angels, God Himself glorified and adored
> in Father, Son and Holy Spirit by the infinite powers, these ascend like lights
> of the third order thanks to lights of the second order. Having arrived, they
> prostrate themselves before the throne of His glory in chaste fear and the joy
> of the Holy Spirit; round about them are the Cherubim and the Seraphim
> and all the powers from on high imbued with fear and trembling, filling the
> souls that ascend with boldness. Then abruptly, at a sign from God, each of
> them proceeds to be united in a close and pure manner, like friend meeting
> friend, with the angelic order whose glory and rank it has received by the
> communication of the Holy Spirit during our present life and with which it was
> manifested in the Church of the faithful for the building up of Christ's body.
> It is joined to this hierarchic rank to the extent of having the same kind of life,
> rejoicing and resting with it in the future, under the shadow of its wings, until
> the general restoration to occur at the command of God. But the other souls,
> obscured and terribly plunged in darkness because of the wickedness of their
> acts, words and thoughts, their habits, occupations and dispositions, these are
> the souls of sinners. When they are violently torn from their body they give off
> a stench as well; this they communicate to it in leaving, along with every kind
> of unpleasantness. These souls, filled with gloom, stench and corruption, are led
> away against their will by punishing and dark angels, in the midst of a horrible
> fear, with fright and trembling, toward the depths of hell as into a gloomy and
> pitiless prison. They are handed over to the unclean and evil spirits that guard
> this prison, there where the prince of darkness is held fast by eternal bonds to
> be prey to the fire with his fellows, the angels of darkness. They are delivered up
> to them to remain with them eternally in the future. They have, in fact, accepted

them as friends during their life in their acts and words; they have preferred their suggestions, they have implemented them to their loss and that of others by putting themselves forward as a bad example in this life and by leaving only an evil trail of unfortunate memories.[29]

He returns to this teaching in a chapter entitled: 'What is the nature of the place where the soul rests after this life?':

Among the souls some, being condemned, dwell in the lightless and deep dark places of hell, as is said. They remain there as if in chains and prison, ceaselessly tormented by regret, afflictions and sighing; memory ceaselessly brings before them and nakedly depicts their wicked and ill-fated actions, just as they were committed in this life. Beside them are the demons, fire darting from their eyes and mouth, who grind their teeth against them and shake before them threats of punishment. In their circumstances there is no other consolation that might speak to their sorrow and alleviate it outside of supplications made to God and good done to the poor. Nevertheless, in the expectation of a dread sentence that is to be heard from the mouth of the incorruptible Judge with that terrifying cry: 'Depart from me, you cursed, into the everlasting fire prepared for the devil and his angels,' with the return to consciousness of this reminder alone, an appalling fright withers them and freezes them with terror. Other souls, being friends of God and companions of the angels, abide in the luminous places of the powers from on high with these beloved powers in joy and gladness; they recall their good works, their justice during life, their virtuous conduct, and this fills them with unspeakable joy. Clearly from that moment they find themselves beneath this primal light with the divine angels, archangels and the infinite powers of God, with peaceful gaze and in glorious company, who sing their hymn, *alleluia* for the latter, the *trisagion* for the former and the *gelgel* [wheel], as is written (Ezek. 10:13), for those who are close to God. These souls remain there, living in order to welcome the promise of God, the promise He made to them: they turn over in their minds these intelligible intellections more perfectly, with a perfect knowledge, almost like the angels; in them, in fact, what was partial has come to an end and the perfect has made its appearance in the revelation and contemplation of the Spirit. Henceforth they only expect to hear this sweet voice which calls them in this manner: 'Come you blessed of my Father, inherit the kingdom prepared for you from the foundation of the world.'[30]

St Mark of Ephesus describes the situation of the just and sinners after the particular judgment more soberly:

Now [the just and sinners] are in places appropriate to them. The first, in complete and free repose, are in heaven with the angels and in the presence of God Himself, and already as if in the paradise from which Adam fell (and into which the good thief has entered before the others) ... The second, they are confined in Hades, abiding 'in the deepest pit, in darkness and the shadow of death' (Psalm 87:7), as holy King David says, and also, as described by Job, 'in a land where brightness itself resembles deepest night' (Job 10:22). The first abide with every delight, rejoicing, already anticipating and having within their grasp the Kingdom and all the good things promised them. The second, to the contrary, all abide in confinement and suffering, inconsolable. Such men await the sentence of the judge and foresee their torments.[31]

Paradise and Hades are not geographically identifiable, physical places: the soul, being by nature incorporeal, is not subject to spatial constraints and, strictly speaking, cannot reside in any place.[32] Paradise and Hades therefore designate immaterial and invisible realities.[33] They are, as St Mark of Ephesus says, "intelligible and incorporeal places,"[34] more precisely states,[35] conditions, or modes of existence where the soul is happy and at peace, or to the contrary suffers and is tormented. The modalities of this happiness and this suffering are inaccessible to man in his present condition, and those saints who have had a revelation present them as inexpressible. This is why the scriptural, liturgical and patristic texts present them under a symbolic form and obviously should not be taken literally.

One can say that in Paradise the soul is in the presence of Christ (cf. John 14:2–3, 2 Cor. 5:8) and sees His glory (cf. John 17:24). It participates then in the divine light[36] and all the other energies of God: life, peace, love, blessedness... But, as St Paul says, what it perceives and experiences in this state is ineffable (cf. 2 Cor. 12:4). In Hades the soul is deprived of the intimate presence of God, His light and His energies; this is why Hades is likened to a place of darkness (cf. Matt. 22:13), death, torment and suffering (cf. Matt. 25:46).

Thus, for St Gregory of Nyssa, the suffering of those who are in Hades results from the privation of the Good, about which they have knowledge at this time; the good, he says, "becomes... a flame, which burns the soul."[37] Likewise for St John Chrysostom, the sufferings of sinners come from being prevented from "seeing the glory of God."[38] St Dorotheos of Gaza adopts another viewpoint. He thinks that man suffers chiefly from his own passions. He explains that the soul, "when it goes out of the body," does not lose the spiritual state acquired at the time of its earthly life; if the just soul emigrates with its virtues, the sinful soul is left "alone with its own passions and ... is tormented by them forever."[39] Just as someone who has an ill-humored body[40] is tormented by it his whole life, "so also the soul under the influence of strong emotions [the passions]; the conflict, arising from its own bad habits, punishes it all the time, the memory being always embittered, the mutterings of its passions constantly emerging, always burning it and enraging it."[41] The nature of fallen earthly existence means that the passions are for the soul a source of pleasure and, in any case, that their harmful character remains hidden from it and that it does not feel their unfortunate effects. In the new modality of existence that follows death, this nature becomes apparent in the light of Judgment and of the true good which have been is revealed to it, and the passions, just like the memory of past sins that it retains,[42] become a source of suffering for it. Other Fathers or theologians, like Michael Glykas[43] or St Symeon of Thessalonica,[44] think that the souls of sinners suffer remorse after having acquired in their new state a clear awareness of their sins.

The blessedness of those in Paradise, as well as the suffering of those in Hades, are experienced to varying degrees according to the spiritual state of those found there.[45] We might understand Christ's assertion in this way with regard to Paradise: "In my Father's house there are many mansions" (John 14:2), and St Paul's: "Every man shall receive his own reward, according to his own labor" (1 Cor. 3:8). As concerns Hades, St Macarius received a revelation that it comprises several levels of suffering [46] St Gregory of Nyssa explains that "the suffering is proportional to the amount of evil in each individual," for "it is unlikely that the torment would be equal for someone who has gone far in forbidden vices and for someone else who has yielded to violations of lesser importance, when they are being purged for their perverse condition; but it is according to the quantity of material[47] that that agonizing flame will be burning for a longer or shorter time; that is, as long as there is fuel to feed it. In the case of the man who has acquired a heavy weight of material, the consuming fire must necessarily be very searching; but where that which the fire has to feed upon has spread less far, there the penetrating fierceness of the punishment is mitigated in proportion to the smaller measure of evil in the subject."[48]

2 The Intermediate State's Temporary and Partial Character.

Although, after their death, sinners are placed in Hades and the just in Paradise, in both cases a temporary state is involved where the happiness of the just is only 'partial' or 'incomplete', just as the suffering of sinners is only 'partial' or 'incomplete'. We find this teaching among various other authors such as St Justin,[49] pseudo-Justin,[50] pseudo-Anthanasius,[51] Andrew of Caesarea,[52] St Photius,[53] Arethas of Patrae,[54] St Theophylact of Bulgaria,[55] Theophanes

Kerameus, Euthymius Zigabenus,[56] Philip the Solitary,[57] Michael Glykas,[58] St Symeon of Thessalonica,[59] St Mark of Ephesus; Meletios Pigas, Patriarch of Alexandria;[60] Dositheus, Patriarch of Jerusalem; Eugenius Bulgaris or, closer to us, Metropolitan Philaret of Moscow. St Justin expresses in a nuanced manner the fact that neither the reward and delight of the just, or the torment and suffering of the sinner are complete in the intermediate state: "The souls of the pious remain in a better place, while those of the unjust and wicked are in a worse, waiting for the time of judgment."[61] The pseudo-Athanasius (who has inspired numerous authors) notes: "The joy felt by the souls of the saints today is a partial delight, just as the sadness of sinners is only a partial torment. The souls of the just are like those favored people the king has invited to his table and who wait with rejoicing, in front of the palace, for the hour of the feast; likewise, the souls of sinners resemble those condemned people the king has imprisoned before imposing on them the penalty they deserve."[62] Philip the Solitary writes regarding the just: "The just have now only a small portion of the glory that they will receive at the Last Judgment along with their resurrected bodies. Their happiness, their glory will be much greater then. . . . Surely, they abide now in heaven, where full of joy they contemplate their Creator; but only after the Resurrection will their reward be full and will they receive their crown."[63] Theophanes Kerameus presents the just as still uncertain of the definitive lot that will be ascribed to them at the universal Last Judgment.[64] St Symeon of Thessalonica affirms that, after death, each just soul receives from God joy and consolation according to the degree of perfection of the life led, but that all the souls of the just are still imperfect until the coming of the Lord[65] and possess only the first fruits of eternal life;[66] as for the souls of sinners, "they are in Hades and in other dark and sad places, where they suffer from the tyranny of the demons in proportion to their sins and their faithlessness; but they have not at this time been handed over to the complete torment that awaits them."[67]

This teaching has also been professed in a more developed manner by St Mark of Ephesus who more particularly writes: "We say that, for the moment, neither the just have received the fullness of their happy lot and that blessed condition for which they have prepared themselves here through their works; nor have the sinners, after death, been led into eternal punishment in which they will be tormented eternally. Neither are they then in the situation they must necessarily assume after the Judgment of the last day and the resurrection of all."[68] Dositheus of Jerusalem can also be cited on this topic, who writes in his *Enchiridion*: "the souls of those that have fallen asleep are either at rest or in torment, according to what each has wrought; —for when they are separated from their bodies, they depart immediately either to joy, or to sorrow and lamentation; though confessedly neither their enjoyment nor condemnation are complete. For after the common resurrection, when the soul shall be united with the body, with which it had behaved itself well or ill, each shall receive the completion of either enjoyment or of condemnation."[69] Again we find the same conception in Eugenius Bulgaris: "Before the end of the world, what will be the condition of those souls who have lived in justice and those who have died in sin? As our Orthodox Church teaches, the first have not yet been introduced into perfect blessedness, nor have the second been consigned to the terrifying and horrifying Gehenna."[70] The *Longer Catechism* of the illustrious Metropolitan Philaret of Moscow expresses the same doctrine: "*Question*: In what state are the souls of the dead till the general resurrection? *Answer*: The souls of the righteous are in light and rest, with a foretaste of eternal happiness; but the souls of the wicked are in a state the reverse of this. *Question*: Why may we not ascribe to the souls of the righteous perfect happiness immediately after death? *Answer*: Because it is ordained that the perfect retribution according to works shall be received by the perfect man after the resurrection of the body and God's last judgment. The Apostle Paul says: Henceforth there is laid up for me a crown of righteousness, which the Lord, the righteous Judge, shall give me at that day; and not to me only, but unto all them also that love his appearing (2 Tim. 4:8). And again: We must all appear before the judgment-seat of Christ; that every one may receive the things done in his body, according to that he hath done, whether it be good or bad (2 Cor. 5:10). *Question*: Why do we ascribe to the souls of the righteous a foretaste of bliss before the last judgment? *Answer*: On the testimony of Jesus Christ himself, who says in the parable that the righteous Lazarus was immediately after death carried into Abraham's bosom (Luke 16:22)."[71] St Macarius of Moscow, in his *Dogmatics*, after having examined the positions of the Fathers, concludes that "the reality of the (imperfect) glorification of the just in heaven, soon after the particular judgment and before the universal judgment, is a point beyond all doubt."[72]

This position is maintained by modern Orthodox theologians.[73] For example, Archimandrite Justin Popovich writes in his *Dogmatics of the Orthodox Church*: "As divine revelation shows, the life of the soul beyond the grave consists either in an incomplete blessedness, or in a partial torment, for our complete blessedness and our total torment will only come about after the Last Judgment; deprived of its body, the soul can only be a soul and not a complete person. At the particular judgment, souls are divided into two categories: just souls and sinful souls. This is why only the two corresponding situations are possible in the hereafter: the state of blessedness and the state of torment, each one being comprised of countless nuances, and this in two places only, hell and Paradise, each one again including countless dwelling-places."[74]

This conception is not, however, peculiar to the Christian East: important Latin Fathers have likewise shared it and defended it. Thus, St Hilary considers that the just, after their death, go to repose in the bosom of Abraham, while sinners go to hell,[75] but that these are only temporary states while awaiting the Judgment to fix them for eternity.[76] St John Cassian thinks that after death souls "have already begun to taste something of what is reserved for them at the general judgment."[77] St Gregory the Great likewise affirms that, for the just, their beatitude will be greater after the Judgment than before, for they will be enjoying then with their bodies, while immediately after death only the soul enjoys it.[78]

The partial character of the intermediate state is expressed by a good many Orthodox Fathers and theologians by a certain reserve in mentioning the happiness known to the just in Paradise and the pains sinners are subject to in Hades. Many among them, on the one hand, refer to Paradise in terms of 'rest', 'refreshment', 'consolation', 'freedom', 'hope in the good things promised', 'joy', 'contentment', 'rejoicing,' and 'happiness,'[79] and prefer, when they express themselves with greater precision, to restrict the term 'beatitude' to the Kingdom to come.[80] On the other hand, they conceive of the sufferings of Hades as consisting above all in pains of a moral order, like the torments of conscience, regrets, remorse, shame, confinement and privation of freedom, sadness, bitterness, groanings, ignorance, darkness, fear, uncertainty about the future, despair[81]... The Church itself has integrated this conception, as is seen for example in the troparion sung many times during the various services for the intention of the deceased: "Give rest, O Christ, to the soul of Thy servant, where sickness is no more, neither sorrow nor sighing, but life everlasting."

The intermediate state and the ultimate state, strictly speaking, can be designated by different terms: one can say that the just enter *Paradise* after their death and will enter the *Kingdom of Heaven* after their resurrection, while sinners enter *Hades* after their death and will enter *hell* or *Gehenna* after their resurrection. Although the Fathers of the early centuries are seen to be flexible in their use of terms, by contrast, Orthodox Fathers and theologians starting with St Photius tend to manifest and require more rigor in their use, a tendency found again among certain present-day theologians.[82] Thus, St Photius urges that the Paradise where the good thief went not be confused with the Kingdom of Heaven. Referring to the word of St Paul regarding the just: "God having provided something better for us, that they should not be made perfect apart from us" (Heb. 11:40), he notes: "It was inappropriate that, alone of all those who had pleased God in the course of the centuries, the thief should attain the height of supreme beatitude before the time set for the general distribution of eternal rewards, and that he arrive at perfection without the countless multitude of the saints, as the divine Paul teaches."[83] Euthymius Zigabenus likewise distinguishes between the Paradise promised to the good thief and the Kingdom of Heaven "which is the ineffable enjoyment of those eternal good things that eye has not seen, nor ear heard, nor the heart of man tasted. For, as the great apostle Paul teaches, none of the just have as yet received the promise. It is later, at the time of universal recompense that this Kingdom of Heaven will be entrusted to the saints."[84] This distinction is again found with John Zonaras,[85] as well as with Michael Glykas[86] and Meletios Pigas, patriarch of Alexandria,[87] who was inspired by Pseudo-Athanasius.[88]

By making this distinction in so precise a manner, it must not be understood, however, that Paradise and the Kingdom of Heaven are different states and without continuity: there is only a difference of duration and intensity between them; it is the same for Hades and hell. On the one hand, Paradise and Hades are temporal; they become eternal after the Last Judgment; on the other, Hades is only an antechamber and foretaste of hell, just as Paradise is only an antechamber and foretaste of the Kingdom of Heaven. But there is no difference of nature between them. This is why the foregoing terminological distinction does not seem judicious to St Theophylact the Bulgarian, who restricts himself to recognizing a difference in degree between them:

> Some will ask, "How can the Lord say to the thief, *Today thou shalt be with Me in paradise*, when Paul said that none of the saints had received the promise?" Some say that the Apostle was not referring to all the saints when he said that none of them had received the promise, but was speaking only of those whom he there enumerated. Though he listed many, the good thief was not among them. Listen to the words that Paul uses, *And these all...* By this he refers expressly, they say, to those whom he had just enumerated, and the thief was not one of those. Others have said that the thief has not yet attained the life

in paradise, yet the Lord could still say, *Today shalt thou be with Me in paradise*, because his promise is immovable and irrevocable. For the Lord, they explain, often employs this kind of speech when He speaks of things that will be as if they had already occurred. For example, the Lord says, *He that believeth not is condemned already*; and again, *He that heareth My word, and believeth... shall not come into condemnation, but hath passed from death unto life*. Others have done violence to the context of these words, pausing after *today*, so that it might read, *Verily I say unto thee today, Thou shalt be with Me in paradise*. Others, who appear to have hit the mark, explain it this way: the good things that are promised to us are not a life in paradise, or a return to paradise, but instead the kingdom of heaven. This is why we pray, *Thy kingdom come*, and not, 'May we live in paradise.' Let no one say to me that paradise and the kingdom are one and the same. For *eye hath not seen, nor ear heard, neither have ascended into the heart of man*, the good things of the kingdom. But the eye of Adam saw paradise, and his ear heard the words, *Of every tree which is in paradise thou mayest eat for food*. Even if you say, 'Yes, but one tree was denied him,' still he could see it, and he did hear about it, and delight in it rose up in his heart. And Adam had every reason to be delighted; for was not this tree both his work and pleasure, as husbandman of paradise? Therefore, the Lord does not contradict what Paul says. The repentant thief did obtain paradise, but he has not yet obtained the kingdom. But he will obtain the kingdom, along with all those whom Paul enumerated. In the meantime he has paradise, which is a place of spiritual rest. Many have spoken about these things. We may add that, even if the kingdom of heaven and paradise are one and the same, this does not prevent both the Lord's words and Paul's from being in agreement. For the good thief is in paradise, that is, in the kingdom, and not only he, but all those mentioned by Paul. But he does not yet enjoy the full inheritance of good things. It is not the condemned that live in kingly palaces, for these are locked in prisons where they await their appointed punishments. It is, rather, men of honor and nobility who enter palaces and pass their time within them. Then, when the time is at hand for the distribution of royal gifts, they are found worthy of them. So too with the saints: although they do not yet enjoy their reward in full, nevertheless in the meanwhile they pass their time in places of light, of fragrance, of royalty, in short, in the tabernacles of the righteous, although they are not yet entitled to the full measure of the gifts of the kingdom. Therefore the thief was in paradise, and yet did not enjoy completion, so that he *without us should not be made complete*. This, I think, is the truest understanding of all ... In truth all those who were found worthy of spiritual gifts received those gifts already in this life as an earnest and pledge of the Holy Spirit. They are in paradise, although they have not yet been brought to completion and perfection and have not yet received the kingdom. As Paul says in the Letter to the Hebrews, that *these all ... have not yet received the promise*. When he says *the promise* he means 'the whole promise'. The saints, therefore, have not yet received the full promise, although they are in the kingdom and in paradise.[89]

Theophylact clarifies his thinking when he goes back over the passage cited from the Letter to the Hebrews: "God [has] provided something better for us, that they should not be made perfect apart from us:" "This something better about which the Apostle speaks signifies that God has wished to honor us. In order that they might not seem to prevail over us by being crowned first, the Lord has fixed a single day in which the crowns will be distributed for all. And the Apostle did not say: 'That they should not be crowned', but clearly: 'That they should not be made perfect.' Hence it follows that they will appear as perfect at that time. For the moment, they possess an earnest of future glory. For, without that, how explain their power to help those who call upon them, the efficacy of their intercession? Later they will receive recompense in its fullness."[90]

There are several reasons for the temporary and partial character of the intermediate state:

1) There is a certain solidarity between all men in the reception of the promised good things. God actually has in view the salvation and deification of each person, but also of all humanity and, in the thought of the Fathers, the former has never been dissociated from the latter. "There is 'one body' which is waiting to be justified," says Origen.[91] And St Hippolytus of Rome writes: "[God] desires to save all, wishing to make all the children of God... unto one perfect man."[92] It is for this reason that the good things stored up for us have not been given individually and immediately in full, but there is a delay which is that of the full unfolding of humanity, of the possibility to be saved and deified offered to all human persons. St Gregory of Nyssa explains[93] that originally, by creating man, God did not create an individual but "all the fullness of the nature together;" "in the Divine foreknowledge and power all humanity is included in the first creation." God not only knew that Adam was going to sin and would beget children after that, but He also knew, the One "who holds all limits in His grasp ... how great in number humanity will be in the sum of its individuals." "Now seeing that the full number of men pre-conceived by the operation of foreknowledge will come into life ... God, Who governs all things in certain order and sequence... He who beholds the future equally with the present... also foreknew the time coextensive with the creation of men, so that the extent of time should be adapted for the entrances of the pre-determined souls, and that the flux and motion of time should halt at the moment when humanity is

no longer produced." And so the end of time will occur "when the generation of men is completed;" "humanity also should be changed from the corruptible and earthly to the impassable and eternal " when "the full complement of human nature has reached the limit of the pre-determined measure, because there is no longer anything to be made up in the way of increase to the number of souls." This solidarity among all men and consequently the delay in receiving the fullness of good things are emphasized by the Psalmist: "The righteous shall patiently await until you shall deal richly with me" (Psalm 141:8), and above all by Paul who, recalling the holy patriarchs, writes that they "did not receive the promise... that they should not be made perfect apart from us" (Heb. 11:39–40). It is in this sense that this last passage is understood by St Gregory of Nyssa,[94] but also by St John Chrysostom who comments in this way: "Do you also consider what a thing it is, and how great, that Abraham should be sitting, and the Apostle Paul, waiting till you have been perfected, that then they may be able to receive their reward. For the Savior has told them before that unless we also are present, He will not give it them ... [God] appointed one time of crowning for all ... For they also wait for the brethren. For if we are 'all one body,' the pleasure becomes greater to this body, when it is crowned altogether, and not part by part."[95] This last idea is taken up again by St Theophylact of Bulgaria following the passage previously cited: "Is not God unjust in their respect by making [the saints] wait for the crown that they have deserved to receive before us by their works? By no means; for they themselves desire to find fulfillment only in the company of their brothers. All of us form only a single body. The joy of this body will be greater by the fact that all its members will receive their crown at the same time. God is a father full of tenderness who has various children. Some have returned more quickly from the fields, their tasks completed; others are still at work. The Father of the family has served a kind light meal to the first, telling them to await their brothers for the grand feast; and they themselves, animated by true fraternal charity, are glad to await the hour of joy in common."[96]

2) A second reason for the temporary character of the happiness or pain known to the souls of the deceased soon after their death is that they are in expectation of the Judgment of which they will be the object at the time of Christ's Second Coming; it is this Judgment that will decide their definitive, eternal state.

This Judgment will confirm for the Just the state in which they are already, but will enable them to obtain its fullness; for the souls found in Hades, it might decide another destiny, better than that temporary state in which they have found themselves: for this the prayers of the Church and those close to the deceased can play a determining role, as we will see later.

3) But the temporary and partial character of this state is also the result of souls at present being without their bodies (all the while preserving, as we have seen, a certain connection to it). For the soul, and for man as a whole, this is an unnatural state: by nature man is at once soul and body, and the post-mortem condition, in which the two elements that compose it are dissociated, should not be definitive. In the intermediate state the soul alone experiences the joy or pain corresponding to the condition in which it finds itself, while what remains of the body is in the grave and is devoid of any sensitivity. In the grave, the bodies of the just and those of sinners might 'as objects' know different conditions: the former can remain intact, incorrupt, while the latter decomposes; but there is no rule on this subject[97] and the incorruption of saints' bodies is still certainly considered to be a miracle rather than a natural and necessary consequence of their spiritual state.

St Irenaeus clearly stresses that the intermediate state is for the soul a temporary state of waiting: waiting for the Resurrection, when it will regain the body, and for the Last Judgment to which both together will be subject. "For as the Lord 'went away in the midst of the shadow of death' (Psalm 22:4) where the souls of the dead were, yet afterwards arose in the body, and after the resurrection was taken up [into heaven], it is manifest that the souls of His disciples also, upon whose account the Lord underwent these things, shall go away into the invisible place allotted to them by God, and there remain until the resurrection, awaiting that event; then receiving their bodies, and rising in their entirety, that is bodily, just as the Lord arose, they shall come thus into the presence of God [to be judged]."[98] St John Chrysostom notes similarly that, "upon its going out of the body, the soul, invisible to fleshly eyes, is gathered up by the angels and established either in the bosom of Abraham, if it was faithful, or else in the prison of Hades, if it was sinful, and that until the arrival of the day fixed for it to resume possession of its body and render an account of its acts at the tribunal of Christ, the incorruptible judge."[99]

One might think, in view of the diverse teachings of Orthodox Fathers and theologians, that there is a divergence and even an opposition between those who affirm an immediate retribution for souls after death (even considering that the just have an experience of the vision of God and know blessedness, while sinners know the pains of hell) and those who affirm a delay in this retribution.[100] The two positions are in fact perfectly reconcilable (and the authors who uphold them by turns are not contradicting themselves) seeing that gradations in blessedness and suffering are admitted, which the Fathers have always done, in this context or in others.[101] One can in a coherent manner therefore admit at once to an immediate (but partial) blessedness and to a delay in obtaining it (this time conceived of as eternal and perfect), or to an immediate (but partial and temporary) pain and to a delay in receiving pain (in this case conceived of as greater and eternal).

3 A False Conception: Soul-Sleep.

The idea that, after death, the soul enters into a kind of lethargy, into a sleep in which it would be inactive until the resurrection, has been developed in the East by some marginal theologians, chiefly of Syriac origin and of a Nestorian persuasion,[102] and has been favored in the West by a faction in Protestantism, Luther having expressed his preference for this theory[103] and certain Protestant groups, the Anabaptists for one, having adopted it.

The Fathers certainly speak at times of sleep in connection with death, and the Orthodox Church, in the treating of the Mother of God and the saints, prefers to speak of 'dormition' rather than 'death'. But here we are dealing with a symbolic expression that wishes to signify that the awakening of the resurrection will ensue, or that the soul is in a state of repose but is not, as it would be if entirely dead, completely inactive; it is only inactive with respect to this world, but in fact displays another form of activity in the hereafter.

Against the false conception of soul-sleep the Fathers have given a certain number of clarifications on the capacities and energies that the soul preserves in the hereafter. St John Chrysostom affirms that even if "the soul of someone who sleeps sleeps, in return the soul of someone who is dead is not so, but has been awakened."[104] Against the theory of soul-sleep, St Justin advances a moral argument: "If [death] issued in insensibility, [this] would be a godsend to all the wicked."[105] St John Cassian specifies that "the souls of the dead are not only not deprived of their feelings, but do not even lack the dispositions of hope, sadness, joy, and fear."[106] St Nicetas Stethatos explains that "the properties of the soul's reasonable part, as has been stated, are therefore reflection, knowledge of beings, inner language [that is to say thought], intellectual sensations [the capacity for intellectual intuition in the mind (*nous*)], concepts about what is intelligible, the cardinal virtues ... deliberation, preferences and memory. The soul, when it quits the body and the present life, retains some of these properties and carries them away, others not... It retains for itself, in being brought closer to God, a knowledge of beings, inner language [or thought], intellectual sensations, concepts about what is intelligible and above all memory; but it ceases exercising its other properties as well as works of the body."[107] Nevertheless the soul retains a memory of actions it accomplished with the body.[108] One contemporary Orthodox theologian, Archimandrite Justin Popovich, rounds out these remarks: "So to pursue with their whole being their life in the world hereafter, souls have their entire personality and their self-consciousness available to them: they perceive, know, conceive, discern and, in a general manner, exercise all psychic activities. We find a characteristic example of this in the parable where our Lord speaks to us of Lazarus and the wicked rich man: the latter is able to see and recognize Lazarus and Abraham, he feels his torments and the flame that burns him, he remembers his brothers still on earth and is anxious about the judgment that awaits them ... The holy apostle Peter speaks of the proclamation the Savior has addressed "to the spirits in prison" (that is to say to the souls of the dead); and this clearly shows that they are conscious and reasonable, free, and capable of receiving or rejecting this proclamation."[109]

From a certain point of view, one can say the soul, by the very fact of its separation from the body, is deprived of all those capacities that its union with the body gave it, and that its activity is therefore impoverished. But from another point of view one can say that the soul gains access to a greater awareness and that the new world in which it lives offers it new and more expansive possibilities. As Father Sergius Bulgakov writes, "when the body's curtain falls, 'an opening of the [spiritual] senses', a broadening of experience occurs."[110]

4 Another False Conception: Metempsychosis.

Certain Fathers were also involved in criticizing another theory, quite widespread in antiquity,[111] on man's development after death: metempsychosis.[112] Seeing that this theory has been revived by Theosophy and above all the New Age movement under the influence of Far Eastern religions

(Hinduism and Buddhism), we should briefly mention these critiques and clarify the Christian position on the subject.

St Irenaeus of Lyons, that ardent defender of the unity of the human being, notes: "The Lord has taught with very great fullness, that souls not only continue to exist, not by passing from body to body, but that they preserve the same form as the body had to which they were adapted, and that they remember the deeds which they did [with it] in this state of existence."[113] St Theophilus of Antioch denounces the quite irrational, dreadful and monstrous character of this doctrine in which "he who was once a man shall afterwards be a wolf, or a dog, or an ass, or some other irrational brute."[114]

As for Dionysius the Areopagite, he advances a spiritual argument: observing that "among the unholy ... [some] would assign other bodies to souls," he reproaches them for "holding an unfair view of the bodies which have shared in the struggles of divine souls. They wrongly deny them the sacred rewards which they have earned at the end of the divine race."[115]

It is from an anthropological point of view that St Gregory of Nyssa criticizes metempsychosis at length,[116] which was likewise criticized by his brother St Basil of Caesarea[117] and St Gregory of Nazianzus.[118] He first remarks that a theory that holds that, after death, the soul of man assumes the body of animals or even plants confuses the natures of these different beings and mixes together their specific characteristics.[119] It means that the soul itself, in an absurd manner and according to the bodies it assumes, changes nature, being first rational, then devoid of reason, and even deprived of sensitivity.[120] This amounts to judging "everything to be the same and the nature of all beings to be one, mixed in a confused and undifferentiated association with itself, with no property distinguishing one thing from another."[121] The meaning of the hierarchy of beings is lost in the behavior of people who adopt such a belief, and if as much value is given to plants and animals as to man, this can work in the positive direction of an enhanced value and greater respect for plants and animals, but also in a negative direction of a devaluing of man, providing an excuse for ill-treatment or cruelty against him.[122]

Gregory next attacks those who see metempsychosis as a 'fall' of a body's soul into another body because of 'wickedness'. He counters that if "the fall comes through evil, then these people must suppose that evil begins the constitution of the things that exist,"[123] and God's providence plays no role in this.[124]

The theories of metempsychosis (especially the one that gives evil the initiative) often implies a determinist conception of the fall or the passage into other bodies, and no longer leaves any place for human freedom.[125] Such a conception destroys morality and renders the spiritual life nonsensical.[126] This is all the more true when the soul has supposedly passed into an animal body, since it is subject then to the instincts and passions and has no possibility of choosing the good, it being given that, for animals, there is neither choice or virtue. We do not see then how the soul might be able to climb back up the slope that would restore it to a better condition, nor how it might stop on the path that makes it descend toward the worst (after the condition of the animals, that of the plants, and finally nonexistence). [127]

To this conception Gregory opposes the Christian conception that enhances the freedom of the human person who "by his free will chooses that which accords with his inclination, becoming whatever he wishes by his power of choice" according to what is good, and is able to progress in virtue.[128]

Gregory refutes, moreover, the conception of the pre-existence of souls presupposed by the theory of metempsychosis, strongly affirming a basic principle of Christian anthropology: the simultaneous coming into existence of soul and body.[129]

Gregory also stresses, as already shown,[130] the indivisible character of soul and body, and the subsistence of their ties even beyond the separation to which death subjects them. This conception, in relation to a very strong feeling about the identity and permanence of the human hypostasis (or person), is another powerful argument against the theory of metempsychosis. To affirm that an individual could change bodies would be to: 1) deny the tie that the soul always retains with the body; 2) deny the hypostatic dimension of the body, in other words, that the body not only belongs rightly to a person, but is itself an element and dimension of this person;[131] 3) deny the identity of this person (since it would be, through different bodies, several human persons in succession, or a particular man, next a particular animal or plant ...); 4) deny the permanence of personal identity over the course of time. In other words, metempsychosis denies the human person as well as human nature, two realities to which Christianity is profoundly attached since they have their foundation in God himself, in the image of Whom man was created.

These anthropological arguments were considerably broadened and deepened by St Maximus the Confessor, who especially insists on the simultaneity of the coming into existence of soul and body, on their union at the core of the hypostasis to which they belong in an inalienable manner, and on the indestructible subsistence of their ties even beyond death. Having amply set forth these arguments elsewhere,[132] we will not reiterate them here.

We will only point out that modern Orthodox theologians remain quite attached to this anthropology which: 1) enhances the unity, unicity, and identity of the hypostasis (or person); 2) considers that the body and soul inalienably belong to it and remain, in this hypostasis and through it, indissolubly tied to each other beyond their separation by death (a separation that is only temporary); 3) considers that the soul can have only a single body and the body only a single soul, the risen body being itself identical, although it exists according to a new mode, to the earthly body.[133]

Chapter Eight

PURGATORY

AS WE HAVE seen in the preceding chapter, for the Orthodox Church there are only two conditions in which souls are to be found while awaiting the Resurrection and the Last Judgment: paradise and hell. The Orthodox Church rules out any third, intermediate condition, as the Roman Catholic Church believes which designates it under the name of Purgatory and which, in its most precise formulations, see in it an independent place characterized by the activity of a temporal 'purifying fire'.

1 The Latin Position.

a) *The Latin doctrine of Purgatory.* At the end of the year 1231, we encounter a trace of the first controversy between a Greek, George Bardanes, Bishop of Corfu, and a Latin, Friar Bartholomew, a papal envoy, on the question of Purgatory. The positions of the Latin theologian in favor of the existence of a Purgatory were reported by the Greek bishop to Patriarch Germanus II who refuted them in a treatise,[1] while the rumor that the Greeks denied Purgatory spread among the Latins[2] who then wrote treatises to refute this 'error' of the Greeks. One of them was published in 1252 by the Dominicans of Pera under the title *Contra errores Graecorum.*[3] It inspired the opuscule by Thomas Aquinas under the same title ten years later, and one chapter of which (the 69th) also focuses on the question of Purgatory.

Belief in Purgatory was expressed for the first time in an official document of the Catholic Church in 1254. It was a letter from Pope Innocent IV to his envoy on Cyprus, Odo, Cardinal of Tusculum, where we can read this instruction: "Considering that the Greeks assert that they cannot find in the works of their doctors any certain and proper name to designate the place of this purgation, and that, moreover, according to the traditions and authority of the Holy Fathers, this name is Purgatory, we wish that in the future this expression be also accepted by them. For, in this temporary fire, sins, not of course crimes and capital errors, which could not previously have been forgiven through penance, but slight and minor sins, are purged; if they have not been forgiven during existence, they weigh down the soul after death."[4]

At the Council of Lyons (1274) a profession of faith prepared by Pope Clement IV for the unionist emperor Michael Paleologos was submitted to the Greeks. The section of text dealing with Purgatory was drawn up in this way: "[The lot of the deceased]. If they die truly repentant in charity before they have made satisfaction by worthy fruits of penance for (sins) committed and omitted, their souls are cleansed after death by purgatorial or purifying punishments, as Brother John [Parastron] has explained to us. And to relieve punishments of this kind, the offerings of the living faithful are of advantage to these, namely, the sacrifices of Masses, prayers, alms, and other duties of piety, which have customarily been performed by the faithful for the other faithful according to the regulations of the Church. However, the souls of those who after having received holy baptism have incurred no stain of sin whatever, also those souls who, after contracting the stain of sin, either while remaining in their bodies or being divested of them, have been cleansed, as we have said above, are received immediately into heaven. The souls of those who die in mortal sin or with original sin only, however, immediately descend to hell, yet to be punished with different punishments."[5] As we know, the *de fidei* definition of the unionist Council of Lyons, signed by the representatives of the emperor of Byzantium, was rejected shortly afterward by the Orthodox Church. Anyhow, it is plain that the cited text remains prudent, since neither the questions of Purgatory as place or the purging fire (two controversial points) are directly expressed here, but only "purgatorial or purifying punishments." We must not forget that what we have here is a compromise text, intended to give rise to a broad agreement within both Churches.

The same prudence for the same reasons characterizes the definition of the unionist Council of Florence (1439): "If those truly penitent have departed in the love of God, before they have made satisfaction by the worthy fruits of penance for sins of commission and omission, the souls of these are cleansed after death by purgatorial punishments."[6] The Council of Florence having been held with a view to the reunion of Latin and Orthodox Churches (its *de fidei* definition having been, however, ultimately rejected by the latter), the preceding formulation stems from contradictory discussions and presents the Latin position in a watered-down manner.

The Council of Trent's definition is clearer: "Since the Catholic Church, instructed by the Holy Spirit, in conformity with the sacred writings and the ancient tradition of the Fathers in sacred councils, and very recently in this ecumenical Synod,[7] has taught that there is a purgatory, and that the souls detained there are assisted by the suffrages of the faithful, and especially by the acceptable sacrifice of the altar, the holy Synod commands the bishops that they insist that the sound doctrine of purgatory, which has been transmitted by the holy Fathers and holy Councils, be believed by the faithful of Christ, be maintained, taught, and everywhere preached."[8]

The recent *Catechism of the Catholic Church* reaffirms the doctrine of Purgatory, presenting it as an article of Catholic faith by referring to these definitions.[9] These definitions remain mute as to the nature of Purgatory, but an entire very precise theology of Purgatory has been developed, before[10] and after them,[11] in the Latin Church and is therefore bound up with these definitions; even more than these it is stamped upon Catholic consciousness. This theology is, moreover, accompanied by a whole imagery and a whole piety relative to Purgatory; even though the former (with respect to which the Council of Trent, impelled by Protestant criticism, has explicitly distanced itself[12]) is on its way to disappearing, the latter is, still today, quite prevalent in the bosom of Catholicism.

b) *The novelty of the Latin doctrine of Purgatory.* However, despite the assertions of the *de fidei* definition of the Council of Trent and a certain number of Catholic historians,[13] there is no convincing basis for the doctrine of Purgatory either in Scripture or the writings of the early Fathers. The numerous scriptural and patristic references collected *a posteriori* by Catholic theologians with an eye to justifying it[14] only succeed, on the one hand, in showing that Scripture and the Fathers deem the Church's prayers advantageous to the deceased (which has been always acknowledged by the Orthodox Church and by no means implies the existence of a Purgatory), and, on the other, in benefiting from the ambiguity of certain texts mentioning a punishment by fire in the hereafter (but which actually allude to the infernal condition posterior to the Last Judgment and, in any case, do not at all imply the existence of a Purgatory).

The doctrine of Purgatory arose in fact in the second half of the twelfth century and truly corresponds to an 'invention'. This reproach was made to the Latin theologians by the Orthodox theologians, once they had become aware of this theory, and polemics ensued. But this involves a historical fact acknowledged today by most historians. One highly acclaimed Catholic historian, Jacques Le Goff, has masterfully demonstrated this after composing a vast dossier appropriately titled: *The Birth of Purgatory*.[15] He informs us point blank: "Until the end of the twelfth century the noun *purgatorium* did not exist: *the* Purgatory had not yet been born."[16]

c) *Agreement with the principles of Latin theology.* Although it was in the second half of the twelfth century that the word 'Purgatory' was created and used for the first time and Purgatory was conceived as a 'third place', this invention was nonetheless facilitated by certain statements or expressions of some earlier Latin Fathers like St Ambrose,[17] St Augustine,[18] and St Gregory the Great[19] (who have not however elaborated any systematic theory and whose positions remain ambiguous in many respects, which Catholic historians of every persuasion recognize[20]).

As to its basic theological presuppositions, the doctrine of Purgatory can be seen as being in agreement with the post-Augustinian orientation of Latin theology.[21] The Augustinian theory of theophanies (created intermediaries between God and man), adopted by western theology, lends itself to the concept of a created and material purging fire, while the eastern concept of the divine energies does not allow such a concept: for Orthodox theology in fact, the divine energy, which can be perceived as a light or a fire, is one and uncreated but takes on different qualities according to its effects. It is called 'purifying' when it purifies man, 'illuminating' when it illumines him, 'deifying' when it divinizes him. There is not then one fire for the just and another fire for sinners, but one sole divine uncreated energy which acts upon them differently—because they receive it differently—according to their spiritual state.[22] This conception which has roots in Fathers like St Basil the Great, St Gregory of Nyssa, Pseudo-Dionysius, St Maximus the Confessor, St John Damascene and, of course, St Gregory Palamas, was likewise the basis for the positions St Mark of Ephesus in his refutation of the Latin theory of a purging fire[23] at the Council of Florence.[24]

But the factors contributing most to the birth, in the West, of the doctrine of Purgatory were, in the high middle ages, the theories of penal 'satisfaction' and expiation,[25] the formation of the concept of 'venial sins',[26] and the developing of a distinction between 'fault' and 'guilt'.[27] The notion of venial sin induced the placing of a third category of the faithful between the just (purified of all sin) and the damned (guilty of mortal sins), and find for them, *post-mortem*, a status and place of residence (Purgatory) different from the other two. The second distinction induced the imagining of a place for 'satisfaction' where they would be cleansed of their punishment and be purified of those venial sins that had been forgiven but the 'guilt' of which remained.

The development of the doctrine of Purgatory also seems tied to factors of ecclesiastical 'politics' at the heart of the Latin Church, expressed by the doctrine and practice of 'indulgences' that appeared shortly after the 'birth of Purgatory.'[28]

This doctrine and practice consist in regarding the pope as having the power to ease and even totally free the souls in Purgatory from their pains, which he does in exchange for various 'gestures' of the faithful—as for example "praying for the intention of the Sovereign Pontiff, " or giving gifts for the construction of church buildings—or at times in a gratuitous manner under certain solemn circumstances (major feasts, jubilees …). We know that this practice aroused Luther's ire and was surely one of the chief causes for the birth of Protestantism. Far from being obsolete today, it remains strongly anchored in Catholic piety and was quite recently brought to mind on the occasion of the Jubilee of the Year 2000.

The appearance of this doctrine and practice is historically tied, on the one hand, to the wish to reinforce the power of the papacy (henceforth extended not only over souls, but over their *post-mortem* progress), and, on the other, to the more prosaic concern to encourage gifts at a time when the papacy had embarked on an ambitious policy of the construction and decoration of churches and palaces. These practices and the doctrine of Purgatory are known to have been rejected not only by Orthodox theologians, but likewise by theologians of the Reform. More recently, certain Catholic theologians hav also shown themselves critical of these matters, such as Father Yves Congar[29] who proposed to his Catholic brothers to "accept a certain questioning of positions that are neither the most authentic or profound of [their] tradition."[30] It does not seem that much attention was paid to their remarks, but it must still be observed that a certain erosion of popular piety has put an end to some of the excesses of the doctrine and practices at issue.

2 The Defense of the Theory of Purgatory by the Latins and Its Refutation by the Orthodox at the Council of Florence.

From its advent the doctrine of Purgatory aroused a critical reaction on the part of the Orthodox Church. We have referred to the treatise composed around 1233 by the patriarch Germanus II. After the Council of Lyons, several critiques were drafted by Orthodox theologians to refute this doctrine. Of particular note is that of St Symeon of Thessalonica who, in chapter 23 of his *Dialogue against the Heresies*, asserts that, for sinful souls, none of the saints recognize any other punishment than that of being confined, as in a prison, in places of desolation, in sadness, while awaiting their ultimate punishment; the souls of the just, to the contrary, being in places of light and rejoicing, in expectation of the promised blessings which they will enjoy when reunited with their bodies. Among sinners, God allows a certain relief in their fear and sadness to those who have left this life with feelings of true but imperfect repentance, but there is no fire that purifies them, as the Latins assert.[31]

At the time of the Ferrara-Florence council of union, the question of Purgatory was discussed, along with those of the Filioque, azymes, and papal primacy, as one of the four chief subjects of divergence between the Orthodox and Roman Catholic Churches. This was the most extensive and thorough debate to have directly taken place between Catholic and Orthodox theologians on the question of Purgatory, and it therefore merits to be set out in detail.

a) *The report on the Latin position by Cardinal Cesarini.* When this question was broached, the Latin position was framed, in a memorandum submitted to the Greeks by Cardinal Julius Cesarini[32] in terms that reiterated almost word for word the profession of faith made in the name of Michael VIII Paleologus at the second Council of Lyons: "Those sincerely repentant souls who die in charity, before being acquitted by the meritorious results of penitence for their faults of commission or omission, are purified after their death by purifying punishments and by the suffrages of the faithful yet alive, namely the offering of masses, prayers, alms and other pious works serving to relieve the punishment of this kind; however, the souls who are not tainted by any sin after baptism, as well as those who after being tainted by sin have been purified during their bodily existence, or by the means previously described, are soon received into heaven; to the contrary, the souls who leave this life in a state of true mortal sin, or with original sin, soon descend to hell to suffer various punishments. Nevertheless, at the Last Judgment all men will appear together with their bodies before the just tribunal of Christ to render an account of their own acts." The rest of the memorandum presented seven proofs drawn from Scripture and the Fathers, justifying the first part of the declaration relative to Purgatory and focused on demonstrating two particular points: a) that there is an intermediate state (between Paradise and Hades); b) that it includes a punishment by fire:

1) The text of 2 Machabees 12:46: "He made atonement for the dead so that they might be delivered from their sins."

2) The text of Matthew 12:32: "Whoever blasphemes against the Holy Spirit, it will not be forgiven him, either in this age or in the age to come," which leads us to believe that other sins will be forgiven in the age to come, which implies the existence of a Purgatory.

3) The text of 1 Corinthians 3:13–15: "Every man's work shall be manifest. For the day of the Lord shall declare it, because it shall be revealed in fire. And the fire shall try every man's work, of what sort it is. If any man's work abide, which he hath built thereupon, he shall receive a reward. If any man's work burn, he shall suffer loss: but he himself shall be saved, yet so as by fire." These words can only be understood concerning the fire that purifies souls hereafter.

4) The tradition of both Churches has always recommended prayer for the dead, which would not make any sense if there were not a purification after death.

5) The authority of the Roman Church, which has always professed this doctrine.

6) The teachings of the Latin Fathers (St Augustine, St Ambrose, St Gregory the Great) and the Greek Fathers (St Basil the Great, St Gregory of Nyssa, Dionysius the Areopagite, St Epiphanius, St John Damascene, Theodoret of Cyrrhus).

7) The demands of Divine Justice which must leave no sin unpunished but adjusts the expiation to the fault according to Deut. 25:2, Ezek. 33:14–15, and Wisd. 7:25. One should concede then that there is another place between heaven and hell where purification is completed and from which it can, once this purification is completed, rejoin the souls of the blessed.

b) *The first memorandum of St Mark of Ephesus.* St Mark of Ephesus drew up a memorandum replying to these arguments.[33] The beginning of this memorandum presents the Orthodox position clearly and merits being cited fully:

In point of fact, those who have entered their rest while confessing the faith are, without any doubt, assisted by liturgies, prayers and alms done for their intention. Since this custom has been in effect from the earliest times, there is a host of testimonies and numerous and varied utterances from both Latin and Greek Doctors. These verbal and written testimonies have been referred to at different times and places. But, that souls are delivered thanks to a certain purgative suffering and by a temporary fire possessed by Purgatory which is in the nature of an aid, this we find neither in the holy scriptures, the prayers of the Church, in the hymns for the dead, or in the words of the Doctors. Conversely, we accept that even the souls held in Hades and already subject to eternal torment, either in fact and experience, or in a hopeless expectation [of torment], can be helped and receive a certain minor relief, even though this cannot deliver them completely from torment, or give them hope for a final deliverance. This was shown by the words of the great St Macarius of Egypt, a famous ascetic who, finding a skull in the desert, was instructed about these things by the activity of the Divine Power.[34] And St Basil the Great, in connection with the kneeling prayers read on the day of Pentecost, writes: Thou 'Who makest us worthy that our propitiatory prayers, of this all-perfect day of salvation, be acceptable for those who are imprisoned in Hades, and Who grantest those imprisoned therein a great hope in receiving from Thee consolation and relief of their confining grief.'[35] But if the souls who have quit this life with faith and love, yet bearing away with them certain sins, either minor sins for which they have not repented at all, or major sins for which, although they had repented of them, they had not however undertaken to show the fruits of repentance; we believe such souls are cleansed (ἐκκαθαίρεσθαι = whitened) of these kinds of sin, but not by means of some 'purgatorial' fire or a specific punishment somewhere, for this, as we have already said, has not been handed down to us at all. Among these souls, some will be [made clean] at the very time of their departure from the body, thanks to the fright of death, as indicated by St Gregory the Dialogist.[36] Others have to be made clean after their departure from the body, either by abiding in the same earthly place, before coming to adore God and being honored with the lot of the blessed, or, if their sins are more serious and are held back for a greater duration, these souls will be kept in Hades, but not in such a way as to remain forever in fire and torment, but as if imprisoned there, confined and under guard. Such souls, we declare, receive assistance thanks to prayers made for their intention and to liturgies, with the cooperation of God's goodness filled with love for men. God grants the remission of certain sins, like those committed through human weakness, as stated by St Dionysius the Areopagite in his contemplations on the mystery of those who repose in peace.[37] Other sins are however, after a certain time by a just judgment, completely discharged and pardoned, or else the sinners are held responsible for them until the Last Judgment. Hence we see no need whatever for another punishment or purifying fire, for some sinners are made clean by fear, while their conscience gnaws at others with more torment than any fire whatsoever might bring; still others are made clean by the great terror experienced before the divine glory and the uncertainty about what the future will be. Experience shows that this torments and punishes much more than anything else. St John Chrysostom bears witness to it in the majority of his ethical homilies. The same holds true for the holy ascetic Dorotheos in his discourse *On the conscience*.[38] And, that the damned are more tormented by uncertainty over their future than by any torture, this is affirmed by Doctors such as Gregory the Theologian in his discourse *On the Plague of Hail*[39]... And so we implore God and think to deliver [from eternal torment] those who have left us, and not from any other torment or from any other fire than those which have been proclaimed eternal. Moreover, we believe that the souls of the departed are delivered, through prayer, from being shut away in Hades as if from a kind of prison. From all this testimony, among so many others, Theophanes the Confessor, also called *Graptos* [the Branded]... In one of his Canons on behalf of those who have entered into their rest, he prays for them in this way: "Deliver, O Savior, Thy servants who are in Hades from tears and sighing." Do you hear? He says: 'tears and sighing'. He speaks of no other kind of punishment or purging fire. And if in these hymns and prayers some allusion is found to a fire, this is not to a temporary fire that holds sway in Purgatory, but rather to that eternal fire of everlasting punishment. The saints, moved by love for men and by compassion for their fellow citizens, daring and wishing for what is nearly impossible, pray for the deliverance of all those who have departed in the faith. St Theodore the Studite thus bears witness to this when he writes at the very beginning of his canon for the departed: "As we celebrate today the memory of the dead from the beginning, let us all entreat Christ to deliver from the everlasting fire those who have fallen asleep in faith and in the hope of eternal life."[40] Next, in another troparion of the canon, he says: "From the ever-burning fire, from the darkness without light, from the gnashing of teeth and the worm that torments without ceasing, from every punishment deliver, O our Savior , all who have died in the faith."[41] Where is the fire of Purgatory here? And, if it actually existed, where if not here would there be a more appropriate place for the saint to speak of it? It is not for us to seek to know if the saints are heard by God when they pray with this intention. But they themselves know it, like the Spirit who dwells in them and through Whom they were moved, speaking and writing then with this knowledge. Just as Christ the Lord gives us the commandment to pray for our enemies and prayed for those who crucified Him, so He inspired the first martyr Stephen when he was being stoned to death to do the same. Even though no one can say we are heard when we pray for such people, despite that we should do everything in our power. And here we have, offered for our imitation, the example of certain saints who prayed not only for believers, but also for the impious. And they were heard, and these others, the objects of their prayers, were saved from eternal torment. Thus, the first female martyr, Thecla, saved Falconille, and holy Gregory the Great saved the emperor Trajan, as he recounts in his *Dialogues*.[42]

c) *Bessarion of Nicea's discourse.*   Bessarion of Nicea also composed a memorandum.[43] It was he who was charged with presenting the official Greek reply to the memorandum of Cardinal Cesarini. His reply was a synthesis of his own memorandum (for the preamble and account of the question) and St Mark of Ephesus (for the argumentation).

From the very first, Bessarion points out that the Greeks like the Latins acknowledge that the prayers of the Church benefit the deceased, but that, on the other hand, they have encountered among none of their doctors the belief in an temporal expiation accomplished through fire after this life.

The controversy, he notes, can be reduced to two points, the second in its turn capable of being subdivided into two parts: 1) Is there a remission of sins after this life? 2) If this is the case, how is it accomplished? a) Simply as an effect of the divine mercy responding to the prayers of the Church, b) either by means of a punishment, which are in such a case: captivity, darkness, and ignorance, or, as the Latins think, fire, material fire?

The Greeks rule out this last opinion: on the one hand, they have never encountered among any of their doctors the belief in a material and temporal fire, and on the other, such a notion favors the Origenist doctrine of apocatastasis which rejects eternal punishment.

As for the first point, the Greeks readily admit, according to the teaching of their doctors, that after this life there is a remission for minor faults.

The only remaining point of debate is then: how is the remission of certain sins effected, a remission that both Orthodox and Catholic Churches admit as a possibility.

Bessarion opens the debate by presenting first what in the teachings of the Latins concerning the cleansing by fire seems unacceptable to the Greeks. For this he restates the different points of Cardinal Cesarini's memorandum.[44]

(1–2) The passages cited from 2 Macc. 12:46 and Matt. 12:32 clearly have in mind the remission of certain sins granted under certain conditions after death, but nowhere mention a cleansing by fire.

(3) As for the passage cited from 1 Cor. 3:11–15, Bessarion defers to the incontestable authority of one of St Paul's best exegetes: St John Chrysostom. Now the latter deems that the fire mentioned by St Paul is the eternal fire,

which does not give up its victims. True, St Augustine has understood this text otherwise. His mistake arises from a praiseworthy concern: to refute the error of those who apply this text to all the faults, in this way denying eternal punishment; to do this he found nothing better than to avail himself of a middle term: that of a temporal fire.

In the expression of St Paul: "he himself will be saved (σωθήσεται), yet so as through fire," the verb σῴζεσθαι must not be understood in the usual sense of 'to be saved' but in the sense of, which it often possesses as well, 'to be safeguarded', in other words 'protected' or 'preserved'. The Apostle—there is no indication that he has in mind a temporal fire—meant that the damned will not be exterminated, but will be preserved in eternal fire. Such is the exegesis of St John Chrysostom and, along with him, all of the Greek Fathers. St Paul himself ratifies such an interpretation (1 Cor. 3:13) as do other scriptural passages that mention the fire of the Last Judgment (Dan. 7:10, Psalm 49:3, 2 Pet. 3:7).

(6) The Latins appeal to several texts of the Fathers, but these do not have the meaning attributed to them by the Latins: St Basil, St Epiphanius, St Dionysius and St John Damascene affirm that, for the remission of certain faults, the prayer of the living is advantageous for the deceased, but they go no further than that. As for Theodoret's text, it needs supplementary clarifications, which are not to be found however in any of his numerous writings. It has then no decisive value.[45] There remains St Gregory of Nyssa, some of whose positions seem to actually go in the direction of Latin positions. Unfortunately, these positions also tend towards apocatastasis, a doctrine developed by Origenism and so condemned by the fifth ecumenical council. The fact that St Gregory of Nyssa is a venerable Father does not preclude that, like other Fathers (among whom are Irenaeus of Lyons, Dionysius of Alexandria …), he might be mistaken on certain points; under the circumstances he has the excuse that, in his time, the Church's dogma on the eternity of punishment was not yet settled. The Greeks intended to cling to the teaching of the Church and the rule of Scripture, and not to the assertions of a particular doctor.

Personal opinions are likewise being expressed by St Ambrose, St Augustine, and St Gregory the Great when they refer to a purification by fire. These opinions however do not for all that confirm the Latin doctrine of Purgatory. The only thing that clearly emerges from their texts is that the prayers of the living are profitable for the deceased. True, St Gregory the Great in his *Dialogues* cites numerous examples of purification by fire, but one suspects that they are, in his thinking, little else than allegories.

(5) The Latins invoke the authority of the Latin Church, but, under the circumstances, this amounts to a custom. One cannot argue on this basis, for one custom can always be opposed to other customs. It behooves us to examine the basis of the matter by taking Scripture and the Fathers as guides.

(7) The Latins make an appeal to reason. But the Greeks for their part are not short of reasons.

Bessarion presents then ten arguments borrowed from the memorandum of St Mark of Ephesus:[46]

> I. It is less fitting for the goodness of God to disregard a slight merit than to punish a slight fault. Now, the little good in great sinners obtains no reward by reason of the overabundance of evil: therefore it is not appropriate that the little evil in the saints is punished despite the preponderance of the good, for in the absence of serious sin, a slight fault seems negligible. Therefore it is inappropriate to admit a purifying fire.

> II. This is about the slight evil of the good and the slight good of the wicked alike. But the slight good of the wicked should not call for a reward, but only a difference in punishment. And so the slight evil in the good should not call for a punishment, but only a difference in blessedness. Therefore, there is nowhere to admit a purifying fire.

> III. The justice of eternal punishment is above all apparent in the irrevocable disposition of the unruly will of sinners; for to the eternal perversion of the will is due an eternal punishment. Conversely and as a result, although the will immutably fixed in evil is punished with an eternal punishment, anyone not punished eternally does not then have an irrevocable will. For an irrevocable will for evil would be destined to an eternal punishment, while an irrevocable will for good calls for no punishment, since it merits a crown. But you yourselves recognize that those who would be purified by this fire have an irrevocable will; they do not have to be purified then by fire.

> IV. If the perfect reward for purity of heart and soul consists in seeing God, and if all do not share equally in this, this is then because all are not equally pure. Therefore there is no need for a purifying fire, even though for some purification leaves a lot to be desired, for this very fire would produce an equal purification in all and would dispose all to see God equally. As on the mountain of the Law, in symbol and in figure, what transpires is that all do not appear in

the same place or on the same tier, but on various tiers according to the extent of their respective purifications, following Gregory the Theologian.[47]

V. The great saint Gregory the Theologian, in his theoretic and anagogic oration *On Pascha*, has this to say: "Neither let us carry anything of it abroad, nor leave it till the morning;"[48] and he explains in clear and plain terms that after this night there is no purification, by 'night' meaning the present life of each person, and making no allowance for any further purification.

VI. This is expressed in the same way in his oration *On the Plague of Hail*: "I do not dwell on the judgments to come, to which indulgence in this world delivers us, as it is better to be punished and cleansed now than to be transmitted to the torment to come, when it is the time of chastisement, not of cleansing,"[49] making it clearly understood that there is no purification beyond this life, but nothing else than eternal punishment.

VII. The Lord, in the Gospel according to St Luke, on the rich man and Lazarus, teaching about the destiny of the one and the other, says that Lazarus upon dying was carried by the angels into the bosom of Abraham, and that the rich man upon dying was imprisoned and his soul tormented in hell: thus, by the bosom of Abraham, He has indicated the exaltation in goodness reserved for the friends of God; by hell and torment, the final condemnation and eternal punishment of sinners. He did not leave a place of temporary torments between the two, but nothing save a great and impassable abyss separating the one from the other and showing the profound and irreconcilable opposition between their destinies.

VIII. The soul delivered from the body, totally incorporeal and immaterial, does not seem able to be punished by a corporeal fire after its body, which would make it vulnerable to fire, has perished. But, after the Resurrection, it will be joined to an imperishable body; all creation will be transformed: the fire will be apportioned, we are told. Then it will surely experience a corresponding punishment. And not only it, but even the demons, they too [will be] darkened, clothed with matter, with coarseness, with airy or fiery bodies, according to Basil the Great. But before regaining its own body, being only a form exempt from matter although subsisting by itself, how would the soul be chastised with a corporeal fire?

IX. Our holy Fathers, who have led an angelic life on earth, initiated in many places and at many times by visions, dreams and other miracles into the eternal punishment and lot of the impious and afflicted sinners, and imparting their illuminations, contemplating and expounding these mysteries as real and present (just as the parable of Luke's Gospel describes the condition of the rich man and Lazarus), have never alluded to a purifying temporal fire.

X. The doctrine of the apocatastasis and the end of eternal punishment, due to Origen and accepted by some churchmen like Didymus and Evagrius, a doctrine that brings God's goodness to the fore and finds a warm welcome among the lax, according to the word of godly John [Climacus], architect of the heavenly Ladder,[50] has nonetheless been proscribed and anathematized by the holy Fifth Ecumenical Council as soul-destroying and encouraging laxity among the lax, who anticipate deliverance from their torments and the promised apocatastasis. For the same reasons it seems that the proposed doctrine of a divine purifying fire ought to be rejected by the Church as disturbing to valiant souls, diverting them from making every effort to purify themselves in this life, with the prospect of another purification.

d) *Second Memorandum of St Mark of Ephesus.* The task of responding to the Greek arguments presented by Bessarion was entrusted by the Latins to John of Torquemada.[51]

The clarifications asked of the Greeks by the latter were provided by St Mark of Ephesus in a second and a third memorandum.

In the second memorandum,[52] St Mark of Ephesus again expounds the Orthodox position:

> We affirm that neither the righteous have as yet received the fullness of their lot and that blessed condition for which they have prepared themselves here through works, nor have sinners, after death, been led away into the eternal punishment in which they shall be tormented eternally. Rather, both the one and the other must necessarily occur after the Judgment of the last day and the resurrection of all. Now, however, both the one and the other are in places proper to them: the first, in absolute repose and free, are in heaven with the angels and before God Himself, and already as if in the paradise from which Adam fell (into which the good thief entered before others) and often visit us in those temples where they are venerated, and hear those who call on them and pray for them to God, having received from Him this surpassing gift, and through these relics perform miracles, and take delight in the vision of God and the illumination sent from Him, more perfectly and purely than before, when they were alive; while the second in their turn, being confined in hell remain *in the lowest pit, in darkness and in the shadow of death* (Psalm 87:7), as David says, and then Job: *to the land where light is as darkness* (Job 10:21–22). And the first remain in every joy and gladness, already expecting and only not having in their hands the Kingdom and the unutterable good things promised them; while the second, on the contrary, remain in total confinement and

inconsolable suffering, like condemned men awaiting the Judge's sentence and foreseeing their torments. Neither have the first yet received the inheritance of the Kingdom, and those good things which "eye has not seen, nor ear heard, nor have entered into the heart of man" (1 Cor. 2:9); nor have the second yet been given over to eternal torments, or to burning in the unquenchable fire. And this teaching, handed down as such from our Fathers in antiquity, we can easily show it as proceeding from the Divine Scriptures themselves. And so we transmit this doctrine in our turn by pointing out how simple and just it is.[53]

St Mark then cites a certain number of scriptural texts and patristic sources establishing this point of Orthodox faith: St Athanasius of Alexandria,[54] St Gregory the Theologian,[55] and St John Chrysostom.[56] In the rest of his memorandum, St Mark clarifies other points.

1) He shows that, neither in Scripture or among the Fathers, do we find a belief in purification by a temporal and material fire. St Peter, for example, referring to the impious awaiting final sentence (2 Pet. 2:4), speaks only of their captivity. Along with him the Greeks readily speak of punishment already begun, of shame, remorse and other pains, but it is unnecessary to ask them to admit a material fire acting on spiritual souls. The texts of the saints relating visions of punishment by fire should be taken in a figurative and allegorical sense.

2) The Church, in the liturgy and other circumstances, does not pray for just one category of souls, but for all the deceased without distinction, and therefore also for the sinners in hell, to gain for them, for want of a complete deliverance, at least a slight relief. We know of instances of prayers for sinners that were heard, like those of St Thecla for Falconille or St Gregory the Dialogist for the emperor Trajan. The Church does not, however, offer its public prayer for such souls, being content to pray for all the faithful departed, even great sinners: they ask God, either in public or in private, that He pardon them, which is brought out in the words of liturgical prayer addressed to God "for all those who have fallen asleep in the faith" or in the words of the prayer of St Basil read on the day of Pentecost at the *Kneeling Service*: "You who, on this most perfect and salutary feast, have been pleased to receive our intercessory prayers for those who are immured in Hell, granting us great hopes to see You grant to the departed deliverance from the pains which overwhelm them and their alleviation, hear our prayers ..."[57]

If the Church's prayers have, for souls found guilty of serious sins, the power to bring about an alleviation of their pain and a more consoling hope (before their final lot is settled at the Last Judgment), *a fortiori* they can help the least guilty souls join the righteous. As for holy souls, they also reap the benefit of these prayers, for they have still not achieved perfect blessedness, according to the teaching of St Dionysius the Areopagite.[58]

There is then no reason to restrict the efficacy of prayers and the holy sacrifice to one category of souls consigned to purgatorial fire.

3) The Latins appeal to the authority of St Basil who, in the previously cited prayer, asks God to introduce the souls of the departed into a place of refreshment. But there is nothing here that implies the Latin doctrine of purgatorial fire: St Basil was only thinking of David who also spoke of refreshment (Psalm 28:14).

4) The Latins are shocked that the Greeks deem Gregory of Nyssa deceived about the point of doctrine under consideration. But this was also the case with other points of doctrine with other Fathers whose teachings are otherwise authoritative. However it is with the doctrine of St Gregory of Nyssa, it is quite different from that of the Latins since, according to him, these are not only slight faults but all faults that can be purified by fire, it is all punishment that must cease and desist, since punishment is for him nothing but a purification intended for impious and perverse people, but even for demons, which must end in their final restoration (apocatastasis). Likewise on this point Gregory's thinking is quite far from that of the Latins, who restrict the purgatorial fire to slightly guilty souls; on the other hand, it is close to the teaching of Origen who was officially condemned by the Church.

5) Surprisingly, the Latins present their doctrine of purification by fire as one of the Church's early doctrines and as keeping to the middle way between two errors, whereas the most numerous and most illustrious Doctors believe that eternal fire and unending punishment should be explained in an allegorical sense. They in fact teach that we have here neither a material fire or an outer darkness other than ignorance of God, neither worm or venomous and devouring reptile except for the torment of a guilty conscience and the bitterness of remorse, nor the grinding of teeth except for a vengeful frenzy with the grief it engenders and bitter groaning.

6) Concerning the texts from Maccabees and St Matthew, the Greeks find in these no trace of punishment or purification, but only the pardon of sins.

7) The Greeks are surprised at the odd distinction made by the Latins between fault and pain[59] and of their notion according to which, after the pardon of an offense, a pain is left to be suffered. We do not see princes continue to

punish an offense once they have pardoned it; so much the more God, one of whose most obvious attributes is Goodness. This distinction is contradicted by numerous scriptural passages: the publican goes back not only absolved but justified (Luke 18:14); Manasses, after being humbled, is delivered from his chains and reestablished on his throne (2 Chr. 33:12–13); the Ninivites, thanks to their repentance, are spared the blows that threatened them (Jon. 3:5–10); the paralytic receives, along with the pardon of his sins, a rectifying of his body (Matt. 9:6).

8) Lastly, as to Paul's text upon which nearly the Latins' whole teaching on purgatorial fire relies, it never occurred to any of the Greek Fathers when commenting on it (St John Chrysostom in particular, Paul's preeminent exegete) to interpret it in this way. The work and the worker consigned to the fire by the Apostle are respectively a monstrous sin and a worker of iniquity; this is not an average soul to which St Paul would promise salvation after purification. The fire he speaks of is clearly the eternal fire.

e) *Third memorandum of St Mark of Ephesus.*

The third memorandum of Mark of Ephesus[60] provides some clarifications requested by the Latins. In particular he stresses:

— that the lot of souls destined for blessedness remains, until the Last Judgment, provisional and imperfect (§ 1);

— that the saints do not see God by essence (§ 2) but by illumination[61] (§ 4);

— that the souls of those who have died in mortal sin are, in hell, tortured by the expectancy and fear of their sad lot (§ 6), while the souls of the saints enjoy a blessed happiness in advance in the hope of the promised good things (§ 7);

— that the privation of the divine vision is for the damned a pain greater than eternal fire or any other torment (§ 8);

— that the pains endured by the average category of souls (ignorance, sadness, shame of conscience, and the rest) are varied and unequal, like the faults that have merited these pains for them (§ 9).

— that they suffer besides from uncertainty about the future, that is from the ignorance in which they abide as to a time when they might be united with the choir of the elect (§ 10).

— that the prayers of the living can obtain for the damned themselves some alleviation of their pain before the Last Judgment (§ 12).

— that the Greeks do not agree that sins may be consumed by charity in the souls of those who have died with love for God, for they attribute the virtue of wiping away sins to repentance, not charity; now repentance does not arise out of charity, it arises out of fear (§ 13).

— that the Greek priests impose a penance while absolving sinners for therapeutic reasons above all. Faced with immanent death, sacramental penitence can be dispensed with: one absolves and gives communion to the dying by having confidence that God will deign to welcome them as He welcomed the good thief (§ 14).

Debate broke off at this point and, despite what the final definition of faith of the Council of Florence might lead us to believe, no agreement was found between Greeks and Latins on the issue of Purgatory. [62] This debate did, however, have the merit of enabling the Latins to understand the criticism of the Greeks against their doctrine, and of enabling the Greeks to make the Orthodox position explicit concerning the situation of souls awaiting the Last Judgment.

The Greeks have been reproached for presenting negative arguments against the doctrine of Purgatory rather than positively presenting their own faith on this issue.[63] But this reproach is doubly unjustified: on the one hand, it was perfectly normal for the Greeks to be interested foremost in criticizing a doctrine that seemed an unacceptable innovation and that they were being urged to accept; on the other, they did not have to explain their own doctrine of Purgatory positively since the very notion of Purgatory was foreign to them. All that they could do was to clarify how they conceived of the situation of the departed before the Last Judgment and how, according to them, prayers for the departed might be of assistance. Catholic theologians have also accused St Mark of Ephesus of presenting new positions for the Orthodox;[64] in fact, he made explicit and precise a point of doctrine which circumstances had not obliged the easterners, up until that time, to give a systematic account of their position.

3 The Teaching of Orthodox Theologians after the Council of Florence.

The relative diversity of positions on the situation and progress of the souls of the deceased before the Last Judgment, to be observed in reading treatises of

Orthodox theology subsequent to the Council of Florence,[65] may be explained in part by the Latin influences experienced by a certain number of Orthodox prelates and theologians, many of whom were formed in western theological schools.[66] These Orthodox often concede for intermediary souls the existence of an expiation and a purification; they sometimes consider this to be achieved through fire; but almost unanimously reject, however, the idea that this transpires in a third place, Purgatory.[67] In the treatises most authentically Orthodox, we rediscover the overall notion defended by St Mark of Ephesus at the Council of Florence,[68] a notion in the line of thinking of the Greek Fathers that remains dominant today among Orthodox theologians who have dealt with this topic.[69]

Among the most outstanding works that have dealt with Purgatory after the Council of Florence, and that reiterate and clarify the positions expressed by Bessarion and St Mark of Ephesus, we will cite the *Orthodox Catechism* of Meletios Pigas, the Patriarch of Alexandria (Vilna, 1596), and the new revised, corrected and enlarged edition (1690) of the *Confession of Faith* of Dositheus, Patriarch of Jerusalem.[70]

Meletios Pegas, the Patriarch of Alexandria, sees Christ as having achieved a total and full satisfaction, which excludes every secondary satisfaction provided by the sinner pardoned for sins committed after baptism. The sacramental penance imposed by the confessor is in no way vindictive, but solely pedagogical and prophylactic. After sacramental absolution, no pain of temporal satisfaction remains to burden the sinner, either in this world or the next. Not only the sacramental *epitimia* (penance), but even the trials of this life are devoid of all punitive and satisfactory quality for sin. There is no need to see in the fruits of repentance spoken of in Scripture a satisfactory compensation for sin, but purely and simply indications of a true repentance. If a sinner therefore dies with a contrite heart without having had time to provide these indications, God will grant him a full remission of his faults because of the sacrifice of Jesus Christ, and this is in keeping with divine justice: heaven is open to him. Whoever reaches the end of the present life must necessarily go into the bosom of Abraham with the poor man Lazarus, or descend into hell with the wicked rich man. After death there is, for souls, only two states and two abodes. Purgatory is superfluous and akin to Origenism. It is superfluous because those who die repentant are completely purified by the blood of Jesus Christ and have no need of any other purification. It 'Origenizes' because it introduces purifying torments that last only for a time and leads to a universal apocatastasis. One might even say it Judaizes: the Pharisees in fact, admitting in principle that no son of Israel can perish, deliver sinners up to purifying torments after death. Passing to the scriptural texts upon which Latin theologians customarily base the doctrine of Purgatory, Meletios turns them against this very doctrine. In the gospel passage of Matthew 5:26: "You will by no means get out of there till you have paid the last penny," the word 'till' does not indicate a limited period of time, but signifies: "In prison, that is to say in hell, you will be punished for all your sins, even the very least." As for the text of 2 Maccabees 12:43 ff, far from supporting Purgatory, it destroys it: Judas Maccabeus actually offers a sacrifice not for the expiation of a venial sin, but a serious sin of idolatry committed by people who died impenitent. The fire involved in 1 Corinthians 3:13–15 is not the fire of Purgatory, but a trial by fire, to which the just as well sinners will be subject as regards their good or bad works. Lastly the text of Matthew 12:32: "whoever speaks against the Holy Spirit, it will not be forgiven him, either in this age or in the age to come," means only one thing, namely that the sin against the Holy Spirit will never be forgiven, as is brought out in the parallel passages of Mark 3:28–29 and Luke 12:10.

Of what use, then, are the suffrages of the living for the dead? First of all, every good work accomplished on behalf of the deceased who died a pious death glorifies the God who beatified them. If the deceased are in hell, the suffrages can gain for them an alleviation and even deliver them entirely if their lives were not totally evil. This is seen by the examples of Trajan and Falconille. Surely the flames of hell are eternal, but those that God delivers from them spend only a certain time there. The Church in fact prays for all Christians dead in the faith and excludes only those who have departed obviously unrepentant.[71]

Dositheus, the Patriarch of Jerusalem, in the new revised and corrected edition (1690) of his *Confession of Faith*, shows four differences between Orthodox and Catholic doctrines.

1) The first difference, he says, is that we Orthodox do not admit a third place, separated from or close to hell, from which souls can be delivered, but we assert that this redemption is effected among the denizens of hell itself, provided that no definitive sentence has as yet been pronounced by the Savior against the reprobate.

2) The second difference is that there exists no purifying fire outside of God, who is rightly by Himself the purifying fire working the perfect redemption,

or refreshment, or remission and reconciliation of souls. Only by way of metaphor can we give the name of 'purification' to the sadness and groanings of those imprisoned in hell.

3) The third difference is the most serious: according to Orthodox doctrine, venial sins are not taken into account after death. God makes them of no account, and they involve no punishment, no pain for the souls of the deceased who have committed them. These peccadilloes, from which no mortal is exempt, are generously forgiven by God at the hour of death, in light of the preponderant good to be found in just souls. If this were not so, no one would ascend to heaven after death. These are then the souls of sinners guilty of mortal sins who are comforted and drawn out of hell by the prayers of the Church and the suffrages of the living.

4) The fourth difference follows from the third and does away with the other raison d'être for Purgatory, namely the temporal pain due to sin already blotted out by repentance or priestly absolution. To those who, forewarned about death, have been able to bear fruits worthy of repentance, Christ completely forgives every sin and every pain. He sanctifies them, glorifies them, and gives to them the joy of the blessed. To say, while making a distinction between 'guilt' and 'pain', that the sins of such people are forgiven and that the pain of their sin remains is absurd. We confess therefore, concludes Dositheus, that those who have repented of their faults are not punished in hell, expecting that the faithful have their abode in the heavenly Church of the first-born. That there are in hell, to the contrary, only those who are punished for great sins, and that it is from hell that sinners are drawn is what the account of the Maccabees highlights. Although they are truly in hell, the reprobates delivered by the prayers of the Church do not suffer the pain of fire, for the infernal fire becomes active only after the Last Judgment. The pains of the reprobates are currently only of a moral order: sadness, regrets, remorse of conscience, imprisonment, darkness, fear, and uncertainty about the future.[72]

4 Recapitulation of the Catholic and Orthodox Positions.

a) *The Catholic Position.* After death, souls undergo a particular judgment. The souls of the just (those who, after Baptism, have committed no stain of sin) are placed in heaven, while the souls of those who have not been baptized and are therefore bearers of original sin, or those who are guilty of mortal sins, descend into hell.

The souls of those who are neither altogether good or altogether bad, and who are guilty of 'venial' (slight and trivial) sins, who have not received absolution for these sins before their death, or who have been pardoned for them but who have not had time to satisfy divine justice by doing penance, that is, according to the Latins, by suffering the expiatory pain owed to God for these sins; these souls are put in a place distinct from heaven and hell called 'Purgatory', where they are purified of these sins and purge away the pain through fire. This 'purgatorial fire', source of a pain at once purifying and expiatory, is temporal — it will disappear at the time of the Last Judgment—and material. These souls can be relieved of their pains by the prayers of the living and the holy sacrifice of the Mass, and also by the will of the pope granting 'indulgences' ('plenary' indulgences being able to totally and immediately remit the pains of a given deceased person, or a category of deceased people). Prayers and the holy sacrifice of the Mass are, on the other hand, useless for the just in heaven and for the damned in hell, for both have already, in their souls, attained the fullness of the state to be theirs after the Last Judgment (the just have obtained blessedness in the vision of the divine essence, while the damned are being punished by eternal, infernal fire), the only difference being that, after the Last Judgment, they will experience their respective conditions with their bodies. After having purged away their pain and having been purified by it, the souls who abide in Purgatory are able to rejoin the souls of the just.[73]

b) *The Orthodox Position.* There are only two places or conditions for the souls of the departed before the Last Judgment: paradise and hell. The souls of the just abide in paradise; the souls of sinners abide in hell. These two conditions are partial and provisional: the just receive an imperfect blessedness and sinners an incomplete punishment. Only at the Last Judgment will their lot be definitively set and will they gain access to the fullness and eternity of their respective conditions.

Neither in Scripture or the Fathers is there mention of a third place or third condition like the one the Latins call 'Purgatory'. The souls of those guilty of minor sins (which the Latins call 'venial'), who have repented of these sins before their death and have been pardoned, are exonerated and have no need of being purified after death or punished. They therefore join the souls of the just in paradise, where there are nevertheless numerous dwellings, the souls of the just being on differing levels; they enjoy freedom and rest, are in the proximity of God and see Him in proportion to their purity. The souls of those guilty of minor sins, but have not repented and whose sins have not been pardoned, join the souls of the great sinners in hell. But in hell there are likewise 'numerous dwellings'; the souls of great unrepentant sinners are situated in the lower levels of hell, those of sinners guilty of small faults in its higher levels. The pains that souls endure there are those of imprisonment in places of desolation and sadness, where they suffer from fear of their judgment and of their future condition, as well as the remorse of their conscience; but the souls suffer these pains to varying degrees, according to the importance of the sins committed and that are unforgiven. These pains are not punitive pains or meant to satisfy divine justice (notions foreign to the Orthodox Church); nor are they purifying pains. And we must not lose sight of the symbolic nature of the various expressions referring to them: fire, worm, grinding of teeth, etc. The fire is the uncreated energy of God which is manifested as suffering among those deprived of it by their sinful state (this same energy being perceived as light and a source of joy by the just in paradise). The deceased are no longer able to do anything for their own salvation; they can no longer even repent. On the other hand, the prayers of the living and the holy sacrifice of the liturgy are beneficial for them. They are accomplished on behalf of all those who have died in the faith and abide in hell, whatever the importance of their sins. They can however lessen the pains of all those who abide in hell. The great sinners themselves can receive a slight relief from them in lieu of a complete deliverance.[74] Less guilty souls can *a fortiori* benefit from them and be united with the souls of the just, the passage from hell to paradise being possible even before the Last Judgment. As for the souls of the just, they equally benefit from the prayers made for their intention, since they have still not attained perfect blessedness. In any case, the benefits that souls in hell receive from prayers from the living depend only on the mercy of God solicited by these prayers.

Chapter Nine

RELATIONS BETWEEN THE LIVING
AND THE DEAD

1 Relations of the Living with the Dead.

a) *Proscription by the Church of 'occult' relations.* The Church has at all times denounced as vain and dangerous those practices claiming to entertain a physical or psychic relation with the souls of the deceased. Especially because these practices (like spiritualism, necromancy[1] ...) have been most often connected with delusions (with autosuggestion at the heart of many cases), superstitions, but also magical practices comprising grave risks for the intervention of demons[2] who are able to injure their participants physically, psychically[3] and spiritually.[4]

b) *The necessity of prayer for the dead.* The Church has at all times felt it necessary to pray for the deceased. According to St John Chrysostom, this is a custom of the Church instituted by the Apostles themselves: "Not in vain did the Apostles order that remembrance should be made of the dead in the dreadful Mysteries. They know that great gain results to them, great benefit."[5] The treatise *Concerning Those who have Died in the Faith*, attributed to St John Damascene, asserts the same thing.[6] In the second letter to Timothy, we see St Paul himself pray for his deceased disciple Onesiphorus (2 Tim. 1:18). The opinion according to which it would be inappropriate to pray for the dead has even been condemned by certain Fathers, such as St Epiphanius attacking the doctrine of Arius: "As to naming the dead, what could be more helpful? What could be more opportune or wonderful than that the living believe that the departed are alive and have not ceased to be, but are with the Lord and live with him—and that the sacred doctrine should declare that there is hope for those who pray for their brethren as though they were off on a journey."[7]

c) *The different 'suffrages' on behalf of the deceased.* 'Suffrages' on behalf of the deceased traditionally take three principal forms: prayer (liturgical or private), the offering of the holy sacrifice, and almsgiving.

LITURGICAL PRAYER FOR THE DECEASED. In the previous chapters, we have seen that, since earliest times, the Orthodox Church celebrates a liturgical service for the deceased not only at the time of their burial, but even on the third, ninth and fortieth days, and during the third, sixth and ninth month following their death, as well as each year on the anniversary of their death.[8]

In addition, a short commemorative service called a 'Panikhida' that may be requested by a family at any time.

Add also the office of the *Kolyva*, often celebrated at the end of the liturgy, at the request of the deceased's family, or on days when the Church commemorates all of the deceased (see *infra*). *Kolyva* is a kind of boiled wheat[9] cake with dried fruits, sugared, flavored with cinnamon and other seasonings, and decorated. This cake, blessed by the priest in memory of one, several, or all of the deceased, was formerly placed on the graves for the intention of the poor and the officiants, but today is consumed by the faithful at the end of the service. It has a symbolic meaning that always includes a sharing, but in a more spiritual sense of the solidarity of the ecclesial community: 1) in prayer for the deceased, and 2) with the families of the latter.[10] The Saturday of each week (because it is the day of rest, σάββα- τον), is specifically devoted to the deceased, with special prayers for their intention in the different services.[11]

On the other hand, several days of the liturgical year are devoted specifically to commemorating the deceased: the Saturday preceding *Apocreo* (Sunday of the Last Judgment or Carnival), the Saturdays of the third and fourth weeks of Great Lent, Tuesday of Thomas week (following the second Sunday after Pascha), the Saturday before Pentecost, called 'Saturday of Souls' (ψυχοσάββατον) and the Saturday before St Demetrius (October 26th according to the Gregorian calendar, November 8th according to the Julian calendar). An important place should be reserved here for the liturgy properly speaking. Certain Fathers especially recommend offering the holy eucharistic sacrifice on behalf of the deceased.[12]

The Liturgy of St John Chrysostom, generally celebrated, and that of St Basil the Great, celebrated at certain times of the liturgical year defined by the *Typikon* (during Great Lent in particular), include numerous prayers for the deceased.

At the end of the liturgy of the catechumens, a long 'ectenia' (or litany) for the deceased takes place for whose intention the faithful have asked the priest to pray and for whomever the priest himself wishes to pray (deceased parishioners or spiritual children):[13]

—Again we pray for the respose of the souls of the departed servants of God N., and that they may be forgiven every transgression, both voluntary and involuntary.

—That the Lord God commit their souls to where the righteous repose.

—The mercy of God, the kingdom of heaven, and the remission of their sins, let us ask of Christ the immortal King and our God.

—God of spirits and of all flesh, Who hast trampled down death, and overthrown the devil, and given life to Thy world: Do Thou Thyself, O Lord, give rest to the souls of Thy departed servants N., in a place of light, a place of green pasture, a place of repose, whence all sickness, sorrow, and sighing are fled away. Pardon every sin committed by them in word, deed, or thought, in that Thou art a good God, the Lover of mankind; for there is no man that liveth and sinneth not, for Thou alone art without sin, Thy righteousness is an everlasting righteousness, and Thy word is truth.

—For Thou art the resurrection, and the life, and the respose of Thy departed servants N., O Christ our God, and unto Thee do we send up glory, together with Thine unoriginate Father, and Thy Most holy and good and life-creating Spirit, now and ever, and unto the ages of ages.[14]

At the center of the Liturgy of St John Chrysostom, after the epiclesis (corresponding to the consecration in the Latin liturgy), the priest pronounces this prayer: "Again we offer unto Thee this rational service for them that in faith have gone to their rest before us: the forefathers, fathers, patriarchs, prophets, apostles, preachers, evangelists, martyrs, confessors, ascetics, and for every righteous spirit made perfect in faith."[15]

A little after this the priest requests: "And remember all that have departed in the hope of the resurrection unto life everlasting (and he commemorates by name whomever he wishes from among the departed), and grant them rest where the light of Thy countenance shall visit them"[16] a prayer equally represented in the liturgy of St Basil.[17]

At the time of the preparation (Proskomedia or Prothesis) of both liturgies, the priest commemorates "all our Orthodox fathers and brethren who have departed in the hope of resurrection, life eternal, and communion with Thee, O Lord, Lover of mankind," and sets aside for the intentions of the latter from a 'prosphora' (a small round bread made of two superposed parts symbolizing the two united natures of Christ and upon which is impressed a Cross with the inscriptions IC XC NIKA, 'Jesus Christ Victor'), by means of the 'holy lance' (a small knife in the form of a lance symbolizing the centurion's that pierced the side of Christ), a triangular particle (symbolizing the Holy Trinity). The priest does likewise for the intention of the deceased designated by name in a list[18] handed over to him by the faithful and accompanied by smaller prosphora. After communion, all these set aside particles will be immersed by the officiant in the chalice, while asking that the sins of the faithful for whom these particles were set aside be washed in the blood of Christ and wiped away by His holy sacrifice: "Wash away by Thy precious Blood, O Lord, the sins of all those commemorated, through the prayers of Thy saints."

INDIVIDUAL PRAYERS. Alongside these collective prayers of the Church for the deceased, individual prayers are offered. The formularies for morning and evening prayers make mention of the deceased, but it is customary for the faithful to pray for the deceased of their family in various other circumstances.

Devout Christians, anxious to love all men, extend their prayers beyond the circle of their near and dear. The great spiritual figures in the Orthodox Church are always distinguished by the volume and intensity of their prayers for the deceased, known or unknown to them, testifying to a truly disinterested love with respect to all men. Many saintly priests have distinguished themselves by praying for long hours, within the setting of the preparation for each liturgy, for the thousands of faithful designated by name appearing on the lists of the deceased of their parish and on their personal lists (including their deceased spiritual children).[19]

ALMSGIVING. Numerous Orthodox Fathers, theologians and spiritual figures recommend, beside prayers, the practice of almsgiving to the poor, looking upon it as benefiting the deceased.[20] This is an ancient custom, a trace of which we already find in this recommendation of the *Apostolic Constitutions*: "And let alms be given to the poor out of his goods for a memorial [of the departed]."[21] In the eyes of St John Chrysostom this involves concretely accomplishing an act of charity (the preeminent Christian virtue) the deceased are no longer able to accomplish, substituting oneself in some manner and in their name, with the goal that the grace received from God in response to this practice might be attributed to them.

CANDLES AND LAMPADA. It is customary for the faithful in the Orthodox Church to light two candles before each liturgical service: one for the intention of the living, the other for the intention of the dead. This act is accompanied with a prayer. The candle, by burning throughout the service, symbolizes the perpetuity of the prayer and its integration with that of the community and the entire Church. It is the same for the oil lamps lit upon the tombs of the deceased.[22]

OFFERINGS FOR THE CHURCH. It is also customary to offer, on behalf of the deceased, gifts for the upkeep or construction of churches. Otherwise or in addition, these gifts are represented by the prosphoras offered by the faithful before the liturgy so that the priest might set aside, in reading the dyptichs on behalf of the living and dead inscribed on them, the particles which will be subsequently immersed in the blood of Christ.[23]

d) *Prayers for the dead have for their object all of the deceased.* The liturgical prayers for the deceased make it seem that the former are pronounced in the very first place for the 'faithful who have died in the faith', or the 'faithful departed', or the 'faithful piously fallen asleep', the 'faithful who have fallen asleep in the hope of the resurrection', or the 'faithful who have died in righteousness and in faith', or the 'servants' of God: the majority of the prayers include these details. Some have claimed that the Church should stop there, and that the impious and the faithless should be excluded from its public prayers to become solely the object of the private prayers of the faithful. But it is incontestable that the Church also prays, in the liturgy itself, 'for the salvation of all' mankind. In fact, if the Church, at the liturgy, celebrates the holy Sacrifice of Christ and if Christ has died for all mankind, it would be somewhat inconsistent to exclude certain people from its prayer…

If the order of liturgical prayers is followed, one will notice that the Church most certainly prays first for the just (one of the prayers of the liturgy for the intention of the deceased mentions exclusively "the ancestors, fathers, patriarchs, prophets, apostles, preachers, evangelists, martyrs, confessors, ascetics, and every righteous spirit made perfect in faith"). Several reasons have been given to explain this seemingly paradoxical fact (do the just, who are in paradise, still need someone to pray for them?). The reason for these prayers has been variously explained by the Fathers. According to St Cyril of Jerusalem, their goal is that "God through their [the ancestors, fathers, etc.] intercessory prayers may accept our supplication."[24] For St Epiphanius, we commemorate the just, but "we worship our Lord Jesus Christ to distinguish him from the whole of humanity by our honor of him, remembering that the Lord is not on a level with any man—even though each man has [performed] a million righteous deeds and more."[25] For St Nicetas Stethatos, this involves both honoring the just and calling upon their intercession: "Each year we celebrate the just with praises and hymns on the day of their remembrance, in conformity with the sacred sentence: "'The memory of the just is with praises' [Prov. 10:7]; we congratulate them, we offer incense and light [candles and lampadas] to God and to them, so that they remember us in their intercessions on behalf of the world. They stand in fact before the throne of God with an unutterable joy and confidence, in a position to accept the thanksgiving that we raise with gratitude towards God for their feast, as well as the alms made to the poor in their honor."[26] Other Fathers have proposed a quite different reason, namely that the just have need of prayers from the living since, although abiding in Paradise, they have not yet reached perfection, a consideration referred to by Hebrews 11:40, but also by the Orthodox conception according to which, before the Last Judgment, the condition of those in Paradise as much as in Hell is incomplete.

But the Church also prays for sinners. The ectenia[27] for the intention of the deceased that appears in the liturgy has in mind those of the deceased who have a need for "their sins, both voluntary and involuntary ... [to] be pardoned," asks God to "pardon every transgression which they have committed, whether by word or deed or thought" while reminding God that "there is no man who lives yet does not sin" and that He alone is "without sin." In his commentary on the liturgy, St Cyril of Jerusalem points out: "Then we commemorate also those who have fallen asleep: first of all, the patriarchs, prophets, apostles, and martyrs, that God through their intercessory prayers may accept our supplication. Next we pray also for the holy Fathers and Bishops who have fallen asleep, and generally for all who have gone before us, believing that this will be of the greatest benefit to the souls of those on whose behalf our supplication is offered in the presence of the holy, the most dread Sacrifice."[28]

This prayer for sinners also includes the great sinners. St Theophylact of Bulgaria esteems that the suffrages of the living are presented to God not only for those who have committed slight faults, but likewise for those who have committed serious sins.[29] This opinion is in conformity with the practice of the Church which, on the Saturday of Apocreo/Souls (the day dedicated to the deceased), prays for those who have merited the pains of hell: "From the ever-burning fire, from the darkness without light, from the gnashing of teeth and the worm that torments without ceasing, from every punishment deliver, O our Savior , all who have died in faith."[30] Calling to mind the prayer for the departed during the holy liturgy, St John Chrysostom notes that if one prays for the living who have committed sometimes significant sins, one does not see why one should not pray for the deceased guilty of similar sins. It might be thought that these considerations, like the previous, apply only to sinners who belong to the Church. But the following clarifications indicate that St John Chrysostom has a wider circle in mind: "For God wills that we should be mutually assisted; else why has He ordered us to pray … on behalf of all men? Since in this number are included robbers, violators of tombs, thieves, men laden with untold crimes; and yet we pray on behalf of all; perchance they may turn. As then we pray for those living, who differ not from the dead, so too we may pray for them."[31]

As for St Mark of Ephesus, he observes that the Church, in the liturgy and other circumstances, not only prays for one category of people, but for all the deceased without distinction, and therefore also for the sinners in Hell.[32] He deems it truly fitting to pray above all for those sinners who have died in the faith, but he notes that the saints pray for all sinners without exception and show us the path to follow. However, the outcome of such prayers is uncertain; some particularly serious sins are probably not forgiven; but, on the other hand, there are cases of grave sinners delivered from Hell through the prayers of the faithful or saints. The salvation of all should not be affirmed as a certainty (this would be to profess the condemnable doctrine of apocatastasis), but it can be legitimately hoped for, and should be unquestionably asked of God: "The saints, moved by love for men, and by compassion for their fellow citizens, daring and wishing for what is nearly impossible, pray for the deliverance of all those who have departed in the faith. St Theodore the Studite gives testimony in this way, writing at the very beginning of his Canon for the departed: 'Let us all entreat Christ to deliver from the everlasting fire those who have fallen asleep in faith and in the hope of eternal life.' And next, in another troparion of the Canon, he states: 'From the ever-burning fire, from the darkness without light, from the gnashing of teeth and the worm that torments without ceasing, from every punishment deliver, O our Savior , all who have died in faith.' . . . It is not our concern to seek to know if the saints have been heard by God when they pray for this intention. But they themselves know it, like the Spirit abiding in them and through Whom they were moved, speaking and writing then with this knowledge. Just as Christ the Lord gives us the commandment to pray for our enemies and as He Himself prayed for those who crucified Him, He inspired the first martyr Stephen when they stoned him to death to do the same.

Even though no one can say that when we pray for a particular person we are heard, despite that we should do everything within our power. And offered here for our imitation is the example of certain saints who prayed not only for believers, but also for the impious. And they were heard, and those others, the objects of their prayers, were saved from eternal torment. Thus the first woman martyr Thecla saved Falconille, and the godly Gregory the Great saved the emperor Trajan, as told by him in his Dialogues."[33]

Other later theologians restate this point of view, such as I. Perov who specifies that only those who have blasphemed against the Holy Spirit and those who have willingly and intentionally rejected the grace of the Redemption are excluded from the possibility of being taken out of Hell.[34] One of the most ancient texts that we have on this subject, the *Apostolic Constitutions*, holds that the impious are excluded from the benefits of the suffrages of the living, but by impious it means the enemies of God: "These things we [recommend] concerning the pious; for as to the ungodly, if you give all the world to the poor, you will not benefit him at all. For to whom the Deity was an enemy while he was alive, it is certain it will be so also when he is departed."[35]

e) *The usefulness of prayer and other suffrages for the deceased.* The Fathers insist on the usefulness of suffrages for the deceased. St John Chrysostom writes: "Not in vain are the oblations made for the departed, not in vain the prayers, not in vain the almsdeeds: all those things has the Spirit ordered, wishing us to be benefited one by the other."[36] St Mark of Ephesus makes the same remark and considers that this is confirmed by the fact that an ancient and universal tradition is involved: "There are a multitude of testimonies from Greek and Latin Doctors, expressed in numerous and varied ways, about the fact that those who have entered into their rest in confessing the faith are, without any doubt, helped by the liturgies, prayers and almsgiving made for their intention, since this is a custom in force since antiquity. These verbal and written testimonies have been recorded at different places and in different periods."[37]

1) On the one hand, the deceased can obtain from God, in response to the prayers of the living, pardon of their sins.[38] This is a fact for the Church which, in various liturgical services where it prays for the deceased, asks God to pardon "all their sins, both voluntary and involuntary."

A question has been posed about knowing whether all sins might be pardoned in this way.

For the eastern Fathers and theologians there is no doubt that the pardon of not very grave sins can be easily obtained, at the moment of their death or a little after, by those who have led good lives, considering the excess of their good works over their sins.[39] Patriarch Dositheus of Jerusalem considers, for those in whom the Good predominates, that sins of this sort no longer matter in the hereafter, that they are generously forgiven by God at the hour of death: if this were not so, no one would be admitted to Paradise after death[40] for, as it is said in the liturgy "there is no man who lives yet does not sin" (cf. 1 John 1:8).

Orthodox Fathers and theologians are equally in agreement in thinking, because Christ Himself has said so, that the sin of blasphemy against the Holy Spirit can be pardoned neither in this world or the other (Matt. 12:31).

As for the other serious sins, they think that they are able to be pardoned by God in response to the suffrages of the living.[41] Their certainty on this subject is based in particular on this word of Christ: "Every sin and blasphemy shall be forgiven men, but the blasphemy of the Spirit shall not be forgiven. And whosoever shall speak a word against the Son of man, it shall be forgiven him: but he that shall speak against the Holy Spirit, it shall not be forgiven him neither in this world, nor in the world to come" (Matt. 12:31–32), a word from which we can deduce that serious sins other than that of blasphemy against the Spirit might be pardoned in the hereafter.

St Theophylact of Bulgaria insists especially on the fact that the power to pardon everything belongs to God: "For not all sinners who die are cast into Gehenna: God has power to do this, but also to forgive. I say this because of the offering of prosphora loaves and the giving of alms on behalf of the dead. These things have no small effect even on those who have died in grievous sins. God does not always cast into Gehenna such a sinner after he has died, but He has the power to do so."[42] Patriarch Dositheus of Jerusalem who, as we have seen, considers that non-serious sins are pardoned at the very hour of death, considers that the raison d'être for the suffrages of the Church are truly serious sins: the souls of sinners guilty of mortal sins are able to be relieved and drawn from hell by the prayers of the living; before the Last Judgment the sentence of Christ against the reprobate is still not definite and everything therefore remains possible; only after the Last Judgment will all hope of deliverance be lost for the damned.[43]

Other Fathers or theologians show themselves to be more reserved however, for fear that such considerations might be understood in the sense of the heretical theory of apocatastasis. Thus, Michael Glykas,[44] referring to the authority of Dionysius the Areopagite, considers that prayers for the deceased should be made for the intention of all, but that serious sins will not be pardoned: "Not to be doubted is the efficacy of good works that some people offer for the pious who have died, surely, but are sinners. Our confidence is based above all on the disciples of Christ and the Apostles who have established that the dead would be remembered publicly on the third, ninth and fortieth days, and on the anniversary... But do not say: since the sacrifices are offered universally to God for the deceased, therefore everyone also attains salvation. To dispel this objection, here we have, before any other one, the opinion of the great Dionysius who teaches admirably well which, among sinners, can be pardoned and which do not receive forgiveness. For he says this about those who quit this life still stained with sin: 'If they are stained with only slight sins, good works done for their intention will be of use to the deceased; but, if their sins are serious, God will thrust these far from them.'"[45]

St Mark of Ephesus proves to be even more nuanced: he thinks that minor sins will be surely forgiven by God at the moment of death, and as for serious sins, some will be forgiven at the request of the living or by God's mercy alone, but others will not be: "or even [serious] sins, after a certain time, by a just judgment, are discharged and pardoned, and that completely, or else the responsibility of sinners for them persists until the Last Judgment."[46]

With respect to the previous considerations, certain Orthodox Fathers and theologians do not hesitate to affirm that the souls abiding in Hell and for whom the Church prays are purified and see their spiritual state changed and improved.[47] But they reject, on the one hand, the idea of an automatic, systematic and universal purification through a punishment suffered by the deceased after their death—an idea leading to the heretical doctrine of the apocatastasis—, and on the other the Latin idea, connected to the idea of Purgatory, according to which this purification should be accomplished in a particular place (Purgatory), and by means of a material fire either at least created and temporary (the 'purgatorial fire') and/or by means of a punishment produced by this fire.[48] They equally think that the souls of the deceased so disposed (for this should not be imposed upon them),[49] receive this purification and transformation from God passively, from without, on behalf of the living, for they themselves are no longer in a position to actively obtain this through their own works.[50] This passivity is, however, not total. Father Sergius Bulgakov notes: "prayer, of course, supposes not only intercession before the Creator, but a direct action on the soul, an awakening of the powers of the soul, capable of making it worthy of pardon."[51]

Among all the 'suffrages', the Fathers and theologians think the holy liturgy is most in a position to obtain from God this pardon and purification.[52] St Gregory the Great affirms this more than anyone else and, for this, bases himself on various apparitions and revelations.[53] We have seen that the priest, at the time of the celebration of the Holy Sacrifice, asks for the sins of those commemorated to be washed in the very blood of Christ while immersing, in the holy chalice, the particles previously set aside when listing their names.

2) On the other hand, the deceased in hell can receive, to a more or less significant extent, a consolation and a lessening of their pains.[54] This is affirmed by a very ancient text enjoying great authority concerning a revelation made to St Macarius the Great: "Whenever you take pity on those who are in torments, and pray for them, they feel a little respite."[55] St John Chrysostom elucidates this theme on many occasions. Several texts more particularly mention the consolation that the prayer of the living can obtain for the deceased: "Help him [the one who has departed] as far as possible, not by tears, but by prayers and supplications and alms and offerings. For not unmeaningly have these things been devised, nor do we in vain make mention of the departed in the course of the divine mysteries, and approach God on their behalf, beseeching the Lamb Who is before us, Who takes away the sin of the world—not in vain, *but that some refreshment may thereby ensue to them.* Not in vain does he that stands by the altar cry out when the tremendous mysteries are celebrated, 'For all that have fallen asleep in Christ, and for those who perform commemorations in their behalf.' For if there were no commemorations for them, these things would not have been spoken: since our service is not a mere stage show, God forbid! Yea, it is by the ordinance of the Spirit that these things are done. Let us then give them aid and perform commemoration for them. For if the children of Job were purged by the sacrifice of their father, why do you doubt that when we too offer for the departed, *some consolation arises to them?*"[56] The same Father writes elsewhere: "Let us weep for [our dead]; let us assist them according to our power; let us think of some assistance for them, small though it be, yet still let us assist them. How and in what way? By praying and entreating others to make prayers for them, by continually giving to the poor on their behalf. *This deed has some consolation.*"[57]

Other texts by the same saint insist above all on a lessening of pain that the prayers of the living can obtain for souls dwelling in Hell: "Here is a [sinner] who has lost all the labor of a whole life ... Then, say, shall we not bewail this man? Shall we not try to snatch him from his perils? For it is, yes, it is possible, if we will, to *mitigate his punishment,* if we make continual prayers for him, if for him we give alms. However unworthy he may be, God will yield to our importunity ... This will overcome God: though it [not be] done by the man himself, yet because of him another is the author of the almsgiving ... Many have profited even by the alms done by others on their behalf: for even if they have not got perfect (deliverance), at least they have found some comfort thence."[58] St Cyril of Jerusalem goes further in affirming that prayers for sinners, especially those uttered at the time of the eucharistic sacrifice, even enable us to obtain from Christ the remission of their punishment:[59] "For I know that many say, what is a soul profited, which departs from this world either with sins, or without sins, if it be commemorated in the prayer? For if a king were to banish certain who had given him offense, and then those who belong to them should weave a crown and offer it to him on behalf of those under punishment, would he not grant a remission of their penalties? In the same way we, when we offer to Him our supplications for those who have fallen asleep, though they be sinners, weave no crown, but offer up Christ sacrificed for our sins, propitiating our merciful God for them as well as for ourselves."[60] The certainty that the deceased in Hell receive from God, in response to the suffrages of the living, a consolation and a more or less great alleviation of their punishment is expressed several times by St Mark of Ephesus in the memorandums that he presented to the Council of Florence.[61]

The two factors—both the pardon of sins, and the alleviation of punishment—are closely linked in the eyes of the eastern Fathers (who do not distinguish between fault and punishment as do the western theologians starting with the high Middle Ages), the second following from the first.[62] Thus, St Nicetas Stethatos notes: "For the ungodly, we implore the pardon and remission of their faults, having fallen down in prayer before God, so that an alleviation of punishment might be granted them, so that they might benefit from a ray of God's goodness for mankind and obtain His mercy and pity; to this end we offer alms and donations to the poor, supplications and prayers all night long, following the apostolic tradition, and bloodless sacrifices for their intention; for we are indeed convinced that their intellectual feelings are affected by these and that they benefit from a slight respite in the afflictions that surround them, as the apostles of Christ think and as revealed to numerous Fathers."[63]

The texts cited speak of a 'consolation', an 'alleviation' of punishment, or a 'slight respite in the afflictions' endured by sinners in Hell. The Fathers consider however that, in certain cases, the prayers of the living, of saints in particular, can obtain from God more than that, namely that certain sinners whose lives were not totally evil may be totally pardoned of their sins and freed from their punishment, and can either at the time of the Last Judgment avoid Gehenna, or from now on depart from the 'places of torment' and enter into the dwellings of the just.[64] For Orthodox Fathers and theologians hell in fact remains open, and it will be closed definitively only after the ultimate Judgment.[65] For example, Theophilus of Campania writes: "Ever since it was trampled underfoot by the all-powerful soul of Christ, hell remains always open; it has not been shut by the general sentence of Christ. This is why the prayers, the liturgies of the holy Church and alms given to the poor for the Orthodox departed remain efficacious, and by them many souls are delivered from the torments consistent with the character and seriousness of their sins."[66] These Fathers and theologians often cite the case of Falconille, delivered from hell by the prayers of St Thecla, that of the emperor Trajan liberated from there following the prayers of St Gregory the Great[67] and that of the iconoclast emperor Theophilus, whose pardon was obtained after his wife Theodora had asked the monks, clergy, and all the faithful to pray for him.[68] These cases are, however, considered exceptional. In the treatise *Concerning Those who have Died in the Faith* long attributed to St John of Damascus and which, under this sponsorship, has had a great influence on later theologians, it is asserted that impenitent sinners are not usually delivered by suffrages for the deceased.[69] A good many theologians affirm however that, although the majority of great sinners cannot avoid Gehenna or be totally freed from their present torments, they are however able to receive a little relief from the prayers of the faithful. Thus St Mark of Ephesus writes: "We understand that even souls detained in hell and already delivered up to eternal torment, either in fact and experience, or in a hopeless expectation (of the latter), can be helped and receive a certain small relief. However, this cannot deliver them completely from torment, or give them hope in a final deliverance."[70] St Mark of Ephesus is here referring to a revelation made to St Macarius[71] and to a prayer of St Basil read on Pentecost at the time of the Kneeling Service.[72] We can conclude with

St Epiphanius of Cyprus that, in every instance, "prayer for the deceased is beneficial to them, even if it does not obtain everything that it asks."[73]

f) *The responsibility of the living towards the condition and progress of the deceased.* As we have seen, when an individual dies the faculties of his soul unrelated to the body and life in the sensible world remain in his possession and retain the possibility of being exercised. On the other hand, the deceased is no longer able to act spiritually for or against his salvation:[74] he is no longer able to sin,[75] but neither is he any longer able to do whatever he can to cure the passions and sins he carried within himself at the time of his death and which subsist in him after this has occurred. After death, numerous Fathers clearly affirm, to repent is impossible.[76] The deceased person who has not repented in time finds himself in the situation of the foolish virgins who, at the moment when the bridegroom arrives, no longer have any oil in their lamps and no longer have the means to obtain some (Matt. 25:1–13).[77] This is the reason why numerous spiritual figures invite the faithful to repent continually for fear that they be carried off unexpectedly by death. "As long as we are in this world, even if we commit countless sins it is possible to wash them all away by manifesting repentance for our offenses: but when once we have departed to the other world, even if we display the most earnest repentance it will be of no avail," notes St John Chrysostom.[78] Only the living are henceforth able to do something for the deceased and ask God to pardon their sins and free them from their passions, so that they may be made worthy of obtaining a better condition. This is why the prayer of the living for the deceased assumes such a great importance and why the living have such a great responsibility towards the condition and final lot of the dead.

On this subject, St John Chrysostom refers to the solidarity that unites the members of the one Body of Christ, and to the fact that, as St Paul says, within this body certain members that are stronger can and should come to the aid of the weaker (cf. 1 Cor. 12:12–26) and have the possibility, to a certain extent, of substituting themselves for them and obtaining from God the benefit of those graces they have asked for and received in their name, those who are stronger being either the living themselves who pray, or the saints whose intercession they have asked for: "Since God is wont to grant the petitions of those who ask for others. And this Paul signified saying, 'that for this gift obtained for us by the means of many persons thanks may be given by many in our behalf' (2 Cor. 1:11). Let us not then be weary in giving aid to the departed, both by offering on their behalf and obtaining prayers for them ... Therefore with boldness do we then entreat for the whole world, and name their names with those of martyrs, of confessors, of priests. For in truth one body are we all, though some members are more glorious than others; and it is possible from every source to gather pardon for them, from our prayers, from our gifts in their behalf, from those whose names are named with theirs."[79] St John Chrysostom notes that in the Bible are to be found examples of God sparing sinners because of the prayers and good deeds of some of the just: "Hear the words of God Himself, when He says, 'I will defend this city for My own sake, and for My servant David's sake' (2 Kings 20:6). If the remembrance only of a just man had so great power when deeds are done for one, how great power will it not have [for the dead]?"[80]

g) *Under what conditions the deceased profit from the suffrages offered for their intention.* The effect of prayers and other 'suffrages' of the living on behalf of the deceased cannot be imposed on the latter against their will. Respect for the freedom of each person is a principle highly valued by Orthodox anthropology and theology which stress that even God does not wish to impose anything on man against his will, were it for his own good. The deceased can then benefit from the suffrages of the living (or more exactly from the grace that God bestows upon them in response to these suffrages) only to the extent that their will is not opposed to this and it does not run counter to their deepest desire. For this reason the prayers of the living are of no benefit to the great sinners who have refused to repent or whose will, at the moment of their death, was directed towards a denial of any repentance and by a rejection of God and His mercy. On the other hand, those who have died without having had time to repent, but who would have done so had they had the opportunity, those in general whose will and desire, at the moment of death, are directed towards the divine good things and who have prepared themselves as much as possible to receive them, can directly benefit from these suffrages. This point is the object of a long explanation on the part of Dionysius the Areopagite when he clarifies the meaning of the prayers of the priest on behalf of the deceased during the funeral ceremony:

> Coming forward then the divine hierarch offers sacred prayer over the deceased ... The prayer is to the divine goodness, asking pardon for the deceased for all the sins caused by human frailty, beginning that he be established 'in the light ... in the land of the living,' 'in the bosom of Abraham,' Isaac, and Jacob,

'where pain and grief and lamentation shall flee away'... While agreeing with what I am saying you might nevertheless declare yourself unable to understand why it is that the hierarch beseeches the divine goodness to pardon the sins of the deceased and to grant him the same order and the same lot as those who have lived in conformity with God. If under the workings of divine justice each one receives a return for whatever good or bad he did in this life and if it is the case that the deceased has terminated his lifetime activity, then by what prayers could the hierarch win for the dead person such a change of condition that it would be different from what he had earned during his life here? Now I know well that each one will receive what he deserves, for scripture says that the Lord has shut the door on him and 'each one will receive good or evil, according to what he has done in the body.' And scriptural truth has passed on to us the fact that the prayers of the just are of use only to those who are worthy of them, and only in this life, not after death. Did Saul profit in any way from Samuel? Were the Hebrew people helped at all by the prayers of the prophet? And just as it would be silly for a man whose eyes have been torn out to pretend that he shares in the light which the sun bestows only on those with unharmed eyes, so too would it be foolish to cling to the impossible and empty hope of gaining the intercession of the saints when one has driven aside their naturally sacred activities by one's refusal to accept the gifts of God and by contempt for the most lustrous of God's good commandment. Nevertheless, following scripture, I say that the prayers of the saints in this life are extremely valuable for the one who has a longing for the sacred gifts, who has made a holy preparation to receive them, and who, knowing his own weakness, has sought out some holy man to beg him to be his helper and to join him in his prayers. Such help can only be of the greatest possible assistance to him, since it will gain for him the most divine gifts which he desires. The divine goodness will accept him because of his well-shaped disposition, because of the respect he shows for the saints, because of the praiseworthy eagerness with which he begs for those longed-for gifts, and because of the life he lives in harmony with this and in conformity to God ... So, then, regarding this prayer under discussion which the hierarch offers for the deceased, it is to be explained in accordance with what has been handed down to us by those godlike men, our leaders. As scripture says, the divine hierarch makes known the judgment of God, for he is 'the angel of the all-powerful Lord God.' From what God has told him in scripture he knows that to those who have lived in a most pious fashion there are given a bright, divine life under the most just guidelines, for in his kindly love for man the divinity closes his eyes to the faults coming from human weakness. "No one," says Scripture, "is free of filth." The hierarch knows well what the true scriptures have promised and he prays that they be fulfilled and that those who have lived holy lives may receive their blessed reward.[81]

h) *What benefit the living derive from their prayers for the dead.* To pray for the dead is equally beneficial for the living. This, notes St Epiphanius, supports and reinforces the hope of the living in another life and in the resurrection.[82]

But also and above all this prayer maintains, establishes, or reestablishes a bond of love between the living and the dead.

2 The Relationships of the Dead with the Living.

a) *Forgetfulness of the world but concern for the living.* In the state that is theirs, whatever its nature, the souls of the deceased have in large part forgotten the world; they no longer exist in its living conditions and subsist in another modality of space and time; they are estranged from its preoccupations and activities. Nonetheless, they retain the possibility of knowing about it. Under their new conditions, the deceased have acquired a new "clear and profound" knowledge of the living,[83] at least of those who are their near and dear or who enter into relationship with them through prayer. This is a spiritual knowledge that has as its object the spiritual reality of the living. Thus the dead do not see every detail of our material life,[84] but know of our situation, our state, our dispositions and our spiritual needs.[85]

It is from this spiritual point of view, and in terms of what they know in their present condition about the possible destinies of the living, that the deceased retain and even develop a concern for them.

This is true for the souls suffering in hell: Christ Himself reveals this in the parable of Lazarus and the wicked rich man, where we see that the latter is preoccupied with the lot and future of his five brothers who have remained on earth, and he asks Abraham to send Lazarus to "testify unto them, lest they also come into this place of torments" (Luke 16:27–28).

If those in hell, especially busy deploring their own lot to the point of forgetting everything else,[86] are anxious for the living to avoid their circumstances, on the other hand, the just in Paradise are expressly preoccupied about the salvation of everyone living on earth. "I am convinced," writes St Gregory Nazianzus, "that the holy souls of the departed closely follow, understand and feel concern for our souls."[87] We find in the *Sayings of the Desert Fathers* and the *Lives* of the saints numerous testimonies of these preoccupations: many saints, before their death, affirm that they will continue to watch over the members of their circle and assist them from wherever they are, and a majority of the accounts of the apparitions of saints to the living testify to their solicitude regarding them.[88] Origen expresses in this way the feeling of solidarity within the body of Christ itself and the solicitude experienced by the saints towards those on earth: "One of the most supreme virtues according to the divine Word is the love of neighbor. And we must suppose that it is far more present in the saints who have already fallen asleep toward those struggling in life than in those who are still in human weakness and struggle alongside their inferiors. For it is not only here below that there applies to those who love the brethren the saying 'If one member suffers, all the members suffer together; and if one member is honored, all the members rejoice together' (1 Cor. 12:26). Indeed, it is fitting also for the love of those outside this present life to speak about 'the anxiety for all the churches. Who is weak, and I am not weak? Who is made to fall, and I am not indignant?' (2 Cor. 11:28–29). And Christ says the same when He confesses that with each of the saints in sickness He is sick and, similarly, that He is in prison, naked, a stranger, hungry, and thirsty (Matt. 25:35–36)."[89] As for St Cyprian of Carthage, he mentions the continuity of a solidarity and mutual intercession established during everyone's lifetime: "Let us be mindful of one another, being united in heart and one in spirit; let us on either side pray constantly for one another; let us lighten the burden of our trials and tribulations by our mutual love. And if any one of us, blessed through God's favor with a speedy death, should go on ahead before the others, let our charity continue still before the presence of the Lord, let our prayers not cease on behalf of our brothers and sisters in the presence of our merciful Father."[90]

b) *The intercession of the dead on behalf of the living.* The interest of the deceased faithful in the living and their preoccupation with their salvation is shown in the spiritual assistance given to them, either by inspiring, guiding, and directly protecting them,[91] or by praying and interceding for them before Christ, the Mother of God, and the saints to whom they are now closer.[92] Since Christ is the sole Mediator, "the saints who have fallen asleep in the Lord are not called mediators, but intercessors and petitioners before God on our behalf, for they are as if ambassadors," writes the patriarch Dositheus of Jerusalem.[93] One might even say that "the whole existence of saints after their death is one unceasing prayer, a continual co-assitance" for the world.[94]

This is why for their part the living pray to the deceased faithful, the saints in particular, asking them to intercede for them. St Nicetas Stethatos writes: we celebrate the memory of the just "so that they will remember us in their intercessions on behalf of the world; they truly stand before the throne of God with an unutterable joy and confidence, in a position to welcome [the prayers] that we raise up with gratitude."[95]

We have seen in previous chapters that, in certain cases, the righteous deceased, the saints in particular, can appear to the living. But this remains exceptional. In the parable of Lazarus and the wicked rich man, it is revealed to us by the voice of Abraham that God restricts these apparitions, and we have heard St John Chrysostom explain why, generally, these apparitions are not desirable. The presence and activity of the saints in the world on behalf of the living is exercised most often invisibly, and when they have to express themselves visibly, they generally do so through the intermediary of their relics and icons which manifest to the minds of the living, through the intermediary of their senses, the divine energies of which the saints are bearers and which they communicate on behalf of God to those who ask for them.

c) *The common life of living and dead Christians in the bosom of the Church.* As Father Georges Florovsky writes, "earthly death, the separation of soul and body, do not destroy the relationship of the believer with the Church; it does not alienate him from his condition and familiar place; it does not separate him from the other members of the Church."[96] The Church is composed at once of the living and the dead which, together, are the body of Christ. The living and the dead are in communion among themselves, just like the living among themselves and the dead among themselves. One of the expressions of this communion—frequently called 'the communion of the saints'—is mutual prayer. According to Nicholas Cabasilas, however, it has a still more profound reality: according to him the deceased faithful, invisibly, and mystically share beside the living in eucharistic communion:

> We have seen that this divine and holy sacrifice sanctifies in two ways. First by intercession; the offerings we make, by the very fact of being offered, sanctify those who offer them, as well as those for whom they are offered, and cause God to look favorably upon them. Secondly, by participation; for the offering becomes for us true meat and drink, as the Savior said. Of these two ways, the first is common to the living and the dead, since the sacrifice is offered for both; but the second is possible only to the living, since the dead can no longer eat or drink. What then? Because of this, are the dead not to benefit from the sanctification that comes from communion? Are they to be in this worse off than the living? By no means; for Christ himself communicates with them in a mysterious way known only to him. To make this clear, let us consider the essential causes of this sanctification, and see whether the souls of the dead as

well as of the living cannot possess it. Does it come because one has a body, approaches the holy table on one's feet, receives the holy species in one's hands, takes them in one's mouth, and eats and drinks them? Certainly not; for many who communicate in this fashion and come thus to the holy mysteries gain no benefit from it, but return the worse for grave sins. What then are the causes of sanctification in those who are made holy? What conditions does Christ demand? Purity of heart, love of God, desire for the sacrament, zeal for communion, a glowing ardor, a burning thirst. These are the means by which we draw sanctification to ourselves; these are necessary if we are to partake of Christ; without them true communion is impossible. Yet none of these is the property of the body; all are characteristic of the soul. Therefore there is nothing to prevent the souls of the dead from possessing them as well as those of the living. If then the soul is ready and prepared to receive the sacrament, and if he who has the power to sanctify and perfect wishes to do so, and desires to continue to give himself, what can hinder such a communion? Absolute nothing. Then, you will say, if a living man has the dispositions which you mention in his soul, and yet does not partake of the holy mysteries, will he nevertheless receive the sanctification which the sacrament gives? Not in all cases; only when it is physically impossible for him to receive the elements, as it is for the dead. Such was the case of the solitaries who lived in the desert, or in caves and grottoes in the mountain-side, and could not avail themselves of priest or altar. Christ gave them this sanctification in an invisible manner. We know this because they had life, which they could not have had without partaking of the sacrament, for Christ himself said: "Except ye eat the flesh of the Son of Man and drink his blood, ye have no life in you." Another proof is the fact that God sent angels to several of these men with the sacrament. If, however, a man could come to the altar but does not, it is impossible for him to receive the sanctification which the sacrament brings; this is not because he does not come, but because he could come and will not; for this shows that his soul is void of the good dispositions required for the sacrament. What desire, what longing for the holy table does he possess who could easily come to it but will not? What faith in God has he who does not fear the Savior's threats concerning those who despise this banquet? How can one believe in the love of him who, although able to receive the sacrament, does not bother to do so? It is not then surprising that Christ should grant to those departed souls who are innocent of such faults a share in this sacred banquet. It is amazing and supernatural that a man living in corruption can nourish himself on incorruptible flesh; but what is strange in the idea of an immortal soul nourishing itself on immortal food, as is its nature? And if the first thing, which is marvelous and beyond nature, has been accomplished by God in his ineffable love and hidden wisdom, why should he not accomplish the other, which is both logical and likely? ... As far as sanctification is concerned, those souls which are free of the body have an advantage over those still living in the flesh. It is true that they receive, through the prayers of the priest and the intercession of the holy offerings, purification and the remission of their sins, just as the living do. But they can no longer sin, and do not add new wrongdoing to the old, as most of the living do; they are either entirely absolved from all blame, or at least freed for ever from the possibility of further sin. Because of this, they are better disposed for communion with the Savior, not only than the majority of the living, but also than they would themselves have been if they were still in the flesh. The very fact of being free from the bonds of the flesh makes them far more worthy to receive the holy mysteries than they could possibly have been if they were still housed in their bodies. We know that in the next world there are many mansions, so that every degree of goodness may be glorified, and none may go unrewarded by the most just and loving Judge. Thus, those worthy of the greatest rewards, who are perfect, and who inherit perfect blessedness, such as St Paul, enjoy this happiness more purely after death than they did while still in this life. So also those who are called to a lower position in this place of rest naturally gain more fruit from the mysteries than they did while they were alive. We have shown that all peace of soul and the entire reward of virtue, be it great or small, consists only in this Bread and this Chalice, which is partaken of by both living and dead. This is why our Lord himself describes the future happiness of the saints as a banquet; it is in order to show that in the next life there will be nothing save the Holy Table. Thus, the holy sacrifice of the Eucharist is for the dead as well as the living, and just as the latter, as we have said, receive a two-fold satisfaction, so do the former. The dead are in no way inferior to the living; rather, they possess certain advantages over them.[97]

3 The Relationships of the Dead among Themselves.

In the parable of Lazarus and the wicked rich man, the latter, who is in hell, can see Lazarus who abides in the bosom of Abraham and even converses with the latter (Luke 16:23). One might ask, however, if this involves an exceptional situation, a knowledge given through revelation, as some claim,[98] or an habitual state of affairs, as others assert,[99] which consequently would be for those who abide in hell one of the sources of their suffering.

The relationships of the deceased among themselves undoubtedly varies according to their circumstances and their spiritual state.

According to the revelation given to St Macarius of Egypt by a soul dwelling among the great sinners in the depths of hell, souls there are in a state of isolation, deprived of any relationship with each other and even, under usual conditions, unable to see each other. This circumstance is one of the sources of their suffering, which can only be temporarily lessened by the prayer of the

living that enables them to see each other partially: "As far as the sky is removed from the earth, so great is the fire beneath us, we are ourselves standing
in the midst of the fire, from the feet up to the head. It is not possible to see
anyone face to face, but the face of one is fixed to the back of another. Yet when
you pray for us, each of us can see the other's face a little. Such is our respite."[100]
The impossibility of seeing other people face to face symbolically expresses
the situation of withdrawal into oneself, egocentrism, ignorance and mutual
insensitivity, egoist self-love (philautia) and therefore absence of a love for
others produced by sin and basic to the latter; this state, when revealed beyond
the grave in its true nature—that is, in its spiritual negativity, in its opposition
to the first divine commandment and also to the nature and will of God—
becomes for man the source of a terrible suffering.

In Paradise, the condition of souls is quite different: this is characterized by
mutual love, love by which souls resemble God and share in His bounty, and
is then a source of their happiness. This love goes hand in hand with a mutual,
deepened, supernatural knowledge realized in the divine light. St Symeon
the New Theologian refers to this mutual knowledge of the just at length, by
showing how it is based in God upon the relationship that the Father and the
Son have between themselves, and by refuting those who falsely imagine that
anyone who has attained the vision of God would be isolated in their ecstasy
and would remain ignorant of those around them:

> To those who say that the saints will neither see nor know one another, but
> only Him, as supposedly they will be wholly united in all their perceptions to
> Him alone, He will somehow respond clearly and say: 'Have you known Me,
> O men? Have you seen my light? Have you received Me into yourselves?
> Have you learned of the energies of My Holy Spirit by experience, or not?' I
> do not think they will be able to respond and say: 'Yes, Lord.' For, if they do,
> He will answer them in return: 'How then, if you have come to these things
> by experience, do you say that those who are going to have Me within
> themselves will not know one another? I am God Who does not lie; God
> Who is true; Who is holy, and Who dwells in His saints. How then do I dwell
> in them? Just as I have said that I am in the Father, and the Father in Me, so
> also are the saints in Me and I in them; and just as the Father is in Me and I,
> again, in Him, so too I shall dwell in all the saints, and they shall all abide in
> Me.' In addition, He will also say the following: 'If then I am in My saints and
> My saints are in Me, I in the Father and the Father in Me, and as the Father
> knows Me even as I know the Father, then clearly the saints, too, know me and
> I the saints, and just so ought the saints to be known by and know one another

... Therefore, if the saints are like God, and if they shall know Him as well as He knows them, as the Father knows the Son and the Son the Father, then the saints ought both to see and to know each other. Indeed, those who have not yet seen one another in the body ought to know each other then. So, how is it that you do not blush at talking, and inquiring, and teaching about matters concerning which you know nothing? For heaven's sake, it is as if you were already enriched by the knowledge of things which are beyond us all ... Just as the Father is never ignorant of the Son, nor the Son of the Father, just so neither are the saints. They are become gods by adoption through having God indwelling them. They can never be ignorant of each other, but shall look on one another and on each one's glory, like the Son on the Father's glory and the Father on the Son's ... It therefore follows that they who say that the saints will not see or even know one another when they are come to the contemplation of God in fact are simply whistling in the dark. Since they themselves have not arrived at participation in, nor contemplation, nor knowledge of God, they are still chattering about, and giving testimony to matters which they neither understand nor have ever seen.[101]

Chapter Ten

THE RESURRECTION AND THE LAST JUDGMENT

I. THE RESURRECTION

It is an article of faith, included in the *Credo*, that Christ will come again in glory (Matt. 25:31; cf. 24:27) at the end of time to raise the dead, judge all men and inaugurate a Kingdom that will have no end, where all men will live for eternity in a henceforth final condition.

The resurrection of all men has been heralded by the Prophets, especially by Isaiah (Isa. 26:19), Daniel (Dan. 12:2–3), and above all Ezekiel, whose impressive prophecy (Ezek. 37:1–14) is solemnly read in Orthodox churches at the end of the office of matins on Great Saturday.[1] It has been announced by Christ Himself (Mark 12:25–26, John 5:25–29, 11:25), and next by His Apostles (Acts 4:2, 17:31–32, 23:6, 24:14–16; Rom. 6:5; 1 Thes. 4:13, 18; Heb. 6:2; 11:35). His own resurrection is the first accomplishing of it (He is "the firstborn from among the dead" [Col. 1:18, Rev. 1:5], the "firstfruits of those who have fallen asleep" (1 Cor. 15:20, 23]), the source, basis, and guarantee (see 1 Cor. 15:12–22). Its pledge and prefiguration[2] are those resurrections of the dead performed by Him already (see Matt. 9:23–25, Luke 7:11–15, John 11:17–44), then, in His name and through His grace, by the Apostles (Acts 9:36–42) and the saints; but those who have been resurrected have died anew, while those resurrected at the end of time will die no longer; death will be ultimately destroyed by Christ (1 Cor. 15:26).

1 The Time and Modalities of the Resurrection.

The resurrection will be accomplished at the time of the second coming (Parousia)of Christ (Matt. 24:29–31, Mark 13:24, 27, Luke 21:25–27), at a time known to the Father alone (Matt. 24:36) and decided by God alone.

It is through Christ (1 Thes. 4:14), with Him (1 Thes. 4:14) and in Him (1 Cor. 15:22), by the power of the Holy Spirit (Rom. 8:11),[3] that God will give life to those who are dead (Rom. 8:11).

We do not know how the resurrection will be accomplished. "All that is extraordinary and the mode of its realization is unknown to us, whereas, for the Creator, this is obviously very easy and quite simple to accomplish."[4] The process of resurrection is described in the prophecy of Ezekiel, but in an image-filled, symbolic manner. This does not imply, for all that, a resurrection symbolic in nature. Confronted by the criticisms of other religions, the apologists of the early centuries have shown that, for Christianity, the resurrection has indeed a real and not a symbolic sense, that it is indeed a resurrection of the body and not an inner, spiritual resurrection in the minds of believers. St Paul had developed, prior to them, a line of argument to show that, if there is no resurrection of the dead, our faith is vain (cf. 1 Cor. 15:1–18). To the sceptical currents that have traversed western Christianity in the twentieth century, especially the attempt at 'demythologizing' carried out by some Catholic and Protestant theologians (R. Bultmann in particular), the arguments of the Fathers[5] can be opposed almost unchanged, for modern critical arguments are essentially identical to those developed in the course of the early centuries by the enemies of Christianity.

To those for whom the resurrection of the body—the components of which have not only been dispersed, but corrupted and almost annihilated by death—seems an impossibility, the Fathers pointed out that to God, who is all-powerful, everything is possible; it is easier for Him to reconstitute something which had existed and transform it than to create, as He has done, the entire world out of nothing.[6] "If God produced all things whatever out of nothing," writes Tertullian, "He will be able to draw forth from nothing even the flesh which had fallen into nothing; or if He molded other things out of matter, He will be able to call forth the flesh too from somewhere else, into whatever abyss it may have been engulfed."[7]

2 Resurrection Involves All Men.

All men will be resurrected, whatever their state or spiritual destiny.[8] Christ Himself attests to this: "The hour is coming in which all who are in the graves will hear His [the Son of Man's] voice and come forth—those who have done good, to the resurrection of life, and those who have done evil, to the resurrection of condemnation" (John 5:28–29). St Paul reaffirms it: "There will be a resurrection ... both of the just and the unjust" (Acts 24:15). And the Church sings: "Everyone set in the earth, his mother, will again return thence to receive punishment or reward for his life's actions."[9]

As for those living at the time of Christ's second coming, they will be re-united with the deceased who have risen, their bodies transformed so to be made similar, in their mode of existence, to the risen bodies. "For if we believe that Jesus died and rose again, even so God will bring with Him those who sleep in Jesus. For this we say to you by the word of the Lord, that we who are alive and remain until the coming of the Lord will by no means precede those who are asleep. For the Lord Himself will descend from heaven with a shout, with the voice of an archangel, and with the trumpet of God. And the dead in Christ will rise first. Then we who are alive and remain will be caught up together with them in the clouds to meet the Lord in the air. And thus we shall always be with the Lord" (1 Thess. 4:14–17). The Apostle clarifies elsewhere: "We shall not all sleep, but we shall all be changed" (1 Cor. 15:51).

3 The Nature of the Resurrected Body.

a) *Each person will again find his own body.* At the resurrection, each person will again find the body that was his during his earthly life.[10] The *same* body is resurrected.[11] "It is a clear and fixed point," writes Tertullian, "that the body which is to rise again is that which was sown in death."[12] St John Chrysostom asserts that, if it were otherwise, there would be no victory over death and corruption, but both would be triumphant;[13] he also contends it would be unjust and incomprehensible for the body that enjoys glory in the Kingdom of heaven to be other than the one that suffered and endured tribulations on earth.[14] The risen body will have, then, the same nature or essence (it will be a human body);[15] it will, moreover, retain its personal identity:[16] it will be the body of a particular person, enabling it to be identified,[17] and not the body of some other person.[18] In the totality of his being, body and soul, "Peter is Peter, and Paul, Paul, and Philip is Philip. Each person in his own unique nature and personality remains," St Macarius of Egypt makes clear.[19] No metempsychosis or reincarnation is involved here, the Fathers insist.[20] Athenagoras notes that the future resurrection points to the unicity of the person and human existence which has been marred by division and discontinuity, the extreme form of which is death.[21] He even sees resurrection as the only means by which the same soul will find again the same body and by which the identity of the human person is assured: "It is impossible for the same men to be reconstituted unless the same bodies are restored to the same souls. But that the same soul should obtain the same body is impossible in any other way, and possible only by the resurrection."[22]

b) *The mode of existence of this body will differ from that of earthly life.* The resurrected body will be the same and yet different. It will retain the same essence, substance, or nature, but will have another mode of existence. To return to the vocabulary of St Maximus the Confessor, it will have the same *logos* of nature (λόγος φύσεως), but a different mode of existence (τρόπος ὑπάρξεως). Tertullian explains that "a thing may undergo a complete change, and yet remain still the same thing. In like manner, a man also may be quite himself in substance even in the present life, and for all that undergo various changes— in habit, in bodily bulk, in health, in condition, in dignity, and in age, in taste, business, means, houses, laws and customs—and still lose nothing of his human nature. And so he does not cease being himself, does not become someone else, but exists otherwise ... [C]hanges, conversions and reformations will necessarily take place to bring about the resurrection, but the substance of the flesh will still be preserved safe."[23] What the resurrection changes, says Tertullian, is "our condition, not our nature."[24] St Isaac the Syrian likewise notes that, through resurrection, Christ "will bring us into another state."[25]

We have only a few indications about the resurrected body's mode of existence. Some of them are provided by what the Scriptures tell us about Christ after His resurrection, since our bodies will be similar to His.[26] We see then that His body transcends material laws, by entering "when the doors were shut where the disciples were assembled" (John 20:19, 26) or by suddenly making himself invisible (Luke 24:31). And, even though He takes nourishment in the company of His disciples (Luke 24:41–43), this is not by necessity but by economy, so that they will not think that this is a ghost that has appeared to them (cf. Mark 6:49; Luke 24:37), as the *eothinon* in the eighth tone for Sunday matins points out: "Thy disciples thought they were seeing a spirit, but Thou didst calm the turmoil of their souls by showing them Thy hands and feet. Yet when they still doubted, Thou didst take nourishment with them."[27] These indications have, however, only a relative value since Christ, before His ascension, is moving within the framework of this world; living conditions will be otherwise in the future world and bodies will behave differently, in a manner unknown to us from our present living conditions.

St Paul can only give us a presentiment of what the resurrected body will be like by insisting above all on its difference from our present earthly body: "All flesh is not the same flesh, but there is one kind of flesh of men, another flesh of animals, another of fish, and another of birds. There are also celestial bodies and terrestrial bodies; but the glory of the celestial is one, and the glory of the terrestrial is another. There is one glory of the sun, another glory of the moon, and another glory of the stars, for one star differs from another star in glory. So also is the resurrection of the dead. The body is sown in corruption, it is raised in incorruption. It is sown in dishonor, it is raised in glory. It is sown in weakness, it is raised in power. It is sown a natural body, it is raised a spiritual body. There is a natural body and there is a spiritual body ... The first man Adam ... was of the earth, made of dust; the second Man is the Lord from heaven. ... and as is the heavenly Man, so also are those who are heavenly ... we shall all be changed—in a moment, in the twinkling of an eye, at the last trumpet. For the trumpet will sound, and the dead will be raised incorruptible, and we shall be changed. For this corruptible must put on incorruption, and this mortal must put on immortality" (1 Cor. 15:39–53).

To sum up, by setting these two series of indications side by side we are able to deduce that the resurrected body will be a spiritual body, not dependant on the present conditioning of matter, space and time, a powerful, incorruptible and immortal body.

The Fathers return to and explain these scriptural indications. First of all they present the resurrection as "a restoration of the being as a whole,"[28] where the soul and body are reunited anew, the body being however totally renewed.[29] St Gregory of Nyssa thinks that it will be a restoration of the body to its paradisal state. "The resurrection," he writes, "is nothing other than the restoration of our nature to its original state."[30] The resurrected body will be delivered from its infirmities and defects[31] inherited from the Fall and will find its original wholeness once more;[32] and "integrity, whether the result of preservation or restoration, will be able to lose nothing more, after the time that it has given back to it whatever it had lost."[33] But the body, moreover, will no longer exist according to its own present material mode, and will therefore no longer recognize the determinations, necessities or limitations of any sort tied to our current world.[34] It will become "so subtle that it will no longer appear to be at all material."[35] It "will become like the soul;"[36] however, this will not be a psychic but a spiritual body.[37] No longer bearing the image of the earthly but of the heavenly (cf. 1 Cor. 15:49), it will be impassible[38] and incorruptible,[39] no longer having any physical needs (such as hunger, thirst, and sleep)[40] or sickness,[41] physical suffering,[42] weakness,[43] or negative changes of any kind.[44] It will also be immortal,[45] death having been definitively destroyed by Christ. Incorruptibility and immortality are not to be seen here as qualities attributable to man as a dignity or reward, but as a means of gaining access to a condition no longer knowing any alteration or end,[46] whether this condition is blessed or unfortunate.[47]

By the very fact of the resurrection, the body will be perfectly united with the soul.[48] And it will be totally transparent to the divine energies.[49]

4 The State Resulting from the Resurrection.

Resurrection is not only a transformation for the body; it gives man as a whole access to a particular mode of life, different from the mode of earthly life.

The body no longer being subject to material conditions, it will no longer have to be fed, to breath, to reproduce itself, etc. The Fathers, then, have had to pose the question of knowing if, under these conditions, the body would be resurrected with all its faculties—since many of them would be in that case useless to it—and if it would be indeed restored in the fullness and integrity of its nature.[50] The Fathers affirm that the body's organs will subsist.[51] Tertullian specifies that they will be henceforth without function;[52] he points out that even today "it is possible to do without the use of stomach and generative organs" in periods of fasting and abstinence, remaining no less a whole man.[53] By utilizing a more precise vocabulary (to be found among the Cappadocians, St Maximus the Confessor, St John Damascene, and the later Fathers), we can say that the body will preserve its powers (or faculties) but their energies will remain inactive. Tertullian, however, voices a doubt regarding the just formulated hypothesis: it is possible that the organs will "have something to do; for in the presence of God there will be no idleness."[54] Put more judiciously, in the body that has become spiritual and heavenly, the organs, while remaining identical as to their essence, will be transfigured (cf. Phil. 3:21),[55] as well as their functions and energies. They will have then a spiritual function about which Scripture and mystical experience give us some insight when they speak of spiritual sensations[56] and the spiritual use of all the body's organs.[57]

The new mode of resurrected human life will also be marked by a change in the mode of interpersonal relationships. For example, sexual relations between men and women or relations of a familial kind will be abolished in favor of purely spiritual relationships which will not necessarily abolish their intimacy, but will endow the latter with another nature, exempt from the carnal dimension. "When they rise from the dead, they neither marry nor are given in marriage, but are like angels in heaven," Christ affirms (Mark 12:25; cf. Matt. 22:30; Luke 20:35–36).

5 The Spiritual Significance and Finality of the Resurrection.

Resurrection has for its first (in chronological order) finality to reconstitute the human being in his totality, body and soul, which corresponds to his nature, the intermediate state in which body and soul were separated being an unnatural and even anti-natural state. "Man, therefore, who consists of the two parts," notes Athenagoras, "must continue for ever. But it is impossible for him to continue unless he rise again. For if no resurrection were to take place, the nature of men as men would not continue."[58]

The resurrection's second finality is that man is able to be judged by Christ at once in body and soul, the co-actors of his earthly existence and co-responsible for sins and passions as well as for virtues.[59] By way of an anthropological preamble, Tertullian writes: "Since the entire man consists of the union of the two natures, he must therefore appear in both, as it is right that he should be judged in his entirety; nor, of course, did he pass through life except in his entire state. As therefore he lived, so also must he be judged, because he has to be judged concerning the way in which he lived. For life is the cause of judgment, and it must undergo investigation in as many natures as it possessed when it discharged its vital functions."[60] The resurrection is necessary, notes Athenagoras for his part, so that "the parts that were separated and entirely dissolved having been again united, each one may, in accordance with justice, receive what he has done by the body, whether it be good or bad,"[61] "or that which practiced each of the things in life on which the judgment is passed was man, not soul by itself."[62]

The resurrection's third finality is to enable man to participate as a whole, with the fullness of his recovered being, in the condition that will be conferred on him by the final judgment of Christ. In the intermediate state the deceased experience with their souls alone the repose, freedom and rejoicing of paradise, or the torments, bonds and pains of hell. Henceforth, those who must eternally submit to the sufferings of hell, and those who will experience the blessedness of the kingdom of heaven will do so not only in their soul but also in their body.[63] Each one must, says St Paul, "receive the things done in the body, according to what he has done, whether good or bad" (2 Cor. 5:10). "Of course the retribution will have to be paid by the body," comments Tertullian, "since it was by the body that the actions were performed."[64] The soul itself, notes St John Chrysostom, could not by itself alone possess the lasting fullness of the good things of the kingdom of heaven or receive the eternal pains of hell: "Even if the soul abide, even if it be infinitely immortal, as indeed it is, without the flesh it shall not receive those hidden good things;" "for if the body rise not again, the soul abides uncrowned without that blessedness which is in heaven;" without the flesh, "neither truly shall it be punished."[65]

II. THE LAST AND UNIVERSAL JUDGMENT

1 The Author of the Judgment.

After being resurrected, mankind will be judged. It is Christ Himself, coming in His glory (Matt. 25:31), who will carry out this judgment,[66] as proclaimed by the Creed: He "shall come again with glory to judge both the living and the dead." It is He Himself, as St Peter says, "who was ordained by God to be Judge of the living and the dead" (Acts 10:42). He will perform this function on the Father's behalf,[67] for "the Father judges no one, but has committed all judgment to the Son" (John 5:22). The Son will be seated upon a throne (Psalm 9:7–8, Matt. 25:31, Rom. 14:10, 2 Cor. 5:10, Rev. 20:11–12), the symbol of His glory (cf. Matt. 25:31), His supreme authority and universal power. He will be surrounded by all the angels (Matt. 16:27, 25:31),[68] apostles (cf. Matt. 12:27, 19:28) and all the saints (cf. 1 Cor. 6:2).[69]

2 All Men Will Be Judged.

All the men of all time will be judged then by Christ. "All the nations will be gathered before Him" (Matt. 25:32), symbolized by the twelve tribes of Israel (cf. Matt. 19:28). No one shall escape this judgment. "We must all appear before the judgment seat of Christ," St Paul points out (2 Cor. 5:10). Christ "will pass judgment on the whole human race", St Justin affirms.[70] And St Clement of Rome writes: "Where can any of us escape from His strong hand? And what world would receive any of them that desert from His service? ... where shall one flee from Him that embraceth the universe?"[71]

3 The Object of Judgment.

Man will be judged on the totality of his life on earth, from his birth until his death, and for the totality of his conduct during his existence.[72] "The Son of Man will come in the glory of his Father with His angels, and then He will reward each according to his works" (Matt. 16:27).

Christ will reward each according to his deeds,[73] as St Paul affirms (Rom. 2:6), and as St Basil repeats in a prayer of the Midnight Office: Christ "will come in glory, as judge of the universe, to render to each the fruit of their works."[74]

Not only all the acts of man,[75] but all his thoughts[76] and all his words,[77] good or bad, will be taken into account,[78] including the smallest and most insignificant, as revealed symbolically by this word of Christ: "I say to you that for every idle word men may speak, they will give an account of it on the day of judgment" (Matt. 12:36); including also the most hidden. On that day "God will judge the secrets of men by Jesus Christ," affirms St Paul (Rom. 2:16); and St John Chrysostom notes that at this moment "even our most secret thoughts ... will be revealed and laid bare."[79] Men will then, writes St Basil, confirm the truth of this prophecy of Hosea: "Their deeds encompass them, they are before my face" (Hos. 7:2).[80]

The incalculable number of these acts, thoughts, and words, the fact that they have been recorded and memorized, and the fact that they will be recalled at that time are symbolized by the 'books' which will then be opened before Christ:[81] "Then I saw a great white throne and Him who sat on it, from whose face the earth and the heaven fled away. And there was found no place for them. And I saw the dead, small and great, standing before God, and books were opened. And another book was opened, which is the Book of Life. And the dead were judged according to their works, by the things which were written in the books" (Rev. 20:11–12; cf. Dan. 7:9–10).

But, as we have seen in the previous chapter, the suffrages carried out by the living for the dead while the latter abide in paradise or hell will be likewise taken into account in their favor and for their acquittal.

4 The Nature of Judgment.

According to the Fathers, all the works of men, performed throughout their lives, from birth until death, will be supernaturally revealed at that time in the presence of Christ.

Christ is the Word. We can also say that man's spiritual state will be made manifest by the Word of God insofar as the expression of His will and the source of His commandments. St Paul has this to say on the subject: "The word of God is living and powerful, and sharper than any two-edged sword, piercing even to the division of soul and spirit, and of joints and marrow, and is a discerner of the thoughts and intents of the heart. And there is no creature hidden from His sight, but all things are naked and open to the eyes of Him to whom we must give account" (Heb. 4:12–13). And St Symeon the New Theologian elaborates: "neither the style nor composition of belles lettres, nothing of the affairs or riches of the earth will provide you with any help then, when my God will judge all things and all men ... [A]s the commandment of God, alas, comes to meet our life, it will point out the unfaithful from the truly faithful, those who obeyed or disobeyed the words of the Master, those who were industrious or those who were negligent and in this way the unjust will be separated from the just, the disobedient from those who truly obey Christ; those who now are lovers of the world from the friends of God."[82]

But Christ is also light (John 1:4–5, 8:12, 12:46). At the time of the Judgment, says Scripture, He will appear with glory, that is to say in uncreated light. This light will illumine every man and reveal in the presence of God and other men everything each one has done and all that he is even to his most secret depths. Men, say the Fathers following St Paul (Heb. 4:13), will find themselves completely naked.[83] "At the feet of our Judge," writes St John Chrysostom, "all our deeds will be disclosed and exhibited in broad daylight. For, not only will we appear, but even our souls will be exposed."[84] "Happy," says St Basil, "is the one who, on the day of the just judgment of God, when the Lord will come to illumine the secrets of darkness and show the intentions of our hearts, will withstand being under this light that reproaches us for our faults and will return from it without having had to be ashamed of a conscience soiled by perverse actions."[85] For his part, St Symeon the New Theologian notes: "When the Lord comes to those who now hate the light and are unwilling to come to it, the light that is now hidden will be revealed and all that they have hidden will become manifest. Whatever each of us men is now, as we wrap ourselves up and refuse to reveal our condition by penitence, the light will then make it clear and manifest to God and to all men ... Every act of each person, whether good or bad, every word, every thought, every memory that has arisen in us from our very birth till our last breath, will then be gathered together and be revealed in every member of mankind."[86]

We can say then, from a certain point of view, that men will be judged by Christ to the extent that they will be judged by the light of His glory, and, from another point of view, that they will be judged by themselves to the extent that their deeds and spiritual condition will be revealed according to their true nature and will show where their destiny lies. St Gregory of Nyssa thus thinks that the separation of the 'sheep' from the 'goats' will be easy, for each person possesses "a distinctive mark" according to his or her deeds, virtues and passions.[87] St Cyril of Jerusalem points out in the same vein that the 'sheep' and the 'goats' single themselves out to the shepherd by the quality of their fleece.[88]

Having judged themselves, those who deserve condemnation will also condemn themselves. Christ indicates that, basically, it is not He who judges and condemns, and that condemnation is contrary to His intention: "If anyone hears My words and does not believe, I do not judge him; for I did not come to judge the world but to save the world" (John 12:47). And St John Chrysostom reminds us that "He who will be our judge" is "the one who at present forgives our sins," that the one "who will come to judge all mankind" is "the one who died for us," and therefore "unto them that look for Him, says the Apostle, shall He appear the second time without sin unto salvation" (Heb. 9:28).[89]

We find in Scripture different notations that point, in some manner, to the passive role of Christ who simply sits upon His throne and judges by His presence alone, as a revealer of the spiritual condition of those who appear before Him. For example, St Paul writes: "We must all appear before the judgment seat of Christ, that each one may receive the things done in the body, according to what he has done, whether good or bad" (2 Cor. 5:10).

This is the reason why men will be able to be judged simultaneously and in the blink of an eye.

We find among the Fathers, moreover, remarks indicating the role played by the condition and conscience of a person in his judgment when he will find himself in Christ's presence. St Basil of Caesarea affirms that we will have no other accuser than our sins made manifest in their own nature.[90] And St Cyril of Jerusalem writes: "Out of your own conscience shall you be judged, your thoughts the meanwhile accusing or else excusing, in the day when God shall judge the secrets of men (Rom. 2:15–16). The terrible countenance of the Judge will force you to speak the truth; or rather, even though thou speak not, it will convict you. For you shall rise clothed with your own sins, or else with your righteous deeds."[91]

The divine light that will reveal the deeds of men will also be a fire that will test them. "Each one's work will become clear," writes St Paul, "for the Day will declare it, because it will be revealed by fire; and the fire will test each one's work, of what sort it is. If anyone's work which he has built on it endures, he will receive a reward. If anyone's work is burned, he will suffer loss; but he himself will be saved, yet so as through fire" (1 Cor. 3:13–15). St Nicetas Stethatos comments on this passage in this way: "Since the day of judgment will be one of fire, what each of us has done, as St Paul says, will be tested by fire. Thus, if what we have built up is of an incorruptible nature, it will not be destroyed by fire; and not only will it not be consumed, but it will be made radiant, totally purified of whatever small amount of filth may adhere to it. But if the work with which we have burdened ourselves consists of corruptible matter, it will be consumed and burnt up and we will be left destitute in the midst of the fire."[92]

5 Criteria for the Judgment.

As shown by the four symbols used in the parables to refer to those who will be distinguished and separated at the Judgment—the sheep and the goats (Matt. 25:32–46), the wheat and the tares (Matt. 13:24–30), the wise and foolish virgins (Matt. 25:1–13), the invited guests who have put on the wedding garment and those who have not (Matt. 22:1–14) —Christ will judge according to the dispositions acquired by men with respect to God, with respect to their neighbor, and as a preparation for entering into the Kingdom of heaven. To the question: "Why then are some sheep and others goats?", St John Chrysostom answers: "These terms indicate not a difference in nature, but a difference in dispositions."[93] In what do these dispositions of those who will be judged consist? In the purity of their mind and of their heart, in their virtues,[94] that is, in the fact that they have conformed themselves in a lasting manner to the will of God, have practiced His commandments so far as to resemble Him in their interior states, their intentions, their behavior, thus manifesting by participation the qualities that are His by nature. Sheep are at once a symbol of purity (by their whiteness), of richness in virtue (by the abundance of their fleece), of humility (by their docility), and of the practice of the divine commandments (by the fact that they follow the shepherd).[95]

Each person will have to answer for the way in which he will have exercised the virtues appropriate to the functions conferred on him in the course of his life. Those exercising these virtues in an ideal manner will serve then as the norm and criterion for the judging of others, as St Symeon the New Theologian explains so beautifully:

To the patriarchs He [the Judge] will likewise oppose the sainted patriarchs: John of the golden mouth, John the Almsgiver, Ignatius, Tarasius, Methodius, and the rest, who not only by word but by deed were the reflection of the true God. Against the metropolitans He will set the saintly metropolitans: Basil, Gregory his brother and his namesake the Wonderworker, Ambrose, and Nicholas. In short, each patriarch, each metropolitan, each bishop, God will judge by the apostles and the holy Fathers who were illustrious before them in each metropolitan see and diocese. He will set them all opposite each other when you hear Him say, 'The sheep on the right hand, the goats on the left ' (Matt. 25:33). He will say, 'The place where these have worshipped and served me, is it not the same as where you have spent your lives? Did you not sit on their thrones? Why did you not imitate their life and conduct as well? ... Depart from Me, you workers of iniquity, depart!' (Luke 13:27). Thus fathers will be judged by fathers, friend and relatives by friends and relatives, brothers by brothers, slaves and free men by slaves and free men respectively, the rich by those who were rich and the poor by those who were poor, the married by those who have excelled in the married state, the unmarried by those who have lived unmarried. In short, on the awesome day of judgment every sinful man will see one who is like him opposite to him in eternal life, in that unutterable light, and will be judged by him. What do I mean? As every sinner looks on him who is like him, the king upon the king, the ruler upon the ruler, the impenitent whoremonger on the whoremonger who repented, the poor man on the poor man, and the slave on the slave, he will remember that the other one was also a man, with the same soul, the same hands, the same eyes, in short with all other things in common, the same kind of life and the same rank, the same occupation, the same resources. Yet, since he was unwilling to imitate him, his mouth will at once be stopped (Psalm 107:42) and he will remain without excuse (Rom. 1:20), without a word to speak![96]

Among the virtues, the fruits of practicing the commandments, the most important one is charity: the love of God is presented by Christ as the first commandment, and the love of neighbor as the second (Matt. 22:34–40). And charity is traditionally presented by the Fathers as the summit and sum of all the virtues. It is also primarily on the criterion of charity (conceived of indissociably as love of God and neighbor) that men will be judged.[97] The person who, on the day of judgment, will be found naked, "really deprived of divine glory, expelled out of the Kingdom and the heavenly wedding hall," will be so, St Symeon the New Theologian points out, because he will be destitute of the virtues and charity foremost: "Even if he is sinless but is without virtues, he is considered as stark naked. And the first of all the virtues, the queen and the mistress, really is love. It is the head of all the others, both their apparel and their glory. Headless, a body is dead indeed and deprived of respiration. A body without a robe, how will it not be naked? Without charity the virtues are withered and useless. He is devoid of divine glory, the one who has not charity; even if he had all the virtues he is completely naked, and, not bearing his nakedness, he prefers to hide. For, bearing his shame thus, he also bears his condemnation and he hears the 'I do not know you' from the mouth of the judge of the universe."[98]

Christ Himself has revealed this primal importance of love as a criterion of the future Judgment:

> When the Son of Man comes in His glory, and all the holy angels with Him, then He will sit on the throne of His glory. All the nations will be gathered before Him, and He will separate them one from another, as a shepherd divides his sheep from the goats. And He will set the sheep on His right hand, but the goats on the left. Then the King will say to those on His right hand, 'Come, you blessed of My Father, inherit the kingdom prepared for you from the foundation of the world: for I was hungry and you gave Me food, I was thirsty and you gave Me drink, I was a stranger and you took me in; I was naked and you clothed Me; I was sick and you visited Me; I was in prison and you came to Me.' Then the righteous will answer Him, saying, 'Lord, when did we see You hungry and feed You, or thirsty and give You drink? When did we see You a stranger and take you in, or naked and clothe You? Or when did we see You sick, or in prison, and come to You?' And the King will answer and say to them, 'Assuredly, I say to you, inasmuch as you did it to one of the least of these My brethren, you did it to Me.' Then He will also say to those on the left hand, 'Depart from Me, you cursed, into the everlasting fire prepared for the devil and his angels: for I was hungry and you gave Me no food, I was thirsty and you gave Me no drink; I was a stranger and you did not take Me in, naked and you did not clothe Me, sick and in prison and you did not visit me.' Then they will also answer Him, saying, 'Lord, when did we see you hungry or thirsty or a stranger or naked or sick or in prison, and did not minister to You?' Then He will answer them, saying, 'Assuredly, I say to you, inasmuch as you did not do it to one of the least of these, you did not do it to Me.' . . . And these will go away into everlasting punishment, but the righteous into eternal life (Matt. 25:31–46).

6 'The Dread Judgment Seat of Christ.'

The Judgment of Christ is presented by the Fathers and by the Church in its liturgical prayers as dreadful.[99]

The Fathers intentionally repeat frightening expressions and images apt for inspiring fear.[100] The pedagogical role of this material is obvious and at times acknowledged explicitly:[101] this involves encouraging their audience to do what must be done in this life to avoid bringing upon themselves a condemnation to eternal fire in the other. Nevertheless, the Judgment of Christ will be actually dreadful for several reasons:

1) This judgment will cast on man a light that lays bare his interior state and will leave none of his bad actions in the dark; his entire life will be unveiled before Christ, the angels, the saints and all other men, and this will be for him a grounds for shame.[102]

2) While, at the time of the particular judgment, a person benefitted from the defense of the angels, at the time of the Last Judgment he will be defenseless. On that day, writes St John Chrysostom, there will be only "a terrible judgment seat, an incorruptible court, and the deed of each one set before our eyes, no one to help, neither neighbor, nor counsel, nor relative, not a brother, not a father, not a mother, not a friend, not anyone else."[103]

3) The particular judgment was provisional and the lot of the deceased was not definitively set at that point. Although the just will have every good reason to hope to be placed in the Kingdom of heaven, sinners will dread being ultimately cast down into hell. "That day," notes St John Chrysostom, "to them that live in good works is to be desired, even as on the other hand to those in sin, it is a subject of fear and terror, because they will hear the eternal and irrevocable decree of their condemnation."[104]

7 The Truthful and Definitive Character of the Judgment.

The Judgment is called 'Last' Judgment first with respect to the particular judgment, which follows soon after death, second because it occurs at the end of time, and third because it is definitive and final.[105]

Those who will have been judged will not even think of appealing the sentence for, in the divine light, the whole truth of their condition will be apparent, and the judgment passed on them will seem entirely just. "Those who will be condemned," writes St Basil, "will be in complete agreement that 'the judgment passed on them was altogether just.'"[106]

The Fathers also state insistently, following Scripture (see John 5:30, Rom. 2:5, 2 Tim. 4:8, Rev. 19:2, 11), that the judgments passed by He who is preeminently

Truth (John 14:6) and the Just One (Acts 3:14, 22:14, James 5:6, 1 John 2:1) will be entirely truthful and just.[107] The judgments of God and those of men have no common measure.[108] God will judge us impartially (cf. Acts 10:34, Rom. 2:11, Gal. 2:6, Eph. 6:9), that is considering everyone on an equal footing.[109] His sentence will be perfect because He will take into account the quality, quantity, and the magnitude of our sins,[110] and will know how to measure exactly the inward responsibility of each person.[111]

8 Outcome of the Judgment.

The Last Judgment will be a discriminating judgment that will separate men into two groups and only two: those found worthy of enjoying the Kingdom of heaven and those eternally suffering the pains of hell. Christ Himself informs us that He "will separate them one from another, as a shepherd divides his sheep from the goats. And He will set the sheep on His right hand, but the goats on the left. Then the King will say to those on His right hand, 'Come, you blessed of My Father, inherit the kingdom prepared for you from the foundation of the world' ... [And] He will also say to those on the left hand, 'Depart from Me, you cursed, into the everlasting fire prepared for the devil and his angels' ... And these will go away into everlasting punishment, but the righteous into eternal life" (Matt. 25:32–46). The outcome was announced in this way elsewhere by Christ: "those who have done good [will come forth] to the resurrection of life, and those who have done evil, to the resurrection of condemnation" (John 5:29). And this separation into two groups was likewise announced by the parable of the wheat and the darnel (Matt. 13:24–30), the good seed symbolizing the just and their virtues, the darnel the sinners and their passions, while the harvest symbolizes the Judgment, the owner Christ, and the harvesters the angels who assist Him at the Judgment. "The harvest is the end of the age, and the reapers are the angels. Therefore as the tares are gathered and burned in the fire, so it will be at the end of this age. The Son of Man will send out His angels, and they will gather out of His kingdom all things that offend, and those who practice lawlessness, and will cast them into the furnace of fire. There will be wailing and gnashing of teeth. Then the righteous will shine forth as the sun in the kingdom of their Father" (Matt. 13:39–43). The separation into two groups is also symbolized by the parable of the wise and foolish virgins (Matt. 25:1–13), the wise having been found worthy through their virtues (the oil of their lamps) of entering into the wedding hall (the Kingdom of God), while the foolish are shut out and condemned to remain in outer darkness. We again find the same symbol in the parable of the wedding feast where the king (that is to say Christ) receives those who wear the wedding garment (the virtues), but excludes from the feast (the Kingdom) the one who has not put it on, saying to the servants (the angels): "Bind him hand and foot, take him away, and cast him into the outer darkness [hell]; there will be weeping and gnashing of teeth" (Matt. 22:1–14).[112]

Chapter Eleven

ETERNAL LIFE:
THE KINGDOM OF HEAVEN AND HELL

1 Introduction.

We must repeat here what we have already said about Paradise and Hades: the Kingdom of heaven and hell are not physical locales, geographically identifiable, but immaterial and invisible realities.[1] They are, as St Mark of Ephesus says, 'intelligible places'[2] that correspond to states of being,[3] conditions of life, modes of existence.

Scriptural texts often refer to them under a material form (for hell: fire [Matt. 25:41, Mark 9:45], worm [Mark 9:45], weeping and gnashing of teeth [Matt. 13:42]). The Fathers often develop their own commentaries under the same form:[4] they describe materially the various torments of hell and the delights of the Kingdom of heaven, presenting the latter, for example, as a garden with luxuriant vegetation or a banquet where one is served delicious foods[5] (the symbol of a banquet having been utilized moreover by Christ Himself [Matt. 22:1–14, Luke 14:16–24])... The aim here is pedagogics: it has to do with inspiring a fear of hell and exciting a desire for the Kingdom of heaven out of those material realities analogous to the spiritual realities of the hereafter, the realities of earthly life being familiar to listeners and readers, whereas the realities of the hereafter, very different from our present living conditions, remain inaccessible or incomprehensible for them.

In other words, we are dealing with a symbolic expression[6] that we must avoid taking literally. The Fathers moreover explain this,[7] including those who dwell on material descriptions.[8] St Gregory of Nyssa, for example, points out: "Those good things which are held out in the Gospels to those who have led a godly life, are not such as can be precisely described. For how is that possible with things which 'eye hath not seen, neither ear heard, neither have entered into the heart of man' [cf. 1 Cor. 2:9]? Indeed, the sinner's life of torment presents no equivalent to anything that pains the senses here. Even if some one of the punishments in that other world be named in terms that are well known here, the distinction is still not small. When you hear the word fire, you have been taught to think of a fire other than the fire we see, owing to something being added to that fire which in this there is not; for that fire is never quenched, whereas experience has discovered many ways of quenching this; and there is a great difference between a fire which can be extinguished, and one that does not admit of extinction. That fire, therefore, is something other than this. If, again, a person hears the word 'worm,' let not his thoughts, from the similarity of the term, be carried to the creature here that crawls upon the ground; for the addition that it 'dieth not' suggests the thought of another reptile than that known here."[9]

2 The Kingdom of Heaven.

The Kingdom of heaven, shared by the just for eternity, is equally called the 'Kingdom of God', 'Paradise' in a higher sense, or 'eternal life' in a positive sense.[10] The ineffable character of life in the Kingdom of heaven is underscored by the Fathers[11] and St Paul himself: "As it is written: Eye has not seen, nor ear heard, nor have entered into the heart of man the things which God has prepared for those who love Him" (1 Cor. 2:9).

The saints, in their visions and ecstatic experiences, have received an earnest and a certain foreknowledge of it, but they nevertheless affirm its indescribable and inexpressible character. Thus, St Paul, carried up to the 'third heaven', "was caught up into Paradise and heard inexpressible words, which it is not lawful for a man to utter" (2 Cor. 12:4). "O Paradise, we will be able to delight in thee, but we will be unable to comprehend thee," exclaims Nicodemus of the Holy Mountain.[12]

And yet these experiences of the saints, the teaching of Christ and the apostles above all, give us a few indications about the Kingdom of heaven.

We know that it consists of good things prepared by God from the beginning for those who will be worthy to receive them: "Then the King will say to those on His right hand, 'Come, you blessed of My Father, inherit the kingdom prepared for you from the foundation of the world'" (Matt. 25:34).

The good things of the Kingdom are sometimes presented negatively by the Fathers as the absence of all the evils known to this world or, more positively, as the sum of good things of which we are deprived by the evils of this world.[13]

In the Kingdom, writes St John Chrysostom, "whence pain, distress and groaning have fled... there is no grief... or faintheartedness, or wailing... all obstacles [are] removed; no alarm anywhere, no disturbance ... *the land of the living*: that is true life, free of death, having good things that are uncontaminated ... no grief remains, no concern, no desire, and so everything will be joy, everything peace, everything love, everything happiness, everything that is true, unalloyed and stable."[14]

But we have only an introduction here, for the good things of the Kingdom are clearly more than all the good things of this world and do not even have anything in common with them. "The Kingdom of heaven," writes St Gregory Nazianzus, "is nothing but the encountering of supreme purity and perfection."[15]

What characterizes the Kingdom of heaven first is the proximity to God enjoyed by the just.

The just, when entering into the Kingdom of heaven, will meet Christ. They will see Him in the light of His glory (cf. John 17:24) which will be revealed to them (Rom. 8:18) in its fullness and in a definitive manner.[16] They will see Him then no longer as in a mirror, in an indirect and dim manner but "face to face" (1 Cor. 13:12).[17] Then, says St Paul, "I shall know just as I also am known" (*ibid.*). They will be in His presence (cf. John 14:2–3, 2 Cor. 5:8). Even more, God will then be "all in all" (1 Cor. 15:28), and conversely the just will be totally in Him. They will also possess the Holy Spirit within themselves,[18] and by the Holy Spirit, in Christ, they will be united to the Father, being equally in Him and having Him equally in them. They will be with Him, united to Him eternally (cf. 1 Thes. 4:17) and they will live with Him forever "a divine and truly eternal life."[19] Christ reveals that the fulfilling of the Christian life results in this intimate union with Him, and in Him with the Father, a union achieved in the glory or the light that makes known the Holy Spirit: "As You, Father, are in Me, and I in You; that they also may be one in Us ... And the glory which You gave Me I have given them, that they may be one just as We are one: I in them and You in Me" (John 17:21–23). And the liturgy likewise presents, in its prayers, this communion with God in the Kingdom: "Grant that we may more perfectly partake of Thee in the never-ending Day of Thy Kingdom."

The just themselves will shine with the divine uncreated light they will see and in which they will see the Triune God[20] (cf. Matt. 5:8) and be united with Him. "Then the righteous will shine forth as the sun in the kingdom of their

Father" (Matt. 13:43). They will partake of this divine light[21] and, being glorified with Christ (Rom. 8:17), they will partake of God's glory (cf. 1 Pet. 5:1).

By partaking of this divine glory they will receive true and total freedom, that of the children of God (Rom. 8:21).

They will share in all divine good things. Thus, St Maximus the Confessor defines the Kingdom of God as "the imparting through grace of those blessings which pertain naturally to God."[22] The just will derive an intense pleasure from this partaking. They will enter with inexpressible joy "where Jesus has entered as a forerunner," St Paul tells us (Heb. 6:20). From their close union in a perfect and mutual love with Christ they will receive a happiness well beyond the greatest earthly happiness, which St John calls 'perfect joy' (John 16:24) and Tradition calls 'blessedness'.[23] After presenting an idyllic description of the Kingdom of heaven by showing that life there includes none of the disadvantages and defects of our current life, St John Chrysostom underscores the most profound reason for the happiness experienced by the just: "Greater than all these [good] things is the perpetual enjoyment of the presence of Christ in the company of angels, archangels, and the higher powers."[24] This joy (or blessedness) will be not only perfect, but definitive, inalienable and eternal. "Your joy," says St John, "no one will take from you" (John 16:22).

It is with the choir of these celestial powers and that of the saints that they will praise God continuously.[25] Nothing of His glory and His virtues being hid from them, this praise will spring spontaneously from their entire being[26] like an outcry of admiration, adoration and love.

St John Damascene summarizes several of the foregoing considerations in this way: "Those who have done good will shine like the sun together with the angels unto eternal life with our Lord Jesus Christ, ever seeing Him and being seen, enjoying the unending bliss that is from Him, and praising Him together with the Father and the Holy Spirit unto the endless ages of ages."[27]

The vision of God in the light of His glory will not only unite the just with God in a perfect manner, but will transform them and make them fully alike to Him.[28] "It has not yet been revealed what we shall be," says St John, "but we know that when He is revealed, we shall be like Him, for we shall see Him as He is" (1 John 3:2).

For the just, in other words, the process of their deification[29] will be brought to completion at that time. They will become by grace what God is by nature, enabling them to have access to God and, through Him, to the fullness of divine life, according to the plan conceived by the Creator since the beginning for man to realize his true nature.[30] "For this is why God has made us: to become participants in the divine nature (2 Pet. 1:4), partaking of His eternity, alike to Him and deified by grace."[31]

The blessedness of the just in the Kingdom of heaven will be experienced in varying degrees according to their spiritual state.[32] Christ Himself reveals this when He says: "In My Father's house are many mansions" (John 14:2), as does St Paul when he writes: "Each one will receive his own reward according to his own labor" (1 Cor. 3:8), or again: "There is one glory of the sun, another glory of the moon, and another glory of the stars, for one star differs from another star in glory" (1 Cor. 15:41). Commenting on this last passage St John Chrysostom observes: "[There is] not only a difference between sun and moon, and stars, but also between stars and stars. For what though they be all in the heaven? Yet some have a larger, others a lesser share of glory. What do we learn from hence? That although they be all in God's kingdom, all shall not enjoy the same reward."[33] St Gregory Nazianzus likewise writes: "All men do not seem to have been deemed worthy of the same rank and position; but one of one place and one of another, each, I think, according to the measure of his own purification."[34] St Gregory of Sinai similarly affirms that "the rewards of the righteous differ"[35] and that "the degree or quality of the requital will accord with the state induced in each by ... the virtues."[36] St Nicholas Cabasilas likewise affirms that "there are many mansions so that every degree of goodness may be glorified."[37] As for Isaac the Syrian, he writes that "just as each man enjoys the sun according to the clarity of his eyesight and perception, and just as the radiance of a single lamp lit in a house is perceived differently, even though the light has always the same intensity," so in the age to come "each man will be illumined in proportion to his own capacity by the one noetic Sun" and "each man will inwardly delight in the grace given him according to his capacity." This grace is unique however, coming from "one place, one dwelling, one vision, and one outward appearance."[38]

Speaking in absolute terms, the spiritual state of the just will be 'perfect' only by comparison to earthly life. If, from a certain point of view, their likeness to God, their union with Him, their deification will be complete; from another point of view they will always remain to be completed, for God, because of His infiniteness, always remains inaccessible and inexhaustible in His nature. Never will man be able to claim that he knows Him or loves Him perfectly;

never will he be able to enjoy the totality of His bounty, but his desire will continue to draw closer to Him eternally. This theme of 'epectasis' was developed especially by Gregory of Nyssa.[39] He writes in particular: "No consideration will be given to anything enclosing [God's] infinite nature. But every desire for the Good which is attracted to that ascent [towards God] constantly expands as one progresses in pressing on to the Good. This is truly the vision of God: never to be satisfied in the desire to see him …. Thus, no limit would interrupt growth in the ascent to God, since no limit to the Good can be found nor is the increasing of desire for the Good brought to an end because it is satisfied."[40] Other Fathers have also developed this theme. Thus, St John Climacus writes: "If love never faileth [1 Cor. 13:8]… we shall never cease to advance in it, either in the present or in the future life, continually adding light to light."[41] On the topic of the glorified just, St Symeon the New Theologian writes: "The beginning of his race is his end and the end is the beginning. Perfection has no end."[42] And elsewhere he teaches: "Progress in fact will be endless, in the course of the centuries, because the cessation of the growth towards this infinite end would be nothing else but the seizure of the unseizable and that the one who can satisfy no one would become the object of satiety; on the contrary, to be filled by Him and to be glorified in His light will dig a bottomless progress and an unlimited beginning; in the same way as, while possessing Christ who was formed within them, they abide near the One who shines with inaccessible light, even so in them the end becomes the beginning of glory, and… they will have the beginning in the end, and the end in the beginning."[43] St Photius observes that in the Kingdom of heaven "we are always full of joy without ever feeling any satiety. To the contrary, the abundance of this rejoicing becomes the cause of a greater and more abundant love for God. While we are filled to the brim by divine knowledge, this satisfaction increases our holy desire for knowledge that never ceases and never weakens."[44] As for St Maximus the Confessor, he speaks of the "perpetually moving repose of the desiring around the Desired,"[45] which is actually the continuous and uninterrupted enjoyment of the Desired."[46] These last remarks of St Photius and St Maximus the Confessor imply that the absence of satiety does not mean for all that a lack of enjoyment. The endless desire that a person experiences at that time is not, like earthly desire, accompanied by dissatisfaction and therefore anxiety and suffering. The enjoyment of the just goes in some manner from fullness to fullness. They incessantly discover with joy that the abounding happiness they have found is increased anew.

Life of the Kingdom of heaven is not then a life of inactivity. Although the natural human energies that activate the faculties of man are at rest, this is to make room for the divine energies which the just, by their purity, are deemed worthy to receive within themselves and to which they are, in complete freedom, fully open, moving from then on—with full agreement of their will—not by their own powers, henceforth insufficient for this celestial activity, but by grace.[47] The life of man is no longer then simply a human life but a divine-human life, since man's human faculties are moved by divine energies, and since man is henceforth able to say: "it is no longer I who live, but Christ lives in me" (Gal. 2:20). Moved by the divine energies, man's activity is then accomplished effortlessly, but with a sheer spontaneity of love.

The activity of the blessed will be, in fact, totally focused on the knowledge and praise of God, as we have said, but also on love for God, for angels, and other men. On this topic Gregory of Nyssa writes: "But when the thing hoped for comes, all the others grow quiet while the operation of love remains, not finding anything to take its place [cf. 1 Cor. 13:8]. For this reason also it has the primacy among all virtuous actions as well as among the commandments of the law. So if the soul should ever reach this goal, it will have no need of the others, as it embraces the fullness of existing things ... For the life of the superior nature is love, since the beautiful is in every respect lovable for those who know it, and the Divine knows Itself. But knowledge becomes love, because that which is known becomes beautiful by nature. Insolent satiety does not touch the truly beautiful. Since satiety does not cut off the attachment of love to the beautiful, the divine life will always operate through love, the divine life which is beautiful by nature and from its nature is lovingly disposed towards the beautiful."[48]

3 Hell.

Hell (or Gehenna) is presented by Scripture and the Fathers as a place of punishment[49] or, more profoundly, as a condition or state where sinners are tormented[50] and have to endure great suffering, and this for eternity, definitively and irremediably.[51]

The immediate cause of this suffering is generally presented as being fire, an inextinguishable and eternal fire.[52] This word of Christ is the point of reference here: "Then He will say to those on the left hand, 'Depart from Me, you cursed, into the everlasting fire prepared for the devil and his angels'" (Matt. 25:41). But Christ also mentions as sources of suffering, besides "the fire [that] is not quenched" (Mark 9:47–48; cf. Isa. 66:24), the "worm [that] does not die" (*ibid.*), and the fact of finding oneself in the company of the Devil and the demons (see Matt. 25:41),[53] while the just are in the company of God, the angels and the saints.

As manifestations of sufferings endured, Christ mentions "weeping and gnashing of teeth" (Matt. 13:42, 25:30).

Another basic characteristic of hell is its gloomy, somber or dark quality. Job refers to it as "the land of gloom and deep darkness, the land of gloom and chaos, where light is as darkness" (Job 10:21–22). Christ Himself designates it by the expression "outer darkness" (Matt. 25:30).

When they refer to hell, the Fathers are most often content to repeat this scriptural data.[54] Some from among them 'add something' when describing the 'torments' or 'tortures' suffered in such a way as to inspire more fear in their audience or readers, often presenting them under a material form.[55]

However all the expressions used by Scripture to describe hell and the sufferings that it causes have, as we said, a symbolic value.

Many of the Fathers stress that the fire of hell, which appears to be the chief source for the suffering of sinners, is not the material fire known to us, but one "such as God might know."[56] On the one hand it is inextinguishable, on the other it does not burn and consume in the manner of a material fire, since the bodies of sinners, like those of the just, have become, after the resurrection, incorruptible.[57]

Nor does it cause a bodily or psychic suffering since, after the resurrection, all have become bodily and psychically impassible.

The source of the sufferings of hell and its effect on both soul and body (for man suffers as a whole then) are therefore spiritual in nature.

Among the sufferings endured some Fathers mention the feeling of an absence of freedom.[58]

They also mention "the shame and eternal regret of the conscience."[59] The shame, experienced before the glorified assembly of the just and the angelic powers, is analogous to the shame experienced by Adam when, after his sin, he found himself naked (cf. Gen. 3:10), that is, divested of the divine gifts and divine glory which he partook of in paradise. The eternal regret of conscience, symbolized in part by 'the devouring worm', is experienced by sinners in the face of their sins and past conduct, the memory of which will no longer leave them, and which are henceforth irreparable. "Let us think about," St Maximus the Confessor writes, "the bitterness of the soul in hell with its awareness and recollection of all the evil that it has done."[60] "Who," he asks, "can bear the eternal shame of a conscience whose secrets have been brought to light? Who can tally up the endless lamentations and these bitter as well as vain tears, these moans and gnashings of teeth of those tortured to the depths of their soul by a heart wrung with burning regret? Who is in a position to tell of the anguish gripping them at seeing neither end to the torment that bears down on them, or hope in a transformation at the end and a change to a better life?"[61]

But all the Fathers concur in saying that the suffering experienced by sinners in hell is basically caused by the fact of being separated and distant from God (cf. 2 Thess. 1:9), deprived of His presence and all the blessings bound up with that, deprived of communion with Him. After having mentioned all manner of sufferings analogous to those we might now experience, St John Chrysostom writes: "Some [torments] bitterer than these have their place in hell: but the loss of the good things involves so much pain, so much affliction and straitness, that even if no other kind of punishment were appointed for those who sin here, it would of itself be sufficient to vex us more bitterly than the torments in hell, and to confound our souls."[62] A little later he likewise observes: "a far more severe punishment than hell is exclusion from the glory of the other world, and I think that one who has failed to reach it ought not to sorrow so much over the miseries of hell, as over his rejection from heaven, for this alone is more dreadful than all other things in respect of punishment."[63] St Maximus the Confessor speaks in the same way of the soul "banished from the divine glory and falling beneath the blow of a dread condemnation to its relational alienation from God for ages without end."[64] As for St Basil the Great, he points out that "the descent to hell is separation from God,"[65] and again that "separation and estrangement from God are more unbearable than the punishment reserved for hell."[66] This is why a great contemporary Serbian monastic, St Justin Popovich, imitating Dostoyevsky, writes: "Nothing is more horrible than an eternity without Christ. I would prefer to be in hell where Christ was—if I might be forgiven this paradox—than in a paradise where Christ was not."[67]

Sinners live in hell for eternity, and yet they are deprived of life, true Life, spiritual life in God. They know then, spiritually a 'second death,'[68]

(Rev. 20:14, 21:8). For "death, properly speaking, is this: for the soul to be unharnassed from divine grace."[69]

It is not only Life, but all the other energies of God (often called 'the glory of God' by the Fathers) that sinners are deprived of in hell. These energies are all of God's active qualities which He manifests and communicates as grace to those who are worthy, but which the unworthy cannot receive. St Nicodemus stresses how detrimental their loss is to sinners: "Is it but a small loss and slight grief for you to lose God, you poor sinner, Who is complete delight, complete joy, complete desire, and complete insatiable satiety? Who is complete light and the origin of light, complete life and the origin of life, complete wisdom and the origin of wisdom? Is it but slight grief to lose God, Whose beauty surpasses every beauty, Whose wisdom surpasses every wisdom, Whose sweetness surpasses every sweetness, a single ray of Whose glory, if it shone in Hades, would immediately change Hades into Paradise? ... Is it but slight grief to lose your God, you poor soul, Who is absolute good, Who is your beginning, your middle, and your end? ... O infinite loss! O immeasurable loss! I am certain, brother, that if you saw but once this great loss which you caused by your sins, you would cry out like that king who said at the time of his death that he had lost everything."[70]

These energies are gathered together and manifested in the divine Light, and the 'damned' have been of course deprived of this Light. This is why hell is likened by Scripture and the Fathers to a place of darkness and gloom.

And yet the divine energies, shown forth from the Father, by the Son in the Holy Spirit, are everywhere present and fill all things. One might even say that, in hell as in the Kingdom of heaven, God is united to all and is "all in all." Objectively, the divine Light shines everywhere, illumines everything, including hell and those who are confined there. God's very Love, which is one of His energies, is lavished on all, those in hell as well as those in the Kingdom of heaven. The divine energies are not then exterior to the damned, but the damned remain exterior to them, because they have made the choice to remain closed to them and have persevered in this choice. St Maximus the Confessor, who has developed profound insights on this subject, explains that, at the end of time, God will unite Himself with all equally. However, for the people worthy of this union and who, from their side, will be disposed to be united with God and receive His grace, blessedness will be the result of this union; conversely, this union will imply great suffering for people unworthy of it, who will reject grace and be 'subjected' to it against their will: "Above nature is the divine and unimaginable rejoicing that it is meet for God to produce by nature when He is united by grace to the worthy; against nature, the inexpressible pain that constitutes its privation and that the One who is God by nature is wont to produce when He is united contrary to grace with the unworthy. For God, being united with all according to the quality of the disposition in the depths of each person, the sensation [of this union] is given to each just as each person has shaped himself to receive the One who must be united with all at the end of the ages."[71]

The damned know God, His love, and all the blessings that He shares with men and that the just receive with gratitude, mutual love and praise. But they suffer, by their own fault, from being deprived of them for eternity. They see then that the divine blessings are immense, infinite and, weighing up all that they have lost, all the harm to themselves following upon this, they suffer atrociously for this immense loss and harm.

Thus, according to St Gregory of Nyssa and St Maximus the Confessor, the suffering of those in hell results from their awareness of now being deprived of these blessings.[72] The Good, says Gregory, "becomes a flame burning the soul."[73]

In a more precise manner, St Isaac the Syrian holds that the damned are tortured by love—God's love for them, fully recognized now but, through their own fault, which they are unable to receive and to which they are unable to respond—and that this is the greatest suffering there is:

> Those who are punished in Gehenna are scourged by the scourge of love. . . . Those who have become conscious that they have sinned against love suffer greater torment from this than from any fear of punishment. For the sorrow caused in the heart by sin against love is more poignant than any torment. It would be improper for a man to think that sinners in Gehenna are deprived of the love of God. Love is the offspring of knowledge of the truth which, as is commonly confessed, is given to all. The power of love works in two ways: it torments sinners, even as happens here when a friend suffers from a friend, but it becomes a source of joy for those who have observed its duties.[74]

In a most beautiful passage from one of his *Letters*, St Maximus evokes in a very concrete manner the refusal, by sinners in hell, of the divine grace directed toward them (and which they recognize as such). And he speaks of this refusal not only as a past attitude, but one in which they persist: "Your judgment, O God, is just, for you call and we do not listen, you speak and we do not draw near; we make fruitless your counsels by not accepting your words. This is why perdition has befallen us, and ruin, the tempest and besieging fear. We who do not want wisdom and have only scorn for fear of the Lord, nor do we want God's counsels. We reap the fruits of our own sowing and we would have our fill of our insanity."[75]

Eternal separation from God is therefore clearly the result of a not only past but present free choice of man. St Irenaeus of Lyons insists on the responsibility of the latter in the punishment he undergoes. He stresses that it is not God who punishes, it is the person who punishes himself and surrenders himself to sufferings by refusing the gift of God, depriving himself of union and communion with Him: "To as many as continue in their love towards God, does He grant communion with Him. But communion with God is life and light, and the enjoyment of all the benefits which He has in store. But on as many as, according to their own choice, depart from God, He inflicts that separation from Himself which they have chosen of their own accord. But separation from God is death, and separation from light is darkness; and separation from God consists in the loss of all the benefits which He has in store. Those, therefore, who cast away by apostasy these aforementioned things, being in fact destitute of all good, do experience every kind of punishment. God, however, does not punish them immediately of Himself, but that punishment falls upon them because they are destitute of all that is good. Now, good things are eternal and without end with God, and therefore the loss of these is also eternal and never-ending."[76] In the same vein, St Maximus the Confessor has sinners abiding in hell tell us: "We collect in this way what our actions have earned, or rather we receive the wage that our own resolute disposition deserves."[77]

The notion of hell found in St Maximus, St Gregory of Nyssa, St Isaac the Syrian, and St Irenaeus is in substance the same. Referring more particularly to St Maximus, who has given it a more precise conceptual expression, V. Lossky, in his *Mystical Theology of the Eastern Church*, presents it as being representative of the Orthodox concept: "[Men will be] raised up in incorruptibility to be united to God who will be all in all. But some will be united by grace, others apart from grace, according to St Maximus.[78] Some will be deified by the energies which they have acquired in the interior of their being; others will remain without, and for them the deifying fire of the Spirit will be an external flame, intolerable to all those whose will is opposed to God."[79]

According to this conception, hell and the Kingdom of heaven "do not exist from God's point of view, but from man's. It is true that Paradise and Hell exist as two ways of life, but it is not God who created them. In the patristic tradition it is clear that there are not two ways, but God Himself is Paradise for the saints and God Himself is Hell for the sinners."[80]

Hell and the Kingdom of heaven are the same divine energies perceived and received differently. Thus the divine Light, in the same way as sunlight, can be perceived as either illuminating or burning. The just will only perceive its illuminating properties and rejoice in all the wonders that it will make them see and they will not suffer from its burning properties. Conversely, the damned like blind men will not perceive its luminous, but only its burning properties. They will not perceive the presence of God's love as a light that illumines them and makes them happy, but only as a fire that burns them and makes them suffer. Along these lines, St Basil notes that the fire of hell is "a fire without light, which has the capacity to burn in darkness, but is deprived of brightness."[81]

The same Father explains this idea in connection with the three youths in the furnace who were refreshed by the fire in which they were placed, whereas the same fire burned everything around them (cf. Dan. 3:46–50). He remarks that the fire is "cut in twain by the voice of God." The fire, he notes, possesses two energies, one that burns and another that illumines. Those who deserve the fire of hell and fall into it will be subject to the burning energy of the fire, which will make them suffer, while those worthy of illumination will experience the second energy in which they will rejoice. "The Lord distributes the flames of fire so that the fire of hell is devoid of light, whereas the light of peace does not burn."[82] St Gregory Nazianzus observes more laconically that the damned incur "the sentence of darkness, or the seeing Him to be fire, Whom he did not recognize as light."[83] And, in a prayer addressed to the Holy Trinity, he cries out: "O Trinity, who will be recognized one day by all the world, by some through illumination, by others through punishment!"[84] Elsewhere, he notes that the same Word "is on the one hand terrible through its nature to those who are unworthy, and on the other through its loving kindness can be received by those who are thus prepared" having purified themselves.[85] And he addresses his readers in this way: "Receive besides this the Resurrection, the Judgment and the Reward according to the righteous scales of God; and believe that this will be Light to those whose mind is purified (that is, God—seen and known) proportionate to their degree of purity, which we call the Kingdom of heaven;

but to those who suffer from blindness of their ruling faculty, darkness, that is estrangement from God, proportionate to their blindness here."[86]

St John Climacus reiterates this conception: "When the holy and super-celestial fire comes to dwell in the souls of [sinners], as says one of those who have received the title of Theologian, it burns them because they still lack purification, whereas it enlightens the [just] according to the degree of their perfection. For one and the same fire is called both the fire which consumes and the light which illuminates."[87]

As several of the previously cited texts indicate, there are various degrees in the sufferings of hell as in the blessedness of the Kingdom of heaven relative to the diversity of spiritual states and the dispositions of sinners on the one hand, and of the just on the other. "Chastisements differ, as do the rewards of the righteous," notes Gregory of Sinai.[88] St John Chrysostom likewise observes that "although all sinners will be in Gehenna, everyone will not be subjected to the same treatment."[89] St Gregory of Nyssa affirms that "the measure of pain is proportional to the quantity of evil in each one,"[90] and St Gregory of Sinai that "the degree or quality of the requital will accord with the state induced in each by either the passions or the virtues."[91]

So to respond in an argued manner to this objection arising from the foregoing considerations: "If someone must be punished much and someone else little (Luke 12:47), how can it be said that there is no end to punishment?", St Basil of Caesarea dwells at length on this subject:

> The things said in a veiled and ambiguous way in certain places of the God-inspired Scripture are clarified by explicit statements in other places. The Lord at one time declares that *These shall go away into eternal punishment* (Matt. 25:46) and at another sends certain ones *to the eternal fire prepared for the devil and his angels* (Matt. 25:41) and elsewhere he invokes a *Gehenna of fire* (Matt. 5:22) and adds: *where their worm does not die and the fire is not quenched* (Mark 9:48), which he had said long before by the prophet: *their worm shall not die and their fire shall not be quenched* (Isa. 66:24). Since these and many such sayings are found everywhere in the God-inspired Scripture, this is surely one of the devil's stratagems: that many human beings, by disregarding such weighty and solemn sayings and declarations of the Lord, award to themselves an end of punishment in order that they may sin with greater bravado. For if ever there were an end of eternal punishment, then surely eternal life would also have an end. Now if we do not tolerate thinking like this about [eternal] life, by what logic shall we assign an end to eternal punishment? For the adjective 'eternal' is attached equally to either term. For *These shall go away*, he says, *into eternal punishment, but*

the righteous into eternal life (Matt. 25:46). In view of such explicit sayings, we must understand that *shall be beaten with many strokes* and *shall be beaten with few* indicate not an end of punishment but a difference of degree. For if God is a righteous judge, not only to the good but also to the evil, *rendering to each according to his deeds* (cf. Rom. 2:6), then one may deserve *unquenchable fire*, which may burn softly or more fiercely, while another may deserve the *undying worm*, which in turn may afflict more moderately or more keenly according to what each deserves; a third may deserve *Gehenna*, which has quite different punishments; yet another deserve *the outer darkness* (Matt. 8:12, 22:13, 25:30), where he may have only the *weeping*, while another also has *the gnashing of teeth* owing to the intensity of pains. And the *outer darkness* surely hints that there is an inner darkness as well. Moreover, the saying in Proverbs *in the depths of Hades* (Prov. 9:18) shows that some in Hades are not in *the depths of Hades*, but endure a lighter punishment instead. It is possible to illustrate this even now with respect to the conditions of the body. For one who has a fever may also have symptoms and other sufferings, while another only has a fever and is not like the other. Then in a manner different from the first a third does not have fever but is oppressed by pain in some limb, and this again may be greater or less. Now in the present case, *many* and *few* were uttered by the Lord according to customary usage, as also many other such terms. For we know that such a manner of speech is often applied to those afflicted by some one illness, as when we say, marveling at one who only has a fever or is suffering from smarting eyes: 'How much he has suffered!', or 'How many troubles he has endured!' So, again I say, *to be beaten with many* or *few strokes* is accomplished not by the protraction or foreshortening of time, but in the difference of punishment.[92]

4 The Question of the Apocatastasis.

The foregoing objection and response allude to a subject debated long and hard in the Church: the apocatastasis.

The theory of apocatastasis (that is to say of the universal restoration to a primal state) was chiefly defended by Origen[93] and by the so-called 'Origenist' current. It was also upheld by St Gregory of Nyssa,[94] but under a more temperate and ambiguous form to such a point that his position could be interpreted in an orthodox sense by some ancient[95] and modern[96] authors. It has likewise tempted, under various forms and in different eras, certain Christian thinkers[97] to whom the idea of an eternal hell seems incompatible with God's sovereign goodness.

According to this theory, hell is not eternal; all those confined there, including the devil and the demons, will be ultimately saved and glorified.

This theory has remained however quite marginal. It has given rise to critiques by numerous Fathers,[98] before and after having been officially condemned by the Church, along with all the other Origenist errors,[99] during the Fifth Ecumenical Council (Constantinople II) in 553.

With the exception of Origen and his disciples, all the Fathers teach the eternity of the pains of hell and the eternity of the condition of those who will suffer them.[100]

One of the chief objections voiced to the assertion of hell's eternity is that the latter is incompatible with the existence of a good and merciful God. However, the origin of hell is not, as we have seen, God's will, but the will of the devil, the demons and certain people. Hell, like evil, is not a positive ontological reality; it has only a privative existence; it exists for those subject to it only as the absence of the benefits of the Kingdom only because of a rejection of God. By this very fact it has not been created by God. As for its eternity, it follows from the possibility of the devil's, the demons' and men's free choice to persist in evil and reject right to the end God's eternal and uncreated grace. Bessarion of Nicaea affirms: "The justice of eternal punishment becomes apparent above all in the irrevocable disposition of the unruly will of sinners, for to the will's eternal perversion is due an eternal punishment."[101]

This argument from angelic and human freedom, upon which the goodness of God refuses to impose itself because He respects it right to the end in its choices and their consequences, the worst included,[102] has been brought to the fore by several Fathers,[103] St Maximus the Confessor for one,[104] and logically follows moreover from the previously explained notion of hell.

Two objections remain: 1) how can it be asserted that hell will exist as a continuation of Hades, whereas nothing is final concerning the future of those abiding there before the Last Judgment? 2) how can we, *a priori*, consider the choice of those found in hell to be final?

As to the second objection, it must be recalled that a person no longer has the possibility of repenting or modifying his choice not only after the Last Judgment, but after the moment of his death, and that, between the moment of death and the Last Judgment, it is only the prayers of the Church, the saints, and the other faithful who are able to obtain from God a change in his condition. That surely limits the freedom of a person, but we know in advance that our freedom will be limited in this way and must make our choices accordingly. The warnings of the Fathers are, moreover, aimed at this, and this is also one of the teachings of the Gospel parable of poor Lazarus and the wicked rich man.

To the first objection we reply that the affirmation of the eternity of hell rests on the teaching of Christ Himself. This teaching rests on the foreknowledge He has, insofar as God, about what the future life will be.[105]

The rejection of the theory of the apocatastasis does not prevent the Church and its members from praying that all might be saved. But there is a twofold difference between this attitude and adherence to the theory of apocatastasis. On the on hand, the latter affirms the certainty of universal salvation, while the former only desires it, wishes it, hopes for it, without having any certainty that this will be realized. On the other hand, in the present situation—and this being until the Last Judgment—the condition of no one abiding in Hades can be seen as absolutely final. Therefore it is perfectly legitimate to hope for the salvation of all and to pray to God for this to be realized.

Chapter Twelve
Preparing Oneself for Death and the Life Beyond

1 The Meaning of Precise Details about the Afterlife.

The preceding lengthy study belies the widespread idea according to which Christianity, in contrast to nearly all other religions, would be almost mute about life after death.

The examination of Scriptures and patristic tradition enable us all in all to define a representation at once broad and precise of the dying process, the stages that follow, and the ultimate destiny of man. It remains no less true that, paradoxically, we find at the same time in Scripture and with the Fathers —including those who show themselves the most prolix on the subject— a certain reticence to describe in detail and in a manner other than symbolic the forms and contents of *post-mortem* life. It is a fact that God has not allowed the deceased to reveal to the living how they live in the afterlife. The request of the wicked rich man: "'I beg you therefore, father [Abraham], that you would send [Lazarus] to my father's house, for I have five brothers, that he may testify to them, lest they also come to this place of torment,'" is rebuffed with a denial: "'They have Moses and the prophets; let them hear them.'" The persistence of rich man— "'No, father Abraham; but if one goes to them from the dead, they will repent.'" —is to no avail: Abraham "said to him: 'If they do not hear Moses and the prophets, neither will they be persuaded though one rise from the dead.'" (Luke 16:27–31). St John Chrysostom, who at certain moments does not hesitate to deliver lengthy descriptions of the tortures of Hell and the delights of the Kingdom of heaven, at other times shows himself reserved when details are involved. To the question: "Where then, in what place is this Gehenna to be found?", he replies: "... *somewhere* out of this world. Seek we not then to know where it is, but how we may escape it."[1]

Although quite different, the two counsels have the same aim: the important thing is not to know what will happen after death, to gain a knowledge about the form and contents of *post-mortem* life, but to be prepared for death and what will ensue. Knowledge about death and the hereafter will be of no use at that moment; these alone will be decisive for us: our spiritual state, the pardon of our sins obtained from God, our degree of inner purity, our virtues, our disposition with respect to God and neighbor, the prayers of the Church, the saints and those close to us, and all the other quite concrete factors that will contribute to assuring us of a good death, a good passage into the hereafter, and lastly, as the liturgy says in several places in its litanies, "a good defense before the dread judgment seat of Christ."

When to the contrary they judge it good to give some details on what awaits us after death, the Fathers have no other end than making us aware that, at each one of the stages that must be crossed until our final and eternal destiny is decided, a quite precise accounting will be asked of our earthly conduct, and that at the very moment of our death our spiritual state will be a determining factor, because it will determine our *post-mortem* development, and because henceforth it will be impossible for us to change it. Their goal is then, by this approach as well, to encourage us starting now, to prepare for death so that we might be found worthy, at the moment that it occurs, of the destiny of the just and not the fate of the sinner. Their aim is to inspire in us the former's ardent desire and the latter's fear. Abba Isaiah recommends in this vein: "Remember the kingdom of heaven, in order that your desire for it may very gradually attract you. Think of Gehenna, so that you may despise its works."[2] And again "Each day, before you do anything, remember and always consider where you are and where you must go when you die, and you will not neglect your soul for even a day. Think of the honor received by all the saints, and their zeal will attract you very gradually."[3]

We clearly need to recognize however that, for pedagogical reasons, knowing that the fear of evil is more familiar to their audience and more apt to influence their conduct than the desire for spiritual benefits which, from the viewpoint of their current situation, seems generally abstract and distant, the Fathers, when they do mention the after-life, more often insist on the need to flee the evils of hell than on the need to seek the benefits of the Kingdom of heaven. Thus, St Gregory Palamas writes: "From this [second death, eternal damnation] let us also flee with all our might. Let us cast away, let us reject all things, bid farewell to all things: to all relationships, actions and intentions that drag us downward, separate us from God and produce such a death. He who is frightened of this death and has preserved himself from it will not be alarmed by the oncoming death of the body."[4] Abba Isaiah recommends: "Attend diligently, always remembering to have before your eyes eternal fire and punishments. In this way, consider yourself as one of the living amidst those who are condemned and tortured."[5]

John Chrysostom is indeed aware of the partial character of such an approach and, to justify it, puts forward pedagogical reasons: "I sense that what I am saying distresses you and that it is painful to listen to this discourse. But what would you have me do? Please God that you were all so virtuous that I would not be obliged to speak of Hell. But since you are for the most part engaged in sin, with all my heart I would that my words, entering into your minds, might impress there a feeling of real sorrow. I would cease then describing these baneful things ... Hell is so horrible a thing that any conversation serving to distance us from it, however hard and unendurable they might seem, should be pleasant. We will draw greater benefits from them. For they make our soul return to itself, render it more innocent, raise its thoughts to heaven, detach it from the earth and all its passions. Lastly they serve as an excellent remedy forestalling evils and preventing us from falling into them."[6] He concludes moreover that "St John [the Evangelist] prods his listener, either by recalling the Last Judgment, or by saying that anyone who does not believe in the Son will not see life, but wrath abides on him."[7] After having touched on the dreadful trials that await sinners, Abba Theophilus equally shows his listeners the meaning and usefulness of such an awareness: "Since this is so, in what manner ought we not to give ourselves to holy and devout works? What love ought we to acquire? What manner of life? What virtues? What speed? What diligence? What prayer? What prudence? Scripture says: 'In this waiting, let us make every effort to be found blameless and without reproach in peace' [2 Pet. 3:14; cf. 1 Cor. 1:7–8]. In this way, we shall be worthy to hear it said: 'Come, O blessed of my Father, inherit the kingdom prepared for you from the foundation of the world' [Matt. 25:34]. Amen."[8] St John Chrysostom stresses in any case the serious danger that there is for someone to be unaware of what awaits at the time of death and afterwards, and hence indirectly shows the usefulness of words aimed at making us aware of the existence of the hereafter and its nature: "Anyone who does not believe that he will be resurrected one day, anyone who does not admit that one day he will render an account for his actions here-below, anyone who thinks that everything that is part of us is enclosed within the bounds of the present life, that there is nothing further, that one is careless about virtue; what is the use, if he can expect no reward for his efforts and fatigue? He will not abstain from doing evil, since he does not expect to undergo any punishment for his bad actions; he will give himself up to his unruly desires, to every kind of perversity. Conversely, anyone who believes in his soul in the Judgment to come, who always has before his eyes the dreadful judgment seat, the reckoning demanded by an inexorable voice, the sentence for which there is no appeal, that one will be most careful about temperance; he will cling to justice, to all the virtues; he would flee immodesty, the brutality of insolence and every perversity."[9] In the same positive direction, he again notes: "[Isaiah says:] 'To me every knee shall bend' (Isa. 45:24). Each of us, then, will have to render an account of ourselves before God. Notice that he does not simply say that we will each have to bow down before God, but we will each also have to render an account for our acts. For this reason, Christians, wake up, be ready for combat; be alert, prepared for spiritual struggle since you see the Lord of all things sitting on the judgment seat."[10]

2 The 'Remembrance of Death.'

From this perspective, the Fathers recommend frequently practicing the 'remembrance of death,'[11] that is, to have an awareness that one will die, with the goal of being prepared to face this ordeal and those that follow in the best spiritual conditions possible, and to be ultimately found worthy of the Kingdom of heaven.[12]

The Fathers emphasize that this practice, to be efficacious, should be continual. St Gregory Nazianzus counsels one of his correspondents: "You must live for the time to come and make of this life a meditation on death."[13] St Athanasius recommends: "Each hour recall your departure; keep death before your eyes daily."[14] And St John Climacus: "Always let the remembrance of death ... go to sleep with you and get up with you."[15]

Saint Hesychios of Batos characterizes the remembrance of death as "a powerful trainer of body and soul."[16] This practice actually enables us to detach ourselves from this world and the desires of the flesh, and thus facilitates the departure of the soul when death separates it from the body and all sensible realities.[17] On the other hand it helps man preserve himself from sin (cf. Sir. 7:36) and the passions,[18] and cling to God and His will in the practice of His commandments.[19] According to Abba Isaiah, "holding death before our eyes" is, along with repentance, what enables man to "protect all the virtues."[20] This practice, of itself, also arouses repentance, one of its most beneficial effects[21] and, as we have seen several times, one of the most important spiritual dispositions for passing through the door of death and entering into the hereafter.

Even though the remembrance of death implies fear of death, this does not involve dreading death itself, but the judgment of God that will follow it and the consequences of this judgment.[22] Abba Isaiah gives details about this by stressing that the remembrance of death should be continual: "the fear of coming before God must be [our] very breathing."[23] St Basil of Caesarea notes in the same vein: "Truly blessed is the soul, which by night and by day has no other anxiety than how, when the great day comes wherein all creation shall stand before the Judge and shall give an account for its deeds, she too may be able easily to get quit of the reckoning of life."[24]

To the same end, the Fathers recommend living each day as if it were the last.[25] St John Cassian notes that one method is "certainly decisive in regard to all vices in general—namely, that a person reflect daily on the fact that he is going to depart from this world."[26] Abba Isaiah counsels more precisely: "Think to yourself daily, 'I only have this day to do something in this world', and you will not sin before God."[27] Indeed, he explains further: "One who keeps death nearby in his expectation does not sin much (cf. Sir. 7:36), but one who expects to live a long time will be entangled in many sins. When a person is prepared to give an account to God for all his deeds, God himself will take care to purify his every way from sin, but the person who pays no attention and says, 'It will be a long time before I die', dwells in evil."[28]

St Antony joins together the two recommendations: "In order that we do not become negligent, it is good to carefully consider the Apostle's statement: *I die daily*. For if we so live as people dying, we will not commit sin. The point of the saying is this: As we rise daily, let us suppose that we shall not survive till evening, and again, as we prepare for sleep, let us consider that we shall not awaken. By its very nature our life is uncertain, and is meted out daily by Providence."[29]

3 Meditation on the Last Things.

As for himself, St Maximus the Confessor advises a detailed meditation on death and the hereafter:

> By the fear of God and the threat [of the chastisements] to come, halt the violent impulses of the senses. In everything and everywhere remember death and the soul's terror upon its leaving the body, and how the powers of the air and the dark forces come to meet it, all dissociated and cut to pieces in proportion to its disastrous familiarity with them through the play of the passions. Let us think of the bitterness of the soul in hell, in the awareness and recollection of all the evil it has done in its body. Let us think of the final consummation of the entire world, of the immense conflagration destroying the universe in a frightful tumult of the elements dissolved by flames: the heavens precipitously fleeing the terrifying envelopment of fire purifying creation for the Parousia of the Pure; the sea disappearing; the earth shaken to its foundations, casting forth the countless myriads of the bodies of all men without exception. Let us think of the dread hour of reckoning at that time, at the dreadful and terrifying judgment seat of Christ, when all the powers of heaven and every human creature since the foundation of the ages will see right down to the most naked of our thoughts; when the ineffable light will welcome some for the brilliance of their works and when the illumination of the holy and blessed Trinity will cause to shine with even more brilliance those who can see It and endure the sight by the purity of their soul. Outer darkness will welcome the others, as well as the gnawing, untiring worm and the inextinguishable fire of Gehenna. Finally, the most serious of all, the eternal shame and regret of conscience. Think of all that so to be worthy of the first and not to be condemned to suffer this trial; let us be with them and with God, or rather wholly with God alone, totally within Him, with no longer anything of the earthly within us; in order to be close to God, become gods, receiving being gods from God. In this way the divine gifts are venerated and are awaited in the love of the Parousia of divine Joy.[30]

St Maximus himself, in the first of his letters, engages in a meditation in which he puts himself—and his reader at the same time—in the position of a repenting damned individual. The aim is clearly, by this imaginary anticipation, to arouse in the soul a movement of conversion which would be impossible when the events mentioned will have actually occurred:

> Your judgment is just, O God, we do not cease saying; called, we have not heard; called back to order, we have refused. We were each day warned of this terrible [falling-due], but we scorned what we were told about it. These warnings mattered little then; all that matters little to us even now; that

which restrains [and threatens] our life, we take it for so much idle talk repeated over and over. O negligence, O deceit, O pernicious advice, O unlawful carnal relations, O how just is the sentence of God and how apt the ordeal for our every kind of evil way! That miserable and abominable carnal pleasure earns for us a just condemnation to Gehenna. We have been condemned to dwell, quaking with fright, in the horrible darkness and night for our delight in shameful words and sights ... We are henceforth in all justice deprived of light for having no regard in our short life for the glory of God, the Author of this creation. No, we have soiled our eyes, ears and tongue, and, even more, we have corrupted a soul created in the image of God, fascinated by these sights, sounds and words hateful to God. Cast into Tartarus, swallowed up and prisoners of this frightful abyss, preferring pride to humility, the mediatrix of sublime and divine benefits, we have thrust aside the solidity and firmness of virtue by the debilitating excess of carnal pleasure. Where is our haughtiness now, where is the debilitating weakness and laxity of the flesh? O lack of judgment! It is the grinding of teeth for us now instead of foolish laughter and unrestrained chatter. Not wanting to train ourselves in the study of divine and salutary speech, preferring to abandon ourselves to drunkenness instead of the divine canticles, here we are chastised, our tongue condemned to a horrible thirst. We have received the worthy fruit of hatred, envy, deceit and hypocrisy towards our brothers, from which comes murders, injuries, and calumnies, both from bitterness, lies and false oaths. And the ever-gnawing worm, the unsleeping worm lies in the innermost recesses of our soul, seeing that we perverted love's honesty, twisted our heart, that, by corrupting the impassibility of the truth, we bent it [to our own views]. We have created this unwanted worm by our self-willed enmity, sinking deeper and deeper in a rut of perversion with lies, by distancing ourselves from union with God who is upright and direct ([for He says] "the twisted heart turned away from me" [Psalm 101:4]). We reap in this way what our actions have earned us, or rather we receive the price that our own resolute tendencies deserve: the fire of Gehenna [which is] one of sensual delight, eternal darkness [which is] that of ignorance and the enticements of the world, the punishing and unsleeping worm [which is] that of hatred and lies warping and twisting the heart, the grindings of the teeth [which are those] of licentious prattle and unrest, the plunge and the yawning abyss, the horror at being fixed there [which are those of] haughtiness and arrogance. In short, for each of our deliberately willed evils accrues its counterpart that we do not will. O miserable lot! Why not extinguish the fire by fasting, vigils, mediation on the divine words which so easily quench this fire, instead of frying down below? Why not see, hear and speak according to nature and not to accustom the eyes, ears and tongue to this, so not to have then this darkness and this silence of the grave, but to enjoy with the saints light, word and wisdom, having becoming spectators, listeners and singers of the divine glory? If through love we kill this worm of hatred and through truth we erase the lies, we are delivered from that other burning worm and those other evil spells that besiege our life. Just is God's judgment. Whatever is not sought for is not found, and the door to the Kingdom of heaven does not open if we do not knock at the door by practicing the virtues. If we do not ask in prayer for the grace of knowledge, we do not enjoy the eternal good things, we have no love for them, and we enchain our spirit to the things of the earth and by that corrupt our whole life. But see how the former passes away as so much smoke dispelled, while the word of justice about the latter subject … it does not pass away. Those who experience the might of divine justice will perhaps reflect among themselves; they have not suffered on account of it. But I, poor wretch, what will become of me? On the basis of what actions shall I hope to escape the dread condemnation, stripped naked as I am of all virtue and knowledge? I fear being thrown bound hand and foot on a smoke-blackened earth, a land of eternal night where there is nowhere a glimmer, where no mortal is seen alive, as if the faculties for acting were intentionally chained down by the passions, and the advance of the soul along the divine course of the evangelic life barred. Alas, this frightful shame without end if I do not change and deliver myself from my many perversions. Alas, what lamenting and bitter tears if I do not fast and shake off, even late in life, the deep sleep of my laziness and throw off the soiled garment of sin. Instead of light, darkness; instead of grace, sadness; instead of remission, punishment and agony are reserved for me. Both the most pitiful and, to say it all, the most serious (I suffer just to say it), how much more grievous (be kind to me, O Christ, and preserve me from this woe) are the separation from God and his angelic powers, and the deep, perpetual union with the devil and the evil spirits, without being able to expect any liberation from such terrible things. It is with them in fact, according to this age and our unwholesome preoccupations, that we are choosing to go by willful tendency and by directly willing; but along with them too, with good reason, we will be condemned in the age to come, and this time without willing it. This is an ordeal crueler than any other punishment: to be in a perpetual relationship with those who hate and those who are hated, without even any other torture than that, and to be separated from those who love and those who are loved. For God, when He pronounces a just judgment, is not hated by those He judges; for by nature He is (and is called) love, and neither does He hate those He judges, being free from such a passion.

We truly believe that this is how it will be. We do not give way then, but from now on escape with zeal and all our strength from the errings of this world and its overlord the devil, for he is in flight and everything in him is withering away. It will come, truly it will come, that hour when the dread trumpet will sound with its unprecedented blast, and this universe will be dissolved, the whole beautiful order that we see now disintegrating, and this world of appearances will pass away in discovering its own completion and its end. And the now hidden intelligible world will manifest itself to our eyes, ears and intelligence, ushering in astonishing mysteries. And the trumpet blast will proclaim the divine decree, suddenly liberating myriads of human bodies, and it will raise them from death as if from a sleep to have them pass in review. And the God of justice will give to each his reward according to what he deserves, for the good or evil done, by giving to everything that exists its great, dread and ultimate conclusion. [Heaven] grant that we all have a salutary fear of Gehenna and a inestimable hope in the Kingdom of heaven—which is rightly the same thing said in two ways, in accordance with God making Himself all in all— constantly before our eyes: fear, so to always reject evil or make it cease, and desire, so to impel us joyously towards the abundance and the practice of the [divine] good things.[31]

As St Maximus emphasizes, meditation on the last things and the fear of judgment and Hell should be accompanied, so to draw profit from this and not sink into despair, by an expectation of the Kingdom and a desire for God's bounty. Here we must recall Christ's counsel to St Silouan: "Keep your mind in Hell, and despair not!"[32]

4 Features Specific to the Christian Conception.

The Christian position is far from that of the wisdom traditions in antiquity, like Epicureanism and Stoicism which focus their reflections on the very moment of death and, by various considerations, aim at dispelling the fear of it. It is also far from the general attitude of our civilization which, with the same aim, obscures the fear of it by various means.

From a certain point of view, Christianity sees the moment of death as not to be feared, for it is only a passage from one modality of existence to another which, to the eyes of faith, is beneficial, since it frees us from the limitations and the evils of the present life, and gives us the possibility of acceding to a better life.

But at the same time Christianity is aware that this transition is an ordeal, and, the more someone is attached to their body and this world in the course of their earthly existence, it will be that much harder to detach themselves from them. It also knows that the outcome of this transition is in fact uncertain: death can lead to a happy life, but also to a more unfortunate life. Everything depends on the spiritual state of a person at the time of their death. And so St John Chrysostom writes this striking formula: "To die is not evil, but it is evil to die an evil death."[33]

Man's earthly existence is of short duration and also seems to him shorter and shorter as he gradually advances in age. The existence that follows death, conversely, is an eternal existence in which the condition that falls to man will be in the end definitive. Therefore it is urgent for man to prepare for his future life and dedicate all his energies and all his time to this. "Now," St Gregory of Nazianzus notes, "there is but one thing to preoccupy us: the departure [from this world], in the prospect of which we retire within ourselves and prepare."[34] There will no longer be time to think and prepare at the moment of one's death. This preparation is the work of each instant. The dispositions required of man to accede to Paradise and the Kingdom are like the oil that feeds the flame of a lamp: he should be vigilant about never lacking it under pain of seeing himself, like the foolish virgins of the Gospel, denied access to the wedding chamber (Matt. 25:1–13). "It is here," writes St John Chrysostom, "that we must prepare this oil, so that we find it ready in our vases when we have need of it. There is no longer time to think of this after our death. It is necessary to do so in this life."[35] "Watch," Christ recommends in drawing the lesson from this parable, "for you know neither the day, nor the hour" (Matt. 25:13).

The preparation for eternal life in the Kingdom of heaven is therefore not the business of an instant preceding death, nor of simple dispositions manifested at the moment of dying (even if it is true that repentance and the attitude of man towards God are, in this last moment, of capital importance), but is a matter of a man's entire earthly life. Founded on faith, hope, and love, it aims at acquiring purity with respect to evil, sins and the passions, and the sum total of the virtues which will enable the faithful to be without reproach at the hour of judgment and found worthy to abide, with the saints and heavenly powers, close to God Himself.

In order to be united with Christ in the life to come in the Holy Spirit, and through Him united with the Father, to live with a divine life, to share in the good things of God and participate in divine beatitude, man should be united with Christ from this world and acquire, as much as possible, likeness to Him. There is eternal life in God only in and through Christ: "God has given us eternal life, and this life is in His Son. He who has the Son has life; he who does not have the Son of God does not have life" (1 John 5:11–12).

This life is not simply a human life, that an individual can lead solely with his own strength. It is a divine-human life that can only be realized through a synergy of his strength and divine grace, and it is only in the Church, through the sacraments, that he can receive this grace.

Human life in the hereafter, as proclaimed by Christianity, is a multiform victory over fallen nature—a victory over the separation of soul and body, over the body's corruption, over the limitations of matter, over time—which is accomplished through the resurrection. Christianity alone enables man to benefit from such a victory. For all the other religions, man, with death, definitively loses his earthly body, since either his soul alone lives then for eternity, or he finds through reincarnation a series of *other* bodies in which he will again find evils or limitations similar to those of his previous life. These religions truly do damage to both man's nature (which loses its integrity by definitively losing its body) and to his person (reincarnation constituting a negation of it). On the other hand, for the Far Eastern religions, the life that follows earthly death is not so much an eternal life as an indefinite series of successive existences that accompany the cycles of reincarnation and new worlds in which man forever remains a prisoner.

The Christian conception of life after death is based on a unique, exceptional fact, absent from all the wisdom traditions and all the other religions: the resurrection of Christ, who, being God and having assumed in His divine person human nature in its totality, and having united it in Himself to the divine nature, has given to all men the possibility of rising from the dead and being united with God forever, with the entirety of their being. By this He has given to those who would be united with Him and live in Him in the Church, which is His body, the power to be partakers for eternity, in their renewed body and in their purified soul, of divine life and beatitude.

What more beautiful text—celebrating the marvelous victory of Christ over death, and the hope that He gives to all men of an eternally happy life in God—might we cite in conclusion than this homily by St John Chrysostom that is read in all Orthodox churches on the night of Pascha?

> If anyone is devout and a lover of God, let him enjoy this beautiful and radiant festival. If anyone is a wise servant, let him, rejoicing, enter into the joy of his Lord."

> If anyone has wearied himself in fasting, let him now receive his recompense. If anyone has labored from the first hour, let him today receive his just reward. If anyone has come at the third hour, with thanksgiving let him keep the feast. If anyone has arrived at the sixth hour, let him have no misgivings;

for he shall suffer no loss. If anyone has delayed until the ninth hour, let him draw near without hesitation.

If anyone has arrived even at the eleventh hour, let him not fear on account of his delay. For the Master is gracious and receives the last, even as the first; He gives rest to him that comes at the eleventh hour, just as to him who has labored from the first. He has mercy upon the last and cares for the first; to the one He gives, and to the other He is gracious. He both honors the work and praises the intention.

Enter all of you, therefore, into the joy of our Lord, and, whether first or last, receive your reward. O rich and poor, one with another, dance for joy! O you ascetics and you negligent, celebrate the day! You that have fasted and you that have disregarded the fast, rejoice today! The table is rich-laden; feast royally, all of you! The calf is fatted; let no one go forth hungry! Let all partake of the feast of faith. Let all receive the riches of goodness. Let no one lament his poverty, for the universal kingdom has been revealed.

Let no one mourn his transgressions, for pardon has dawned from the grave. Let no one fear death, for the Savior's death has set us free.

He that was taken by death has annihilated it! He descended into Hades and took Hades captive! He embittered it when it tasted his flesh! And anticipating this Isaiah exclaimed, "Hades was embittered when it encountered Thee in the lower regions." It was embittered, for it was abolished! It was embittered, for it was mocked! It was embittered, for it was purged! It was embittered, for it was despoiled! It was embittered, for it was bound in chains! It took a body and, face to face, met God! It took earth and encountered heaven! It took what it saw but crumbled before what it had not seen!

'O death, where is thy sting? O Hades, where is thy victory?' Christ is risen, and you are overthrown! Christ is risen, and the demons are fallen! Christ is risen, and the angels rejoice! Christ is risen, and life reigns! Christ is risen, and not one dead remains in a tomb! For Christ, being raised from the dead, has become the First-fruits of them that slept.

To Him be glory and might unto ages of ages. Amen.

NOTES

The French language edition of this work quoted from English sources, those sources being translated into French. The first English edition of the book translated all sources from the French back into English without reference to the original English texts. In bringing this book back into print, Holy Trinity Publications has kept sources as translated from the French.

Preface

1 John Chrysostom, *Homilies on Lazarus*, IV, 3; Theophylact of Bulgaria, *Explanation of the Holy Gospel according to St Luke*, 16.

2 These views seem pertinent judging, on the one hand, by the turmoil caused with the publications of Dr. Moody and his disciples relating to the often contradictory testimonies of borderline experiences between life and death, and, on the other, by the mental distress and demonic phenomena accompanying spiritualism and other practices that claim to give the dead the possibility of manifesting themselves to the living.

3 Cf. Theophylact of Bulgaria, *op. cit.*, 16.

4 Among the ancient exegeses see especially John Chrysostom, *On Wealth and Poverty*, 1–7. Among recent exegeses, see particularly the remarkable one by Metropolitan Hierotheos Vlachos, *Life after Death*, Levadia, 1996, pp. 19–33.

5 The first wide-ranging synthesis in recent times of Orthodox teaching on the hereafter we owe to Ignatius Brianchaninov (1807–1867), in his work *Slovo o smerti* [*Concerning Death*] in *Complete Works*, vol. III, Saint Petersburg, 1886, pp. 69–183 (in Russian). The well-known work of Archimandrite Seraphim Rose, *The Soul after Death*, Platina, 1980, is largely inspired by it, but above all wishes to respond to the theses of Dr. Moody (see *infra*). An excellent synthesis has been achieved more recently by Metropolitan Hierotheos Vlachos, *Life after Death*.

6 See Isaac the Syrian, *Ascetical Homilies*, 2.

7 Although the Fathers find profound reasons for our ignorance about the very moment of death, they hardly find any reason for our lack of knowledge about life after death, except that this involves an experience not possible to have in this world and therefore understand correctly (see Isaac the Syrian, *Ascetical Homilies*, 2). St

John Chrysostom notes moreover that such a knowledge would provide nothing essential to those who have faith and would be unconvincing to those without it (*Homilies on Lazarus*, IV, 3).

8 This motivation was derided by Nietzsche and was one of his chief avenues of assault in his critique of religion. However, if it is not exclusive and leaves room for deeper and more positive motivations, this critique is legitimate.

9 *The Soul after Death* (Platina, CA: St Herman of Alaska Brotherhood, 1980).

10 See Le Goff, *The Birth of Purgatory* (Chicago: University of Chicago Press, 1981).

11 Here is one dismaying anecdote: when D. R. Wheeler, in writing his wellknown book *Journey to the Other Side*, had asked representatives of various religious groups about their position on the situation of the soul after death, the Archpriest of the Greek Orthodox Archdiocese of the United States to whom he had appealed replied that Orthodoxy did not have any precise idea about the hereafter. And so the nevertheless very rich conception of the Orthodox Church is absent from a work in which representatives from all the other religions agreed to collaborate.

Chapter One—Death: Origin and Spiritual Meaning

1 Basil of Caesarea, *God is not the author of evil*, 7, PG 31; Maximus the Confessor, *Ad Thalassium*, 42, CCSG 7, p. 287; Gregory Palamas, *Topics of Natural and Theological Science and on the Moral and Ascetic Life*, 47, 51; *Homilies*, XXXI, PG 151, 396B.

2 See Athanasius of Alexandria, *Against the Heathen*, 2 and 3; Basil of Caesarea, *God is not the author of evil*, 7, PG 31, 344C; Gregory of Nyssa, *Great Catechism*, V, 6 and 8, VIII, 4–5; *The Making of Man*, IV, PG 44, 136D, XVII, 188B; *Treatise of Virginity*, XII, 2; *Pascal Homilies*, I, 4; John of Damascus, *Exact Exposition of the Orthodox Faith*, II, 12; John Chrysostom, *Homilies on the Statues*, XI, 2.

3 St John Chrysostom asserts on the one hand that "in paradise the human body was subject to neither corruption or death" (*Homilies on the Statues*, XI, 2), and on the other that, in this same paradise, he was "clothed with a mortal body" although experiencing none of its "sad necessities" (Homilies on Genesis, XVII, 7).

4 *On the Incarnation of the Word*, IV, 6; cf. *ibid.*, 4.

5 *Ibid.* V, 1.

6 This is the expression of Wisd. 2:23 cited by Athanasius of Alexandria, *On the Incarnation of the Word*, V, 2.

7 Gregory of Nyssa, *Great Catechism*, VIII, 5; *Sermons on the Beatitudes*, III, 5.

8 Cf. Gregory of Nyssa, *Great Catechism*, V, 6; Athanasius of Alexandria, *Against the Heathen*, 2; Gregory Palamas, *Topics of Natural and Theological Science and on the Moral and Ascetic Life*, 47.

9   Cf. Athanasius of Alexandria, *On the Incarnation of the Word*, III, 4; Maximus the Confessor, *Ambigua to John*, 10, PG 91, 1156D.

10 See Gregory Palamas, *Homilies*, 57, 2.

11 *Homilies*, 36, 3.

12 Cf. Basil of Caesarea, *God is not the Cause of Evil*, 7; Maximus the Confessor, *Commentary on the Our Father*, CCSG 23, p. 68 [*Philokalia*, vol. 2, p. 302]; *Ad Thalassium*, Prologue, CCSG 7, p. 27; Gregory Palamas, *Topics of Natural and Theological Science and on the Moral and Ascetic Life*, 46; *Homilies*, 54, 9.

13 *Against the Heathen*, 2.

14 *On the Incarnation of the Word*, V, 1.

15 *Ibid.*, V, 2.

16 Cf. Athanasius of Alexandria, *On the Incarnation of the Word*, III, 4; Maximus the Confessor, *Ad Thalassium*, 61, CCSG 22, p. 89; John of Damascus, *Exact Exposition of the Orthodox Faith*, II, 30.

17 Cf. Wisd. 6:18: "The keeping of her laws is the firm foundation of incorruption."

18 In this respect the Fathers emphasize man's responsibility, tied to his free choice (conditioned by a voluntary attachment to God), as much as the solicitude of God, who does not want man's death but his immortality. See Athanasius of Alexandria, *On the Incarnation of the Word*, III, 4–5; IV, 4; John Chrysostom, *Homilies on Genesis*, XVII, 3, Gregory Palamas, *Topics of Natural and Theological Science and on the Moral and Ascetic Life*, 47; *Homilies*, 31, PG 151, 388D.

19 *Homilies* 57, p. 469. Cf. John of Damascus, *Exact Exposition of the Orthodox Faith*, II, 11.

20 *To Autolycus*, II, 27. Cf. II, 24: "For man had been made a middle nature, neither wholly mortal, nor altogether immortal, but capable of either."

21 *On the Incarnation of the Word*, III, 4. Cf. John of Damascus, *Exact Exposition of the Orthodox Faith*, II, 30.

22 *Homilies*, 31, PG 151, 388D. Cf. *Homilies*, 54.

23 *Homilies* 31, PG 151, 388D; XXIX, PG 151, 369C. Cf. John Chrysostom, *Homilies on Genesis*, XVII, 7.

24 *Homilies*, 31, PG 151, 388D.

25 Cf. Rom. 5:12. *Letter to Diognetus*, XII, 2; Justin, *Dialogue with Tryphon*, 124; Irenaeus of Lyon, Against the Heresies, IV, 38, 4; Athanasius of Alexandria, *On the Incarnation of the Word*, III, 4–5; V, 1–3; Basil of Caesarea, *God is not the author of evil*, 7; Gregory of Nyssa, *Great Catechism*, VIII, 4; *On the Making of Man*, XX, PG 44, 200C; *On Virginity*, XII, 2; *On the Soul and the Resurrection*, 126, PG 46, 149A; John Chrysostom, *Homilies on Genesis*, XVII, 7; *Homilies on the Epistle to the Romans*,

X, 2; Maximus the Confessor, *Ambigua to John*, 7, PG 91, 1093A; 10, 1156D; *Ad Thalassium*, 61, CCSG 22, p. 89, 93, 95, 97; John of Damascus, *Exact Exposition of the Orthodox Faith*, II, 30; III, 1; Gregory Palamas, *Topics of Natural and Theological Science and on the Moral and Ascetic Life*, 46, 50, 51; *Homilies*, XI, PG 151, 125A.

26 *To Autolycus*, II, 25.

27 *Ad Thalassium*, 42, CCSG 7, p. 287; Blowers & Wilken, *On the Cosmic Mystery of Jesus Christ* (Crestwood NY: Saint Vladimir's Seminary Press, 2003), p. 121.

28 *Homilies*, 31, PG 151, 388BC, p. 243. Cf. John Chrysostom, *Homilies on the Statutes*, XI, 2; Theophilus of Antioch, *To Autolycus*, II, 25.

29 Cf. Gregory of Nyssa, *Great Catechism*, V, 11; John of Damascus, *Exact Exposition of the Orthodox Faith*, II, 30; John Chrysostom, *Homilies on Genesis*, XVI, 4; Gregory Palamas, *Topics of Natural and Theological Science and on the Moral and Ascetic Life*, 46; 48; 66; *Homilies*, 16.

30 *On the Incarnation of the Word*, IV, 4.

31 Cf. *ibid.*, 5.

32 Recall that according to a majority of the Greek Fathers evil exists first only through the personal will of the demons or man, and secondly has no positive essence, being only the privation of the good. See especially Basil of Caesarea, *God is not the Author of Evil*, 2; Gregory of Nyssa, *Great Catechism*, V, 11–12; VI, 6; VII, 3–4; Dionysius the Areopagite, *On the Divine Names*, V, 19–35; Maximus the Confessor, *Ad Thalassium*, Prologue.

33 *Great Catechism*, VIII, 19.

34 *Ibid.*, VI, 11.

35 *God is not the author of evil*, 7.

36 *Ambigua to John*, 10, PG 91, 1156D.

37 Cf. John Chrysostom, *Homilies on the Statutes*, XI, 2. Gregory Palamas, *To Xenia*, 9; *Homilies*, 11, PG 151, 125A.

38 *On the Incarnation of the Word*, III, 5.

39 *To Xenia*, 10. Cf. *Topics of Natural and Theological Science and on the Moral and Ascetic Life*, 51.

40 Among others see: John Chrysostom, *Homilies on the Epistle to the Romans*, X, 2; Mark the Monk, *On Baptism*, 18.

41 See Gregory of Nyssa, *The Making of Man*, XVI, PG 44, 185B; XXII, 204CD; Mark the Monk, *On the Hypostatic Union*, 18; Gregory Palamas, *Homilies*, 5, PG 150, 64–65; 52.

42 See Gregory of Nyssa, *The Beatitudes*, VI, 5; Theodoret of Cyrrhus, *Commentary on the Epistle to the Romans*, PG 80, 1245A; Maximus the Confessor, *Ad Thalassium*, 21,

CCSG 7, p. 127; 61, CCSG 22, pp. 85–87, 91; John of Damascus, *Exact Exposition of the Orthodox Faith*, II, 30; Gregory Palamas, *Homilies*, 5, PG 150, 64B; 43; 54.

43 See especially Maximus the Confessor, *Ad Thalassium*, 61, CCSG 22, pp. 87–97.

44 *Ad Thalassium*, 49, CCSG 7, p. 369.

45 *Ambigua to John*, 31, PG 91, 1276AB; *Ad Thalassium*, 31, CCSG 7, p. 129.

46 *Commentary on Psalm 114*, 2. Cf. *Commentary on the Gospel of St Matthew*, XXXI, 3.

47 *Homilies on Genesis*, XVIII, 3.

48 John Chrysostom, *Commentary on the Gospel of St Matthew*, XXXIV, 4; *Homilies on the Statutes*, XI, 2.

49 *Commentary on the Gospel of St Matthew*, XXXIV, 4.

50 *God is not the Author of Evil*, 7. Also see Methodius of Olympus, *On the Resurrection*, XL; XLIII.

51 *Commentary on the Gospel of St Matthew*, XXXIV, 4.

52 *Homily on the Resurrection of the Dead*, 7.

53 See Theophilus of Antioch, *To Autolycus*, II, 26; John Chrysostom, *Commentary on the Gospel of St Matthew*, XXXIV, 4.

54 Methodius of Olympus, *On the Resurrection of the Body*, XL; XLIII; Gregory of Nazianzus, *Discourses*, XXXVIII, 12; XLV, 8; John Climacus, *The Ladder*, XV, 1.

55 *Homilies on the Statutes*, V, 4.

56 *Letters* 10, PG 91, 449BC. Cf. *Ad Thalassium*, 61, CCSG 22, p. 85.

57 *Ad Thalassium*, 42, CCSG 7, p. 287; Louth, p. 120.

58 *Ambigua to John* 10, PG 91, 1157C; Louth p. 127.

59 On the concepts of distance (*diastasis*) and separation (*diastema*) in Maximus, see L. Thunberg, *Microcosm and Mediator. The Theological Anthropology of Maximus the Confessor*, 2nd ed. Chicago and La Salle, 1995, pp. 57–60.

60 *Homilies on Lazarus*, V, 2.

61 See John Chrysostom, *Commentary on the Gospel according to St Matthew*, XXXVIII, 4; Gregory of Nyssa, *On Death*. Notice also that this is the title of a treatise by St Ambrose of Milan (*De bono mortis*, PL 14, 567–596).

62 John Chrysostom, *Commentary on the Gospel of St Matthew*, XXXIV, 4.

63 See Jean Daniélou, 'La doctrine de la mort chez les Pères de l'Église', in *Le Mystère de la mort et sa célébration*, Paris, 1956, pp. 141–151.

64 The word evil does not have, however, the same meaning in both instances: a physical evil in the first instance (death is one of the evils resulting from the ancestral sin), an evil of the moral and spiritual order in the second.

65 See our study: *Dieu ne veut pas la souffrance des hommes*, Paris, 1999.

66 On this interpretation of the Greek text of St Paul's verse, see: S. Lyonnet, 'Le sens de ἐφ' ᾧ en Rm 5, 12 et exégèse des Pères greca', *Biblica* 36, 1955, pp. 436–456; J. Meyendorff, *Byzantine Theology: historical trends and doctrinal themes*, 2nd ed. (New York: Fordham University, 1979), pp. 143–144; ' Ἐφ' ᾧ (Rm 5, 12) chez Cyrille d'Alexandrie et Théodoret', *Studia Patristica*, 4, *Texte und Untersuchungen*, 79, 1961, pp. 157–161.

67 See Meyendorff, *op. cit.*, pp. 144–145.

68 *Commentary on the epistle to the Romans*, PG 66, 801B.

69 *Commentary on the epistle to the Romans*, PG 80, 1245A.

70 *Commentary on the epistle to the Romans*, PG 82, 100.

71 On the previously cited passions, see our study: *Therapy of Spiritual Illnesses*, trans. K. Sprecher (Montreal: Alexander Press, 2012).

72 *Homilies on the epistle to the Hebrews*, IV, 4; *Homilies on the holy martyrs Bernice, Prosdoce and Domina*, 1. St John Chrysostom remarks in several places that the fear of death held sway not only over sinners but the just (*Homilies on the holy martyrs Bernice, Prosdoce and Domina*, 1). He gives the example of Abraham (*Letters to Olympias*, III, 3; *Homilies on the holy martyrs Bernice, Prosdoce and Domina*, 1–2; *Homilies on Genesis*, XXXII, 5), Jacob (*Homilies on the holy martyrs Bernice, Prosdoce and Domina*, 2), Moses (*Homily on Eleazar and the seven youths*, 2), and Elias (*ibid.*).

73 *Homilies on the epistle to the Hebrews*, IV, 4.

74 *Exact Exposition of the Orthodox Faith*, III, 1.

75 See J. Meyendorff, *A Study of Gregory Palamas* (Crestwood NY: St Vladimir's Seminary Press, 1964), pp. 158–159.

76 *Ad Thalassium*, 61, CCSG 22, p.95; Blowers & Wilken, p. 138.

77 See *Ad Thalassium*, 21, CCSG 7, pp.127–129; Blowers & Wilken, pp. 110–111.

78 This passion is at origin natural and non-culpable, since it is a normal expression of the survival instinct, the tendency of all living beings to persist in being, as well as an expression of the inner sense that death is foreign to man's true nature and has been introduced into it as a foreign and parasitical element.

79 See our study: *Dieu ne veut pas la souffrance des hommes*, pp. 39–47.

80 See *Ad Thalassium*, 21, CCSG 7, p. 131 [Blowers & Wilken, p. 112]; 61, CCSG 22, p. 89 [Blowers & Wilken, pp.134–135].

81 See Gregory of Nyssa, *On Death*, PG 46, 517A.

82 *Catechetical Oration*, 32.

83 See Maximus the Confessor, *Ad Thalassium*, 61; John of Damascus, *Exact Exposition of the Orthodox Faith*, III, 1.

84 Cf. Athanasius of Alexandria, *On the Incarnation of the Word*, 20; Cyril of Alexandria, *Commentary on the Gospel according to St Luke*, V, 19.

85 Cf. Gregory of Nyssa, *Pascal Homilies*, II, 5.

86 See John Chrysostom, *Homilies on the epistle to the Romans*, X, 2; *Commentary on the Gospel according to St John*, XXV, 2; *Homily on the Ascension*, 2.

87 See for example Methodius of Olympus, *On the Resurrection of the Body*, III, 23; John Chrysostom, *Homilies on the epistle to the Colossians*, VI, 3; *Homily in honor of all the saints who have suffered martyrdom*, 1.

88 See Athanasius of Alexandria, *On the Incarnation of the Word*, 20.

89 See Maximus the Confessor, *Commentary on the Our Father*, CCSG 23, p.36.

90 See Maximus the Confessor, *Ad Thalassium*, 21, CCSG, 7, p.131 [*On the Cosmic...* p. 112].

91 See Maximus the Confessor, *Ad Thalassium*, 21, CCSG, 7, pp. 129–131 [Blowers & Wilken, pp. 110–112]; 42, CCSG 7, p. 287 [Blowers & Wilken, p. 121].

92 See Gregory Nazianzus, *Oration XXX*; Maximus the Confessor, *Theological and Polemical Opuscules*, VI, PG 91, 65A–68D; VII, PG 91, 80C; XVI, PG 91, 196D; III, PG 91, 48C; XV, PG 91, 160C, 164C, 165AB, 169C.

93 See *Ibid.*

94 See Athanasius of Alexandria, *On the Incarnation of the Word*, 20.

95 See John Chrysostom, *Homilies on the epistle to the Hebrews*, IV, 4.

96 Irenaeus of Lyon, *Against the Heresies*, III, 23, 1.

97 *On the Incarnation of the Word*, 10.

98 See John Chrysostom, *Homily on the word 'cemetery' and on the Cross*, 1; *Homily on the Feast of Pascha*, 2; *Homilies on Genesis*, XXIX, 7.

99 *On the Incarnation of the Word*, 27. Cf. 28–30.

100 *Homilies on the epistle to the Hebrews*, IV, 4.

101 *Homily on the Feast of Pascha*, 2.

102 *Homily on the word 'cemetery' and on the Cross*, 2.

103 *Homily in honor of all the saints who have suffered martyrdom*, 1.

104 *Homilies on the holy martyrs Bernice, Prosdoce and Domina*, 1

105 *Ad Thalassium*, 42, CCSG 7, p. 285; Blowers & Wilken, p. 120.

106 John Chrysostom, *Commentary on the Gospel according to St Matthew*, XXXI, 3.

107 See Theophilus of Antioch, *To Autolycus*, II, 26; Methodius of Olympus, *On the Resurrection*, XL, XLIII; Gregory of Nyssa, *On Death*, PG 46, 516C; John Chrysostom, *Homily on the Resurrection of the Dead*, 7; *Homilies on the second epistle to the Corinthians*, X, 3; Gregory Palamas, *Topics of Natural and Theological Science and on the Moral and Ascetic Life*, 54.

108 See John Chrysostom, *Homily on the epistle to the Hebrews*, IV, 4.

109 See John Chrysostom, *Commentary on Psalm 48*, 5.

110 See Ignatius of Antioch, *To the Romans*, VI, 2.

111 *Homily in honor of all the saints who have suffered martyrdom*, 1.

112 See for example Athanasius of Alexandria, *On the Incarnation of the Word*, 28–29; Basil of Caesarea, *Homily on the holy martyr Barlaam*, 1.

113 'La doctrine de la mort chez les Pères de l'Église', op. cit., pp. 143–144. Recall that the flesh, in the language of St Paul and the Fathers, does not designate the body, but whatever is opposed to the spirit.

114 *To the Romans*, VI–VII [trans. B. D. Ehrman (Cambridge MA: Loeb Classical Library, 2003), pp. 277, 279].

115 *Life of St Macrina*, 23 [W. K. L. Clarke trans.].

116 *Ibid.*, 24.

Chapter Two — The Moment of Death

1   Archimandrite Sophrony, *His life Is Mine* (Crestwood NY: St Vladimir's Seminary Press, 1977), p. 54.

2   Ode 1, Tone 6. *The Great Book of Needs*, vol. III (South Canaan PA: St Tikhon's Seminary Press, 2002), p. 75.

3   *Révélation au sujet des âmes: comment elles sont enlevées des corps*, éd. Lantschoot, p. 178. Also see: *Sayings of the Desert Fathers*, alphabetical collection, Elias, 1.

4   *Ascetic Discourses*, XXVI, 32.

5   *Sayings of the Desert Fathers*, alphabetical collection, Elias, 1.

6   Psalm 69: 2, 6.

7   Psalm 142.

8   Ode 3.

9   Ode 1.

10 Ode 6.

11 Ode 7.

12 See R. Moody, *Life After Life* (Covington GA: Mockingbird Books/Bantam Books, 1973), pp. 64–73.

13 See S. Bulgakov, *The Bride of the Lamb*, trans. B. Jakim (Grand Rapids MI/ Edinburgh: William B. Eerdmans/T & T Clark, 2002), p. 360; Vlachos, *Life after Death*, p. 53, 67, 73.

14 *Life after Death*, p. 53.

15 *Ibid.*, p. 73. Cf. John Chrysostom, *Commentary on the Gospel according to St Matthew*, XLIV.

16 See S. Bulgakov, *The Bride of the Lamb*, p. 360.

17 See S. Bulgakov, *Jacob's Ladder*, trans. T. A. Smith (Grand Rapids MI/Cambridge UK: William B. Eerdmans, 2010), p. 146.

18 See St John Maximovich, *Sermon on Life after Death*, note 2.

19 *Révélation au sujet des âmes: comment elles sont enlevées des corps*, p. 178.

20 *Dialogues*, IV, 36, trans. O. J. Zimmerman (New York: Fathers of the Church, 1959), p. 233.

21 *Ibid.*

22 *Ibid.*

23 See Gregory the Great, *Dialogues*, IV, 12; 17.

24 *Life of St Syncletica*, 113, trans. E. B. Bongie (Toronto: Peregrina, 1995), p. 68.

25 He was already deceased at that time.

26 *Sayings of the Desert Fathers*, alphabetical collection, Sisoes, 14.

27 *The Life of Daniel the Stylite*, 97; in Dawes and Baynes, *Three Byzantine Saints*, Oxford, 1948, p. 68

28 *Dialogues*, IV, 17.

29 *Ibid.* IV, 18.

30 *Ibid.*, IV, 12.

31 *Ibid.*, IV, 14.

32 *Ibid*, IV, 12.

33 *Ibid.*, IV, 13.

34 The *Life St Macarius of Scetis*, 34, in *Saint Macarius, the Spiritbearer*, trans. T. Vivian (Crestwood NY: St Vladimir's Seminary Press, 2004), p. 192.

35 *Life of St Daniel the Stylite*, 96; Baynes and Dawes, p. 68.

36 Angelic apparitions.

37 S. Bulgakov, *Jacob's Ladder*, p. 146.

38 See Gregory of Nazianzus, *Discourses*, XLIII, 79; John Chrysostom, *Homilies on Lazarus*, II, 2; *Homily on Repentance*, PG 60, 727; *Life of St Daniel the Stylite*, 97; *Life of Hypatios*, 51, 3; *History of the Monks of Egypt*, XI, 8 (On Abba Surous). Other references will be given in chapter 4, section 1.

39 See Justin, *Dialogue with Trypho*, 105; Basil of Caesarea, *Homily on Holy Baptism*, PG 31, 441D–444A.

40 *Sayings of the Desert Fathers*, alphabetical collection, Sisoes, 14.

41 *Discourses*, XLIII, 79.

42 *Life of St Macarius of Scetis*, 35; p. 193.

43 *History of the Monks of Egypt*, XIV, 23; trans. Russell, *The Lives of the Desert Fathers*, London/Oxford/Kalamazoo MI, 1980, p. 98.

44 See F. Cumont, 'Les vents et les anges psychopompes', *Pisciculi. Studien dien zur Religion und Kultur des Altertums (Antike und Christentum. Ergänzungsband, 1)*, Münster, 1939; A. Recheis, *Engel, Tod und Seelen reise. Das Wirken der Geister beim Heimgang der Menschen in der Lehre der alexandrinischen und kappadokischen Väter*, 'Temi e Testi' num. 4, Rome, 1958.

45 S. Bulgakov, *Jacob's Ladder*, p. 71.

46 See *infra*.

47 A. Uexkuell, 'Unbelievable for Many, but Actually a True Occurrence', *Orthodox Life*, 26, 1976, p. 22.

48 *Vita Patrum*, trans. S. Rose and P. Bartlett (Platina CA: St Herman of Alaska Brotherhood, 1988), p. 296.

49 Gregory of Thrace, *Life of St Basil the Young*, Account of Theodora from: *Eternal Mysteries Beyond the Grave*; Archimandrite Panteleimon (Jordanville NY: Holy Trinity Publications, 2012) p. 94.

50 *Dialogues*, IV, 40.

51 *Eternal Mysteries Beyond the Grave*; Archimandrite Panteleimon (Jordanville NY: Holy Trinity Publications, 2012) p. 93.

52 *Ibid*, p.94.

53 Ode 1, Tone 6.

54 Ode 3.

55 *Révélation au sujet des âmes: comment elles sont enlevées des corps*, p. 178.

56 *Homily on Patience*, PG 60, 727.

57 *Commentary on the Gospel according to St Matthew*, LIII, 5.

58 *Ibid*.

59 *Life and of St Syncletica*, 113, p. 68.

60 See *infra*, chapter 4.

61 *Ecclesiastical History of the English People*, V, 13; ed. B. Colgrave and R. A. B. Mynors (Oxford: Clarendon Press, 1969), p. 501.

62 See Gregory the Great, *Dialogues* IV, 16.

63 *Ibid.*, IV, 15, 1.

64 *Ibid.*, IV, 15, 4.

65 *Ibid.*, IV, 16.

66 *History of the Monks of Syria*, X, 8; trans. R. M. Price (Kalamazoo MI: Cistercian Publications, 1985), p. 92.

67 See Gregory the Great, *Dialogues*, IV, 16.

68 See *ibid.*, 13; 16.

69 *Homily on Patience*, PG 60. 727.

70 See the *Synaxarion*, May 3/16.

71 First edition Mockingbird Books, Atlanta, 1975.

72 See for example D. R. Wheeler, *Journey to the Other Side*, New York, 1977; K. Osis and E Haraldson, *At the Hour of Death*, New York, 1977; E. Kübler-Ross, *La Mort est un nouveau soleil*, Paris, 1988; and likewise R. Moody, *Reflections on the After Life*, New York, 1985.

73 See for example R. Moody, *Life after Life*, pp. 21–25.

74 As R. Moody honestly recognizes, *ibid.*, p. 3.

75 *Ibid.*, 21–23.

76 *Ibid.*, p. 22 and *passim*.

77 *Ibid.*, pp. 23–24.

78 Accounts analogous to those found on this subject in Dr. Moody's books are also found in the Orthodox world. See for example 'Unbelievable for Many, but Actually a True Occurrence', an English translation, printed in *Orthodox Life* (vol. 26, num. 4, 1976, pp. 1–36), of an account published at the end of the nineteenth century in the *Moscow Journal* and reprinted in 1916 by Bishop Nikon, a member of the Holy Synod, in his publication *Trinitary Pages*; the account's author, K. Ueskuell, became a monk in the Orthodox Church. Also see the account related by Metropolitan Hierotheos Vlachos of a similar experience that happened some years ago to Metropolitan Kallinikos of Edessa (*Life after Death*, pp. 116–117).

79 See Archimandrite Seraphim Rose, *The Soul after Death*, pp. 14–16; Metropolitan Hierotheos Vlachos, *Life after Death*, pp. 111–131.

80 This is also the case for occultist literature as a whole (inspired by Swedenborg, Theosophy or Spiritualism) or that of Far-Eastern inspiration (drawn from the

Tibetan *Book of the Dead*, for example), which Archimandrite Seraphim Rose refutes in his book *The Soul after Death*, pp. 97–135.

81 See the commentaries of Archimandrite Seraphim Rose, *The Soul after Death*, pp. 21–26.

82 See Archimandrite Seraphim Rose, *The Soul after Death*, pp. 14–16.

83 *Synaxarion*, May 3/16.

84 Archimandrite Seraphim Rose, who has devoted a large part of his book *The Soul after Death* to a critical analysis of Dr. Moody's *Life after Life*, is quite hesitant about making 'beings of light' comparable to angels, since these beings of light, devoid of visible form and presented as systematically agreeable, even amusing, do not incline the dying to repentance and lead him nowhere (see *The Soul after Death*, pp. 42–49).

85 See Gregory the Great, *Dialogues*, IV, 13, 16, 20; Leontius of Neapolis, *The Life of St Symeon the Fool*, 41.

Chapter Three — From the First to the Third Day

1 Among others see: Clement of Alexandria, *Miscellanies*, VII, XII, 71, 3; *Sayings of the Desert Fathers*, anonymous collection, num. 1491 (N 491); Athanasius of Alexandria, *Against the Heathen*, 33; Gregory of Nyssa, *Against Apollinarius*, XVII, PG 45, 1153D; Gregory of Nazianzus, *Moral Poems*, XXXXIV, 25, PG 37, 947A; John Chrysostom, *Homilies on the Consolation of Death*, II, 1; *Homilies on the Statues*, V, 3; *Homilies on Second Corinthians*, X, 2; Gregory the Great, *Dialogues*, IV, 7; 9; Gregory Palamas, *To Xenia*, 9. Among recent authors: S. Bulgakov, *Jacob's Ladder*, p. 71; Archimandrite Justin Popovich, *Philosophie orthodoxe de la vérité, Dogmatique de l'église orthodoxe*, vol. 1, Lausanne, 19997, p. 364; Metropolitan Hierotheos Vlachos, *Life after Death*, pp. 51–52; N. P. Vassiliadis, *The Mystery of Death*, Athens, 1993, pp. 95–98.

2 See our *Mental Disorders and Spiritual Healing*, Hillsdale NY, 2005, pp. 26–33.

3 See Gregory of Nyssa, *Catechetical Oration*, VIII, 5–6; John Chrysostom, *Commentary on Psalm XLVIII*, 5.

4 See Athanasius of Alexandria, *Against the Heathen*, 33; Gregory of Nyssa, *Catechetical Oration*, VIII, 8; John Chrysostom, *Homilies on the Consolation of Death*, II, 1.

5 See among others: *Justin, Dialogue with Trypho*, V; Athanasius of Alexandria, *Against the Heathen*, 33; Gregory of Nyssa, *Catechetical Oration*, VIII, 8; John Chrysostom, *Homilies on the Consolation of Death*, II, 1. Some fathers assert that the soul is immortal by nature (see Athanasius of Alexandria, *Against the Heathen*, 33; Gregory of Nyssa, *Catechetical Oration*, VIII, 8). Others consider that, being created, it is by nature mortal, but is made immortal by grace, this grace being accorded to all human souls (see Justin, *Dialogue with Trypho*, V).

6 See Athanasius of Alexandria, *Against the Heathen*, 33; Gregory of Nyssa, *Catechetical Oration*, VIII, 8; John Chrysostom, *Commentary on Psalm XLVIII*, 5; Gregory

Palamas, *To Xenia*, 9: "The separation of the soul from the body is the death of the body" (*The Philokalia*, IV, p. 296).

7   See Nicetas Stethatos, *On the Soul*, XIII, 68; 70; Callistus and Ignatius of Xanthopoulos, *Directions to Hesychasts*, 69.

8   See our works *Mental Disorders and Spiritual Healing*, pp. 31–33, 36–39; *Pour une éthique de la procréation. Éléments d'anthropologie patristique*, Paris, 1998, pp. 107–110.

9   This symbolism, prevalent in Plato's *Phaedrus*, is often used by St Gregory of Nyssa.

10 By way of illustration see: *Sayings of the Desert Fathers*, anonymous collection, N 491. On the rivalry of angels and demons in gaining possession of the soul of the deceased, see *infra*, chapter 4, p. 74 ff.

11 See the anonymous text published by K. Krumbacher, 'Studien zu den Legenden des hl. Theodosios', *Sitzungsberichte der königl. bayr. Akademie der Wissenschaften*, Munich, 1892, pp. 348–350, from the Parisinus graec. 1140 A, f. 82r–v, cited by C. Vogel, 'The Cultic Environment of the Deceased in the Early Christian Period,' *Temple of the Holy Spirit*, trans. M. J. O'Connell (Collegeville, MN: The Liturgical Press, 1983), p. 269; this text seems to be in close rapport with a passage from *De mensibus* (IV, 26, ed. R. Wünsch, p. 84) by J. Lycos (sixth century); also see Macarius of Alexandria, *Révélation au sujet des âmes* p. 177. Hagiographic accounts show, however, some rare cases of saints whose souls were raised to heaven at the moment of death.

12 Canon 162, in J. Papp-Szilagyi, *Enchiridion juris ecclesiae orientalis catholicae*, 1880, p. 38, 48.

13 *Révélation au sujet des âmes*, p. 177.

14 *Ibid.*, p. 179.

15 *Thesaurus*, XV, CCSG 5, p. 127.

16 *Sermon on Life after Death*.

17 *Soul-Profiting Reading* (in Russian).

18 Here again a very ancient tradition is involved. Among the sources, see the *Apostolic Constitutions*, VIII, 42; Macarius of Alexandria, *Révélation au sujet des âmes*, pp. 177, 178–179; Palladius, *Lausiac History*, 21; Theodore of Petra, *Life of St Theodosius*, 8, ed. Usener, p. 22; Theognostus, *Thesaurus*, XV, CCSG 5, p. 127. See also G. Dagron's study, 'Troisième, neuvième et quarantième jours dans la tradition byzantine: temps chrétien et anthropologie', in *Le Temps chrétien de la fin de l'Antiquité au Moyen Âge, IIe-XIIIe siècle*, Paris, 1984, pp. 419–430.

19 See C. Vogel, 'The Cultic Environment of the Deceased in the Early Christian Period,' p. 271.

20 See the *Apostolic Constitutions*, VIII, 42.

21 Macarius of Alexandria, *Révélation au sujet des âmes* , p. 179; Theognostus, *Thesaurus*, XV, CCSG 5, p. 127; John Maximovich, *Sermon on Life after Death*.

22 See the anonymous texts (linked to *De mensibus*, IV, 26 of John Lycos) published by K. Krumbacher, 'Studien zu den Legenden des hl. Theodosios' pp. 345–347 ("When a person dies, on the third day he deteriorates and his external appearance is destroyed.), pp. 348–350 ("On the third day after death the viscera of the human being — stomach and intestines — liquefy; this is what we call dissolution."), cited by C. Vogel, 'The Cultic Environment of the Deceased in the Early Christian Period,' *Temple of the Holy Spirit*, New York, 1983, p. 268.

23 See G. Dagron, 'Troisième, neuvième et quarantième jours dans la tradition byzantine: temps chrétien et anthropologie,' p. 426.

24 See *ibid.*

25 See *ibid.*

26 Like St Anastasius, who returned from the other world at the very end of a full three days (*Apocalypse of Anastasius*, ed. Hamburg, p. 2), or more recently K. Ueskuell (see supra, chapter 2, note 78, p. 45).

27 See *supra*, chapter 2, pp. 43–48.

28 Pseudo-Athanasius, *Questions to Antiochus*, 127, PG 28, 677.

29 On this last point see the critical remarks of Dr. M. Andronikof (at present head of emergency services at a major Paris hospital), who shows that the current definition of death is marked by several contradictions (*Transplantation d'organes et éthique chrétienne*, Paris, 1993, pp. 57–62, and 'La bioéthique devant un regard orthodoxe', *Cahiers de l'Association des philosophes chr.tiens*, 6, 1993, pp. 5–7). See also our *Une fin de vie paisible, sans douleur, sans honte ...*, Paris, 2010, pp. 105–109, 190–198.

30 As the numerous cases of a return to life after being pronounced clinically dead by a doctor attest (see *supra*, chapter 2, p. 41 ff).

31 Pseudo-Athanasius, *Questions to Antiochus*, 127, PG 28, 677.

32 See Dr. M. Andronikof in *Transplantation d'organes et éthique chrétienne*, p. 53. Father N. Hatzinikolaou, 'Prolonging Life or Hindering Death? An Orthodox Perspective on Death, Dying and Euthanasia,' *Christian Bioethics*, 9, 2003 p. 188. See also our *Une fin de vie paisible, sans douleur, sans honte...*, Paris, 2010, pp. 134–135.

33 See C. Vogel, 'The Cultic Environment of the Deceased in the Early Christian Period,' *Temple of the Holy Spirit*, pp. 259–276. See also our *Une fin de vie paisible, sans douleur, sans honte ...*, Paris, 2010, pp. 243–245.

34 *Transplantation d'organe et éthique chrétienne*, p. 93; 'Le médecin face au patient de religion chrétienne orthodoxe', in H. Durant, P. Biclet, C. Hervé (ed.), *Éthique et pratique médicale*, Paris, 1995, p. 24: "By tradition, the separating of the soul from the organic body takes at least three days. Anything that interferes, during this lapse

of time, with the newly deceased person is seen as being possibly harmful for him. Hence the hesitation of some over organ donations and even autopsies." See also our *Une fin de vie paisible, sans douleur, sans honte . . .*, Paris, 2010, pp. 202–203.

35 *On the Practice of the Virtues, Contemplation and the Priesthood*, 61.

36 See *supra*, chapter 2, pp. 25–27.

37 Burial of a Layman, stikhera for the *Apasmos* [last kiss], tone 2, *The Great Book of Needs*, vol. III, p. 209.

38 Burial of a Layman, idiomela stikhera, tone 2, *ibid.*, p. 204; *cf.* Funeral Office over a Departed Priest, stikhera of St John of Damascus, tone 2, *ibid.*, p. 307.

39 *Révélation au sujet des âmes* , p. 178. The same text speaks a little later of the "affliction that affects the soul with regard to its separation from the body (p. 179). See also: *Sayings of the Desert Fathers*, alphabetical collection, Elias, 1; Theophilus, 4.

40 *Homilies Second Corinthians*, X, 3.

41 S. Bulgakov, *The Orthodox Church*, p. 181.

42 *Mikron euchologion*, Athens, 1996, p. 243.

43 *The Orthodox Church*, p. 181.

44 *Révélation au sujet des âmes* , pp. 177–178.

45 This image is found already in Plato's *Phaedrus*.

46 *The Soul and the Resurrection*, 70–71; trans. C. P. Roth (Crestwood NY: St Vladimir's Seminary Press, 1993), pp. 75–76.

47 *Ibid.*, 71; Roth, p. 76.

48 See *ibid.*, 73; Roth, p. 77.

49 Archimandrite Justin Popovich, *Philosophie orthodoxe de la vérité. Dogmatique de l'Église orthodoxe*, tome 5, Lausanne, 1997, p. 369.

50 *Ibid.*

51 *Ibid.*, p. 370.

52 Dionysius the Areopagite, *The Ecclesiastical Hierarchy*, VII, 2.

53 *Catechetical Oration*, VIII, 5.

54 *Homilies on Second Corinthians*, X, 3; cf. *Commentary on Psalm XLVIII*, 5.

55 Dionysius the Areopagite, *The Ecclesiastical Hierarchy*, VII, 2; *The Complete Works*, p. 250.

56 *Ambigua* 7, PG 91, 1101BC; *On the Cosmic Mystery of Christ*, trans. P. M. Blowers and R. L. Wilken (Crestwood NY: St Vladimir's Seminary Press, 2003). pp. 73–74.

57 *The Soul and the Resurrection*, 58; Roth, p. 56.

58 *On the Making of Man*, 27, PG 44, 225B.

59 *The Soul and the Resurrection*, 62; Roth, pp. 68–69.

60 *Ibid.*, 59; Roth, p. 67.

61 *On the Making of Man*, 27, PG 44 225C.

62 J. Daniélou makes a mistake in his translation of *The Making of Man* by translating this word as 'exterior aspect'. *Eidos* is rather a structure, a plan, a kind of 'Idea' or archetype, but personalized, which remains invariable behind the alterations that affect its material expressions and exterior appearance. This notion is also utilized by St Maximus the Confessor in an identical sense (see *supra*, note 52, p. 61 and *Letters* 15, PG 91, 552D; *Ambigua*, 42, 1324AB).

63 *On the Making of Man*, 27, PG 44, 228B (according to the J. Laplace French translation).

64 *The Soul and the Resurrection*, 60; Roth, pp. 67–68.

65 *The Soul and the Resurrection*, 61; Roth, p. 68.

66 It is oriented towards the east, the eyelids and mouth closed, the forearms crossed on the chest (symbolizing the Cross), and the hands holding an icon.

67 According to Orthodox ritual, a small band encircles the head of the deceased at forehead level. It bears the image of the Deisis (Christ in the center, the Mother of God to the right and St John the Baptist to the left), as well as the text of the *Trisagion*: "Holy God, Holy mighty, Holy immortal, have mercy on us!"

68 See J. Kyriakakis, 'Byzantine Burial Customs: Care of the Deceased from Death to the Prothesis', *The Greek Orthodox Theological Review*, 19, 1974, pp. 45–49; C. Vogel, *op cit.*, pp. 261–267; M. Andronikoff, *Transplantation d'organes et éthique chrétienne*, pp. 45–50; V. Bakogiannis, *After Death*, Katerini, 1995, pp. 46–47; N. P. Vassiliadis, *The Mystery of Death*, Athens, 1997, pp. 338–351. This last work contains numerous testimonies drawn from the *Lives* of the saints which witness to the antiquity of these customs and bring out their significance.

69 See also Gen. 50:5; Tob. 4:3–5.

70 See V. Bakogiannis, *After Death*, p. 54.

71 The validity of the veneration of relics was confirmed, as well as that of the veneration of icons, by the *de fide* definition of the Second Council of Nicea.

72 See our *Une fin de vie paisible, sans douleur, sans honte...*, Paris, 2000, chap. 7: "Cremation"pp. 219–248.

74 *The Orthodox Church*, p. 181.

75 *Ibid.*

76 *Ibid.*

Chapter Four — From the Third to the Ninth Day

1 This practice is already attested to in the fourth century. See *Apostolic Constitutions*, VIII, 42, 1: "Let the third day of the departed be celebrated with psalms, and lessons, and prayers." *Révélation au sujet des âmes...*, p. 179.

2 See G. Dagron, 'Troisième, neuvième et quarantième jours dans la tradition byzantine: temps chrétien et anthropologie', pp. 419–423, 427.

3 Anonymous text published by K. Krumbacher, 'Studien zu den Legenden des hl. Theodosios', pp. 348–350 from the Parisinus graec. 1140 A, f. 82r–v, cited by C. Vogel, *op. cit.*, p. 269.

4 Révélation au sujet des âmes..., p. 179.

5 Gregory of Nyssa, *On the Forty Martyrs*, PG 46, 780A.

6 John Chrysostom, *Homilies on the Consolation of Death*, II, I.

7 See S. Bulgakov, *Jacob's Ladder*, p. 71.

8 See *supra*, chap. 2, p. 49, note 44.

9 Gregory of Nyssa, *Life of St Macrina*, 24.

10 See G. Dagron, 'Troisième, neuvième et quarantième jours dans la tradition byzantine: temps chrétien et anthropologie', p. 420.

11 See for example Gregory of Thrace, *Life of St Basil the Young*, Account of Theodora.

12 *History of the Monks of Egypt*, XIV, 17; Russell, p. 97.

13 *Ibid.*, XIV, 24; Russell, p. 98.

14 Theodoret of Cyrrhus, *History of the Monks of Syria*, X, 8; Price, p. 92.

15 Palladius, *Lausiac History*, VII, 6. Cf. *The Lives of the Desert Fathers*, XXII, 9: "When [Amoun] died, completely alone, Antony saw his soul borne up to heaven by angels"; Palladius, *Lausiac History*, VIII, 6: "Such then was the life of the blessed Amoun and such his perfection that the blessed Antony saw his soul carried to heaven by angels."

16 Venerable Bede, *Life of St Cuthbert*, IV.

17 Gregory the Great, *Dialogues*, II, 35. See also IV, 9: "A certain religious man, and one of great credit... told me that certain men sailing from Sicily to Rome, as they were in the midst of the sea, beheld the soul of a certain servant of God carried to heaven, who had been an anchorite in the land of Samnium."

18 *Homilies*, XIV, On the Departure of the Soul.

19 Leontius of Neapolis, *Life of Symeon the Fool*, 9; Krueger, p. 141.

20 See S. Bulgakov, *The Orthodox Church*, p. 182; Justin Popovich, *Philosophie orthodoxe de la vérité*, tome 5, p. 367; Metropolitan Hierotheos Vlachos, *Life after Death*, pp. 23–24, 59–61.

21 Maximus the Confessor, *Letters*, 24, PG 91, 612A.

22 *On Watchfulness and Holiness*, 4; *Philokalia*, vol. 1, p. 163.

23 *Letters*, 7.

24 *Discourses*, XII, 127; Wheeler, pp. 183–184.

25 *On the Practice of the Virtues, Contemplation and the Priesthood*, 61; *Philokalia*, vol. 2, p. 373.

26 *Homilies* (collection III), XXV, 2, 3–4.

27 *Homilies* (collection II), XXII; Maloney, p. 155.

28 *On the Soul*, XIII, 69–72.

29 *Ibid.*, XIV, 79–81.

30 Ode 7, *The Great Book of Needs*, vol. III, p. 80.

31 Ode 1, *ibid.*, p. 75.

32 Ode 3, *ibid.*, p. 76.

33 Ode 5, *ibid.*, p. 78.

34 Ode 6, *ibid.*, p. 79.

35 Canon of Matins, ode 5, tone 8, *Menaion*, vol. 1, p. 237.

36 *Sayings of the Desert Fathers*, alphabetical collection, Theophilus, 4; Ward, p. 81. Also see Maximus the Confessor who, more briefly, likewise shows us a divided soul confronted by its judges (*Letters*, 24, PG 91, 612A).

37 Angels.

38 Demons.

39 Athanasius of Alexandria, *The Life of Antony*, 65; Gregg, p. 78–79. See also *ibid.*, 66.

40 *Ascetic Discourses*, I, 5; Chryssavgis, p. 40.

41 *The Ladder*, V, 22; HTM, p. 60.

42 *Homilies* (collection II), XVI, 13; Maloney, p. 134.

43 *On Watchfulness and Holiness*, 161; *Philokalia*, vol, 1, p. 190.

44 *Homilies on the Gospels*, XXXIX, 8 (on Luke 19:42–47), PL 76, 1298D–1299D; cited in *The Soul after Death*, p. 81.

45 Gregory of Thrace, *Life of St Basil the Young*, Account of Theodora from: *Eternal Mysteries Beyond the Grave*; Archimandrite Panteleimon (Jordanville NY: Holy Trinity Publications, 2012) p. 95.

46 *The Ladder*, VII, 50; HTM, p. 77.

47 *For the Encouragement of the Monks in India*, 25; *Philokalia*, vol. 1, pp. 303–304.

48 See the texts cited *infra*.

49 From the Greek τελώνια which denotes the stations or offices of the publicans, the duty or tax-collectors. See *infra*, note 57, p. 88.

50 See G. Dagron, 'Troisième, neuvième et quarantième jours dans la tradition byzantine: temps chrétien et anthropologie', p. 420.

51 See A. Guilaumont, Introduction to Evagrius of Ponticus, *Traité pratique*, Paris, 1971, pp. 63–84, *passim*.

52 This representation is analogous to the Holy Ladder of St John Climacus, but should not however be confused with it.

53 See *infra* note 57 on the publicans.

54 Maximus the Confessor, *Letters*, 24, PG 91, 612A.

55 See Justin Popovich, *Philosophie orthodoxe de la vérité*, tome 5, p. 366.

56 Anonymous text edited by K. Krumbacher, 'Studien zu den Legenden des hl. Theodosios', pp. 348–350, according to the Parisinus graec. 1140 A, f. 82r–v, cited by C. Vogel, *op. cit.*, p. 269. See also G. Dagron, *op. cit.*, pp. 420–423.

57 In the New Testament, this word designates "a minor Jewish subaltern who should rather be called a 'customs collector'. This was someone scorned and deemed comparable to public sinners by reason of his ties with the occupying pagan and his frequent exactions" (X.-L, Dufour, *Dictionnaire du Nouveau Testament*, Paris, 1975, p. 451).

58 *Homilies on Luke*, XXIII, 5–6; Lienhard, pp. 99–100.

59 *Homily on Psalm 7*, 2, PG 29, 232B, D.

60 *On Spiritual Knowledge and Discrimination*, 100; *Philokalia*, vol. 1, p. 295.

61 *Ascetic Discourses*, XIV, 1; Chryssavgis, p. 111.

62 The angels.

63 The demons.

64 *Ascetic Discourses*, VII, 32; Chryssavgis, p. 85.

65 *Ibid.*, XXIII, 11; Chryssavgis, p. 177.

66 *Ibid.*, XXVI, 3; Chryssavgis, p. 212.

67 *Homilies* (collection II), XLIII, 9; Maloney, p. 222.

68 *Sur la seconde venue du Christ*, éd. Assemani, tome 3, pp. 275–276.

69 *Homilies on those who have died*, PG 89, 1200.

70 *Sacred Parallels*, PG 96, 310.

71 *Homilies*, XIV, On the Departure of the Soul, PG 77, 1073–1076.

72 *Ascetic Discourses*, XVI, 4–18; Chryssavgis, pp. 119–121.

73 Leontius of Neapolis, *Life of John the Almsgiver*, chapter 41; in Dawes and Baynes, *Three Byzantine Saints* (Oxford: Basil Blackwell, 1948), pp. 248–249.

74 In the original patristic text, the word was 'Ethiopians.' In some patristic texts 'Ethiopians' symbolize demons.

75 Text edited by F. Combefis, *Bibliothecae Graecorum Patrum Auctarium Novissimum*, Paris, 1672, vol. 1, pp. 324–326.

76 This has to do with a treasure of prayers, symbolized by a pouch of gold handed over to the angels by St Basil at the death of Theodora. The account of this episode is situated immediately after the text cited supra note 45: "The demons, however, saw this and gnashed their teeth at me. They wanted to tear me instantly from the angels' arms and to carry me down to the bottom of hell. At this time, holy Basil himself appeared unexpectedly and said to the holy angels: 'Holy angels! This soul did great service to ease my old age, and therefore I prayed for her to God, and God has given her to me.' Having said this, he took something out that appeared like a little bag of gold and gave it to the angels with the words, 'Here is the treasure of prayers before the Lord for this soul! As you pass through the torments of the air and the evil spirits begin to torment her, pay her debts with this.'" [Archimandrite Panteleimon, *Eternal Mysteries Beyond the Grave*; 2012, p. 95.]

77 Gregory of Thrace, *Life of St Basil the Young*, Account of Theodora from: *Eternal Mysteries Beyond the Grave*; Archimandrite Panteleimon (Jordanville NY: Holy Trinity Publications, 2012) pp. 96–105.

78 See J. Riviere, 'Rôle de démon au jugement particulier chez les Pères', *Revue des sciences religieuses*, 4, 1924, pp. 57–63.

79 Here we have again the identity between sins (or passions) and demons.

80 Cited by Archimandrite Seraphim Rose, *The Soul after Death*, pp. 85–86.

81 Discourse on Death, *Collected Works*, vol. III, Saint Petersburg, 1886, p. 136.

82 It should be pointed out that the bishop Theophan the Recluse, in one of his shorter works, *The Soul and the Angels are not Corporeal but Spiritual Realities*, Moscow, 1891 (in Russian), criticized certain theses of the *Discourse on Death* by his contemporary bishop Ignatius Brianchaninov (such as the corporeity of the soul), but not what he had to say on the aerial toll-houses.

83 *Interpretation of Psalm 118*, Moscow, 1891 (in Russian), cited in *The Soul after Death*, pp. 95–96.

84 *Dogmatic Theology of the Catholic Orthodox Church*, trans. Vallianos, Athens, 1858, pp. 371–372.

85 *Orthodox Dogmatic Theology*, vol. 2, Saint Petersburg, 1883, p. 535 (in Russian); cited in *The Soul after Death*, p. 83. More recently, in his *Synaxarion*, the Macarius of Simonos-Petra noted: "This doctrine is eminently traditional and found in a good

number of holy Fathers and many *Lives* of the saints" (*The Synaxarion. Lives of the Saints of the Orthodox Church*, vol. III, Thessalonica, 1990, p. 459, note 5).

86 *The Orthodox Church*, p. 182.

87 Vol. 5, Lausanne, 1997, pp. 366–367.

88 Father Justin Popovich cites at length, as we ourselves have done, the testimony of Blessed Theodora. Its absence in the French translation of his *Dogmatics* is due to an initiative of the translator.

89 See John Maximovich, *Sermon on Life after Death*; Archimandrite Vasilios Bakogiannis, *After Death*, Katerini, 1995, pp. 59–67; Archimandrite Seraphim Rose, *The Soul after Death*, pp. 73–96, 253–263; Metropolitan Hierotheos Vlachos, *Life after Death*, pp. 62–80; N. P. Vassiliadis, *The Mystery of Death*, Athens, 1997, pp. 385–392.

90 Tone 4, Friday, ode 8, canon of matins.

91 Tone 3, Friday, ode 9, canon of compline.

92 Tone 1, Monday, kathisma 2, tone 1, matins.

93 Tone 7, Friday, ode 5, canon of compline.

94 Tone 1, Saturday, ode 6, canon of the midnight office.

95 *The Great Horologion*, Holy Transfiguration Monastery, 1997, p. 48.

96 *Akathist to the Guardian Angel*, trans. I. E. Lambertsen, 1992, p. 7.

97 *Menaion*, January 27, Canon of matins, ode 5, tone 8.

98 Ode 4, *The Great Book of Needs*, vol. III, p. 77.

99 Ode 8, *ibid.*, p. 81.

100 From L. Puhalo, *The Soul, the Body and Death*, Dewdney, B.C., 1996, *The Tale of Elder Basil the New and the Theodora Myth. Study of a Gnostic Document*, Dewdney, 1999, and of M. Azkoul, *The Toll-House Myth. The Neo-Gnosticism of Fr. Seraphim Rose*, Dewdney, B.C. (no date). These two authors seek above all to 'settle the score' with Father Seraphim Rose, the author of a bestselling book on this theme. This completely distorts their overall perspective and their interpretation of patristic texts.

101 A first accusation, on the part of the authors cited in the previous note, is that the patristic texts upon which this teaching is based are from the apocrypha which all have their origin in Egypt. This accusation does not hold up: we have seen that the patristic and hagiographic testimonies have a very broad basis in time and space. A second accusation is that this teaching has its origin in the religion of the ancient Egyptians and in Gnostic beliefs. Undoubtedly there is an analogy, but that is also true for many other Christian beliefs (numerous examples of this are to be found in the works of Mircea Eliade), without calling into question their Christian character: the two sets of beliefs are tied to different and irreconcilable theological and spiritual

contexts (see the remarks of Metropolitan Hierotheos Vlachos, *Life after Death*, pp. 77–78). A third accusation is that the soul is inseparable from the body in the human composite and cannot have an independent destiny: the soul would therefore remain in sleep awaiting the Resurrection. It is however a constant teaching of the Fathers that, during the intermediary period between death (which is indeed a separation of soul and body) and the resurrection, the soul and body are found in different states, retaining between themselves all the while a certain relationship. The liturgy of St John Chrysostom teaches that it was the same for Christ during the three days that separated His resurrection from His death: He descended with His soul into Hades while His body remained in the tomb. On these criticisms, see also the responses of Father Seraphim Rose, *The Soul after Death*, pp. 239–266 and P. M. Pomazansky, "'Our War is not Against Flesh and Blood,' On the Question of the Toll-Houses," in *Selected Essays*, Jordanville, NY, 1996, pp. 232–241.

102 See Androutsos, *Dogmas of the Eastern Orthodox Church*, Athens, 1907, p. 415 (in Greek).

103 *The Soul and the Angels are not Corporeal but Spiritual Realities*, Moscow, 1891, pp. 90–92 (in Russian).

104 A symbol's function, let us recall, is to represent concretely, sensibly and materially a metaphysical, spiritual, supersensible and immaterial reality, not only impossible for the senses to grasp, but difficult to apprehend through reason and intellect; the symbol is nevertheless in an analogical relationship with what it represents.

105 *Orthodox Dogmatic Theology*, vol. 2, Saint Petersburg, 1883; cited in *The Soul after Death*, p. 76.

106 *Hymns*, 28, ll. 201–211; Maloney, p. 152.

107 *On Watchfulness and Holiness*, 149; *Philokalia*, vol. 1, p. 188.

109 *On Patience*, PG 60, 727.

110 *On Watchfulness and Holiness*, 149; *Philokalia*, vol. 1, p. 188.

Chapter Five — From the Ninth to the Fortieth Day

1 See John Maximovich, *Sermon on Life after Death*; Archimandrite Seraphim Rose, *The Soul after Death*, pp. 194–195; Metropolitan Hierotheos Vlachos, *Life after Death*, pp. 93–94.

2 *Homilies*, XII, On the Dormition of Our Most Holy Lady, the Mother of God, PG 97, 1049–1052; Daley, pp. 119–120.

3 See John Maximovich, *Sermon on Life after Death*; Archimandrite Seraphim Rose, *The Soul after Death*, pp. 194–195.

4 See *Apostolic Constitutions*, VIII, 42, 1: "Let the third day of the departed be celebrated with psalms, and lessons, and prayers … and let the *ninth day* be

celebrated in remembrance of the living, and of the departed"; *Révélation au sujet des âmes…*, p. 179; anonymous text edited by K. Krumbacher, 'Studien zu den Legenden des hl. Theodosios', pp. 348–350, according to the Parisinus graec. 1140 A, f. 82r–v, cited by C. Vogel, *op. cit.*, in *Temple of the Holy Spirit*, pp. 268–269. Also see G. Dagron, 'Troisième, neuvième et quarantième jours dans la tradition byzantine: temps chrétien et anthropologie', pp. 419–423, 427.

5 Anonymous text edited by K. Krumbacher, 'Studien zu den Legenden des hl. Theodosios', pp. 348–350, according to the Parisinus graec. 1140 A, f. 82r–v, cited by C. Vogel, *op. cit.*, in *Temple of the Holy Spirit*, pp. 268–269.

6 *Révélation au sujet des ames….*

7 Gregory of Thrace, *Life of St Basil the Young*, Account of Theodora.

Chapter Six — The Fortieth Day: The Particular Judgment

1 Archbishop Anthony of Geneva, 'La vie de l'âme dans l'au-delà', p. 7.

2 See Dom L. Beauduin, 'Ciel et résurrection', in *Le Mystère de la mort et sa célébration*, Paris, 1956, pp. 254–255. He notes that Thomas Aquinas only mentions it, that there is in the definitions of the Catholic Church no teaching on this subject and nothing in the liturgical texts of this same Church allude to such a judgment.

3 See J. Rivière, 'Jugement', *Dictionnaire de th.ologie catholique*, 8, 1924, col. 1723–1726.

4 *Ibid.*, col. 1724.

5 See next chapter.

6 M. Jugie, 'La doctrine des fins dernières dans l'Église gréco-russe', *Échos d'Orient*, 17, 1914–1915, p. 14.

7 *Ibid.*, p. 117.

8 Anonymous text edited by K. Krumbacher, 'Studien zu den Legenden des hl. Theodosios', pp. 348–350, according to the Parisinus graec. 1140 A, f. 82r–v, cited by C. Vogel, *op. cit.*, pp. 268–269.

9 Compiled in 1561 on the basis of prior documents.

10 Canon 162.

11 The soul's abiding place while awaiting the Last Judgment.

12 *Consolation or Revelations of Abba Macarius.*

13 See G. Dagron, 'Troisième, neuvième et quarantième jours dans la tradition byzantine: temps chrétien et anthropologie', pp. 419–430; A. van Lantschoot, 'Révélations de Macaire et de Marc de Tarmaqa sur le sort de l'âme après la mort', *Le Muséon*, 63, 1950, pp. 161–165.

14 Paragraph 7. See W. Riedel, *Die Kirchenrechtsquellen des Patriarchats Alexandrien*, Leipzig, 1900, p. 169.

15 *Révélation au sujet des âmes...*

16 This service on the fortieth day has become in the west a service on the thirtieth day. Undoubtedly it was in the middle of the eighth century that this general change occurred, the seventh day being substituted for the ninth and the thirtieth for the fortieth. See C. Vogel, *op. cit.*, in *Temple of the Holy Spirit*, p. 270. The *Apostolic Constitutions* however set the commemoration on the thirtieth day (VIII, 42, 3) but in a manner which, with respect to the east, seems odd (see the note of M. Metzger, *Les Constitutions apostoliques*, tome 3, SC 336, Paris, 1987, p. 261).

17 See M. Jugie, 'La doctrine des fins dernières dans l'Église gréco-russe', *Échos d'Orient*, 17, 1914–1915, pp. 6–22.

18 Trans. Archimandrite Lazarus (Jordanville NY: Holy Trinity Monastery, 2012), p. 6.

19 *Philosophie orthodoxe de la vérité*, vol. 5, pp. 365–366.

20 *On the Practice of the Virtues, Contemplation and the Priesthood*, 61; *Philokalia*, vol. 2, p. 373.

21 See J. Rivière's excellent study: 'Rôle du démon au jugement particulier chez les Pères', *Revue des sciences religieuses*, 4, 1924, pp. 43–64, especially p. 48.

22 Joseph Bryennios for instance, who writes, referring first to the particular judgment and then to the universal judgment: "The merciless duty-collectors that are the spirits of evil perform their office only in the absence of the Judge, but when He will appear, they will be seen to cower and tremble" (*OEuvres complètes*, Bulgaris edition, tome 2, p. 389). Also see Archimandrite Justin Popovich, *Philosophie orthodoxe de la vérité*, tome 5, p. 366; Archimandrite Seraphim Rose, *The Soul after Death*, p. 92.

23 See M. Jugie, 'La doctrine des fins dernières dans l'Église gréco-russe', *Échos d'Orient*, 17, 1914–1915, p. 17.

24 *The Arena, an Offering to Contemporary Monasticism*, p. 6.

25 *The Ladder*, VII, 50; HTM, p. 77.

26 *To the Magnesians*, V.

27 See the *First Apology*, 43–45.

28 *Ibid.*, 43.

29 *Against the Heresies*, IV, 37, 2.

30 *On the Unity of the Church*, 10.

31 *On the Soul and the Resurrection*, 67; Roth, pp. 71–72.

32 *The Conferences*, I, 14; Ramsey, pp. 52–53.

33 *Letters*, 1, PG 91, 384B.

34 *Ibid.*, 384C.

35 *Ibid.*, 388A.

36 *The Explanation by Blessed Theophylact of the Holy Gospel according to Luke,* trans. Fr. C. Stade (House Springs MO: Chrysostom Press, 1997), p. 215.

37 Homily XIV, *On the Leaving of the Soul,* PG 77, 1072.

38 *Discourses,* XII, 126–128.

39 *Second Letter to the Corinthians,* V, 4.

40 *The Ladder,* IV, 86; HTM, p. 44.

41 *Homilies on Lazarus,* IV, 3; Roth, p. 87.

42 *Ibid.,* II, 2; Roth, p. 44.

43 *Commentary on Matthew,* XIII, 6.

44 *Ibid.*

45 *Homilies on Second Timothy,* III, 3.

46 *Ascetic Discourses,* I, 5; Chryssavgis, p. 40.

47 *Ibid.,* XV, 93. Only two paragraphs later the author mentions the resurrection, after which the universal judgment will take place (*ibid.,* XV, 95).

48 *Ibid.,* XVI, 4.

49 *On Those who Have Fallen Asleep in the Faith,* PG 95, 272.

Chapter Seven — From the Fortieth Day to the Last Judgment

1 See Luke 23:43, 2 Cor. 12:4; Gregory of Nyssa, *Life of Moses,* II, 247, who also proposes a whole list of other designations. See also B. Botte, 'The Earliest Formulas of Prayer for the Dead', in *Temple of the Holy Spirit,* pp. 19–21; L. Bauduin, 'Ciel et résurrection', in *Le Mystère de la mort et sa célébration,* pp. 257–259.

2 See Luke 16:22–23; Gregory of Nyssa, *On the Soul and the Resurrection,* 67; *Life of Moses,* II, 247. See also B. Botte, *op. cit.,* pp. 25–27.

3 See Matt. 8:11; *Apostolic Constitut*ions, VIII, 41, 2; Gregory of Nyssa, *Life of St Macrina,* 24; Pseudo-Dionysius the Areopagite, *The Ecclesiastical Hierarchy,* VII, 3, 4. See also B. Botte, *op. cit.,* pp. 25–27.

4 On the term Hades, see Gregory of Nyssa, *On the Soul and the Resurrection,* 51–53.

5 See Ecclesiasticus 21:10, Luke 8:31.

6 On this dual destination of the soul see Nicetas Stethatos, *On the Soul,* XII, 69–70.

7 See G. L. Prestige, 'Hades in the Greek Fathers', *The Journal of Theological Studies,* 24, 1923, pp. 477–478.

8 Archbishop Antony of Geneva, *La Vie de l'âme dans l'au-delà,* p. 64.

9 See the *Divine Liturgy of St John Chrysostom.*

10 See Irenaeus, *Against the Heresies,* IV, 27, 2.

11 See among others: Cyril of Alexandria, *Commentary on Psalm 48*, 16.

12 See G. L. Prestige, 'Hades in the Greek Fathers', pp. 481–484.

13 This is obviously found again among the Fathers. See Gregory of Nyssa, *Life of St Macrina*, 24.

14 *Ibid.*

15 This is also true for the early formulas of western prayers. See B. Botte, 'The Earliest Formulas of Prayer for the Dead', pp. 19–23.

16 *The Great Book of Needs*, vol. III, pp. 180–214.

17 *Ibid.*, pp. 360–382.

18 *Homilies* (col. II), XXVI, 18; Maloney, p. 171.

19 *Sayings of the Desert Fathers*, alphabetical collection, Macarius, 38; Ward, pp. 136–137.

20 *Orations*, VII, 21.

21 *Moral Poems*, II, 141–144.

22 *Conferences*, I, 14; Ramsey, p. 53.

23 *Ascetic Discourses*, V, 47 (cf. 48); Chryssavgis, p. 75.

24 *Homilies on the Consolation of Death*, II, 1. See also *Homilies on Lazarus*, I, 11; V, 3; VI, 6; VI, 4; *Homilies on Philippians*, III, 3–4.

25 *On Worship in Spirit and in Truth*, VI; *Pascal Homilies*, I, 2.

26 See *Commentary on Psalm 48*, 16; *Commentary on the Gospel of John*, XII.

27 *Discourses*, XII, 128 (cf. 127, 129); Wheeler, p. 185.

28 *On the Soul*, XIII, 69–70, 72.

29 *Ibid.*, XIV.

30 *Ibid.*, XV.

31 *Homily 2 on the Purgatorial Fire*.

32 See Gregory of Nyssa, *On the Soul and the Resurrection*, 53.

33 See Theophylact of Bulgaria, *The Explanation of the Gospel according to Luke*, XVI; Nicodemus the Hagiorite, *Eortodromion*, Venice, 1836, p. 400. The latter makes a connection between 'Hades' and *aeides* (formless, invisible).

34 PO 15, p. 153.

35 See Gregory of Nyssa, *On the Soul and the Resurrection*, 55.

36 See Gregory Palamas, *Against Gregoras*, III, 27, ed. Christou, vol. 4, p. 336.

37 *On the Soul and the Resurrection*, 67.

38 *Letter to Theodore*, I, 12.

39 *Discourses*, XII, 126; Wheeler, pp. 183–184.

40 That is to say, according to Hippocratic medicine, sickly.

41 *Ibid.*, XII, 127; Wheeler, p. 184.

42 See *ibid.*, 128; Wheeler, p. 185.

43 *On the Difficulties of Holy Scripture*, XX, ed. Eustratiades, vol. I, p. 242.

44 *Reply IV to Gabriel of Pentapolis*, PG 155, 844–845; *Dialogue against the Heretics*, 23, PG 155, 117.

45 See Gregory of Nyssa, *On the Soul and the Resurrection*, 82; *Sayings of the Desert Fathers*, alphabetical collection, Macarius, 38.

46 See *Sayings of the Desert Fathers*, alphabetical collection, Macarius, 38.

47 The material of sins and passions.

48 *On the Soul and the Resurrection*, 82.

49 *Dialogue with Trypho*, 5.

50 *Questions and Answers to the Orthodox*, 75, PG 6, 1316–1317.

51 *Replies to Antiochus*, 19–20.

52 *Commentary on the Apocalypse*, XVII, 6, 11, PG 106, 272.

53 *To Amphilochius*, XV, 2, PG 101, 136.

54 *Commentary on the Apocalypse*, XVII, 6, 9–11, PG 106, 596.

55 *Explanation of the Holy Gospel according to Luke*, XXIII, 39–43, PG 123, 1104–1105; *Commentary on the Letter to the Hebrews*, XI 40, PG 125, 365. Cited *infra*.

56 *Commentary on the Gospel according to Luke*, XXIII, 43, PG 129, 1092. Cited *infra*.

57 *The Spiritual Mirror*, XIV, 17, PG 127, 866–867.

58 *On the Difficulties of Holy Scripture*, XX, p. 241.

59 *Reply IV to Gabriel of Pentapolis*, PG 155, 844, 873.

60 *Orthodox Catechism*, ed. Ephrem of Jerusalem, 1769, p. 308.

61 *Dialogue with Trypho*, 5.

62 *Questions to Antiochus*, XX.

63 *Loc. cit.*

64 *Homilies*, XVIII, PG 132, 397–400.

65 *Reply IV to Gabriel of Pentapolis*, PG 155, 844.

66 *Ibid.*, 873.

67 *Ibid.*, 844–845.

68 *Homily 2 on the Purgatorial Fire.*

69 Decree 18; in Robertson, *The Acts and Decrees of the Synod of Jerusalem* (London: Thomas Baker, 1899), pp. 150–151.

70 *Adoleschia Philotheus.*

71 *The Longer Catechism*, 1st part, 11th article on the Creed; Schaff, *Creeds of Christendom*, vol. 2, p. 504.

72 *Théologie dogmatique orthodoxe* (French trans.), tome 2, Paris, 1860, pp. 642–651, 702–703.

73 See John Maximovich, *Sermon on Life after Death*; Archimandrite Seraphim Rose, *The Soul after Death*, p. 195; Archbishop Antony, 'La vie dans l'au-delà', p. 64; Metropolitan Hierotheos Vlachos, *Life after Death*, pp. 89–90; N. P. Vassiliadis, *The Mystery of Death*, pp. 400–404.

74 *Philosophie orthodoxe de la vérité*, tome 5, p. 370.

75 *On Psalm 51*, 22–23, PL 9, 322–323; *On Psalm 57*, 5, PL 9, 371.

76 *On Psalm 2*, 48, PL 9, 290.

77 *The Conferences*, I, 14; Ramsey, p. 54.

78 *Dialogues*, IV, 26, 3.

79 See Pseudo-Athanasius, *Questions to Antiochus*, XX, PG 28, 616; Andrew of Caesarea, *Commentary on the Apocalypse*, PG 106, 272; Mark of Ephesus, *Second Reply to the Latins, in which is set forth the true faith of the Greek Church* (= *Second Discourse on Purgatorial Fire*), PO 15, p. 110; *Reply to some difficulties and questions addressed to him by the cardinals and other Latin doctors*, 7, PO 15, p. 163; Patriarch Methodius III, in Migne (ed.), *Perpétuité de la foi de l'Église catholique sur l'eucharistie*, tome 2, Paris, 1841, pp. 1186–1187; Dosithius of Jerusalem, *Confession of Faith*, XVIII; Theophilus Papaphilos, *The Treasure of Orthodoxy*, p. 257; Koidakis, *Orthodox Catechism*, Athens, 1906, p. 74.

80 See Photius, *To Amphilochus*, ques. XV, PG 101, 136; Theophylact of Bulgaria, *Explanation of the Holy Gospel according to Luke*, XXIII, PG 123, 103–106; Gregory of Chios, *Explanation of the Creed*.

81 See Pseudo-Athanasius, *Questions to Antiochus*, XX, PG 28, 616; Nicetas Stethatos, *On the Soul*, XIV–XV; Michael Glykas, *On the Difficulties of Holy Scripture*, XX, vol. 1, p. 242; Symeon of Thessalonica, *Reply IV to Gabriel of Pentapolis*, PG 155, 844–845; *Dialogue against the Heresies*, 23, PG 155, 117; Joseph Bryennios, *Complete Works*, ed. Bulgaris, vol. 2, pp. 392–393; Mark of Ephesus, *Refutation of the Chapters of the Latins* (= *First Discourse on the Purgatorial Fire*), PO 15, pp. 40–41; *Second Reply to the Latins, in which is set forth the true faith of the Greek Church* (= *Second Discourse on Purgatorial Fire*, 3, PO 15, p. 110; 11, p. 118; 18, p. 130; *Reply to the difficulties and questions addressed to him on the subject of his discourses by the cardinals and other Latin doctors*, 6, PO 15, pp. 162–163; 9, p. 164; 10, p. 164; Patriarch Methodius III,

in Migne (ed.), *Perpétuité de la foi de l'Église catholique sur l'eucharistie*, tome 2, Paris, 1841, pp. 1186–1187; Dositheus of Jerusalem, *Confession of Faith*, XVIII; *Enchiridion*, pp. 81–85; Archimandrite Antony, *Dogmatic Theology*, Greek trans. of Vallanios, Athens, 1858, pp. 375–376; Archpriest N. Malinovski, *Outline of Orthodox Dogmatic Theology*, vol. 2, Sergiev Posad, 1908, pp. 469–471; C. G. Koidakis, *Orthodox Catechism*, Athens, 1906, p. 74.

82 See Metropolitan Hierotheos Vlachos, *Life after Death*, p. 90.

83 *To Amphilochius*, XV, 2. Cf. VI 2, 4.

84 *Commentary on the Gospel of Luke*, XXIII, 43, PG 129, 1092.

85 See J. Hergenröther, *Photius, Patriarch von Konstantinopel*, vol. 3, Ratisbonne, 1869, p. 639.

86 *On the Difficulties of Holy Scripture*, XX, ed. Eustratiades, vol. I, p. 241.

87 *Orthodox Catechism*, ed. Ephrem of Jerusalem, 1769, p. 308.

88 *Questions to Antiochus*, PG 28, 616.

89 *Explanation of the Holy Gospel according to Luke*, XXIII,

90 *Commentary on the Letter to the Hebrews*, XI, PG 125, 361–364.

91 *Homilies on Leviticus*, VII, 2, 9; Barkley, p. 137.

92 *On Christ and Antichrist*, 3.

93 In chapters XVI and XXII of *On the Making of Man*.

94 *Ibid.*, XXII, PG 44, 208B–D.

95 *Homilies on Hebrews*, XXVIII, 2.

96 *Commentary on the Letter to the Hebrews*, XI.

97 The bodies of certain sinners have remained intact while the bodies of certain saints have been subject to corruption. The spiritual state of a person cannot be judged from what becomes of his body. Incorruption is traditionally seen in the Orthodox world as an indication of holiness, but this only has a convincing value in conjunction with other indications.

98 *Against the Heresies*, V, 31, 2.

99 *Homilies on the Consolation of Death*, II, 1.

100 The study of the Catholic historian M. Jugie ('La doctrine des fins dernières dans l'Église gréco-russe', *Échos d'Orient*, 17, 1914–1915, pp. 209–228) is built upon this idea.

101 For example, Orthodox theologians recognize for the saints the possibility of a vision of God in this world, which is however neither eternal or lasting, and which, despite its deifying eff ects, does not prevent man from dying.

102 See P. Schantz, 'Seelenschlaf', *Kirchenlexikon*, vol. II, col. 57–58.

103 *Letter to Asdorf of January 13th, 1522* in Enders, *Luther's Briefwechsel*, n. 477, vol. 3, pp. 269–270. Calvin was, however, opposed to this conception (*Psychopannychia*, Strasbourg, 1542, in *Opera Omnia*, vol. 5, Brunswick, 1866., col. 165–233).

104 *Homilies on First Thessalonians*, PG 48, 1018.

105 *First Apology*, 18.

106 *The Conferences*, I, 14; Ramsey, p. 54.

107 *On the Soul*, XIII, 68–70.

108 See Irenaeus of Lyons, *Against the Heresies*, II, 34, 1; Dorotheos of Gaza, *Discourses*, XII, 127–128.

109 *Philosophie orthodoxe de la vérité*, tome 5, p. 370–371.

110 *Jacob's Ladder*, p. 71.

111 The Orphics, Pythagoreans, Plato, the Stoics, Neoplatonists, Gnostics and Manicheans have adopted it with several variations.

112 It is often designated by the word 'reincarnation' or by the expression 'transmigration of the soul'. Strictly speaking, it should rather be called 'metensomatosis'.

113 *Against the Heresies*, II, 34, 1.

114 *To Autolycus*, III, 7.

115 *The Ecclesiastical Hierarchy*, VII, 1, 2.

116 See *The Soul and the Resurrection*, 88–101; *The Making of Man*, 28–29; J. Daniélou, '"Metempsychosis" in Gregory of Nyssa', in *The Heritage of the Early Church, Essays in Honor of the Very Reverend G. V. Florovsky*. Rome, 1973, pp. 227–243.

117 *Homilies on the Hexaemeron*, VIII, 2.

118 *Orations*, XXVII, 10. St John Chrysostom will also criticize this doctrine. See *On the Acts of the Apostles*, II, 5; *On Luke*, LXVI, 3; *To the Ephesians*, XII, 3.

119 *The Soul and the Resurrection*, 89, 91.

120 *Ibid.*, 91.

121 *Ibid.*, 91; cf. 92; Roth, pp. 90–91.

122 *Ibid.*, 92.

123 *Ibid.*, 96; Roth, p. 94.

124 *Ibid.*, 98.

125 *Ibid.*, 99–100.

126 *Ibid.*, 99–100.

127 See *The Making of Man*, 28.

128 *The Soul and the Resurrection*, 101; Roth, p. 96.

129 *Ibid.*, 106–107; *The Making of Man*, 28; 29. We have explained Gregory's conception on this subject in *Pour une éthique de la procréation. Éléments d'anthropologie patristique*, Paris, 1998, pp. 106–110.

130 See *supra*, chapter 3, pp. 61–65.

131 For other reflections and references on this subject, see our study: *Théologie du corps*, Paris, 2009.

132 *Pour une éthique de la procréation. Éléments d'anthropologie patristique*, pp. 110–121.

133 On the Orthodox conception of the body, see my *Théologie du corps*, Paris, 2009, and *Ceci est mon corps. Le sens chrétien du corps selon les Pères de l'Église*. On the incompatibility of the theory of reincarnation with Orthodox anthropology, see also: Archimandrite Seraphim Rose, *The Soul after Death*, pp. 133–135; Metropolitan Hierotheos Vlachos, *Life after Death*, pp. 84–88; N. P. Vassiliadis, *The Mystery of Death*, pp. 440–444.

Chapter Eight— Purgatory

1   See M. Roncaglia, *Georges Bardanès, métropolite de Corfou, et Barthélemy de l'ordre franciscain. Les discussions sur le Purgatoire* (15 octobre–17 novembre 1231). Étude critique avec texte inédit, Rome, 1953.

2   Just like the rumor spread a few centuries earlier that they had suppressed the *'Filioque'* of the Creed!

3   See A. Michel, "Purgatoire", *Dictionnaire de théologie catholique*, tome 13, Paris, 1936, col. 1247–1248.

4   *Denzinger*, 838.

5   *Denzinger* 856–858 (*The Sources of Catholic Dogma*, trans. R. J. Deferrari [St Louis MO & London: B. Herder Book Co., 1957], 464, p. 184).

6   *Denzinger* 1304 (*The Sources of Catholic Dogma*, 693, p. 219).

7   See *Denzinger* 1580 (*The Sources of Catholic Dogma*, 840 Can. 30, p. 261): "If anyone shall say that after the reception of the grace of justification, to every penitent sinner the guilt is so remitted and the penalty of eternal punishment so blotted out that no penalty of temporal punishment remains to be discharged either in this world or in the world to come in purgatory before the entrance to the kingdom of heaven can be opened: let him be anathema."

8   *Denzinger* 1820; (*The Sources of Catholic Dogma*, 983, p. 298).

9   *Catechism of the Catholic Church*, Libreria Editrice Vaticana, 1994, num. 1030–1032.

10 See Le Goff, *The Birth of Purgatory*.

11 See in particular A. Michel, 'Purgatoire', *Dictionnaire de théologie catholique*, 13-1, 1936, col. 2246–2261.

12 See Denzinger, 1820 (*The Sources of Catholic Dogma*, 983, p. 298).

13 Like A. Michel or M. Jugie.

14 See especially the writings of Allatius (*De utiusque Ecclesiae occidentalis atque orientalis perpetua in dogmate de purgatorio consensione*, Rome, 1655), J. Eck (*De purgatorio*, in *Opera*, Rome, 1531), Bellarmine (in *Controverses, De purgatorio*, in *Opera*, vol. 3, Paris, 1869), Suarez (*De paenitentia*, XLV–XLVIII, in *Opera*, vol. 22, Paris, 1856), and more recently with P. Bernard, 'Purgatoire', *Dict. apologétique de la foi catholique*; A. Michel, 'Purgatoire', col. 1163–1326. Regarding our *a posteriori* designation, see Le Goff, *The Birth of Purgatory*, p. 41.

15 *Op. cit.*, page number not given.

16 *Ibid.*, p. 3.

17 See A. Michel, 'Purgatoire', col. 1215–1218; J. Le Goff, *The Birth of Purgatory*, pp. 59–60.

18 See A. Michel, 'Purgatoire', col. 1220–1223; J. Ntedika, *L'Évolution de la doctrine du Purgatoire chez saint Augustin*, Paris, 1966; J. Le Goff, *The Birth of Purgatory*, pp. 61–85, 213.

19 See J. Le Goff, *The Birth of Purgatory*, pp. 88–95, 213. St Cyprian has been placed at times among the precursors of the doctrine of Purgatory, but this is wrong according to P. Jay, 'Saint Cyprien et la doctrine du Purgatoire', *Recherches de théologie ancienne et médiévale*, 27, 1960, pp. 133–136. The same remark applies to Caesarius of Arles, see P. Jay, 'Le Purgatoire dans la prédication de saint Césaire d'Arles', *Recherches de théologie ancienne et médiévale*, 24, 1957, pp. 5–14.

20 For St Augustine see A. Michel, 'Purgatoire', col. 1222; Y. Congar, 'Le Purgatoire', p. 298; J. Ntedika, *L'Évolution de la doctrine du Purgatoire chez saint Augustin*, passim. For Gregory the Great see J. Le Goff, *The Birth of Purgatory*, 93, 94–95, 221.

21 See Metropolitan Hierotheos Vlachos, *Life after Death*, pp. 192–200.

22 *Ibid.*

23 See N. Constas, "Mark of Ephesus', in C. G. and V. Conticello, *La théologie byzantine*, tome 2, Turnhout, 2001.

24 See *infra*.

25 The link between this theory and that of Purgatory is noted by Y. Congar, 'Le Purgatoire', in *Le Mystère de la mort et sa célébration*, Paris, 1956, pp. 299–300. The author observes that these theories were foreign to the Christian East (pp. 301–302).

26 See J. Le Goff, *The Birth of Purgatory*, p. 5: "For a long time there had been a rather vague notion of 'slight', routine', or 'habitual' sins, as Augustine and Gregory the Great were well aware, but it was not until shortly before the emergence of Purgatory that this idea finally gave rise to the category of sin known as 'venial'. On the history

of this notion and its role in the formation of the theory of Purgatory, see J. Le Goff, *op. cit.*, pp. 217–220.

27 The link between this last distinction and the theory of Purgatory was noted by Y. Congar, 'Le Purgatoire', p. 299 and by J. Le Goff, *op. cit.*, pp. 213–214. This distinction was criticized by the Greeks at the Council of Florence within the setting of discussions on Purgatory (see *infra*).

28 In 1300, it seems, with the Jubilee celebrated that year. See J. Le Goff, *The Birth of Purgatory*, pp. 330–331.

29 "Le Purgatoire", pp. 279–336.

30 *Ibid.*, p. 279.

31 *Dialogue against the Heresies*, 23, PG 155, 116D.

32 *Chapters addressed to the Greeks by the Latins on the subject of purgatorial fire.* Document I of the *Documents relative to the Council of Florence. I. The question of Purgatory at Ferrara. Documents I–VI*, texts edited and translated by Mgr L. Petit, Patrologia Orientalis, tome XV-I, Paris, 1920, pp. 25–38.

33 *Refutation of the chapters of the Latins = First discourse on purgatorial fire.* Document II of the *Documents relative to the Council of Florence. I. The question of Purgatory at Ferrara. Documents I–VI*, pp. 39–60.

34 *Sayings of the Desert Fathers*, alphabetical collection, Macarius, 38: "Abba Macarius said, 'Walking in the desert one day, I found the skull of a dead man, lying on the ground. As I was moving it with my stick, the skull spoke to me. I said to it, "Who are you?" The skull replied, "I was high priest of the idols and of the pagans who dwelt in this place, but you are Macarius, the Spirit-bearer. Whenever you take pity on those who are in torments, and pray for them, they feel a little respite." The old man said to him, "What is this alleviation, and what is this torment?" He said to him, "As far as the sky is removed from the earth (Isa. 55:9), so great is the fire beneath us, we are ourselves standing in the midst of the fire, from the feet up to the head. It is not possible to see anyone face to face, but the face of one is fixed to the back of another. Yet when you pray for us, each of us can see the other's face a little. Such is our respite." The old man in tears said, "Alas the day when that man was born!" He said to the skull, "Are there any punishments which are more painful than this?" The skull said to him, "There is a more grievous punishment down below us." The old man said, "Who are the people down there?" The skull said to him, "We have received a little mercy since we did not know God, but those who knew God and denied Him are down below us." Then, picking up the skull, the old man buried it'" (Ward, pp. 136–137).

35 Εὐχολόγιον τὸ Μέγα, Venice, 1862, p. 376.

36 Gregory the Great, *Dialogues*, IV, 46.

37 *The Ecclesiastical Hierarchy*, VII, 7, PG 3, 561: "The divine hierarch ... from what God has told him in scripture... knows that to those who have lived in a most pious fashion there is given a bright, divine life under the most just guidelines, for in his kindly love for man the divinity closes his eyes to the faults coming from their human weakness. 'No one,' says scripture, 'is free from filth.'".

38 This theme is broached in fact by Dorotheos in *Discourse* 12 (On the Fear of the Punishment to Come) and not in *Discourse* 3 (On Conscience) of his spiritual instructions.

39 *Discourse* 16, 9.

40 Saturday of the Dead, Matins, Canticle One; *Lenten Triodion*, p. 129.

41 Canticle Five; *ibid.*, p. 134.

42 *Refutation of the chapters of the Latins = First discourse on purgatorial fire.* Document II of the *Documents relative to the Council of Florence. I. The question of Purgatory at Ferrara. Documents I–VI*, pp. 39–43.

43 *Reply of the Greeks to the Latin position on purgatorial fire.* Document III of the *Documents relative to the Council of Florence. I. The question of Purgatory at Ferrara. Documents I–VI*, pp. 61–79. In the ensuing lines we will summarize this memorandum by closely following the excellent account of A. D'Alès, 'La question du Purgatoire au councile de Florence,' *Gregorianum*, 3, 1922, pp. 14–21.

44 We will refer to their numerical order in parentheses at the beginning of each response.

45 As Jugie remarks, the Greeks should not be reproached for disavowing Theodoret's testimony "since the passage cited by the Latins was one of the apocryphal texts provided by St Thomas Aquinas when he composed his *Contra errores Graecorum*" ('La question du Purgatoire au concile de Ferrare-Florence', *.chos d'Orient*, 21, 1921, p. 273).

46 In document III of the *Documents relative to the Council of Florence. I. The question of Purgatory at Ferrara. Documents I–VI*, pp. 76–79 = Document II of the *Documents relative to the Council of Florence. I. The question of Purgatory at Ferrara. Documents I–VI*, pp. 57–60.

47 PG 36, 637.

48 *Oration* 45, XVI; PG 36, 645.

49 PG 35, 944.

50 *The Ladder*, V, 52.

51 *Reply of the Latins to the memorandum presented by the Greeks on the subject of the purgatorial fi re*, Document IV of the *Documents relative to the Council of Florence. I. The question of Purgatory at Ferrara. Documents I–VI*, pp. 80–107. A summary of it is found in Jugie, 'La question du Purgatoire au concile de Ferrare-Florence', *Échos*

d'Orient, 21, pp. 274–276; A. d'Alès, 'La question du Purgatoire au councile de Florence', pp. 22–31, and A. Michel, 'Purgatoire', col. 1256–1259.

52 *Second reply to the Latins in which is set forth the true faith of the Church of the Greeks = Second discourse on the purgatorial fire.* Document V of the *Documents relative to the Council of Florence. I. The question of Purgatory at Ferrara. Documents I–VI*, pp. 108–151.

53 *Op. cit.*, 3, pp. 109–110.

54 Pseudo-Athanasius, *Questions to Antiochus*, XX–XXI, PG 28, 609.

55 *Panegyric on his brother Caesarius = Oration VII*, 21.

56 *Homilies on the Statues*, VI, 3; *Discourse against the Jews*, VI, 1.

57 Εὐχολόγιον τὸ Μέγα, p. 376.

58 *Ecclesiastical Hierarchy*, VII, 7.

59 This distinction between *reatus poenae* and *reatus culpae* was introduced in the twelfth century by Peter Lombard. It was utilized by John of Torquemada in his brief to assert that it is possible to have a remission of fault (*culpa*) without a remission of pain (*poena*).

60 *Reply to questions and difficulties addressed to him on the topic of his discourses by cardinals and other Latin doctors.* Document VI of *Documents relative to the Council of Florence. I. The question of Purgatory at Ferrara. Documents I–VI*, pp. 152–168.

61 Here St Mark is implicitly referring to the distinction between the divine essence and the divine energies made explicit by St Gregory Palamas. See M. Jugie, 'La question du Purgatoire au concile de Ferrare-Florence', p. 281, and above all N. Constas, 'Mark of Ephesus' in C. G. and V. Conticello, *La Théologie byzantine*, tome 1, Turnhout, 2001.

62 See J. Gill, *Le Concile de Florence*, Tournai, 1964, p. 117.

63 See *ibid.*, p. 114.

64 See M. Jugie, 'La question du Purgatoire au concile de Ferrare-Florence', pp. 281–282; 'Purgatoire dans l'Église gréco-russe après le concile de Florence', *Dictionnaire de théologie catholique*, 13, 1936, col. 1327; J. Gill, *Le Concile de Florence*, pp. 112–113.

65 See M. Jugie, 'Purgatoire dans l'Église gréco-russe après le concile de Florence', col. 1326–1352. Jugie, with polemic intent and in connection with his bias in favor of the Latin doctrine of Purgatory, exaggerates the differences and tends to interpret the texts he cites in light of Latin categories.

66 On this topic, see especially G. Florovsky, *The Ways of Russian Theology*, vol. 1 (Belmont, MA: Nordland, 1979), *passim*.

67 See M. Jugie, 'Purgatoire dans l'Église gréco-russe après le concile de Florence', col. 1329–1336, *passim*.

68 For a summary of this, see M. Jugie, 'La question du Purgatoire au concile de Ferrare-Florence', pp. 278–282; Metropolitan Hierotheos Vlachos, *Life after Death*, pp. 162–192.

69 Among others see: Archimandrite Justin Popovich, *Philosophie orthodoxe de la vérité*, tome 5, pp. 369–383; Hieromonk Seraphim Rose, *The Soul after Death*, pp. 204–205; N. P. Vassiladis, *The Mystery of Death*, pp. 444–447; Metropolitan Hierotheos Vlachos, *Life after Death*, pp. 149–192.

70 We will give a summary of it below, following the account of M. Jugie, 'Purgatoire dans l'Église gréco-russe après le concile de Florence', col. 1337–1342.

71 *Orthodox Catechism*, Jassy, 1769, pp. 269–273, 275–279, 289–297, 300, 309–310. *Letter to the inhabitants of Chios*, Constantinople, 1627, pp. 22–23.

72 *Enchiridion*, Bucharest, 1690, pp. 81–85.

73 For a complete account, see, besides the account of Cardinal Cesarini cited above (and characterized by Jugie as "a brief yet lucid account of the western doctrine"), the synthesis of A. Michel, 'Purgatoire', col. 2246–2261.

74 This was observed however in several cases, like that of the emperor Trajan snatched from hell through the prayers of St Gregory the Great, or the pagan Falconille, saved through the prayers of St Thecla.

Chapter Nine — The Relations between the Living and the Dead

1 See the critiques of St Justin (*First Apology*, 18) and Tertullian (*The Apology*, XXIII, 1).

2 According to St Ambrose of Optina, the entities encountered during spiritualist séances are demons rather than spirits of the dead. See Archimandrite Seraphim Rose, *The Soul after Death*, p. 28.

3 It is not rare that these practices engender serious mental disturbances.

4 On this topic see the position of staretz Ambrose in J. B. Dunlop, *Staretz Amvrosy* (Belmont MA: Nordland, 1972), p. 66.

5 *Homilies on Philippians*, III, 4.

6 Pseudo-Damascene, *Concerning Those who have Died in the Faith*, 3, PG 95, 249BC.

7 *The Panarion*, 75, 7; trans. F. Williams (Leiden/New York/Köln: E. J. Brill, 1994), p. 496.

8 See the *Apostolic Constitutions*, VIII, 43; Gregory Nazianzus, *Discourses*, VII, 17; Symeon of Thessalonica, *Regarding Our Death ...*, 371–372, PG 155, 689C, 692A–D.

9 This is the main ingredient of this mix. It symbolizes birth to another life (cf. John 12:24–25: "unless the grain of wheat falling into the ground die, itself remaineth alone. But if it die it bringeth forth much fruit") and the future resurrection in

a renewed body (cf. 1 Cor. 15:36–38, 42–44: "that which thou sowest is not quickened, except it die firSt And that which thou sowest, thou sowest not the body that shall be: but bare grain, as of wheat, or of some of the reSt But God giveth it a body as he will: and to every seed its proper body... So also is the resurrection of the dead. It is sown in corruption: it shall rise in incorruption. It is sown in dishonor: it shall rise in glory. It is sown in weakness: it shall rise in power. It is sown a natural body: it shall rise a spiritual body. If there be a natural body, there is also a spiritual body").

10 On the meaning of the *kolyva* see Symeon of Thessalonica, *Regarding Our Death* ..., PG 155, col. 688–692; J. Goar, *Εὐχολόγιον sive Rituale Graecorum*, Paris 1647, pp. 658–661; Gabriel Severos, *Sur les colyves*, in R. Simon, *Fides Ecclesiae orientalis*, Paris, 1671, pp. 23–30; Theophilus of Campania, *The Treasure of Orthodoxy*, Tripolitza, 1885 (1780), pp. 161–163; Nicodemus the Hagiorite, *Confession of Faith*, Venice, 1819, pp. 8–50; L. Petit, 'La grande controverse des colybes', *Échos d'Orient*, 2, 1899, pp. 321–331.

11 *Paraclitique ou Grand Octoèque*, Parme, 1995.

12 Among others see Cyprian of Carthage, *Letters*, I, 2; Gregory the Great, *Dialogues*, IV, 57–60; Leontius of Neapolis, *Life of John of Cyprus*, 24; Symeon Metaphrastes, *Life of St Theodore the Cenobiarch*, 17, PG 114, 484–485; Symeon of Thessalonica, *Regarding our Death...*, 369 and 373, PG 155, 688D and 693A; Metropolitan Gabriel of Novgorod and Saint Petersburg, *Explanation of the Liturgy*, Saint Petersburg, 1799, p. 165; Archimandrite Justin Popovich, *Philosophie orthodoxe de la vérité*, tome 5, p. 383. It is to be noted however that, in the Orthodox Church, one speaks more readily of 'prayers for the deceased' or 'commemoration of the deceased' within the framework of the liturgy than of a liturgy offered for the deceased since: 1) as one prayer of the liturgy says it, it is Christ himself "who offers and is offered"; 2) the liturgy cannot be performed specifically for the deceased, for the latter are never dissociated from the living; 3) nor can the liturgy be considered or utilized as a means.

13 This ectenia is identical to the one that appears in the funeral service. It is only pronounced when the liturgy takes place on weekdays.

14 *The Divine Liturgy of Our Father Among the Saints John Chrysostom: Slavonic-English Parallel Text,* 4th Edition (Jordanville NY: Holy Trinity Publications, 2015) pp. 119-121.1;

15 The *Divine Liturgy of Our Father Among the Saints John Chrysostom*, p. 183.

16 *Ibid.*, p. 185.

17 *The Divine Liturgy of Our Father Among the Saints Basil the Great: Slavonic-English Parallel Text* (Jordanville NY: Holy Trinity Publications, 2020), p. 51.

18 These lists of the deceased, because they are accompanied by lists of the living whom the faithful wish to be prayed for and which are therefore dual, are called dyptichs. Formerly, they were listed on two wooden boards tied together.

19 See, among recent examples, that of the recently beatified Father Nicolas Planas (Marthe la Moniale, *Le saint prêtre Nicolas Planas*, Paris, 1987, p. 17).

20 See John Chrysostom, *Homilies on the first epistle to the Corinthians*, XLI, 5; *Homilies on the epistle to the Philippians*, III, 4; Nicetas Stethatos, *On the Soul*, XIII, 77; Theophylact of Bulgaria, *Explanation of the Holy Gospel according to St Luke*, PG 123, 880; Mark of Ephesus, *Refutation of the Chapters of the Latins or the First Discourse on the Purgatorial Fire*, PG 15, p. 40; Theophilus of Campania, *The Treasure of Orthodoxy*, p. 217; John Maximovitch, *Sermon on Life after Death*. More recently, see: Archimandrite Vasilios Bakogiannis, *After Death*, Katerini, 1995, p. 89.

21 *Apostolic Constitution*, VIII, 42, 5.

22 See Archimandrite Vasilios Bakogiannis, *After Death*, pp. 89–90.

23 See *supra*, p. 212.

24 *Mystagogical Catechesis*, V, 9.

25 *The Panarion*, 75, 7, p. 496.

26 *On the Soul*, XIII, 77.

27 Litany.

28 *Mystagogical Catechesis*, V, 9.

29 *Explanation of the Holy Gospel according to Luke*, pp. 141–142; PG 123, 880. Passage cited *infra* pp. 220.

30 Canon of Matins, Canticle 5, in *The Lenten Triodion*, trans. Mother Mary and Archimandrite T. Ware (London: Faber and Faber, 1978), p. 134.

31 *Homilies on Philippians*, III, 4.

32 *Second reply to the Latins, in which is set forth the true faith of the Church of the Greeks = Second discourse on the purgatorial fire*, 12, PO 15, p. 119.

33 *Refutation of the chapters of the Latins = First discourse on the purgatorial fire*, PO 15, pp. 42–43.

34 I. Perov, *Manual of Polemical Theology*, Tula, 1905, pp. 108–109.

35 *Apostolic Constitutions*, VIII, 43.

36 *Homilies on Acts*, XXI, 5. Also see *Homilies on Philippians*, III, 4.

37 *Refutation of the chapters of the Latins = First discourse on purgatorial fire*, PO 15, p. 40.

38 Besides the references given below, see John Chrysostom, *On the Priesthood*, VI, 4; *Homilies on First Corinthians*, XLI, 5; Leontius of Neapolis, *Life of John of Cyprus*, 24.

39 See Pseudo-Dionysius the Areopagite, *Ecclesiastical Hierarchy*, VII, III, 7; Mark of Ephesus, *Refutation of the chapters of the Latins = First discourse on the purgatorial fire*, PO 15, p. 40; Bessarion of Nicea, *Reply of the Greeks to the Latin position on the purgatorial fire*, PO 15, p. 76; Meletius Syrigos, *Refutation of the chapters of Calvin and of the questions of Cyril Lukaris*, Bucharest, 1690, p. 141 s.

40 Dositheus of Jerusalem, *Enchiridion*, pp. 81-85.

41 Besides the references given below, see: I. Perov, *Manual of Polemic Theology*, pp. 108-109; A. Temnomierov, *The Teaching of Holy Scripture on Death and the Life Beyond*, Saint Petersburg, 1899, p. 158.

42 *Explanation of the Holy Gospel according to Luke*, pp. 141-142.

43 *Enchiridion*, p. 82, 85.

44 Said to be "the most lively and original exegete in twelfth century Byzantium."

45 *On the Difficulties of Divine Scripture*, Letter 19; Pseudo-Dionysius the Areopagite, *The Ecclesiastical Hierarchy*, VII, III, 6-7.

46 *Refutation of the chapters of the Latins = First discourse on the purgatorial fire*, PO 15, pp. 40-41.

47 See Mark of Ephesus, *Refutation of the chapters of the Latins = First discourse on the purgatorial fire*, PO 15, p. 40-41 (text cited *supra*, chapter 8, pp. 181-185); Archbishop Antony of Geneva, 'La vie de l'âme dans l'au-delà', pp. 12-13; Metropolitan Hierotheos Vlachos, *Life after Death*, pp. 28-29.

48 See Mark of Ephesus, *Refutation of the chapters of the Latins = First discourse on the purgatorial fire*, PO 15, p. 40-41.

49 See *infra*, p. 229 ff.

50 See *infra*, pp. 227-228.

51 *The Orthodox Church* (Crestwood NY: SVS Press, 188), p. 182.

52 See John Chrysostom, *Homilies on First Corinthians*, XLI, 5; Gregory the Great, *Dialogues*, IV, 57-60; Leontius of Neapolis, *Life of John of Cyprus*, 24; Symeon Metaphrastes, *Life of St Theodore the Cenobiarch*, 17, PG 114, 484-485; Metropolitan Gabriel of Novgorod and Saint Petersburg, *Explanation of the Liturgy*, p. 165; John Maximovich, *Sermon on Life after Death*; Archimandrite Justin Popovich, *Philosophie orthodoxe de la vérité*, tome 5, p. 382-383.

53 *Loc. cit.*

54 Beside the patristic references given *infra*, see, among the eastern theologians: Mitrophanes Critopoulos, *Confession of Faith*, in E.-J. Kimmel-Weissenborn, *Monumenta fidei Ecclesiae orientalis*, vol. 2, Jena, 1851, pp. 194-195; Bishop Sylvester, *Essay on Orthodox Theology*, vol. 5, Kiev, 1897, p. 143.

55 *Sayings of the Desert Fathers*, alphabetical collection, Macarius, 38, cited integrally supra, chapter 8, note 34, p. 182.

56 *Homilies on First Corinthians*, XLI, 8.

57 *Homilies on Philippians*, III, 4.

58 *Homilies on Acts*, XXI, 4.

59 This text is appealed to by Catholic theologians in support of the doctrine of Purgatory, but: 1) no mention is made of a purgatory as an abode for sinners; 2) no mention is made of a purification through the penalties endured. It is God who, in response to the prayers of the Church, pardons sins and remits penalties.

60 *Mystagogical Catechesis*, V, 10.

61 *Refutation of the chapters of the Latins = First discourse on the purgatorial fire*, PO 15, pp. 40–43; *Second reply to the Latins, in which is set forth the true faith of the Church of the Greeks = Second discourse on the purgatorial fire*, 12, PO 15, p. 119; *Reply to the difficulties and questions addressed to him by the cardinals and other Latin doctors on the subject of his discourses*, 12, PO 15, p. 165.

62 See Mark of Ephesus, *Second reply to the Latins, in which is set forth the true faith of the Church of the Greeks = Second discourse on the purgatorial fire*, 12, PO 15, pp. 130–131; Dosithius of Jerusalem, *Enchiridion*, pp. 81–85.

63 *On the Soul*, XIII, 77.

64 See Pseudo-Damascene, *Concerning Those who have Died in the Faith*; Michael Glykas, *Letters*, 20, PG 158, 929; Patriarch Meletios Pegas, *Orthodoxos didaskalia*, Jassy, 1769, p. 297, 300, 301, 309; *Letter to the Christians of Chios*, p. 23; Gregory of Chios, *Summary of the Divine and Sacred Dogmas of the Church*, Venice, 1635; *Dogmatic Letter from the Patriarchs of the East to the Antiochenes* (1722), in Mansi-Petit, *Council*, tome 37, col. 191; Metropolitan Macarius of Moscow, *Orthodox Dogmatic Theology*, Saint Petersburg, 1883, tome 2, pp. 590–610; S. Bulgakov, *The Orthodox Church*, p. 208: the prayer of the Church for the dead "can ameliorate the state of the souls of sinners, and liberate them from the place of distress, snatch them from hell"; cf. *ibid.*, p. 209.

65 See among others: Dositheus of Jerusalem, *Enchiridion*, p. 82; Archimandrite Antony, *Dogmatic Theology of the Catholic Orthodox Church*, Greek trans. of Vallianos, Athens, 1858, p. 386.

66 *The Treasure of Orthodoxy*, p. 217. Recall that this book was quite popular; the Holy Synod of Athens having approved of it in 1860, recommending the reading of it to all the faithful.

67 See among others: Mark of Ephesus, *Refutation of the chapters of the Latins = First discourse on the purgatorial fire*, PO 15, p. 43; *Second reply to the Latins, in which is set forth the true faith of the Church of the Greeks = Second discourse on the purgatorial*

fire, 12, PO 15, p. 119; Dositheus of Jerusalem, *Enchiridion*, p. 83; Theophilus of Campania, *The Treasure of Orthodoxy*, pp. 158–160.

68 These references were introduced in the fourteenth century by Nicephorus Callistus Xanthopoulos in the *Synaxaria* of the *Triodion* (see *Triodion*, Venice, 1870, p. 17). They are also to be found in the unction service for the dead (*Euchelaion*) composed in the thirteenth century by Metropolitan Nicholas of Athens (see Goar, *Euchologion, sive rituale graecorum*, Venice, 1780, p. 441). It should be mentioned that this service, which was very quickly disputed (see Symeon of Thessalonica, *On the Holy Euchelaion*, PG 155, 521), has disappeared today from a majority of the euchologia.

69 Pseudo-Damascene,*Concerning Those who have Died in the Faith.*

70 *Refutation of the chapters of the Latins* = *First discourse on the purgatorial fire*, PO 15, p. 40. Also see Meletius Syrigos (considered to be one of the most outstanding theologians of the seventeenth century), *Refutation of the chapters of Calvin and of the questions of Cyril Lukaris*, p. 138–144.

71 Cited *supra*, chapter 8, note 34.

72 Cited *supra*, chapter 8, note 35.

73 *The Panarion*, 75, PG 42, 513B.

74 See Theophylact of Bulgaria, *Explanation of the Holy Gospel according to St Matthew*, XXII, 13, PG 123, 880.

75 See John Chrysostom, *Commentary on First Corinthians*, XLI, 5.

76 See Theophylact of Bulgaria, *Explanation of the Holy Gospel according to St Matthew*, XXII, 13, PG 123, 880; *Confession of Faith* of Peter Mogila corrected by Meletius Syrigos (1643), 1st part, ques. LXIV–LXV; Meletius Syrigos, *Refutation of the chapters of Calvin and of the questions of Cyril Lukaris*, p. 144 ff ; John of Kronstadt, *My Life in Christ*, trans. E. E. Goulaeff (Jordanville NY: Holy Trinity Monastery, 2000), p. 30.

77 See John Chrysostom, *Commentary on Matthew*, LXXVIII, 1.

78 *First Letter to Theodore*, 9. See also *Commentary on Philippians*, III, 4; *Homilies on Lazarus*, II, 3; *Commentary on Matthew*, XXXVI, 3; *Commentary on the Psalms*, IX, 4.

79 *Homilies on First Corinthians*, XLI, 8.

80 *Homilies on Philippians*, III, 4.

81 *Ecclesiastical Hierarchy*, VII, III, 4–7.

82 *The Panarion*, 75, 7; Amidon, p. 328.

83 Cf. C. Andronikof, "The Dormition as Type of Christian Death", in *Temple of the Holy Spirit*, pp. 14–16.

84 See Augustine of Hippo, *On the Care to be Had for the Dead*, chaps. 13–15.

85 This is true for the just who abide in Paradise, but also for those who are in hell. As an example, we can cite the deceased man who manifested himself to St Macarius after having identified him perfectly: "You are Marcarius, the spiritbearer" (*Sayings of the Desert Fathers*, alphabetical collection, Macarius, 38.

86 See Pseudo-Athanasius, *Questions to Antiochus*, 32.

87 *Letters*, 232.

88 See Archimandrite Vasilios Bakogiannis, *After Death*, pp. 70–73.

89 *On Prayer*, 11; *Origen*, trans. R. A. Greer (New York, Ramsey, Toronto: Paulist Press, 1979), p. 102.

90 *The Letters of St Cyprian of Carthage*, vol. 3, Letter 60, 5.2; trans. G. W. Clarke (New York/Mahwah NJ: Paulist Press, 1986), p. 92.

91 See Gregory of Nazianzus, *Orations*, XXIV, 19; Gregory of Nyssa, *On the Forty Holy Martyrs*, PG 46, 788B; John Chrysostom, *On the Martyrs Juventin and Maximin*, 3.

92 See, among other patristic testimonies: Origen, *Exhortation to Martyrdom*, 38; Eusebius of Caesarea, *Ecclesiastical History*, VI, V, 3–7; Basil of Caesarea, *Letters*, 360; *On the Forty Holy Martyrs*, 8, PG 41, 521C–524A, C; Gregory of Nyssa, *On Great Martyr Theodore*, PG 46, 746D–748C; Gregory of Nazianzus, *Orations*, XVIII, 4; XLIII, 80.

93 *Confession of Faith*, 8.

94 George Florovsky, *Anatomia problematon tes pisteos*, Thessalonica, 1977, p. 125.

95 *On the Soul*, XIII.

96 *Anatomia problematon tes pisteos*, pp. 122–123.

97 *A Commentary on the Divine Liturgy*, 42; 45; trans. J. M. Hussey and P. A. McNulty (London: SPCK, 1960), pp. 96–98, 101–102.

98 See Archimandrite Vasilios Bakogiannis, *After Death*, p. 80.

99 See for example C. Andronikof: among all of the deceased "there is established a communication not subject to space or time" *op. cit.*, p. 15).

100 *Sayings of the Desert Fathers*, alphabetical collection, Macarius, 38.

101 *Ethical Discourses*, 1, 12; *On the Mystical Life*, vol. 1, trans. A. Golitzin (Crestwood NY: St Vladimir's Seminary Press, 1995), pp. 71–72, 73, 74.

Chapter Ten — The Resurrection and the Last Judgment

1 Holy Saturday.

2 See Tertullian, On the Resurrection, XXXVIII.

3 See Irenaeus of Lyons, *On the Apostolic Preaching*, 42.

4 Gregory of Nyssa, *Paschal Homilies*, I, 10.

5 See especially: Athenagoras, *On the Resurrection of the Dead*; Tertullian, *On the Resurrection*.

6 See Justin, *First Apology*, 19; Theophilus of Antioch, *To Autolycus*, I, 8; Athenagoras, *On the Resurrection of the Dead*, II–IX; Tertullian, *On the Resurrection*, XI–XII; LVII; *Apostolic Constitutions*, V, 7, 2; Cyril of Jerusalem, *Baptismal Catecheses*, IV, 30; Gregory of Nyssa, *Paschal Homilies*, I, 5; 7; 10; John Chrysostom, *Homilies on the Consolation of Death*, II, 2–3; *Homilies on First Thessalonians*, VII, 2–3; John Damascene, *Exact Exposition of the Orthodox Faith*, IV, 27; Anastasius of Sinai, *The Guide*, 92.

7 *On the Resurrection*, XI.

8 See Justin, *First Apology*, 52; Tertullian, *On the Resurrection*, XLII, 3–4; Cyril of Jerusalem, *Baptismal Catecheses*, IV, 30; John Chrysostom, *Homily on the Resurrection from the Dead*, 8.

9 *Hymns of Ascent*, Tone 4.

10 See for example Irenaeus of Lyons, *Against the Heresies*, V, 31, 2.

11 See Gregory of Nyssa, *Paschal Homilies*, I, 8; John Chrysostom, *Homilies on First Corinthians*, XLI.

12 See Tertullian, *On the Resurrection*, LIII.

13 *Homilies on Second Corinthians*, X, 3.

14 *On the blessed Job*, PG 64, 620D.

15 See Tertullian, *On the Resurrection*, LII; Macarius of Egypt, *Homilies* (coll. II), XV, 10; Methodius of Olympus, *On the Resurrection*; John Chrysostom, *Homilies on First Corinthians*, XLI, 2.

16 See Athenagoras, *On the Resurrection of the Dead*, XV, 3.

17 See Tertullian, *On the Resurrection*, LV.

18 See Athenagoras, *On the Resurrection of the Dead*, II, 3; XV, 3.

19 *Homilies* (Coll. II), XV, 10; Maloney, p. 112.

20 See Irenaeus of Lyons, *Against the Heresies*, V, 2, 3; Tertullian, *On the Resurrection*, LII; LIII; LV; LXII; Gregory of Nyssa, *The Making of Man*, XXVII; XXVIII; John Chrysostom, *Homilies on First Corinthians*, XLI, 1 and XLII, 2.

21 See Athenagoras, *On the Resurrection*, XVI, 6.

22 See *ibid.*, XXV, 3.

23 See Tertullian, *On the Resurrection*, LV.

24 *Ibid.*, LVII.

25 *Ascetical Homilies*, 37; HTM, p. 180.

26 John Chrysostom, *Homilies on Philippians*, XIII, 2.

27 On the body of the risen Christ, see: Epiphanius of Cyprus, *Against the Heresies*, III, PG 42, 817AB; Nicodemus of the Holy Mountain, *Eortodromion*, Venice, 1836, p. 484 and 594.

28 Tertullian, *On the Resurrection*, LVII. Cf. Gregory of Nyssa, *Treatise on the Word: "Then the Son Himself will subject to Him who put all things under Him"*, 3.

29 Macarius of Egypt, *Homilies* (coll. II), XI, 1; Isaac the Syrian, *Ascetical Homilies*, 37; Symeon the New Theologian, *Ethical Discourses*, I, 4.

30 Gregory of Nyssa, *On the Soul and the Resurrection*, 133; Roth p. 118; cf. *Homilies on Pulcheria*, PG 46, 877A. Cf. Tertullian, *On the Resurrection*, LVII.

31 See Tertullian, *On the Resurrection*, LVII.

32 See *ibid.*, LVII; cf. XXXIV.

33 See Tertullian, *On the Resurrection*, LVII.

34 See Gregory of Nyssa, *On the Departed*, PG 46, 532; 536; *On the Soul and the Resurrection*, 132; Gregory Palamas, *Triads*, I, 3, 36.

35 Gregory Palamas, *Triads for the Defense of the Holy Hesychasts*, I, 3, 36; cf. John Chrysostom, *Homilies on First Corinthians*, XLI. This has nothing to do with the non-Christians theories of the subtle body or astral body.

36 See Maximus the Confessor, *Mystagogy*, VII; Berthold, p. 197.

37 See Symeon the New Theologian, *Ethical Discourses*, I, 4–5.

38 See Athenagoras, *On the Resurrection of the Dead*, X, 6; Gregory of Nyssa, *On the Soul and the Resurrection*, 132; John Chrysostom, *Homilies on the Consolation of Death*, I, 6.

39 See Justin, *First Apology*, 19; Athenagoras, *On the Resurrection of the Dead*, X, 5–6; XVI, 2–3; Tertullian, On the Resurrection, LVI; LVII; LVIII; Gregory of Nyssa, *On the Resurrection*, 132; 133; John Chrysostom, *Homily on the Resurrection of the Dead*, 8; *Homilies on the Consolation of Death*, I, 6; *Homilies on First Corinthians*, XLI; XLII; *Homilies on Second Corinthians*, X; Barsanuphius, *Letters*, 607; Isaac the Syrian, *The Ascetical Homilies*, 37; John Damascene, *Exact Explanation of the Orthodox Faith*, IV, 27; Symeon the New Theologian, *Ethical Discourses*, I, 3–4.

40 See John Chrysostom, *Exhortations to Theodore*, I, 11; Symeon the New Theologian, *Ethical Discourses*, I, 5.

41 See Ammonas, *Letters*, I, 2; John Chrysostom, *Homilies on the Consolation of Death*, I, 6; *Exhortations to Theodore*, I, 11.

42 See Tertullian, *On the Resurrection*, LVIII; Ammonas, *Letters*, I, 2; John Chrysostom, *Homilies on First Corinthians*, XLI, 1; *Homilies on Second Corinthians*, X, 1–2.

43 See Tertullian, *On the Resurrection*, LVIII; John Chrysostom, *Homilies on First Corinthians*, XLI.

44 See Gregory of Nyssa, *Concerning Those Who Have Died*, PG 46, 532; 536; Symeon the New Theologian, *Ethical Discourses*, I, 5.

45 See Tertullian, *On the Resurrection*, XLII, 5; LV; LVI; LVIII; Antony, *Letters*, IV, 1; Cyril of Jerusalem, *Baptismal Catecheses*, IV, 30; Gregory of Nyssa, *Treatise on the Word: "Then the Son Himself will subject to Him who put all things under Him"*, 3; John Chrysostom, *Homily on the Resurrection of the Dead*, 8; *Homilies on the Consolation of Death*, I, 6; *Homilies on First Corinthians*, XLII, 2; Barsanuphius, *Letters*, 607; Symeon the New Theologian, *Ethical Discourses*, I, 4.

46 Cf. Tertullian, *On the Resurrection*, L.

47 John Chrysostom, *Homily on the Resurrection of the Dead*, 8.

48 See Pseudo-Maximus the Confessor, *Scolia on the Divine Names*, I, 4, PG 4, 197.

49 See Macarius of Egypt, *Homilies* (coll. II), XV, 10; Gregory Palamas, *Triads for the Defense of the Holy Hesychasts*, I, 3, 36.

50 See Tertullian, *On the Resurrection*, LX; Gregory of Nyssa, *On the Soul and the Resurrection*, 123.

51 See Tertullian, *On the Resurrection*, LX; Macarius of Egypt, *Homilies* (coll. II), XV, 10; Barsanuphius, *Letters*, 607.

52 Tertullian, *On the Resurrection*, LX.

53 *Ibid.*, LXI.

54 *Ibid.*, LX.

55 See Gregory of Nyssa, *On the Soul and the Resurrection*, 132; John Chrysostom, *Homilies on the Consolation of Death*, I, 6.

56 See H. Rahner, 'Les débuts d'une doctrine des cinq sens spirituels chez Origène', *Revue d'ascétique et de mystique*, 1932, p. 113 ff ; A. Stolz, *The Doctrine of Spiritual Perfection*, trans. A. Williams (New York: Herder & Herder, 1938), p. 211.

57 See my *Therapy of Spiritual Illnesses*, trans. Fr. K. Sprecher (Montreal: Alexander Press, 2017), 2007, vol. 1, pp. 118–120.

58 See Athenagoras, *On the Resurrection of the Dead*, XV, 7.

59 See Tertullian, *On the Resurrection*, XIV–XVII;XXIII; XLIII; Gregory of Nyssa, *Pascal Homilies*, I, 8–9; John Damascene, *Exact Exposition of the Orthodox Faith*, IV, 27.

60 *On the Resurrection*, XIV. This does not prevent Tertullian from considering that, in the period situated between death and the Last Judgment, there is for the soul a

retribution that it alone is subject to: "That souls are even now susceptible of torment and of blessing in Hades, though they are disembodied, and notwithstanding their banishment from the flesh, is proved by the case of Lazarus [Luke 16:29] ... This, in short, will be the process of that judgment which is postponed to the last great day, in order that by the exhibition of the flesh the entire course of the divine vengeance may be accomplished" (*ibid.*, XVII).

61 See Athenagoras, *On the Resurrection of the Dead*, XVIII, 4–5. Cf. John Damascene, *Exact Exposition of the Orthodox Faith*, IV, 27.

62 *Ibid.*, 20, 3.

63 See Athenagoras, *On the Resurrection of the Dead*, XXV, 1; Tertullian, *On the Resurrection*, XXIII; John Chrysostom, *Commentary on the Gospel of John*, LXVI, 3; *Homilies on Genesis*, VII, 4.

64 See Tertullian, *On the Resurrection*, XLIII.

65 *Homilies on First Corinthians*, XXXIX, 4.

66 See Pseudo-Barnabas, *Letter*, VII, 2; Clement of Rome, *To the Corinthians*, I, 1; Polycarp of Smyrna, *To the Philippians*, II, 1; Justin, *Dialogue with Trypho*, 118; John Chrysostom, *Commentary on the Gospel of John*, XXXIX, 3; *Homilies on Romans*, XXV, 3–4; Cyril of Alexandria, *Commentary on St John*, II, 7; *Commentary on Isaiah*, II, 5, 12; III, 2, 16.

67 See Cyril of Jerusalem, *Baptismal Catechesis*, XV, 25.

68 See *ibid.*, 24.

69 See Symeon the New Theologian, *Discourses*, V, 637–654.

70 *First Apology*, 53. Cf. *Dialogue with Trypho*, 124.

71 *To the Corinthians*, XXVIII, 2; 4. Cf. Athenagoras, *A Plea for the Christians*, XII, 2.

72 See Symeon the New Theologian, *Discourses*, XXVIII, 164–175.

73 See Pseudo-Barnabas, *Letter*, IV, 12; Clement of Rome, *To the Corinthians*, XI, 6.

74 *La Pri.re des heures*, Chevetogne, 1975, p. 113.

75 See John Chrysostom, *Commentary on the Psalms*, 48, 4; *Apologia for the Monastic Life*, III, 1.

76 Cf. Basil of Caesarea, *Letters*, XLVI, 5.

77 See John Chrysostom, *Apologia for the Monastic Life*, III, 1.

78 See Cyril of Jerusalem, *Catecheses*, XV, 25; John Chrysostom, *Apologia for the Monastic Life*, III, 1.

79 John Chrysostom, *Apologia for the Monastic Life*, III, 1.

80 *Commentary on Isaiah*, I, 43.

81 Cf. Basil of Caesarea, *Commentary on Isaiah*, I, 43.

82 *Hymns*, XXXI, 154–170: Maloney, pp. 177–178.

83 See John Chrysostom, *Homilies on First Thessalonians*, VIII, 2; Symeon the New Theologian, *Discourses*, XXVIII, 169; *Hymns*, XVII, 462–494.

84 John Chrysostom, *Homilies on Second Corinthians*, X, 3.

85 *Commentary on Psalm 33*, 4.

86 *Discourses*, XXVIII, 141–175; de Catanzaro, pp. 299–300.

87 *On Those Who Weep*, PG 46, 532–536.

88 *Baptismal Catecheses*, XV, 25.

89 *Homilies on the Gospel of John*, XXXIX, 1.

90 *Commentary on Psalm 48*, 2. Cf. Gregory Nazianzus, *Moral Poems*, XXXIV, 254–256.

91 *Baptismal Catecheses*, XV, 25.

92 *Centuries* III, 79; *Philokalia*, vol. 4, p. 165.

93 John Chrysostom, *Homilies on the Demons*, III, 3.

94 The Greek Fathers define the virtues as habitual and stable (*exeis*) dispositions.

95 See Gregory of Nyssa, *On Those Who Weep*, PG 46, 532–536; Cyril of Jerusalem, *Baptismal Catecheses*, XV, 25; Gregory Palamas, *Homilies*, 4.

96 *Discourses*, V, 637–689; de Catanzaro, pp. 107–108.

97 See Gregory Palamas, *Homilies*, 4.

98 *Hymns*, XVII, 462–494.

99 See Gregory of Nyssa, *Commentary on Psalm 6*, PG 44, 612; John Damascene, *Exact Exposition of the Orthodox Faith*, IV, 27. This characterization also made its appearance in many liturgical services and even the liturgy itself, where a litany asks God to grant the faithful "a good defense before the dread judgment seat of Christ."

100 See Basil of Caesarea, *Letters*, XLVI, 5; John Chrysostom, *Apologia for the Monastic Life*, III, 2; *Homilies on Lazarus*, VI, 2; Maximus the Confessor, *Letters*, I.

101 See John Chrysostom, *Apologia for the Monastic Life*, III, 2.

102 See Symeon the New Theologian, *Discourses*, XXVIII, 150–189; *Hymns*, XVII, 482.

103 John Chrysostom, *Homilies on Lazarus*, VI, 2, Roth, p. 98; cf. *Homilies on Second Corinthians*, IX, 4; *Commentary on Psalm 48*, 4; *Homily on the Saying "Fear not, in seeing a man become rich …" and on Hospitality*, 6; Gregory Nazianzus, *Orations*, XVI, 9.

104 John Chrysostom, *Commentary on the Gospel of Matthew*, XC, 2.

105 Cf. John Chrysostom, *Homilies on First Thessalonians*, VIII, 2; Nicodemus of the Holy Mountain, *Eortodromion*, p. 304.

106 *On the Prophecy of Isaiah*, III, 119–120, PG 30, 312B–D.

107 See John Chrysostom, *Homilies on the Demons*, I, 8; *Homilies on the Cross and the Good Thief*, I, 3.

108 See John Chrysostom, *Homilies on the Cross and the Good Thief*, I, 3.

109 Gregory Nazianzus, *Orations*, XIX, 15.

110 Isidore of Pelusium, *Letters*, II, 172.

111 See Basil of Caesarea, *Commentary on Psalm 7*, 5.

112 For a commentary of this parable as a symbol of the Last Judgment, see Gregory Palamas, *Homilies*, XLI.

Chapter Eleven—Eternal Life

1 See Theophylact of Bulgaria, *Explanation of the Holy Gospel according to Luke*, XVI; Nicodemus of the Holy Mountain, *Eortodromion*, p. 400. The latter made a connection between 'Hades' and *aeides*, formless, invisible.

2 PO 15, p. 153.

3 See Gregory of Nyssa, *On the Soul and Resurrection*.

4 See for example John Chrysostom, *Exhortation to Theodore*, I, 10–12; *Commentary on Matthew*, XLIII, 4; *Homilies on Second Corinthians*, X, 4; Maximus the Confessor, *Letters*, I, 24.

5 See, for example, Eusebius of Caesarea, *Commentary on Luke*.

6 The very principle of symbolism is to represent hard to imagine abstract or spiritual realities by means of analogous material realities.

7 See Isaac the Syrian, *The Ascetical Homilies*, 2; Mark of Ephesus, *Second Discourse on Purgatorial Fire*, 18, PO 15, p. 130.

8 See for example John Chrysostom, *Exhortation to Theodore*, I, 10–12.

9 Gregory of Nyssa, *The Great Catechism*, XL, 7–8; Moore and Wilson, p. 54.

10 For the life of those in hell will also be eternal.

11 See for example John Chrysostom, *Homilies on Romans*, V, 7; Theodoret of Cyrrhus, *Cure for Hellenic Illnesses*, XI, 52.

12 *Exomologetarion*, trans. G. Dokos (Thessalonica, Greece: Uncut Mountain Press, 2006), p. 362.

13 See for example John Chrysostom, *Exhortation to Theodore*, I, 11; *Commentary on Psalm 114*, 3; Basil of Caesarea, *Commentary on Psalm 104*, 5.

14 *Commentary on the Psalms*, 114, 3; Hill, vol. 2, pp. 97–98 (under *Psalm 116*).

15 *Orations*, XX, 12.

16 See Gregory Palamas, *Homilies*, 8.

17 On the vision of God according to the Greek Fathers, see V. Lossky, 'Le problème de la "vision face à face" et la tradition patristique à Byzance', *Studia Patristica*, 2 *Texte und Untersuchungen*, 64, Berlin, 1957, pp. 512–537; *The Vision of God*, trans. A. Moorehouse (Crestwood NY: St Vladimir's Seminary Press, 1964).

18 See Symeon the New Theologian, *Discourses*, VI, 112–113; de Catanzaro, p. 122: "The kingdom of heaven consist in partaking of the Holy Spirit."

19 Gregory Palamas, *To Xenia*, 15; *Philokalia*, vol. 4, p. 298.

20 See Gregory Nazianzus, *Orations*, XVI, 9; XX, 12; Maximus the Confessor, *Letters*, 24; Gregory Palamas, *Homilies*, 8.

21 See Gregory Palamas, *Against Gregoras*, III, 27.

22 *Centuries on Theology and the Incarnate Dispensation of the Son of God*, II, 90; *Philokalia*, vol. 2, p. 161.

23 Cf. Basil of Caesarea, *Letters*, VIII, 12; Gregory of Nyssa, *On the Soul and the Resurrection*, 77.

24 John Chrysostom, *Exhortation to Theodore*, I, 11.

25 See Maximus the Confessor, *Letters*, I, PG 91, 388B.

26 See Augustine, *City of God*, XXII, 30.

27 John Damascene, *Exact Exposition of the Orthodox Faith*, IV, 27.

28 See Dionysius the Areopagite, *On the Divine Names*, I, 4.

29 See Gregory Nazianzus, *Orations*, XXI, 2.

30 We will not retrace here what we have already studied at length on the deification of man in *La divinisation de l'homme selon saint Maxime le Confesseur*, Paris, 1997. Also on this theme see: J. Gross, *La Divinisation du chrétien selon les Pères grecs*, Paris, 1938; B. Sartorius, *La Doctrine de la divinisation de l'homme d'après les Pères grecs en général et Grégoire Palamas en particulier*, Genève, 1965.

31 Maximus the Confessor, *Letters*, XXIV.

32 See *Sayings of the Desert Fathers*, alphabetical collection, Macarius, 38; Basil of Caesarea, *On the Holy Spirit*, XVI, 40; Gregory of Nyssa, *On the Soul and the Resurrection*, 82; Maximus the Confessor, *Ad Thalassium*, XLI.

33 John Chrysostom, *Homilies on First Corinthians*, XLI.

34 Gregory Nazianzus, *Orations*, XLV, 11.

35 Gregory of Sinai, *On Commandments and Doctrines*, 33; *Philokalia*, vol. 4, p. 218.

36 *Ibid.* 36; p. 219. See also Maximus the Confessor, *Ad Thalassium*, 11.

37 *A Commentary on the Divine Liturgy*, 45; Hussey and McNulty, p. 101.

38 *Ascetical Homilies*, 6; HTM, p. 56.

39 See J. Daniélou, 'Mystique et Ténèbre chez Grégoire de Nysse', in 'Contemplation', *Dictionnaire de spiritualité*, 2, 1953, col. 1882–1885; *Platonisme et théologie mystique. Essai sur la doctrine spirituelle de Grégoire de Nysse*, Paris, 1954, pp. 291–307.

40 *The Life of Moses*, II, 238–239; Malherbe and Ferguson, p. 116.

41 John Climacus, *The Ladder*, XXVI, 153; HTM, p. 186.

42 *Hymns*, XXIII; Maloney, p. 122.

43 *Hymns*, I; Maloney, p. 15.

44 *Letter 234, To Tarasius the Patrician, to console him on the death of a daughter.*

45 *Ad Thalassium*, 59.

46 *Ibid.* See our commentary on these expressions and other similar ones in *La Divinisation de l'homme selon saint Maxime le Confesseur*, pp. 665–673.

47 This theme has been especially developed by St Maximus the Confessor. See our study: *La Divinisation de l'homme selon saint Maxime le Confesseur*, pp. 527–640, 665–674.

48 *On the Soul and the Resurrection*, 77; Roth, pp. 80–81.

49 Among others see: Theophilus of Antioch, *To Autolycus*, I, 14; *Sayings of the Desert Fathers*, anonymous collection, N 490 (Antony); Maximus the Confessor, *Centuries on Love*, II, 34.

50 Nicetas Stethatos, *Centuries*, III, 79.

51 See *infra*, 49 and 93.

52 Among others see: *Martyrdom of St Polycarp*, XI; Ignatius of Antioch, *To the Ephesians*, XVI, 2; Justin, *First Apology*, 8; 17; 18; *Second Apology*, 1; 8; *Dialogue with Tryphon*, 45; 81; 120; 131, 133, 140; 141; Irenaeus of Lyon, *Against the Heathens*, IV, 40; V, 26, 2; Basil of Caesarea, *Shorter Responses*, 267; Cyril of Jerusalem, *Baptismal Catecheses*, XV, 26; XVIII, 19; Cyril of Alexandria, *Commentary on Psalm 10*, 6; John Climacus, *The Ladder*, VII, 12; 24; Maximus the Confessor, *Letters*, 4; *Questions and Doubts*, 99; Gregory Palamas, *Homilies*, 22; Nicodemus of the Holy Mountain, *New Ladder*, Constantinople, 1844, pp. 188–191.

53 See also on this point: Basil of Caesarea, *Commentary on Psalm 33*, 8; Maximus the Confessor, *Letters*, I, PG 91, 389; Gregory Palamas, *Homilies*, 4.

54 See for example: Abba Isaiah, *Ascetic Discourses*, XXVII, 7; XXIX, 68; 69; Gregory of Sinai, *On Commandments and Doctrines*, 33; Nicetas Stethatos, *Centuries*, III, 79; Gregory Palamas, *To Xenia*, 11.

55 See for example Basil of Caesarea, *Commentary on Psalm 33*, PG 29, 372; John Chrysostom, *Exhortations to Theodore*, I, 10; John Climacus, *The Ladder*, VII, 12; Maximus the Confessor, *Letters*, I; 24.

56 *Exact Exposition of the Orthodox Faith*, IV, 27; Chase, p. 406.

57 John Chrysostom, *Homilies on the Resurrection of the Dead*, 8. See also John Damascene, *Exact Exposition of the Orthodox Faith*, IV, 27.

58 Maximus the Confessor, *Ad Thalassium*, 61.

59 Maximus the Confessor, *Letters*, 24, PG 91, 612C; cf. 1, PG 91, 381D. See also Basil of Caesarea, *Commentary on Psalm 33*, 4; 8.

60 *Letters*, 24, PG 91, 612B.

61 *Letters*, 1, PG 91, 381D–384A.

62 *Exhortations to Theodore*, I, 10.

63 *Exhortations to Theodore*, I, 12; cf. *Homily on the Future Judgment*, PG 63, 751; *Homilies on Second Corinthians*, X, 3.

64 *Ambigua to John*, 21, PG 91, 1252B.

65 *Commentary on Isaiah*, 5, PG 30, 392.

66 *Longer Rules*, 2; Wagner, pp. 235–236.

67 *L'homme et le Dieu-Homme*, Lausanne, 1989, p. 41.

68 Cf. Irenaeus of Lyons, *Against the Heathens*, V, 35, 2; Gregory Palamas, *To Xenia*, 11.

69 Gregory Palamas, *To Xenia*, 11–12.

70 *Exomologetarion*, pp. 317–319.

71 *Ad Thalassium*, 59. See also *Ambigua to John*, 65, PG 91, 1392D, where Maximus says that the damned cannot participate in well-being by being opposed to it.

72 Gregory of Nyssa, *On the Soul and the Resurrection*, 67; Maximus the Confessor, *Questions and Difficult ies*, 19; 99.

73 *On the Soul and the Resurrection*, 67; Roth, p. 72.

74 *Ascetical Homilies*, 28; HTM, p. 141.

75 *Letters*, 1, PG 91, 384BC.

76 Irenaeus of Lyons, *Against the Heathens*, V, 27, 2; cf. 28, 1.

77 *Letters*, 1, PG 91, 385D.

78 *Ad Thalassium*, 59, 609BC.

79 *Mystical Theology of the Eastern Church*, pp. 178–179.

80 Metropolitan Hierotheos Vlachos, *Life after Death*, p. 254.

81 *Commentary on Psalm 33*, PG 29, 372.

82 Basil of Caesarea, *Commentary on Psalm 28*, PG 29, 297A.

83 Gregory Nazianzus, *Orations*, XXI, 2.

84 *Orations*, XXIII, 13.

85 *Orations*, XXXIX, 10.

86 *Orations*, XL, 45.

87 John Climacus, *The Ladder*, XXVIII, 51; HTM, pp. 218–219.

88 *On Commandments and Doctrines*, 33 (*Philokalia*, vol. 4, p. 218); cf. 36 (*ibid.*, p. 219).

89 *Homilies on First Corinthians*, XLI. See also *Homilies on Romans*, V, 3; XXXI, 4.

90 *On the Soul and the Resurrection*, 82; Roth, p. 84.

91 *On Commandments and Doctrines*, 36; *Philokalia*, vol. 4, p. 219. See also Maximus the Confessor, *Ad Thalassium*, XI.

92 *The Shorter Responses*, 267; Anna M. Silvas, *The Asketikon of St Basil the Great* (New York: Oxford University Press, 2005), pp. 418–420.

93 See especially: *On First Principles*, I, vi; II, iii, 3; 4; 7; x, 5; 6; III, v, 4; 8; vi, 3; 6; IV, 23.

94 See Jean Daniélou, 'L'apocatastase chez saint Grégoire de Nysse', *Recherches de science religieuse*, 30, 1940, pp. 328–347; J. Gaith, *La Conception de la liberté chez Grégoire de Nysse*, Paris, 1953, pp. 187–195. This theory has been also wrongly attributed to St Maximus the Confessor as shown by: P. Sherwood, *The Earlier Ambigua of St Maximus the Confessor*, Rome, 1955, pp. 205–221; B. E. Daley, 'Apokatastasis and "Honorable Silence" in the Eschatology of Maximus the Confessor', in C. von Schönborn and F. Heinzer (ed.), *Maximus Confessor, Actes du Symposium sur Maxime le Confesseur*, Fribourg, Switzerland, 1982, pp. 309–339; J.-Cl. Larchet, *La Divinisation de l'homme selon saint Maxime le Confesseur*, Paris, 1996, pp. 653–662; introduction to *Maxime le Confesseur, Questions et difficultés*, Paris, 1999, pp. 18–21.

95 Like St Maximus the Confessor, who deems it good, however, to rectify it. See our introduction to Maxime le Confesseur, *Questions et difficultés*, pp. 18–20.

96 Like Metropolitan Hierotheos of Vlachos, *Life after Death*, pp. 279–312.

97 Like, recently, Father Sergius Bulgakov (see *The Orthodox Church*, p. 185).

98 Among others see: John Chrysostom, *Homilies on Romans*, XXV, 4–6; XXI, 4–5; *Homilies on First Corinthians*, IX, 1–3; Cyril of Alexandria, *Commentary on Psalm 10*, 6; *Commentary on Psalm 35*, 13; *Commentary on Psalm 62*, 10; *Commentary on Isaiah*, LV, 11; Anonymous, *De Sectis*, X, 6; John Climacus, *The Ladder*, V, 52; Anastasius of Sinai, *The Guide*, V; XXII; *On the Hexaemeron*, PG 89, 971 C; Maximus the Confessor, *Ambigua to John*, 7; 42; *Questions and Difficulties*, 19; Theophylact of Bulgaria, *Explanation of the Holy Gospel according to Luke*, XVI.

99 Origenism goes well beyond the doctrine of Origen himself. It must not be forgotten, however, that the latter was already the object of a condemnation by the Alexandrian synods of 231 and 232. On Origenism, see especially: A. Guillaumont, *Les 'Kephalaia gnostica' d'Évagre le Pontique et l'histoire de l'origénisme chez les Grecs et les Syriens*, Paris, 1962.

100 See the patristic dossier established by M. Richard, 'Enfer d'après les Pères', *Dictionnaire de théologie catholique*, 5, 1913, col. 47–83.

101 *Reply of the Greeks to the Latin Position on the Purgatorial Fire*, 19, III, PO 15, pp. 76–77.

102 This also implies the existence and perpetuation of evils here below, except that this world is not eternal. See our study: *Dieu ne veut pas la souffrance des hommes*, Paris, 2nd edition, 2008. Also see our review of A. Glucksmann's book, *La troisième mort de Dieu*, in *Contacts. Revue française de l'Orthodoxie* (tome 52, num. 192, 2000, pp. 359–362) where we show that freedom is indivisble, and that if God withdraws from man the possibility of doing evil and suffering from it, this would also withdraw the possibility of doing good and enjoying it.

103 See in particular John Chrysostom, *Commentary on Philemon*, III, 2; John Damascene, *Dialogue against the Manicheans*, 75; Theophylact of Bulgaria, *Explanation of the Holy Gospel according to Luke*, XVI.

104 See our study, *La Divinisation de l'homme selon saint Maxime le Confesseur*, pp. 658–662.

105 On the non-determining foreknowledge of God, see John Damascene, *Against the Manicheans*, 79.

Chapter Twelve—Preparing Oneself for Death

1 *Homilies on the epistle to the Romans*, XXXI, 4–5.

2 *Ascetic Discourses*, XVI, 33, p. 121.

3 *Ibid.*, 97–98, p. 125.

4 *To Xenia*, 12.

5 *Ascetic Discourses*, XXVII, 7, p. 221.

6 *Commentary on the Gospel according to Matthew*, 43, 5.

7 *Ibid.*, 39, 3.

8 *The Sayings of the Desert Fathers*, alphabetical collection, Theophilus, 4; Bu II 172 (Macarius).

9 *Homily on the resurrection of the dead*, 1.

10 *Homily on the second coming of Christ*, 1, PG 59, 619–620.

11 See *Sayings of the Desert Fathers*, alphabetical collection, Evagrius, 4; Theophilus, 5; Macarius of Egypt, *Letters to his sons*, 17; Basil of Caesarea, *Letters*, 46; Abba Isaiah, *Ascetic Discourses*, 1,5; Ammonas, *Instructions*, IV, 45; John Moschus, *Spiritual Meadow*, 156; Barsanuphius, *Letters*, 232; 242; 256; 790; John of Gaza, *Letters*, 639; 789; Dorotheos of Gaza, *Discourses*, IV, 52; John Climacus, *The Ladder*, I, 14; Iv, 17; V, 18; VI; VII, 21; XI, 3; XXVIII, 49; Isaac the Syrian, *Ascetical Homilies*, 34;

47; 49; Hesychios of Batos, *On Watchfulness and Holiness*, 155; Philotheos of Sinai, *Forty Texts on Watchfulness*, 6; 13; 21; 38; Symeon the New Theologian, *Practical and Theological Chapters*, I, 13; 39; III, 5; 17; Ilias the Priest, *Gnomic Anthology*, II, 11; 12.

12 Remembrance of death has, in the ascetic life, other forms and dimensions that we cannot expand on here. A glimpse into these may be gained by reading the forty-ninth ascetical homily of St Isaac the Syrian which begins significantly in this fashion: "The first thought that by God's loving-kindness descends into a man, that enters into his heart and guides his soul to life, is the thought of his departure from this nature."

13 *Letters*, 31.

14 *On Virginity*, 23.

15 *The Ladder*, XV, 54. See also Isaac the Syrian, *Ascetical Homilies*, 47; Philotheos of Sinai, *Forty Texts on Watchfulness*, 6; 13.

16 *On Watchfulness and Holiness*, 95.

17 Cf. Anthony the Great, *On the Character of Men and on the Virtuous Life*, 91; Isaac the Syrian, *Ascetical Homilies*, 49; Symeon the New Theologian, *Practical and Theological Chapters*, I, 13; Ilias the Priest, *Gnomic Anthology*, II, 11.

18 Cf. Ammonas, *Instructions*, IV, 43; Basil of Caesarea, *Homilies on the Origin of Man*, II, 13; *Letters*, 174; John Chrysostom, *Homilies on the epistle to the Romans*, X, 3; John of Gaza, *Letters*, 789; Hesychios of Batos, *On Watchfulness and Holiness*, 155; Philotheos of Sinai, *Forty Texts on Watchfulness*, 38.

19 Cf. John Chrysostom, *Homilies on the epistle to the Romans*, X, 3; Symeon the New Theologian, *Practical and Theological Chapters*, I, 13.

20 *Ascetic Discourses*, VII, 23, p. 82. Cf. Hesychios of Batos, *On Watchfulness and Holiness*, 155; Philotheos of Sinai, *Forty Texts on Watchfulness*, 38.

21 Cf. Basil of Caesarea, *Letters*, XLVI, 6; Philotheos of Sinai, *Forty Texts on Watchfulness*, 38.

22 Cf. *Sayings of the Desert Fathers*, alphabetical collection, Evagrius, 4; Abba Isaiah, *Ascetic Discourses*, I, 5; John Climacus, *The Ladder*, IV, 17; V, 18; Symeon the New Theologian, *Practical and Theological Chapters*, I, 13.

23 *Ascetic Discourses*, XXVI, 6, p. 212.

24 *Letters*, 174.

25 See, besides the references cited *infra*: Evagrius, *Praktikos*, 29: "[Man] should always live as if he were to die on the morrow"; John Cassian, *The Institutes*, V, 41; Barsanuphius, *Letters*, 346; John of Gaza, *Letters*, 94, 637; Isaac the Syrian, *Ascetical Homilies*, 57.

26 *Conferences*, XVI, 6.

27 *Ascetic Discourses*, IX, 21, p. 96.

28 *Ibid.*, XVI, 97–98, p. 125.

29 Athanasius of Alexandria, *Life of Antony*, XIX, 2.

30 *Letters*, 24, PG 91, 609C–612D. A similar and more developed meditation will be found in Basil of Caesarea, *Letters*, XLVI, 5. He shows the meaning of this, *ibid.*, 6: flee the chastisements, repent and become pure in order to be welcomed by Christ into His Kingdom.

31 *Letters*, 1, PG 91, 384D–392A.

32 On the meanings of this formula, see our work: *Saint Silouane de l'Athos*, Paris, 2001, pp. 41–74.

33 *Commentary on the Gospel according to St Matthew*, XXXV, 1.

34 *Letters*, 168.

35 *Commentary on the Gospel according to St Matthew*, LXXVIII, 1.

BIBLIOGRAPHY

I. SOURCES

1. Liturgical Services and Prayers

Εὐχολόγιον sive Rituale Graecorum, edited by J. Goar, Paris, 1647; Venice, 1780.

[Greater Euchologion] Εὐχολόγιον τὸ Μέγα, Venice, 1862; Athens, 1986; trans. G. V. Shann, Book of Needs of the Holy Orthodox Church, London, 1894, and by St Tikhon's Monastery, Great Book of Needs, 4 vols., South Canaan PA, 2002.

The Great Horologion (Book of Hours), Boston, 1997.

Paraklitike or Great Octoechos, French trans. D. Guillaume, Parme, 1995.

[Lesser Euchologion] Μικρὸν Εὐχολόγιον, Athens, 1992.

The Lenten Triodion, trans. Mother Mary and Archimandrite Kallistos Ware, South Canaan PA, 1977.

The Lenten Triodion. Supplementary Texts, trans. Mother Mary and Archimandrite Kallistos Ware, South Canaan PA, 2007.

2. Councils

Denzinger = H. Denzinger, Symboles et définitions de la foi catholique, Paris, 1996. Trans. R. J. Deferrari, The Sources of Catholic Dogma, St Louis MO & London, 1957.

Mansi = J. D. Mansi, Sacrorum conciliorum nova et amplissima collectio, Florence, 1764.

3. Canons

Manuel Malaxos, Nomocanon. Canon 162. Text in J. Papp-Szilagyi, Enchiridion juris ecclesiae orientalis catholicae, 1880.

4. Fathers and Ancient Authors

Adamnan, Life of Columba. Text edited by A. O. and M. O. Anderson, Oxford, 1991.

Ambrose of Milan, Death is a Good. PL 14, 567–596.

Ammonas, *Instructions.* Greek text and French trans. F. Nau in *Patrologia Orienialis,* xl, 4.

_____, *Letters.* Greek text established by F. Nau, *Palrologia Orienlalis,* XI, 4. French trans. from the Syriac, Georgian and Greek by Dom B. Outtier and Dom L. Régnault in *Lettres des Pères du désert,* "Spiritualité orientale" num. 42, Bellefontaine, 1985.

Anastasius of Sinai, *The Guide.* Text edited by K.-H. Uthemann, "Corpus Christianorum Series Graeca" num. 8, Turnhout, 1981.

_____, *Homily on the Deceased.* PG 89, 1192–1201.

_____, *On the Hexaemeron.* PG 89, 851–1077.

Andrew of Caesarea, *Commentary on the Apocalypse.* PG 106, 216–457. Trans. E. S. Constantinou. Washington, 2011.

Andrew of Crete, *Homilies,* Homily 12, *On the Dormition of the Most Holy Mother of God.* PG 97, 1045–1072. Trans. B. E. Daley, *On the Dormition of Mary, Early Patristic Homilies,* Crestwood NY, 1998, pp. 117–134.

Anonymous, *Apostolic Constitutions.* Book VIII. Roberts and Donaldson (ed.), *The Ante-Nicene Fathers,* vol. 7, New York, 1913, pp. 479–500.

_____, *De sectis.* PG 86, 1193–1268.

_____, *History of the Monks of Egypt.* Greek text by A.-J. Festugière, *Subsidia Hagiographica,* 34, 1961. Trans. N. Russell, *The Lives of the Desert Fathers* "Cistercian Studies" num. 34, Oxford and Kalamazoo MI, 1980.

_____, *Life of Saint Daniel* the *Stylite.* Text established by le P. Delehaye in *Les Saints stylites,* Bruxelles, 1923. Trans. E. Dawes and N. H. Baynes, in *Three Byzantine Saints,* Oxford, 1948, pp. 7–71.

_____, *Life of Saint Macarius of Scetis.* French trans. from the Coptic text by E. Amélineau in *Les Annales du Musée Guimet,* 24, 1894, pp. 203–234. Trans. T. Vivian, in *Saint Macarius, the Spiritbearer,* Crestwood NY, 2004, pp. 151–198.

_____, *Life of Saint Syncletica.* PG 65, 1487–1558, trans. E. B. Bongie, Toronto, 1995.

_____, *Life of the holy mace-bearer.* Text edited by F. Combefi s, *Bibliothecae Graecorum Patrum Auctarium Novissimum,* Paris, 1672, tome 1, pp. 324–326.

_____, *Martyrdom of Saint Polycarp.* Roberts and Donaldson (ed.), *The Ante-Nicene Fathers,* vol. 1, New York, 1913, pp. 39–44.

_____, *To Diognetus,* Roberts and Donaldson (ed.), *The Ante-Nicene Fathers,* vol. 1, New York, 1913, pp. 25–30.

Antony (the Great), *Letters,* Latin version: PG 40, 977–1000; Georgian version established by G. Garine, *Corpus Scriptorum Christianorum Orientalium,* 148 (text) and 149 (Latin translation); Syriac version (1st letter): F. Nau edition, *Revue de l'Orient Chrétien*, 14, pp. 282–297. Trans. S. Rubenson, *The Letters of St Antony*, Minneapolis MN, 1995.

_____, *On the Character of Men and on the Virtuous Life.* Text in *Philokalia ton ieron neptikon*, vol. 1, Athens, 1976, pp. 4–27. Trans. Palmer, Sherrard and Ware in *The Philokalia: The Complete Text*, vol. 1, London & Boston, 1979.

Apophthegmata (Sayings) of the Fathers, Alphabetical series: PG 65, 71–440, completed by J.-C. Guy, "Recherche sur la tradition grecque des Apophtegma Patrum", *Subsidia Hagiographica*, 36, Brussels, 1962, pp. 19–36. Translation B. Ward, *The Sayings of the Desert Fathers*, rev. ed., Kalamazoo MI, 1984. We use J.-C. Guy's numbering.

_____, Anonymous Series. Greek text established by F. Nau, *Revue de l'Orient Chrétien*, 12–14; 17–18 (1907–1913). French trans. Dom L. Régnault, *Les Sentences des Pères du désert, Série des anonymes*, Solesmes, 1985 (apophthegmata numbered N 133 to N 339). Table of correspondence with the numbering of L.-C. Guy in *Les Sentences des Pères du désert*, Troisième recueil, Solesmes, 1976, pp. 254–266. Trans. B. Ward, *The Wisdom of the Desert Fathers*, Oxford, 1986.

_____, Various collections: a) Unpublished or little known Apophthegmata collected and presented by Dom. L. Regnault. Translations from Greek (Ms. Coislin 126 = N; Paul Evergetinos = PE), Latin (R, Pa, M), Syriac (Bu), Armenien (Arm), Copt (Eth. Coll.), Ethiopian (Eth. Coll., Eth. Pat.) by the Monks of Solesmes, *Les sentences des Péres du désert, Nouveau recueil*, Solesmes, 1970; b) Additions to the alphabetico-anonymous series, additions to the systematic Greek series (I–XXI, H, QRT), apophthegmata translated from Latin (PA, CSP), apophthegmata translated from Coptic (Am), by Dom L. Régnault, *Les Sentences des Pères du désert. Troisième recueil.* Solesmes, 1976. This last work includes tables for all series.

Arethas of Patrai (of Caesarea), *Commentary on the Apocalypse.* PG 106, 493–785.

Athanasius of Alexandria, *Against the Heathen.* Text and trans. P. Th . Camelot, "Sources chrétiennes" num. 18 bis, Paris, 1983. Trans. H. Ellershaw, *Nicene and Post-Nicene Fathers*, Series 2, vol. 4, New York, 1924, pp. 1–30.

_____, *The Life of Antony.* Trans. R. C. Gregg, in *Athanasius*, New York, Ramsey, Toronto, 1980, pp. 29–99.

_____, *On the Incarnation.* Trans. P. Lawson, Crestwood NY, 1996.

_____, *On Virginity.* PG 28, 252–281.

Athanasius (Pseudo-), *Questions to Antiochus.* PG 28, 597–708.

Athenagoras, *Embassy for the Christians.* Trans. J. H. Crehan, "Ancient Christian Writers," num. 23, Westminster MD and London, 1956 pp. 29–78.

_____, *The Resurrection of the Dead.* Trans. J. H. Crehan, "Ancient Christian Writers" num. 23, Westminster MD and London, 1956, pp. 79–116.

Augustine of Hippo, *The City of God.* Text of the 4th edition of B. Dombart and A. Kalb. Trans. H. Bettenson, Harmondsworth UK and New York, 1972.

_____, *On Care to be had for the Dead.* PL 40, 591–610.

Barnabas: (Pseudo-), *Letter.* Text and French trans. A. Laurent and G. Oger, "Hemmer-Lejay", Paris, 1926.

Barsanuphius. *Letters.* Greek text established by Nicodemos the Hagiorite, Venice, 1816, Thessalonica, 1984. Trans. John Chryssavgis, *Letters/Barsanuphius and John,* Washington, 2 vols., 2006–2007. The numbering adopted is that of the translation.

Basil of Caesarea (the Great), *Commentary on Isaiah.* PG 30, 117–668.

_____, *God is not the author of evils* (Homily). PG 31, 329A–353A. French trans. M.-C. Rossel in *Dieu et le mal,* "Les Pères dans la foi" num. 69, Paris, 1997.

_____, *Homilies on the Hexaemeron.* Trans. A. C. Way, in *Saint Basil. Exegetic Homilies,* Washington, 1963, pp. 3–150.

_____, *Homilies on the Origin of Man.* Text and French trans. A. Smets and M. Van Esbroeck, "Sources chrétiennes" num. 160, Paris, 1970.

_____, *Homily on Holy Baptism.* PG 31, 424–444.

_____, *Homily on the Holy Martyr Barlaam.* PG 31, 484–489.

_____, *Homilies on the Psalms.* PG 29, 209–493.

_____, *Letters.* Trans. A. C. Way, "The Fathers of the Church, A New Translation", vols. 13 & 28, Washington, 1951 (vol. 13), 1955 (vol. 28).

_____, *The Long Rules.* PG 31, 889–1052. Trans. M. M. Wagner, in *Saint Basil. The Ascetical Works.* "The Fathers of the Church. A New Translation" vol. 9, Washington, 1962, pp. 223–337.

_____, *On the forty holy martyrs.* PG 31, 508–525.

_____, *The Shorter Responses.* PG 31, 1080–1305. Trans. A. M. Silvas, in *The Asketikon of St Basil the Great,* New York, 2005.

Bede the Venerable, *Ecclesiastical History of the English People.* Text edited by C. Plummer, *Baedae Venerabilis Opera Historica,* Oxford, 1896. B. Colgrave and R. A. B. Mynors (ed.), Oxford,1969.

_____, *Life of Saint Cuthbert.* Text edited by B. Colgrave, *Two Lives of Saint Cuthbert: A Life by an Anonymous Monk of Lindisfarne and Bede's Prose Life,* London, 1985.

Bessarion, *Réponse des Grecs à la position des Latins sur le feu purgatoire*. Text edited by L. Petit, *Patrologie Orientalis*, tome XV–L, Paris, 1920, pp. 61–79.

Callinicos, *Vie d'Hypatios*. Text and French trans. G. J. M. Bartelink, "Sources chrétiennes" num. 177, Paris, 1971.

Callistus and Ignatius of Xanthopoulos, *Directions to hesychasts, in a hundred chapters*. Greek text in *Philokalia ton ieron neptikon*, tome 4, Athens, 1976, pp. 197–295. Trans. E. Kadloubobsky and G. E. H. Palmer, *Writings from the Philokalia on Prayer of the Heart*, London, 1951, pp. 164–273.

Cesarini (Cardinal Julius), *Chapters addressed to the Greeks by the Latins on the subject of purgatorial fire*. Text edited by L. Petit in *Patrologia Orientalis*, tome XV–L , Paris, 1920, pp. 25–38.

Clement of Alexandria, *Stromata* VII. Roberts and Donaldson (ed.), *The Ante-Nicene Fathers*, vol. 2, New York, 1913, pp. 523–556.

Clement of Rome, *Epistle to the Corinthians*. Roberts and Donaldson (ed.), *The Ante-Nicene Fathers*, vol. 1, New York, 1913, pp. 5–21.

Cyprian of Carthage, *Letters*. Trans. vol. 1 by R. B. Donna, "Ancient Christian Writers" num. 43, New York/Mahwah, 1964; vols. 2, 3, 4 by G. W. Clarke, "Ancient Christian Writers" num. 44, 46, 47, New York/Mahwah, 1984, 1986, 1983.

_____, *On Death*. PL 4, 583–602. French trans. M. H. Stébé in Cyprien-Ambroise, *Le chrétien devant la mort*, "Les Pères dans la foi", Paris, 1980.

_____, *On the Unity of the Church*. Text edited by von Hartel, "Corpus Scriptorum Ecclesiasticorum Latinorum" num. 3, Vienna, 1869. Trans. M. Bevenot, *The Lapsed, The Unity of the Catholic Church*, "Ancient Christian Writers" num. 25, New York/Mahwah, 1957.

Cyril of Alexandria, *Commentary on Isaiah*. PG 70, 9–1449.

_____, *Commentary on the Psalms*. PG 69, 717–1276.

_____, *Commentary on Romans*. PG 74, 775–856.

_____, *Commentary on Saint John*. PG 73; 74, 9–756.

_____, *Commentary on Saint Luke*. Edition of the Syriac version by R. P. Smith, University Press, 1983. Trans. R. P. Smith, Studion Publishers, 1983.

_____, *Homily XIV, On the Leave-taking of the Soul*. PG 77, 1073C–1076D.

Cyril of Jerusalem, *Baptismal Catecheses*. PG 33, 332–1057. Trans. A. P. McCauley and A. A. Stephenson, *The Works of St Cyril of Jerusalem*, "Fathers of the Church", num. 61 and 64, vol. 1 (1969), vol. 2 (1970).

_____, *Mystagogical Catecheses*. Text established by A. Piédagnel, "Sources chrétiennes" num. 126 bis, Paris, 1988. Trans. E. Yarnold, *Cyril of Jerusalem*, London and New York, 2000, pp. 169–187.

Dionysius the Areopagite (Pseudo-), *The Celestial Hierarchy.* Text established by G. Heil. Trans. C. Luibheid and P. Rorem, *Pseudo-Dionysius. The Complete Works*, New York, 1987, pp. 145–191.

———, *The Divine Names.* Text edited by B. R. Suchla, *Corpus Dionysiacum*, I, *De divinis nominibus*, "Patristische Texte und Studien" num. 33, Berlin/New York, 1990. Trans. C. Luibheid and P. Rorem, *Pseudo-Dionysius. The Complete Works*, New York, 1987, pp. 49–131.

———, *The Ecclesiastical Hierarchy.* PG 3, 396–569. Trans. C. Luibheid and P. Rorem, *Pseudo-Dionysius. The Complete Works*, New York, 1987, pp. 195–259.

Diadochos of Photiki, *On Spiritual Knowledge and Discrimination.* Trans. Palmer, Sherrard and Ware, *The Philokalia. The Complete Text*, London and Boston, 1979, pp. 253–296.

Dorotheos of Gaza, *Discourses and Sayings.* Trans. E. P. Wheeler, Kalamazoo, 1977.

———, *Letters.* Text and French trans. L. Régnault and J. de Préville, "Sources chrétiennes" num. 92, Paris, 1963.

Dositheus of Jerusalem, *Confession of Faith*, Jerusalem, 1672.

———, *Enchiridion*, Bucarest, 1690.

Ilias the Ecdicos (the Presbyter), *A Gnomic Anthology.* Greek text in *Philokalia ton ieron neptikon*, tome 2, Athens, 1976, pp. 289–314 and PG 127, 1129–1176. Trans. Palmer, Sherrard and Ware, in *The Philokalia. The Complete Text*, vol. 3, pp. 34–65.

Ephrem the Syrian (of Nisibis), *On the Second Coming of ChriSt* Syriac, Greek and Latin text edited by J.-S. Assemani, *Oeuvres complètes*, tome 3, pp. 275–276.

Epiphanius of Cyrus (of Salamis), *Panarion* [= *Against the Heresies*]. PG 41, 173–200 ; 42, 9–773. Partial trans. F. Williams, Leiden/New York/Köln, 1994.

Eugenius Bulgaris, *Adoleschia Philotheos*, 2 vols., Moscow, 1801.

Eusebius of Caesarea, *Commentary on the Gospel according to Luke.* PG 24, 529–605.

———, *Ecclesiastical History.* Translation P. Schaff and H. Wace (ed.), *Nicene and Post-Nicene Fathers, Second Series*, vol. 1, Grand Rapids MI, 1976.

Evagrius Ponticus, *The Praktikos*, trans. J. E. Bamberger, in *Evagrius Ponticus: The Praktikos and Chapters on Prayer*, Kalamazoo, 1981, pp. 12–42.

Gabriel of Saint Petersburg and Novgorod (Metropolitan), *Explanation of the Liturgy*, Saint Petersburg, 1799.

Gabriel Severos (of Philadelphia), *On the Kolyvas*, in R. Simon, *Fide, Ecclesiae orientalis*, Paris, 1671, pp, 23–30.

Gregory of Chios, *Summary of the Divine and Sacred Dogmas of the Church*, Venice, 1635.

Gregory of Nazianzus (the Theologian), *Moral Poems.* PG 37, 522–968.

_____, *Oration 7*. Text and French trans. M.-A. Calvet, "Sources chrétiennes" num. 405, Paris, 1995. Unless otherwise noted, English translations of *Orations* in P. Schaff and H. Wace (ed.), *A Select Library of Nicene and Post-Nicene Fathers*, Second Series, vol. 7, New York, Oxford and London, 1894.

_____, *Oration 16*. PG 35, 933–964.

_____, *Oration 18*. PG 35, 985–1044.

_____, *Oration 21*. Text and French trans. J. Mossay and G. Lafontaine, "Sources chrétiennes" num. 270, Paris, 1980.

_____, *Orations 23–24*. Trans. M. Vinson, in *Select Orations*, "Fathers of the Church" num. 107, Washington, 2003, pp. 131–156.

_____, *Oration 27*. Text and French trans. P. Gallay, "Sources chrétiennes" num. 250, Paris, 1978.

_____, *Orations 38-40*. Text established by C. Moreschini. French trans. P. Gallay, "Sources chretiennes" num. 358, Paris, 1989.

_____, *Oration 43*. Text and French trans. J. Bernardi, "Sources chrétiennes" num. 384, Paris, 1992.

_____, *Oration 45*. PG 36, 624–661. French trans. E. Devolder, "Les écrits des saints", Namur, 1961.

Gregory of Nyssa, *Against Apollinarius*, PG 45, 1124–1269 and *Gregorii Nysseni Opera*, III, 1, pp. 131-233.

_____, *Catechetical Discourse*. Text and French trans. L. Méridier, Paris, 1908.

_____, *Concerning Those who have Died*. PG 46, 497–537.

_____, *Homilies on the Beatitudes*. PG 44, 1193–1303. Trans. H. C. Graef, *St Gregory of Nyssa. The Lord's Prayer. The Beatitudes*, "Ancient Christian Writers" num. 18, New York/Ramsey, 1954, pp. 85–175.

_____, *Homily of Consolation concerning Pulcheria*, PG 46, 864–877.

_____, *Homily on the Great Martyr Theodore*, PG 46, 736–748.

_____, *On the Forty Holy Martyrs*. PG 46, 749–788.

_____, *On the Making of Man*. PG 44, 128–256. French trans. J. Laplace, "Sources chrétiennes" num. 6, Paris, 1943. Trans. H. A. Wilson, in P. Schaff and H. Wace (ed.), *A Select Library of Nicene and Post-Nicene Fathers*, Second Series, vol. 5, New York, 1917, pp. 387–427.

_____, *Life of Moses*. Trans. E. J. Malherbe and E. Ferguson, New York/Ramsey/Toronto, 1978.

_____, *Life of Saint Macrina*. Trans. K. Corrigan, Toronto, 1987.

_____, *On the passage: "Then the Son Himself will also be subject to Him who put all things under Him".* PG 44, 1304–1325. French trans. M. Canévet in Gregory of Nyssa, *Le Christ pascal,* "Les Pères dans la foi" num. 55, Paris, 1994.

_____, *On Virginity.* P. Schaff and H. Wace (ed.), *A Select Library of Nicene and Post-Nicene Fathers,* Second Series, vol. 5, New York, 1917, pp. 343–371.

_____, *Paschal Homilies.* PG 46, 581–589, 600–628, 652–681 and *Gregorii Nysseni Opera,* IX, 1, pp. 245–270, 600–628, 309–311. Trans. S. G. Hall. *Easter Sermons of Gregory of Nyssa,* Cambridge MA, 1981.

_____, *The Soul and the Resurrection.* PG 46, 12–160. Trans. C. P. Roth, Crestwood NY, 1993.

_____, *Treatise on the Inscriptions of the Psalms.* PG 44, 432–616. Trans. R. E. Heine, Oxford, 1995.

Gregory of Thrace, *Life of Saint Basil the New.* Account of Theodora. Greek text in the manuscript Synod. 249, folios 66v-113v. Slavonic translation. English translation by Archimandrite Panteleimon within the title: *Eternal Mysteries Beyond the Grave;* Holy Trinity Publications:Jordanville NY, 2012.

_____, Metropolitan Makarios in *Cheti Meneya,* 26 March.

Gregory of Tours, *History of the Franks.* PL 71, 159–575. Trans. L. Thorpe, Harmondsworth UK/Baltimore MD, 1974.

Gregory the Great, *Dialogues.* Translated by O. J. Zimmerman, "Fathers of the Church, a New Translation", vol. 39, New York, 1959.

_____, *Homilies on the Gospels.* PL 76, 1075–1314. Trans. D. HurSt In *Forty Gospel Homilies,* Piscataway, NJ, 2009.

Gregory of Sinai, *On Commandments and Doctrines, Warnings and Promises; on Thoughts, Passions and Virtues, and also on Stillness and Prayer.* Greek text in *Philokalia ton ieron neptikon,* tome 4, Athens, 1976, pp. 31–62 and PG 150, 1240–1300. Trans. Palmer, Sherrard and Ware, *The Philokalia. The Complete Text,* vol. 4, London, 1995, pp. 212–252.

Gregory Palamas, *Against Gregoras.* Discourse III. Text edited by P. Chrestou, *Gregoriou tou Palama Suggrammata,* tome 4, Thessalonica, 1988, pp. 321–340.

_____, *Homilies.* PG 151, 9–549 and S. Oikonomos edition, *Gregoriou tou Palama omiliai,* Athens, 1861. Trans. C. Veniamin. *Saint Gregory Palamas: The Homilies,* South Canaan PA, 2009.

_____, *Theophanes.* PG 150, 909–960.

_____, *To the Most Reverend Nun Xenia.* Greek text in *Philokalia ton ieron neptikon,* tome 4, Athens, 1976, pp. 91–115 and PG 150, 1044–1088. Trans. Palmer, Sherrard and Ware, *The Philokalia. The Complete Text,* vol. 4, London, 1995, pp. 293–322.

_____, *Topics of Natural and Theological Science and on the Moral and Ascetic Life.* Text edited by R. E. Sinkewicz, *The One Hundred and Fifty Chapters*, Toronto, 1988. Trans. Palmer, Sherrard and Ware (of the text edited in *Philokalia ton ieron neptikon,* tome 4, Athens, 1976, pp. 134–187) in *The Philokalia. The Complete Text*, vol. 4, London, 1995, pp. 347–417.

_____, *Triads in Defense of the Holy Hesychasts.* French text and trans. J. Meyendorff , Louvain, 1973. Partial English translation N. Gendle, *Gregory Palamas. The Triads*, Mahwah NJ, 1983.

Hesychios of Batos (of Sinai, the Priest), *On Watchfulness and Holiness.* Greek text in *Philokalia ton ieron neptikon,* tome l, Athens, 1976, pp. 141–173 and PG 93, 1480–1544. Trans. Palmer, Sherrard and Ware, in *The Philokalia. The Complete Text*, London and Boston, 1979, pp. 162–198.

Hilary of Poitiers, *Commentary on the Psalms.* PL 9, 231–908.

Hippolytus of Rome, *The Apostolic Tradition.* Trans. G. Dix and H. Chadwick, *The Treatise on the Apostolic Tradition*, New York/Abingdon UK, 1991.

_____, *Demonstration on Christ and the AntichriSt* PG 10, 725–788.

Ignatius Brianchaninov (Bishop), *Offering to Contemporary Monasticism,* in *Complete Works*, vol. 5, *Ascetic Works*, Saint Petersburg, 1886 (in Russian); English translation by Archimandrite Lazarus under the title: *The Arena: Guidelines for Spiritual and Monastic Life*, Jordanville NY, 2012.

_____, *Slovo o smerti* [*Concerning Death*]. in *Complete works,* vol. 3, *Ascetic Works*, Saint Petersburg, 1886, pp. 69–183 (in Russian).

_____, *Pribavlenie k slovy o smerti* [*Supplement to "Concerning Death"*], in *Complete Works.* vol. 3, *Ascetic Works*, Saint Petersburg, 1886, pp. 183–312 (in Russian).

Ignatius of Antioch, *Letters.* Trans. J. B. Lightfoot, in *The Apostolic Fathers*, London, 1891, pp. 63–88.

Irenaeus of Lyon, *Against the Heresies.* Trans. D. J. Unger, "Ancient Christian Writers" num. 55, New York, 1992.

_____, *On the Apostolic Preaching.* Trans. John Behr, Crestwood NY, 1997.

Isaac of Nineveh (the Syrian), *The Ascetical Homilies.* Text of the Greek version, edited by N. Theotokis, Leipzig, 1770, reedited by J. Spetsieris, Athens, 1895. Trans. the Holy Transfiguration Monastery, 1984. NB This Greek version has been retained in preference to the original Syriac text, since that is the text accepted by all Hellenic monasticism since the ninth century.

Isaiah of Scetis (Abba), *Ascetic Discourses.* Text edited by Augustinos, Jerusalem, 1911, reprinted by S. N. Schoinas, Volos, 1962. Trans. J. Chryssavgis and P. Penkett, Kalamazoo MI, 2002.

Isidore of Pelusium, *Letters*. PG 78.

John of Karpathos (or Karpathos), *For the Encouragement of the Monks in India*. Greek text in *Philokalia ton ieron neptikon*, tome 1, Athens, 1971, pp. 276–296 and PG 85, 1837–1856. Trans. Palmer, Sherrard and Ware in *The Philokalia. The Complete Text*, vol. 1, pp. 298–321.

John Cassian. *The Conferences*. Trans. B. Ramsey, "Ancient Christian Writers" num. 57, Washington/Mahwah NJ, 1997.

John Chrysostom, *Apology for the Monastic Life*. PG 47, 319–386.

_____, *Commemary on John*. PG 59, 23–482.

_____, *Commentary on Matthew*. PG 57 and 58.

_____, *Commentary on the Psalms*. PG 55.

_____, *Discourse against the Jews*. PG 48, 843–942.

_____, *Exhortations to Theodore*. PG 47, 277–316.

_____, *Homilies on Colossians*. PG 62, 299–392.

_____, *Homilies on First Corinthians*. PG 61, 9–380.

_____, *Homilies on First Thessalonians*. PG 62, 391–500.

_____, *Homilies on Genesis*. PG 53, 23–385 and 54, 383–580.

_____, *Homilies on Hebrews*. PG 63, 9–236.

_____, *Homilies on Lazarus*. PG 48, 963–1051. Trans. C. P. Roth, *On Wealth and Poverty*, Crestwood NY, 1984.

_____, *Homilies on Philemon*. PG 62, 70 1–720.

_____, *Homilies on Philippians*. PG 62, 177–298.

_____, *Homilies on Romans*. PG 60, 39 1–682.

_____, *Homilies on Second Corinthians*. PG 61, 381–610.

_____, *Homilies on the Acts of the Apostles*. PG 60, 13–384.

_____, *Homilies on the Consolation of Death*. PG 56, 293–306.

_____, *Homilies on the Demons*. PG 49, 241–276.

_____, *Homilies on the Statues*. PG 49, 15–222.

_____, *Homily in "honor of all the saints who have suffered martyrdom"*. PG 50, 705–712.

_____, *Homily on Eleazar and the seven youths*. PG 63, 523–530.

_____, *Homily on Patience*. PG 60, 723–730.

_____, *Homily on the Ascension*. PG 50, 44 1–452.

_____, *Homily on the Cross and the Good Th ief*. PG 49, 399–418.

_____, *Homily on the Future Judgment.* PG 63, 743–754.

_____, *Homily on the Holy Martyrs Bernice, Prosdoce et Domnina.* PG 50, 629–640.

_____, *Homily on the passage: "Be not thou afraid, when a man shall be made rich …" and on Hospitality.* PG 55, 499–518.

_____, *Homily on the Resurrection of the Dead.* PG 50, 417–432.

_____, *Homily on the Word "Cemetery" and on the Cross.* PG 49, 393–398.

_____, *Letters to Olympias.* Text and French trans. A.-M. Malingrey, "Sources chrétiennes" num. 13 bis, Paris, 1968.

_____, *On the Blessed Job.* PG 64, 505–656.

_____, *Treatise on the Priesthood.* PG 48, 623–692.

John Climacus, *The Ladder of Divine Ascent.* Text edited by Sophronios the Hermit, Constantinople, 1883, re-edition, Athens, 1979. Trans. Holy Transfiguration Monastery, rev. ed., Boston, 2001.

John Damascene, *Dialogue against the Manichaeans.* Text edited by B. Korrer, *Die Schrift en des Johannes von Damaskos,* IV, "Patristischen Texte une Studien" num. 22.

_____, *Exact Exposition of the Orthodox Faith.* PG 94, 789–1228 and the critical edition of B. Kotter, *Die Schrift en des Johannes von Damaskos,* II, "Patristischen Texte une Studien" num. 12. Trans. F. H. Chase, *Saint John of Damascus. Writings,* Washington, 1958, pp. 165–406.

_____, *Sacred Parallels.* PG 95, 1040–96, 441.

John Damascene (Pseudo-), *On those who have fallen asleep in the faith,* PG 95, 248–277.

John of Gaza, *Letters.* Text edited by Nikodemos the Hagiorite, Venice, 1816; new ed.. Thessalonica, 1984. Trans. John Chryssavgis, *Letters/Barsanuphius and John,* Washington, 2 vols., 2006–2007. The numbering adopted is that of the translation.

John Moschos, *The Spiritual Meadow.* PG 87, 2851–3116. Trans. J. Wortley "Cistercian Studies Series" num. 139, Kalamazoo MI, 1992.

Joseph Bryennos, *Complete Works,* 3 vols., E. Bulgaris edition, Leipzig, 1768–1784.

Justin (the Philosopher), *First Apology.* Roberts and Donaldson (ed.), *The Ante-Nicene Fathers,* vol. 1, New York, 1913.

_____, *Second Apology.* Ibid.

_____, *Dialogue with Trypho.* Ibid.

_____, *On the Resurrection.* Text established by K. Holl, *Texte und Untersuchungen,* N. F., V, 2, Leipzig, 1899.

Justin (Pseudo-), *Questions and Answers for the Orthodox.* PG 6, 1249–1400.

Leontius of Neapolis, *Life of Saint John of Cyprus, 'the Almsgiver'*. Trans. E. Dawes and N. H. Baynes, in *Three Byzantine Saints*, Oxford, 1948, pp. 199–262.

_____, *Life of Saint Symeon the Fool*. Text and Trans. A.-J. Festugière, Paris, 1974. Partial English Trans. D. Krueger, *Symeon the holy fool: Leontius's Life and the late antique city*, Berkeley, 1996.

Macarius of Alexandria, *Révélation au sujet des âmes: comment elles sont enlevées des corps*. Text and Trans. A. Van Lantschoot, "Révélations de Macaire et de Marc de Tarmaqa sur le sort de l'âme après la mort", *Le Muséon*, 63, 1950, pp. 176–181.

Macarius of Egypt (the Great, Pseudo-), *Spiritual Homilies* of Collection II (1–50). Text established by H. Dörries, E. Klostermann, M. Kroeger, *Die 50 geistlichen Homilien des Makarios*, "Patristische Texte und Studien" num. 4, Berlin, 1964. Trans. G. A. Maloney, in *Pseudo-Macarius: The Fifty Spiritual Homilies and the Great Letter*, New York and Mahwah, 1992, pp. 37–246.

_____, *Spiritual Homilies* 51–57 (Supplement to Collection II). Text established by G. L. Marriott, *Macarii Anecdota, Seven Unpublished Homilies of Macarius*, "Harvard Theological Studies" num. 5, Cambridge, Mass., 1918.

_____, *Spiritual Homilies* of Collection III (1–28). Text, French Trans. V. Desprez, "Sources chrétiennes" num. 275, Paris, 1980.

Macarius of Moscow (Metropolitan), *Dogmatic Theology of the Orthodox Church*, 2 vols., Saint Petersburg, 1883 (in Russian); French translation, 2 vols. Paris, 1860.

Mark of Ephesus, *Refutation of the of the Latins = First discourse on purgatorial fire*. Text edited by L. Petit in *Patrolgia Orientalis*, tome XV–L, Paris, 1920, pp. 39–60.

_____, *Another reply to the Latins, in which the true faith of the Church of the Greeks is set forth* [= *Second discourse on purgatorial fire*]. Text edited by L. Petit in *Patrologia Orientalis*, tome XV-l, Paris, 1920, pp. 108–151.

_____, *Reply to the difficult ies and questions posed on the suject of the previous discourse by the cardinals and other Latin doctors*. Text edited by L. Petit in *Patrolagia Orientalis*, tome XV–L, Paris, 1920, pp. 152–168.

Mark the Monk (the Hermit, the Ascetic), *Concerning Holy Baptism*. In *Counsels on the Spiritual Life*, Trans. T. Vivian and A. Casiday. Crestwood NY, 2009, pp. 290–327.

_____, *On the Hypostatic Union* (*On the Incarnation*). Text established by J. Kunze, *Markus Eremita*, Leipzig, 1895. Trans. T. Vivian and A. Casiday in Mark the Monk, *Counsels on the Spiritual Life*, Crestwood NY, 2009, pp. 254–285.

Maximus the Confessor, *Ambigua to John*. PG 91, 1061A–1417C. French trans. E. Ponsoye, Paris-Suresnes, 1994. Partial English translation in *On the Cosmic Mystery of Jesus Christ. Selected Writings from St Maximus the Confessor*, trans. P.M. Blowers and R. L. Wilken, Crestwood, NY, 2003.

_____, *Commentary on the Our Father*, PG 90, 872–909. Trans. G. C. Berthold, in *Maximus Confessor: Selected Writings*, New York, Mahwah and Toronto, 1985, pp. 101–119.

_____, *Four Hundred Texts on Love*. PG 90, 960–1080; critical edition by A. Ceresa-Gastaldo, Rome, 1963. Trans. Palmer, Sherrard and Ware, in *The Philokalia. The Complete Text*, vol. 2, London and Boston, 1981, pp. 52–113, and G. C. Berthold, in *Maximus*

Confessor: Selected Writings, New York/Mahwah NJ/Toronto, 1985, pp. 35–87.

_____, *Letters*. PG 91, 364–649. French trans. E. Ponsoye, Paris, 1997.

_____, *Mystagogy*. PG 91, 657–718 critical edition by C. G. Sotiropoulos, Athens, 1978. Trans. G. C. Berthold, in *Maximus Confessor: Selected Writings*, New York, Mahwah, and Toronto, 1985, pp. 183–214.

_____, *Quaestiones et dubia*. "Corpus Christianorum Series Graeca" num. 10. Trans. D. D. Prassas, *Questions and Doubts*, DeKalb IL, 2009.

_____, *Ad Thalassium*. Text edited by C. Laga and C. Steel, "Corpus Christianorum Series Graeca" num. 7 and 22. Partial English trans. P. M. Blowers and R. L. Wilken, in *On the Cosmic Mystery of Jesus Christ Selected Writings from St Maximus the Confessor*, Crestwood, NY, 2003.

_____, *Texts on Theology and the Incarnate Dispensation of the Son of God* (I-II). PG 90, 1084–1173 and *Philokalia ton ieron neptikon*, tome 2, Athens, 1976, pp. 52–90. Translation Palmer, Sherrard and Ware, in *The Philokalia. The Complete Text*, vol. 2, London and Boston, 1981, pp.

_____, *Theological and Polemical Opuscules*. PG 91, 9–285. French trans. E. Ponsoye, Paris, 1997.

Maximus the Confessor (Pseudo-), *Scholia on the Works of Dionysius the Areopagite*. PG 4, 29–576.

Meletios Pigas, *Letter to the Inhabitants of Chios*, Constantinople, 1627.

_____, *Orthodox Catechism*, Vilna, 1596; Jassy, 1769.

Meletios Syrigos, *Refutation of the Chapters of Calvin and of the Questions of Cyril Lukaris*, Bucarest 1690.

_____, Corrected version of *The Orthodox Confession* of Peter Moghila, 1643.

Methodius III (Patriarch), Texts cited in J.-P. Migne, *Perpétuité de la foi de l'Église catholique sur l'eucharistie*, tome 2, Paris, 1841.

Methodius of Olympus, *The Banquet*. Roberts and Donaldson (ed.), *The Ante-Nicene Fathers*, vol. 6, Buffalo NY, 1886, pp. 309–355.

_____, *On the Resurrection of the Body* [= *Agloaphon*]. Text established by G. N. Bonwetsch, *Methodius von Olympus*, Erlangen, 1891. Roberts and Donaldson (ed.), *The Ante-Nicene Fathers*, vol. 6, Buffalo, 1886, pp. 364–377.

Michael Glykas, *Letters*. PG 158, 643–957.

_____, *On the Difficulties of Divine Scripture*. Text edited by S. Eustratiades, 2 vols. , 1902.

Mitrophan Critopoulos, *Confession of Faith*. Text in E.-J. Kimmel-Weissenborn, *Monumeta fidei Ecelesiae orientalis*, vol. 2, Iena, 1851.

Nikitas Stithatos, *On the soul*. French text and trans. J. Darrouzès, "Sources chrétiennes" num. 81, Paris, 1961.

_____, *Practical, Physical and Gnostic Centuries*. Greek text in *Philokalia ton ieron neptikon*, tome. 3 , Athens, 1976, pp. 273–355 and PG 120, 852–1009. Trans. Palmer, Sherrard and Ware in *The Philokalia. The Complete Text*, vol. 4, London, 1995, pp. 79–174.

Nicodemos the Hagiorite, *Confession of Faith*, Venice, 1819.

_____, *Eortodromion*, Venice, 1836.

_____, *Exomologitarion*, Venice, 1855. Trans. G. Dokos, Thessalonica, 2006.

_____, *The New Ladder*, Constantinople, 1844.

Nicholas Cabasilas, *A Commentary on the Divine Liturgy*. Trans. J. M. Hussey and P. A. McNulty, London, 1960.

Origen, *An Exhortation to Martyrdom*. PG 11, 564–637. Trans. R. A. Greer, in *Origen*, New York, Ramsey and Toronto, 1979, pp. 41–79.

_____, *Homilies on Leviticus*. Trans. G. W. Barkley, "Fathers of the Church" num. 83, Washington, 1990.

_____, *Homilies on Saint Luke*. Trans. J. T. Leinhard, "Fathers of the Church" num. 94, Washington, 1996.

_____, *On First Principles / De principiis*. Text and French trans. H. Clauzel and M. Simonetti , "Sources chrétiennes" num. 252, 253, 268, 269, Paris, 1978, 1980, 1984. Roberts and Donaldson (ed.), *The Ante-Nicene Fathers*, vol. 4, New York, 1913, pp. 239–382.

_____, *On Prayer*. PG 11, 416–561. Trans. R. A. Greer, in *Origen*, New York, Ramsey and Toronto, 1979, pp. 81–170.

Palladius, *Lausiac History*. Trans. R. T. Meyer, "Ancient Christian Writers" num. 34, Westminster MD, 1965.

Philaret of Moscow, *The Longer Catechism*, Moscow, 1900 (in Russian). Trans. P. Schaff , in *The Creeds of Christendom*, vol. 2, New York, 1877, pp. 445–542.

Philip the Solitary, *The Spiritual Mirror*. PG 127, 709–878.

Philotheos of Sinai, *Forty Texts on Watchfulness.* Greek text in *Philokalia ton ieron neptikon,* tome 2, Athens, 1976, pp. 274–286. Trans. Palmer, Sherrard and Ware, *The Philokalia. The Complete Text,* vol. 3, London/Boston, 1984, pp. 16–31.

Photius, *To Amphilochius.* PG 101, 45–1190, 1277–1296.

_____, *To Tarasius the Patrician, to console him on the death of a daughter, Letter 63.* PG 102, 969–981.

Polycarp of Smyrna, *Epistle to the Philippians.* Trans. J. B. Lightfoot, in *The Apostolic Fathers,* London, 1891, pp. 95–99.

Symeon of Thessalonica, *Dialogue against the Heresies.* PG 155, 33–176.

_____, *On the Holy Euchelaion.* PG 155, 516–536.

_____, *Regarding Our Death and the sacred funeral rites.* PG 155. 669–696.

_____, *Replies to Gabriel of Pentapolis.* PG 155, 829–952.

Symeon the New Theologian, *The Discourses.* Critical text and notes by Mgr. Basil Krivocheine, French trans. J. Paramelle, "Sources chrétiennes" num. 96, 104, 113, Paris, 1963, 1964, 1965. Trans. C. J. deCatanzaro, New York/Ramsey/Toronto, 1980.

_____, *The Ethical* Discourses, 3 vols. Trans. A. Golitzin, Crestwood NY, 1995, 1996, 1997.

_____, *Hymns.* Text established by J. Koder: *Hymnes* 1–15, "Sources chrétiennes" num. 156, Paris, 1969; *Hymnes* 16–40, "Sources chrétiennes" num. 174, Paris, 1971; *Hymnes* 41–58, "Sources chrétiennes" num. 196, Paris, 1973. Trans. G. Maloney, *Hymns of Divine Love,* Denville NJ, n. d.

_____, *The Practical and Theological Chapters.* Trans. P. McGukin, Kalamazoo, 1982, pp. 33–103.

Symeon Metaphrastes, *The Life of Saint Theodosius the Cenobiarch.* PG 114, 469–553.

Tertullian, *Apologetics.* Trans. R. Arbesmann and E. J. Daly, *Apologetical Works,* "Fathers of the Church, a New Translation" num. 10, Washington, 1950.

_____, *On the Resurrection of the Flesh.* Trans. Holmes, *The Ante-Nicene Fathers,* vol. 3, New York, 1918, pp. 545–594.

Theodoret of Cyrrhus, *Commentary on the Epistle to the Romans.* PG 82, 43–225.

_____, *Cure for Hellenic Maladies.* Text and French trans. P. Canivet, "Sources chrétiennes" num. 57, Paris, 1958.

_____, *History of the Monks of Syria..* Text and French trans. P. Canivet and A. Leroy-Molinghen, "Sources chrétiennes" num. 234, 257, Paris, 1977, 1979. Trans. R. M. Price, Kalamazoo MI, 1985.

Theodore of Petra, *The Life of Saint Theodosius.* Text established by H. Usener, *Der heilige Theodosios, Schrifi en des Theodoros und Kyrillos,* Leipzig, 1890. French trans. A.-J. Festugière, *Les Moines d'Orient,* III/3, Paris, 1961.

Theognostos, *On the Practice of the Virtues, Contemplation, and the Priesthood*. Text in *Philokalia ton ieron neptikon*, tome 2, Athens, 1976, pp. 255–271. Trans. Palmer, Sherrard and Ware, in *The Philokalia. The Complete Text*, London/Boston, 1981, pp. 359–377.

_____, *Thesaurus*. Text edited by J. A. Munitiz, "Corpus Christianorum Series Graeca" num. 5, Turnhout, 1979.

Theophan the Recluse, *Discourse on Death*, Saint Petersburg, 1886 (in Russian).

_____, *Interpretation of Psalm 118*, Moscow, 1891 (in Russian).

_____, *The Soul and the Angels are Not Bodily but Spiritual Realities*, Moscow, 1891 (in Russian).

_____, *Soul-Profiting Reading*, Moscow, 1894 (in Russian).

Theophilus of Antioch, *To Autolycus*. Text established by Otto, "Corpus Apologetarum" num. 7, Iena, 1871. Roberts and Donaldson (ed.), *The Ante-Nicene Fathers*, vol. 2, New York, 1913, pp. 85–121.

Theophilus of Campania (Papaphilos), *The Treasure of Orthodoxy*, Tripolilza, 1888.

Theophylact of Bulgaria (of Ochrid), *Commentary on the Letter to the Hebrews*. PG 125, 185–404.

_____, *The Explanation of the Holy Gospel according to Luke*. PG 123, 684–1125. Trans. C. Stade, House Springs MO, 2007.

II. STUDIES

Andronikof (C.), "The Dormition as Type of Christian Death", in *Temple of the Holy Spirit*, trans. M. J. O'Connell, Collegeville, MN, 1983, pp. 1–16.

Andronikof (M.), "La bioéthique devant un regard orthodoxe", *Cahiers de l'Association des philosophes chrétiens*, 6,1993, pp. 3–7.

_____, "Le médec in face au patient de religion orthodoxe", in H. Durant, P. Biclet et C. Herve (ed.), *Éthique et pratique medicale*, Paris, 1995, pp. 22–25.

_____, *Transplantation d'organes et éthique chrétienne*, Paris, 1993.

Androutsos (C.), *Dogmatics of the Eastern Orthodox Church*, Athens, 1907.

Antony (Archimandrite). *Dogmatic Theology of the Orthodox Catholic Church*. Greek translation of Vallanios, Athens, 1858.

Antony of Geneva (Archbishop), "Ce que nous pouvons savoir sur la vie de l'âme dans l'au-delà", *La Lumière du Thabor*, 3, 1984, pp. 62–78 , reprinted in a booklet under the title "La vie de l'âme dans l'au-delà", Monastère Saint-Antoine-le-Grand, Saint-Laurent-en-Royans, 1994.

Bakogiannis (Archimandrite Vasilios), *After Death*, Katerini, 1995.

Beauduin (L.), "Ciel et résurrection", in *Le Mystère de la mort et sa célébration*, Paris, 1956, pp. 253–272.

Botte (B.), "The Earliest Formulas of Prayer for the Dead", in *Temple of the Holy Spirit*, trans. M. J. O'Connell, Collegeville, MN, 1983, pp. 17–31.

Bulgakov (S.), *The Bride of the Lamb*, trans. B. Jakim, Grand Rapids MI/Edinburgh, 2002.

_____, *The Orthodox Church*, Crestwood NY, 1997.

_____, *Jacob's Ladder*, trans. T. A. Smith, Grand Rapids MI/Cambridge UK, 2010.

Breck (J.), *The Sacred Gift of Life. Orthodox Christianity and Bioethics*, Crestwood NY, 1998.

Cavarnos (C.), *The Future Life According to Orthodox Teaching*, Etna, 1985.

Clément (O.), *Corps de mort et de gloire*, Paris, 1995.

Collectif, *Le Mystère de la mort et sa célébration*, Paris, 1956.

Congar (J.-Y.), "Le Purgatoire", in *Le Mystère de la mort et sa célébration*, Paris, 1956, pp. 278–336.

Constas (N.), "Mark of Ephesus", in C. G. et V. Conticello (ed.), *La Théologie byzantine*, tome 2, Turnhout, 2001.

Cumont (F.), "Les vents et les anges psychopompes", *Pisciculi. Studien zur Religion und Kultur des Altertums (Antike und Christentum*, Ergänzungsband, 1), Münster, 1939.

D'Alès (A.), "La question du Purgatoire au concile de Florence en 1438", *Gregorianum*, 3, 1922, pp. 9–50.

Dagron (G.), "Troisième. neuvième et quarantième jours dans la tradition byzantine temps chrétien et anthropologie", in *Le Temps chrétien de la fin de l'Antiquité au Moyen âge, IIe–XIIe siècle*, Paris, 1984, pp. 419–430.

Daley (B. E.), "Apokatastasis and 'Honorable Silence' in the Eschatology of Maximus the Confessor", in C. von Schonborn and F. Heinzer (ed.), *Maximus Confesseur, Actes du Symposium sur Maxime le Confesseur*, Fribourg, Suisse, 1982, pp. 309–339.

Daniélou (J .), "L'apocatastase chez saint Grégoire de Nysse", *Recherches de science religieuse*, 30, 1940, pp. 328–347.

_____, "La doctrine de la mort chez les Pères de l'Église," in *Le Mystère de la mort et sa célébration*, Paris, 1956, pp. 134–156.

_____, "'Metempsychosis' in Gregory of Nyssa", in *The Heritage of the Early Church, Essays in Honor of the Very Reverend G. V. Florovsky*, Rome, 1973 , pp. 227–243.

_____, "Le Traité 'Sur les enfants morts prématurément' de Grégoire de Nysse", *Vigiliae christianae*, 20, 1966, pp. 159–182.

Féret (H.-M.), "La mort dans la tradition biblique", in *Le Mystère de la mort et sa célébration*, Paris, 1956, pp. 15–133.

Florovsky (G.), *Anatomia problematon tes pisteos*, Thessalonique, 1977.

_____, "Eschatology in the Patristic Age: an Introduction", *Studia Patristica*, 2, 1957, pp. 235–250.

Freistedt (E.), *Altchristliche Totengedächtnisstage und ihre Beziehung zum Jenseitsglauben und Totenkult der Antike*, Münster, 1928.

Gill (J.), *Le Concile de Florence*, Tournai, 1964.

Habra (G.), *La Mort et l'au-delà*, Fontainebleau, 1977.

Hierotheos Vlachos (Metropolitan), *Life after Death*. Trans. E. Williams. Levadia: Birth of the Theotokos Monastery, 1996.

Jay (P.), "Le Purgatoire dans la prédication de saint Césaire d'Arles", *Recherches de théologie ancienne et médiévale*, 24, 1957, pp. 5–14.

_____, "Saint Cyprien et la doctrine du Purgatoire", *Recherches de théologie ancienne et médiévale*, 27, 1960, pp. 133–136.

John Maximovich (St), *Sermon on Life after Death*, "Жизнь после смерти," Чаю воскресения мертвых и жизни будущаго века », in *Архиепископ Иоанн (Максимович)*. Moscow, 2006. English trans. in Hieromonk Seraphim Rose, *The Soul after Death*, Platina, 1980, pp. 184–203.

Jugie (M.), "La doctrine des fins dernières dans l'Église greco-russe", *Échos d'Orient*, 17, 1914–1915, pp. 5–22, 209–228, 402–421.

_____, "Purgatoire dans l'Église gréco-russe après le concile de Florence", *Dictionnaire de théologie catholique*, 13, 1936, col. 1326–1352.

_____, "La question du purgatoire au concile de Ferrare-Florence", *Échos d'Orient*, 24, 1921, pp. 269–282.

Justin Popovich (Archimandrite), *Philosophie orthodoxe de la vérité, Dogmatique de l'Église orthodoxe*, tome 5, Paris, 1997.

Koidakis (C. G.), *Orthodox Catechism*, Athens, 1906.

Krumbacher (K.), "Studien zu den Legenden des hl. Theodosios", *Sitzungsberichte der königl. bayr. Akademie der Wissenschaften.*, Munich, 1892, pp. 341–355.

Kyriakakis (J.), "Byzantine Burial Customs: Care of the Deceased From Death to the Prothesis", *The Greek Orthodox Theological Review*, 19, 1974, pp. 45–49.

Larchet (J.-Cl.), *Ceci est mon corps. Le sens chrétien du corps selon les Pères de l'Église*, Genève, 1996.

_____, *Dieu ne veut pas la souffrance des hommes*, Paris, 1999.

_____, *La Divinisation de l'homme selon saint Maxime le Confesseur*, Paris, 1996.

_____, Introduclion to Maxime le Confesseur, *Questions et difficultés*, Paris, 1999.

_____, *Pour une éthique de la procreation. Éléments d'anthropologie patristique*, Paris, 1998.

_____, *Therapy of Spiritual Illnesses.* Trans. K. Sprecher, Montreal, 2012.

_____, *Une fin de vie paisible, sans douleur, sans honte…*, Paris, 2010.

Le Goff (J.), *The Birth of Purgatory*, trans. A. Goldhammer, Chicago, 1981.

Lossky (V.), "Dominion and Kingship: An Eschatological Study", *In the Image and Likeness of God*, St Vladimir's Seminary Press, 1974, pp. 211–227.

_____, *The Mystical Theology of the Eastern Church*, Cambridge & London, 1957.

Makarios of Simonos Petra (Hieromonk), *The Synaxarion: The Lives of the Saints of the Orthodox Church*, 7 vols., trans. C. Hookway, 1998–2008.

Malinovski (Archpriest Nicholas), *Essay on Orthodox Dogmatic Theology*, Sergiev Possad, 1908.

Michel (A.), "Purgatoire", *Dictionnaire de th.ologie catholique*, 13-1, 1936, col. 1163–1326.

_____, "Résurrection", *Dictionnaire de th.ologie catholique*, 13-2, 1937, col. 2501–2571.

Mohrmann (C.), "Locus refrigerii, lucis et pacis", *Questions liturgiques et paroissiales*, 39, 1958, pp. 196–214.

Ntedika (J.), *L'Évolution de la doctrine du Purgatoire chez saint Augustin*, Paris, 1966.

Peckstadt (I.), "Quelques réflexions orthodoxes concernant la crémation", *Contacts*, 49, 1997, pp. 264–274.

Perov (I.), *Manual of Polemical Theology*, Tula, 1905.

Petit (L.), "La grande controverse des colybes", *Échos d'Orient*, 2, 1899, pp. 321–331.

Prestige (G. L.), "Hades in the Greek Fathers", *Journal of Theological Studies*, 24, 1923, pp. 476–485.

Recheis (A.), *Engel, Tod und Seelen reise. Das Wirken der Geister beim Heimgang der Menschen in der Lehre der alexandrinischen und kappadokischen Vater*, "Temi e Testi" num. 4, Rome, 1958.

Richard (M.), "Enfer", *Dictionnaire de th.ologie catholique*, 5, 1913, col. 28–120.

Rivière (J.), "Jugement", *Dictionnaire de th.ologie catholique*, 8, 1924, col. 1721–1828.

_____, "Le rôle du démon au jugement particulier chez les Pères", *Revue des sciences religieuses*, 4, 1924, pp. 43–64.

Roncaglia (P.), *Georges Bardanés, métropolite de Corfou, et Barthélemy, de l'ordre franciscain. Les discussions sur le Purgatoire (15 octobre–17 novembre 1231). Étude critique avec texte inédit*, Rome, 1953.

Schanz (P.), "Seelenschlaf", *Kirchenlexikon*, 11, col. 57–58.

Seraphim Rose (Hieromonk), *The Soul after Death*, Platina, 1995 (1980).

Sylvester (Bishop), *Essay on Orthodox Theology*, vol. 5; Kiev, 1897.

Tmenomierov (A.), *The Teaching of Holy Scripture on Death and the Life Beyond*, Saint Petersburg, 1899.

Ueskuell (A.), "Unbelievable for Many but Actually a True Occurrence", *Orthodox Life*, vol. 26, num. 4, 1976.

Van Lantschoot (A.), "Révélations de Macaire et de Marc de Trumaqa sur le sort de l'âme après la mort", *Le Muséon*, 63, 1950, pp. 159–189.

Vassiliadis (N. P.), *The Mystery of Death*, Athens, 1997.

Vogel (C.), 'The Cultic Environment of the Deceased in the Early Christian Period,' in *Temple of the Holy Spirit*, trans. M. J. O'Connell, Collegeville, MN, 1983, pp. 259–276.